ISBN 978-1-5284-8683-5
PIBN 10925929

1 MONTH OF
FREE
READING

at
www.ForgottenBooks.com

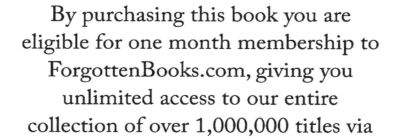

By purchasing this book you are eligible for one month membership to ForgottenBooks.com, giving you unlimited access to our entire collection of over 1,000,000 titles via our web site and mobile apps.

To claim your free month visit:
www.forgottenbooks.com/free925929

Circulation of this Issue 1900 Copies

OCT 13

THE
SUGAR
BULLETIN

Dr. Chas. E. Coates
Baton Rouge, La.

Entered as second-class matter April 13, 1925, at the postoffice at
New Orleans, La., under Act of March 6, 1879.

We stand for the encouragement of Home Industries as against Foreign Competition.

Vol. 9	NEW ORLEANS, LA., OCTOBER 1, 1930	No. 1

TO WHOM IT MAY CONCERN

The variety of cane known as C. O. 281 has been officially released for commercial planting.

The American Sugar Cane League is prepared to distribute its supply of this cane for fall planting to those who desire it. The price is $6.50 per ton, cut and loaded at the place where grown. The cane the League will distribute is located as follows:

At Godchaux Sugars Inc., Raceland, approximately	26	tons
" McCollam Brothers, Ellendale	220	"
" J. M. Burguieres Co., Ltd., Franklin	66	"
" Estate H. C. Minor, Houma	110	"
" Sterling Sugars, Inc., Franklin	93	"
" Ardoyne Planting Co., Ellendale	11	"
" Glenwood Sugars, Inc., Napoleonville	33	"
" Miles Planting Co., Vacherie	55	"
" Standard Sugars Co., Thibodaux	83	"
" South Coast Co., Houma	121	"
" Erath Sugar Co., Erath	22	"
" Houma Station	44	"

OCT 1

Everyone who desires to obtain some of this cane should immediately communicate with the American Sugar Cane League, stating number of tons desired and enclosing check for one-fourth the purchase price thereof at the rate of $6.50 per ton, which will be returned if, for any reason, we cannot make delivery. The remainder of the purchase price is to be paid when cane is ready for delivery which will be some time between October 15th and November 10th, 1930. The cane will be at purchaser's risk after November 10th, 1930.

Owners of plantations given in above list are entitled to deduct from their final payment the current price of mill cane, figured at a dollar a cent on the prevailing market for 96 test sugar at date of delivery in accordance with the terms of their contracts with the League for the growing of the cane.

Allotments will be made October 11th at noon and all orders must be in prior to that date.

THE AMERICAN SUGAR CANE LEAGUE OF THE U. S. A., INC.,

407 Carondelet Street,

New Orleans, La.

=====THE=====

SUGAR BULLETIN

407 Carondelet St., New Orleans

Issued on the 1st and 15th of each month.   Official Organ of the American
Sugar Cane League of the U. S. A., in which are consolidated
The Louisiana Sugar Planters' Assn.
The American Cane Growers' Assn.
The Producers & Mfgrs. Protective Assn.
Subscription Price, 50 Cents Per Year.

Reginald Dykers, General Manager & Editor of the Bulletin
301 Nola Bldg., New Orleans
Frank L. Barker, Secretary and Treasurer
Lockport, La.
C. J. Bourg, Manager Washington Office
810 Union Trust Building

CHAIRMEN OF COMMITTEES:
C. D. Kemper, Franklin, La.
President of the League and Ex-Officio Chairman of Executive Committee
Andrew H. Gay, Plaquemine, La,
Chairman Agricultural Committee
David W. Pipes, Jr., Houma, La.
Chairman Industrial Committee
Frank L. Barker, Lockport, La.
Chairman Finance Committee.
Edward J. Gay, Plaquemine, La.
Chairman Tariff Committee
H. Langdon Laws, Cinclare, La.
Chairman Legislative Committee
J. C. LeBourgeois, New Orleans, La.
Chairman Freight Rate Committee
R. H. Chadwick, Bayou Goula, La.
Chairman Membership Committee
A. H. Rosenfeld, New Orleans, La.
Chairman Publicity Committee

Members of the League desiring action on, or information on, any subject are invited to communicate with the League or with the Chairman of the Committee to which it seems to appertain.

Errata

Through an oversight, which we greatly regret, the name of Mattingly and Whilden was omitted from the list of members of the American Sugar Cane League who have paid their dues for 1930, published in our issue of September 15th, 1930. The firm of Mattingly & Whilden has been a consistent and loyal member of the League for years.

Another omission that we greatly regret was that of the name of the Edward J. Gay P. & M. Co. We offer our apologies for these errors.

Some Field Practices Affecting the Quality of Cane

By George Arceneaux, Agent.
Office of Sugar Plants, Bureau of Plant Industry,
U. S. Department of Agriculture

With the fact completely established that satisfactory yields of cane can readily be produced with varieties now under cultivation, the problem of quality production must still be faced. The experience of most planters with low purity cane and its rapid deterioration following the freeze of last season, emphasizes the importance of producing cane of the maximum sucrose content and purity. Furthermore, with

most factories taxed to capacity, it would seem logical in the future to attach more importance to an improvement in quality rather than to an increase in quantity of cane.

Studies are in progress at the U. S. Sugar Plant Field Station near Houma, La., and on several cooperating plantations to determine which of the current field practices influence the quality of the cane at harvest and what possible modifications of the customary procedure may lead to increased yields of sugar per ton of cane, and per acre.

Tables 1, 2, and 3 summarize the results of the date-of-planting tests conducted during the past two years. It will be observed that, in every case, the cane planted in early October yielded substantially more sugar per ton of cane and, generally speaking, much more sugar per acre than plantings of the same variety made in November or December.

In Table 4, are given the results of preliminary rate-of-planting tests conducted with the varieties, C.P. 807, Co 281, and P.O.J. 213. A considerable improvement in the quality of the cane and a significant increase in quantity of available sugar per acre
(Continued on Page 5)

TABLE 1. (a)RESULTS OF DATE-OF-PLANTING TESTS WITH P.O.J. 213 PLANT CANE ON MIXED SOIL AT THE U. S. SUGAR PLANT FIELD STATION, HOUMA, LOUISIANA.

DATE PLANTED	INDICATED AVAILABLE 96 SUGAR—Nov. 26, 1928	
	Per ton of Cane	Per Acre
	pounds	pounds
October 4, 1927_____	161.0	6,773
October 17, 1927_____	158.0	6,650
November 1, 1927___	132.2	5,149
November 15, 1927___	135.6	5,457
December 6, 1927____	123.0	4,513

(a)Arceneaux, George, and Stevens, F. D. Variety Tests of Sugar Cane in Louisiana During the Crop Year 1927-1928. U. S. Dept. Agr. Circular 88, November, 1929.

TABLE 2. (a)RESULTS OF DATE-OF-PLANTING TESTS WITH P.O.J. 213 PLANT CANE ON LIGHT SOIL AT THE MARY PLANTATION, RACELAND, LA.

DATE PLANTED	INDICATED AVAILABLE 96 SUGAR—Dec. 15, 1928	
	Per ton of Cane	Per Acre
	pounds	pounds
September 10, 1927___	171.7	4,052
September 22, 1927___	174.1	4,333
October 5, 1927_____	167.6	4,529
October 17, 1927_____	155.9	4,081
October 29, 1927_____	152.0	4,092

(a)Arceneaux, George, and Stevens, F. D. Op. Cit.
(Continued on Page 4)

331052

TABLE 3. (b)RESULTS OF PRELIMINARY DATE-OF-PLANTING TESTS WITH PLANT CANE ON MIXED SOIL AT U. S. SUGAR PLANT FIELD STATION, HOUMA, LOUISIANA.

DATE PLANTED	TESTS WITH C. P. 807		TESTS WITH C. O. 281		TESTS WITH C. P. 177	
	Indicated available 96 sugar on Nov. 19, 1929.		Indicated available 96 sugar on Nov. 19, 1929.		Indicated available 96 sugar on Nov. 19, 1929.	
	Per ton of cane	Per acre	Per ton of cane	Per acre	Per ton of cane	Per acre
	pounds	pounds	pounds	pounds	pounds	pounds
October 4, 1928	147.0	7,651	174.3	6,153	148.5	4,605
October 25, 1928	140.1	6,568	163.9	5,799	129.7	3,632
November 17, 1928	133.9	6,412	165.3	5,862	133.3	4,732
December 28, 1928	127.8	4,418	163.8	5,853	129.4	4,274

(b)Arceneaux, George, and Gibbens, R. T., Jr. Variety Tests of Sugar Canes in Louisiana During the Crop Year 1928-1929. (U. S. D. A. Circular to e published.)

TABLE 4. (c)RESULTS OF PRELIMINARY RATE OF PLANTING TESTS WITH PLANT CANE ON LIGHT SOIL AT U. S. SUGAR PLANT FIELD STATION, HOUMA, LOUISIANA. PLANTED NOV. 17-20, 1928.

RATE OF PLANTING	TESTS WITH P. O. J. 213		TESTS WITH C. P. 807		TESTS WITH C. O. 281	
	Indicated available 96 sugar on Nov. 20, 1929.		Indicated available 96 sugar on Nov. 20, 1929.		Indicated available 96 sugar on Nov. 20, 1929.	
	Per ton of cane	Per acre	Per ton of cane	Per acre	Per ton of cane	Per acre
	pounds	pounds	pounds	pounds	pounds	pounds
One "running stalk"	141.4	3,842	153.4	5,619	175.2	4,389
Two "running stalks"	152.2	4,663	153.3	6,843	182.7	5,158
Three "running stalks"	151.0	4,578	155.8	7,541	185.7	5,582

(c)Arceneaux, George, and Gibbens, R. T., Jr. Op. Cit.

was achieved by increasing the quantity of cane planted from one to two "running stalks." Increasing the rate-of-planting Co 281 from two to three "running stalks" gave a further improvement in cane quality as well as an increase in sugar per acre, but with P.O.J. 213, no significant difference was observed when the rate was increased from two to three "running stalks."

With C.P. 807, while the quality of the cane was not materially improved by increasing the quantity of cane planted, each increase resulted in a considerable increase in sugar per acre.

Stalk counts were made at various dates on all the experiments and the results show that, with a given variety, there is a high correlation between the number of stalks per acre early in the season and the indicated available sugar per ton of cane and per acre at harvest. In the date-of-planting tests with the early October plantings, the plants in most cases got well established in the fall and developed lateral buds before winter. The terminal buds were generally killed back by the winter freezes and in the spring, generally speaking, from two to four buds germinated from each of the fall "mother stalks" resulting virtually in a stubble crop.

In connection with the preliminary rate-of-planting tests, it was observed that an adequate rate of planting will result in a generally older stalk population and consequently riper cane at harvest than a thin planting by (1) providing for a large number of "mother stalks" which will reduce to a minimum the time required to reach the maximum number of stalks per acre, and (2) reducing to a minimum the number of gaps, which are generally the source of unduly late and consequently green "suckers." The results indicate that even with the hardy varieties studied, two "running stalks" is the minimum quantity of sound cane which should be planted.

These studies furthermore seem to justify the assumption that, generally speaking, any practice which will make for a greater number of stalks per acre early in the season will result in a higher quality of cane at harvest.

The Election of Officers

At the Annual Meeting of the American Sugar Cane League held on Thursday, September 25th, at the office of the League, 407 Carondelet St., New Orleans, the following officers and members of the Executive Committee were elected to serve during the ensuing year:

President, C. D. Kemper;
1st Vice-President, Percy A. Lemann;
2nd Vice-President, H. Langdon Laws;
3d Vice-President, R. H. Chadwick;
4th Vice-President, C. J. Bourg;
5th Vice-President and General Manager, Reginald Dykers;
Treasurer, Frank L. Barker.

Executive Committee

A. H. Gay, E. A. Burguieres, Jules Godchaux, John D. Minor, J. C. LeBourgeois, E. J. Gay, C. P. Burguieres, C. F. Dahlberg, E. A. Rainold, S. C. Munson, M. V. Marmande, Ulysse Landry, A. H. Rosenfeld, Charles Billeaud, Albert Levert, Emile Sundbery, J. W. Jay, D. W. Pipes, Jr., E. Newton Kearny.

Annual Report of the General Manager of the American Sugar Cane League

(Delivered at the Annual Meeting, Sept. 25th, 1930.)

New Orleans, Sept. 25, 1930.

To the Officers and Members of the American Sugar Cane League of the U. S. A., Inc.

During the Fiscal Year ending today the American Sugar Cane League has continued, and, in fact, enhanced, the activities in behalf of the domestic sugar industry, and particularly the Louisiana sugar industry, which it has engaged in since its formation eight years ago.

The principal accomplishments of the League during the past twelve months, listed in the order of their importance, as it seems to me, have been:

(1) The conduct of the tariff fight, which resulted in an increase of the tariff.

(2) The sale of a large quantity of Louisiana raw sugar of both the 1929-30 crop and the 1930-31 crop direct to the American Sugar Refining Co., at the full New York price.

(3) Obtaining Federal appropriations for sugar work.

(4) The payment in full for the second laboratory building erected at Houma for the use of the scientists of the U. S. Department of Agriculture.

(5) The distribution of such new varieties of cane as have been released for commercial planting and the continuation of the varietal tests and experiments looking to future releases.

(6) The formal proceedings instituted before the Louisiana Public Service Commission asking for lower and more equitable freight rates on raw sugar from Louisiana producing points to New Orleans.

(7) The maintenance of a membership in behalf of the Louisiana sugar industry in the Domestic Sugar Producers' Association.

(8) The perpetuation of the so-called "White Sugar Committee," which brings about the public posting of the prices at which direct consumption sugars are being offered.

(9) The supervision of the expenditure of the $40,000 voted by the Legislature for sugar experimental work.

(10) The collection of complete and detailed information as to the steps it is necessary to take to form a sugar co-operative association to work with the Federal Farm Board, if one be desired.

It is probable, of course, that opinions will differ in regard to the comparative importance of the above activities, but all will agree that in the entire category there is not one that is not material to the welfare of our industry. I might add an eleventh to the ten I have enumerated, and that is the dissemination of all information on the above subjects as developed, and a large amount of other information, to the members of the organization twice a month by means of a neatly printed and newsy Bulletin, which is so managed that it did not cost either its recipients or the League a cent during the past year, and on the contrary has shown a small profit for the League's treasury.

I think it is proper to say a few words concerning each of the ten projects or activities that I have above enumerated.

(1) The Tariff Fight

As we all know, this was a long drawn out affair. Hearings on the sugar schedule of the Hawley-Smoot Bill were inaugurated before the Ways and Means Committee of the House of Representatives on January 21st, 1929, and it was not until June 17th, 1930, that the measure became law by the addition of President Hoover's signature. During all of those eighteen months there was never a day nor an hour nor a minute during which the domestic sugar interests could afford to relax their vigilance. Men and resources designed to carry on a fight in Washington of three or four months duration, which, at the outset was considered about the length of time the legislation would be in process, were found utterly inadequate to carry it on for a year and a half. Yet the League had its representatives, sometimes one, sometimes three or four, always in Washington and on the job. All expenses were met. Nobody was asked to contribute a cent beyond his regular League dues. There was no passing of the hat for special contributions. The quarter cent additional tariff secured, if reflected in the price, as it theoretically ought to be, means about 80c a bag on raw sugar.

(2) The Sale of Raws

Since the last annual meeting of the League it has effected two sales of Louisiana raw sugar in bulk to the American Sugar Refining Co., at the full New York price, one at the outset of the last grinding and one for this year. The sale last year was 30,000 tons and the sale this year was 55,000 tons. The sales were made by the League's Raw Sugar Committee, and were negotiated directly with the President of the American Sugar Refining Co., Mr. J. F. Abbott, at his office in New York. The members of the League had this service performed for them absolutely free of all expenses other than their regular League dues.

(3) The Federal Appropriations

It is possible that many members of the League do not realize that through the League's efforts, as a powerful organization representing the whole sugar industry of our State, the U. S. Government has been led to make appropriations for sugar work in Louisiana that total every year several times as much as all the annual dues paid into the League by all its members put together. In fact there is over half a million dollars annually spent by the Federal Government for sugar experimental work and although all of this is not spent in Louisiana, the sum spent here annually is, as I have said, many times as large as the total expense of carrying on the League, and during this past year, through the efforts of this organization, a representative of which appeared before the Congress and before the various Committees, bureau heads and others whose approval the appropriations must have before they can be secured, the sum of $10,000, extra, was obtained for use by the Office of Sugar Plants to extend its investigations and researches to obtain new and better varieties of cane for us; $10,000, extra, was obtained for the Office of Forage and Cereal Insects to bring into Louisiana parasites to exterminate the cane borer, and $2,500, extra, to extend drainage experiments on our Louisiana sugar plantations.

(4) The Laboratories at Houma

The erection of the two modern laboratory buildings near Houma, by the League, and on land belonging to the League, is a corrollary of the Federal appropriations referred to in the previous paragraph, because those appropriations included no provision for the housing of the Government scientists who were to carry on the work here. The League stepped into this breach and has built and paid for two buildings designed in accordance with the Government's ideas, the second one being completed and paid for last fall. The League is now trying to finance the erection of a third building of the same type. The buildings are rented from the League by the U. S. Government and equipped with the necessary laboratory apparatus by the U. S. Government. The importance of the League's action in providing the buildings can hardly be over-estimated.

(5) The Distribution of New Cane Varieties

The only new variety of cane released for distribution since our last annual meeting is the variety known as 36M. The supply of this variety available was distributed by the League last fall in time for fall planting, and the work of distribution was done fairly and equitably and apparently to the satisfaction of all applicants. The League's accomplishments in connection with this varietal work consist not so much in the actual distribution as in the co-operation necessary to carry on the field trials during the several years that must elapse before the value of any given variety can be definitely determined and its release ordered. It is believed that another variety will shortly be released by those who decide this matter, namely, the President of the League, Dr. E. W. Brandes of the U. S. Department of Agriculture and the Director of the Louisiana Experiment Station. Without the League's participation there would be hopeless confusion in the handling of these varietal releases.

(6) The Matter of Freight Rates

The League pays an annual retainer to the New Orleans Joint Traffic Bureau, an organization of freight rate experts, to handle for it such matters as pertain to the complicated science of rate making. Every member of the League has, individually, the privilege of consulting the Bureau about any freight rate matters he may want information on. At the present time a very important case involving rates on raw sugar from Louisiana producing points to New Orleans is being handled for the League by the New Orleans Joint Traffic Bureau. Should the case be won there will be a material saving effected for many factories in the Louisiana sugar district on the cost of shipping their raw sugar to the New Orleans refineries. These savings, on an average, will be large enough every year to cover the League dues of the factories affected five or six times over. The case will perhaps have been heard by the Louisiana Public Service Commission before this report is published.

(7) The Domestic Sugar Producers' Association

In the great tariff struggle, in which the domestic sugar interests found all sorts of powerful forces arrayed against them, it became apparent that a united front was imperative. An organization was therefore effected embracing all the domestic sugar producing interests, beet and cane. The League undertook to pay the share of the expenses of this organization which was allotted to the Louisiana sugar producers. The League has not asked for contributions from the individual producers for this purpose. It has paid Louisiana's share out of its treasury.

(8) White Sugar Committee

This Committee was formed to do away with certain abuses that had crept into the marketing of Louisiana direct consumption sugars. Its efforts have been confined to persuading all sellers of such sugars to post publicly every day the prices at which their sugars are being offered. There is no influence brought to bear to affect the offering price. The Committee only asks that it be made known so that everybody will know the figures at which everybody else is offering sugar. The plan has worked excellently, and at least one participant in it tells us that it has saved him several thousand dollars every year.

(9) The Louisiana Appropriation

A Committee of the League known as the "Contact Committee" has met every month throughout the year with the officials of the Experiment Station at Baton Rouge for the purpose of determining just how the $40,000 a year appropriated by the Louisiana Legislature for sugar experimental work (at the League's request) should be expended. The Contact Committee has used its best endeavors to see that this considerable sum of money, obtained entirely through the efforts of the League, was spent to the very best advantage. At the last regular session of the Legislature the League was successful in getting this sum again appropriated for two years, but the money is not available because of the Governor's veto. It is hoped and expected however that it may be made available shortly through the State Board of Liquidation, with the full approval of Governor Long.

(10) The Efforts to Form a "Sugar Co-operative"

The League, as an organization, cannot function as a co-operative association in conjunction with the Federal Farm Board because its charter does not authorize it to do so. It did undertake during the past year however to gather all the data and information necessary for the guidance of those who might desire to form a sugar co-operative and all this data, the results of several months of work and several visits to Washington, is on file and available whenever required.

This concludes a brief outline of the League's accomplishments during the Fiscal Year ending today. There are innumerable other things to which reference might properly be made and which have all contributed to the welfare of the industry in which we are engaged and which has been, and still is, in need of every helpful agency, every constructive thought and every human endeavor which can be availed of in its behalf. Although I have referred specifically to less than a dozen of the League's activities there are contained in the brief list many which have, singly and alone, produced monetary returns alongside of which the expense of maintaining the American Sugar Cane League appears as a bagatelle. One has only to run through the list, as given in this report, to verify this fact. In the aggregate the practical gains and benefits accruing from the League's work, as contrasted with the negligible League dues of 1c a ton are overwhelming. It is a pleasure to me to be able to report such a highly desirable state of affairs.

REGINALD DYKERS,
Vice-President and General Manager.

An Open Letter to the Chairman of the Federal Farm Board

Hon. Alexander Legge,
Chairman, Federal Farm Board,
Washington, D. C.   Sept. 26, 1930.

Dear Sir:

We observe, with the same absorbing interest that is felt by a seriously ill patient listening to the consultations of his doctors, the various movements now in being for the rectification of the evils besetting the domestic sugar industry of the United States. These movements range from attempts to bring about a voluntary restriction of domestic sugar production in a country that is producing less than half the sugar it consumes, to proposals that the Federal Farm Board buy up a million tons of sugar, both ideas conceived primarily in the interest of foreign sugar producers who can see no other way of escaping from their own difficulties.

It seems to this organization, which represents the cane sugar element in the sugar production of the United States, that it is incumbent on it to express itself to you officially, without delay, along such lines as will lead you to perceive that while the producers of sugar outside the United States may be at a loss as to how to secure help for themselves except through such untenable plans as those we have above mentioned, the sugar industry of the United States, the welfare of which alone is the concern of the Governmental Boards, Commissions, Legislators, Executive Officers, and other official agencies of the United States, is dependent on no such strained expedients, but is salvable through simpler and saner and sounder methods of procedure.

We protest emphatically against the assumption that the solution of the troubles confronting the sugar industry of the United States must be one which will suffice to also solve the difficulties of the sugar industries of various foreign countries; particularly Cuba. We declare that to be a fundamentally wrong assumption. If it be repudiated, as it should immediately be, then the way to remove the troubles of the domestic sugar industry is opened. If that false assumption is not repudiated then you shall see the amazing spectacle of a domestic industry of vast extent and vaster potentialities allowed to die by a Governmental policy that would not rescue it merely because the means of rescue were inapplicable to foreign industries of like complexion. That is a responsibility so tremendous and an attitude so unpatriotic that we are convinced no agency of our Government will assume it if the case is clearly understood. The purpose of this letter is to clarify the situation.

The sugar industry of the United States is prostrate not because its product lacks a market here at home; not because of over production or expansion to unhealthy proportions; not because the demand for sugar has lessened; not because speculative ventures have turned out disappointingly; not because of lack of business acumen; not because of faulty distribution; not because of lack of modern methods; not because of any inherent fault listed in the whole lexicon of business. It is prostrate because the sugar produced abroad, notably in Cuba, is being sold at prices that are far below the cost of producing sugar in Cuba or anywhere else and this sugar is flooding the United States and is sold at a price which is the lowest in all history and if this continues—if this is allowed to continue by the Government of the United States—the domestic sugar industry will soon draw its last flickering breath and cease to be.

It is easy enough to stop it; it is easy enough to keep that cheap foreign sugar out. That is all that is necessary to solve the problem of the domestic sugar industry; keep the foreign sugar out. There is ample law now on the books to make this possible. If a solution is sought for the troubles of the domestic sugar industry alone, it is ready to our hand. And, at the risk of being charged with needless repetition, we declare again that the Government of the United States has no rightful concern with any sugar industry other than that of its own people, and that any Board, Commission, Legislator or Executive Officer of the United States, if petitioned to take steps to alleviate the troubles of the sugar industry, should confine those steps to such as will most simply, easily and effectually facilitate the sugar industry of the United States, without considering foreign sugar industries in any way whatever.

The Tariff Act of 1922, as well as the Tariff Act of 1930, fixed a rate of duty on sugar that was based upon the theory that the rate then fixed equalized the difference between the cost of production of sugar in Cuba and the cost of production in the United States.

The idea of a tariff that will equalize production costs at home and abroad is the lowest theory of protection possible if there is to be any protection at all. We do not subscribe to this theory of what properly constitutes protection, because it discourages the American policy of building up a high level of community life through the payment of liberal wages. It inevitably leads domestic producers of all sorts to an excess of caution lest they be accused of uneconomical methods, and they pinch and scrape in every direction so that their cost figures when presented will not be assailable on the ground that they are unnecessarily high. We express this view merely as a matter of record.

Congress realized that no fixed figure would exactly cover the difference in cost of production. They realized that Congress had no exact knowledge of the existing difference in cost and Congress realized further that the Tariff Act as passed would carry this fixed rate of duty for a term of years, and that during the life of the Act the difference in cost of production would be varying. Therefore, Congress also passed as a part of the Tariff Act a flexible provision, and authorized the President to appoint a Tariff Commission, which is supposed to ascertain the exact difference between the cost of producing sugar in Cuba and in America, and then recommend to the President that the tariff be increased or decreased to meet the then existing conditions.

When Cuban raw sugar sells c. & f. New York at $1.15 per hundred pounds, or at $3.15 per hundred pounds duty paid, as is the case when this is written, it only nets them about 80 cents per hundred pounds at the mill in Cuba—a figure so inconceivably low that in any year previous to this it would have been regarded as fantastic. The Cubans say themselves that their cost of producing a pound of raw sugar is double the 80 cents they are selling it for. Yet in the face of that situation ,which has prevailed for some time and which shows no indication of alteration, the President of Cuba has come out with an official statement within the past ten days that it is Cuba's intention and expectation to produce 840,000 tons more sugar next year than this year. Is it any wonder that the sugar industry of the United States stands paralyzed before such a reckless and destructive threat? Is it possible that there are not agencies in our Government to nullify it?

Our Tariff Law declares that the U. S. Tariff Commission shall protect producers in the United States against unfair practices, "the effect or tendency of which is to destroy or substantially injure an industry efficiently and economically operated in the United States." To deliberately flood our markets with sugar in tremendous amounts, at prices half of its cost of production, and then declare through the Presidential voice itself that nearly one million extra tons will be forthcoming in 1931 to carry on this devastation is surely an unfair practice on the part of Cuba, "the tendency of which is to destroy or substantially injure an industry efficiently and economically operated in the United States." The Department of Justice at Washington has declared on numerous occasions that an unfair practice has been indulged in whenever an American concern deliberately sells on the American market any product at a price below its cost. We admit that we have not the same jurisdiction over foreign producers as we have over the citizens of the United States, but at least this defines what may be called unfair practice.

We realize that the adjustment of the tariff does not come within the province of the Federal Farm Board, and our object in reciting the facts given above is for the purpose of demonstrating to you that pleas made to the Federal Farm Board to induce it to take action along such lines as it may in behalf of the resuscitation of the sugar industry should be scrutinized carefully to make sure that they are not pleas in behalf of some foreign sugar industry with which our Government has nothing to do. As far as our domestic sugar industry is concerned, both beet and cane, its salvation lies in the imposition of an adequate degree of protection against foreign sugar that is sold below its own cost of production. It is the Machiavellian practice of the Cuban sugar producers of selling below their own production cost that is extinguishing the domestic sugar industry by swift degrees. Of what avail is a 2-cent tariff on sugar, enacted to protect us against a legitimate Cuban production cost of 2 cents a pound, when the Cubans proceed to make sugar and sell it delivered in New York harbor at 1.15 cents? Either their real costs are far below 2 cents, justifying an increase in the tariff accordingly, or they are engaged in a deliberate campaign of annihilation. The remedy lies with the United States Tariff Commission. It should be applied with all possible expedition.

While it is true, as we have said above, that the Federal Farm Board has no official connection with the adjustment of tariffs, yet it may very well be that in its operations it will find its interest in the existence of a protective tariff that really protects is vital. The Federal Farm Board can hardly be a disinterested spectator of a situation which renders abortive any effort it may make through the functional channels allowed it by law to benefit and salvage a domestic agricultural industry by loans and similar assistance when the industry is suffocated and robbed of ability to repay such loans by the influx over the existing tariff wall of a competitive foreign commodity sold at less than it costs to produce it in the country of its origin.

We are convinced that the Federal Farm Board in its economic wisdom must have long ago perceived that sugar beets and sugar cane are unique and conspicuous among the agricultural crops of the United States because of the fact that the area in them may be vastly expanded without reaching the consumption needs of this country in the way of sugar, and the most interesting aspect of the matter is that these crops can be grown with success on great areas of the land that is now in wheat or corn or cotton, thus bringing about the greatly desired reduction in the acreage devoted to those products.

How reasonable it is, therefore, for us to earnestly desire that the Federal Farm Board shall understand that the foundation on which we hope to see it build an expanded sugar acreage, with corresponding reduction of acreage in certain surplus crops, must be secured against the destructive effect of ruthless and extraordinary foreign competition, else the edifice of sugar that the Board may construct will be like a house built upon the sand.

We hope that in writing you this letter we are taking a step that you will regard as logical and timely and we hope that you will be sufficiently impressed with our statements to give them your thoughtful consideration. The moral effect of your acquiescence in our point of view will, we are sure, be far reaching and helpful in the highest degree.

With my best respects and good wishes, I am

Yours truly,

REGINALD DYKERS,
Vice President and General Manager.

Varietal Proportions for This Fall's Plantings

(By Arthur H. Rosenfeld)

A decision as to the acreage of the three released *P.O.J.* varieties to plant in this fall's program depends upon several factors, among which the following are the most important:

First. Acreage in each variety which will be cultivated next year as stubble cane;

Second. Geographical location of plantation as affecting length of growing season; and

Third. Soil types on plantations.

From amongst the numerous planting programs outlined in the past month, those contained in the two letters below, the first applying to a plantation in the northern section of the belt and the second in the more southerly part, have been selected as more or less typical of the suggestions made under the varying conditions:

August 27, 1930.

Dear Sir:

I want to confirm the suggestions I gave you by telephone this morning regarding the proportion of the various *P.O.J.* varieties to be employed in your planting this fall.

In the first place, I think it is best to view the problem from the standpoint of your total cane acreage for next year. Then, in view of your rather northerly location and, hence, shorter growing season than in Terrebonne or Lafourche, I would recommend that you plant an amount of the earliest maturing of the three varieties—the *P.O.J.* 234—in such an acreage as will bring the percentage of that variety in your total under cane for the 1931 crop to 40%.

The greater part of your stubble acreage next year will be in *P.O.J.* 213, and I would recommend only such fall planting of this variety as is necessary to bring the percentage of 213 to the whole to about 35%.

I understand that you have sufficient seed for planting about 50 acres of the 36M variety and would suggest that you plant sufficient of the ordinary 36 to bring the total 36 and 36M acreage to approximately 25% of the total 1931 cane acreage.

I was delighted to have your inquiry and feel that it is unnecessary to assure you again that it is always a pleasure for me to be able to give you any information which may be of assistance to you.

Very truly yours,
ARTHUR H. ROSENFELD,
Consulting Technologist.

September 17, 1930.

My dear Sir:

I have now had time to study over carefully the problem of your varietal proportions in your fall plantings this year, which you state to be a total of some 800 acres. I would suggest that these plantings be made in the following amounts for each released variety:

P.O.J. 234—425 acres making about 20% of the 2327 acres you expect to have in cane for the 1931-32 crop;

P.O.J. 36M—250 acres or 13% of total;

P.O.J. 213—125 acres making about 50% of total;

	800 acres or 83%
P.O.J. 36—Stubble	16%
	99%

You may or may not be somewhat surprised that I recommend your planting 425 out of the 800 acre planting program in *P.O.J.* 234 but even this will give you, with the dangerously small amount of but 48 acres of first year stubble which you project carrying forward, less than 1/5 of your total acreage in this early maturing variety on which we depend so much for being able to make an early start of grinding. Frankly, I think that with anything less than this amount of 234 you will be facing the danger of having to start your grinding later than other places having the proper proportion of this earliest maturing of the varieties, and I think you should work toward arranging your plantings in future years so as to increase this proportion to about 1/3 of your total area for each crop.

You will note that I am recommending 250 acres of 36M and no planting of the regular 36 this fall. I do this because the 250 acres of 36M plus the 56 acres of stubble of this variety gives you a 13% proportion of this variety to your entire 1931 acreage, which, added to the 16% which you will have in stubble of the regular *P.O.J.* 36, gives you just about 30%, which I think you should have in these two varieties combined. It is pretty definitely established that 36M is rather earlier maturing than 36 although there are some indications that it may not stubble quite so well as the straight 36. One of the great advantages of 36 and 36M is their resistance to early cutting and the excellent prospects we have of getting good second and even third year stubble from these varieties. This has been evidenced very strongly during the past unfavorable season, when as second year stubble all over the State 36 has stood out very clearly as the best.

Now as to *P.O.J.* 213, I am recommending only 125 acres, as stated above, because this will give you a total of about 50% of your 1931 cane area of this heavy tonnage, but recumbent and rather late maturing variety. I view with considerable alarm any tendency to go beyond ½ of the cane acreage in this variety on any one plantation due largely to its habit of lodging. I have just returned from a trip up the river and down the bayou, and I was very grieved to see, though not surprised, that the good 213 has already begun to lodge badly. I am very much inclined to believe that—just as happened last year—this lodging will have the effect of delaying the maturing of the cane, which, in turn, will mean a delay in starting to mill it and which again means that if we get a freeze before December we are likely to have the larger portion of this twisted variety still in the field and will find it almost impossible to windrow it properly.

I trust you will pardon this rather lengthy explanation of the reasons for my recommendations in each case, and, if there is any point which I have not made clear, I shall be delighted to have you write me in regard to same or discuss the matter with you in person.

Thanking you for giving me this opportunity to be of some assistance to your company, I am

Very truly yours,

ARTHUR H. ROSENFELD,
Consulting Technologist.

Angola (Africa) Sugar Industry

We have in recent issues published several interesting letters from Mr. Edgar Jacobs, formerly Agriculturist for Godchaux Sugars, to Dr. A. H. Rosenfeld, containing some pertinent sidelights on the sugar industries of South Africa, Mauritius and Reunion.

The following excerpts are from a letter from Mr. L. H. Powell, of Durban, South Africa, to Mr. Jacobs regarding a recent visit to the Angola sugar country and fit in nicely with the letters which we have already published. Mr. Powell says:

"I had a very interesting trip in Angola—the going was hard, but not so bad as some people have found it, as I have been used to rough conditions in the 'back of beyond' in other countries.

The factories are not up to much, in fact very inefficient, but on two estates especially they certainly have got the cultivation up to a very high state of efficiency.

The estates are mainly on, or near the coast, where there is very little rainfall, but any amount of water available for irrigation. Inland it is very mountainous, with a high rainfall.

The cane grown is usually about fifty-fifty Uba and Cheribon, Lousier, and other purple canes. I was very much taken with the extraordinary heavy crops of Uba, running up to 75 and 80 tons per acre. The same applies to the other kinds of cane, but I had never seen Uba of such a size. Many of the Uba canes were 1 1-2" to 2" in diameter x 14'/16' long without the top. It was also the first time I had seen Uba in flower.

As far as I could gather, no fertilizer was used, and the soil was exceedingly rich.

The climate in the northern part of the country, towards the Congo is not very healthy—plenty of big hungry mosquitoes.

I visited both, Lobito and Loanda, the capital of the Colony. I was everywhere most hospitably received, and everything was done to make my visit as pleasant as possible.

It is a wonderful cane growing country, with plenty of cheap labor. There is only one up-to-date factory grinding about 800 tons of cane per day, which was supplied and erected by the Mirrlees-Watson Company in 1928."

Freight Rates

Louisiana Public Service Commission,
Baton Rouge.   September 22, 1930.
American Sugar Cane League,
New Orleans, La.
Dear Sirs:

With reference to your letter of September 17th: This Commission's Order No. 1117, providing half rate on machinery, was cancelled, in part, by the Interstate Commerce Commission in its Docket 8845, known as the Natchez Case. The part cancelled applied to machinery to be purchased from original owner and reconstructed for manufacturing purpose. This cancellation was made effective to Western Classification territory, that is, between points west of the river and from points east of the river to points west of the river, and from points west of the river to points east of the river. As to points in Southern Classification territory, the order is effective in full as written.

Yours very truly,
HENRY JASTREMSKI,
Secretary.

THE
SUGAR
BULLETIN

La. State University,
Baton Rouge, La.

Entered as second-class matter April 13, 1925, at the postoffice at
New Orleans, La., under Act of March 6, 1879.

We stand for the encouragement of Home Industries as against Foreign Competition.

| Vol. 9 | NEW ORLEANS, LA., OCTOBER 15, 1930 | No. 2 |

C. P. 807 RELEASED

The cane variety known as C.P. 807 has been released for commercial planting, on the recommendation of Dr. E. W. Brandes of the United States Department of Agriculture, concurred in by Mr. C. D. Kemper, President of the American Sugar Cane League, and Dr. C. T. Dowell, Director of the Louisiana Experiment Station.

The American Sugar Cane League has only a very small amount of this cane available for distribution, as follows:

At Godchaux Sugars, Inc., Raceland, about - - - - - - - - 40 tons
" Ardoyne Planting Co., Ellendale, about - - - - - - - 40 "
" Standard Sugars Co., Thibodaux, about - - - - - - - - 20 "
" Erath Sugars Co., Erath, about - - - - - - - - - - 40 "
" Estate H. C. Minor, Houma, about - - - - - - - - - 180 "
" The U. S. Sugar Plant Field Station, Houma, about - - - 30 "

Of the cane at the United States Field Station and the Estate of H. C. Minor a considerable portion will not be available for distribution until after November 10th, 1930, but all the other cane listed above will be ready for distribution on and after October 27th, 1930. Applications will be received up to 12 o'clock noon October 25th, 1930, from parties desiring to secure some of this cane.

The price is $6.50 per ton, cut and loaded, at place where grown, and check for 25% of the purchase price should accompany application.

Address applications to

The American Sugar Cane League
of the U. S. A.

407 CARONDELET ST.   NEW ORLEANS

THE
SUGAR
BULLETIN

407 Carondelet St., New Orleans

Issued on the 1st and 15th of each month. Official Organ of the American Sugar Cane League of the U. S. A., in which are consolidated The Louisiana Sugar Planters' Assn. The American Cane Growers' Assn. The Producers & Mfgrs. Protective Assn. Subscription Price, 50 Cents Per Year.

Reginald Dykers, General Manager & Editor of the Bulletin
301 Nola Bldg., New Orleans
Frank L. Barker, Secretary and Treasurer
Lockport, La.
C. J. Bourg, Manager Washington Office
810 Union Trust Building

CHAIRMEN OF COMMITTEES:
C. D. Kemper, Franklin, La.
President of the League and Ex-Officio Chairman of Executive Committee
Andrew H. Gay, Plaquemine, La.
Chairman Agricultural Committee
David W. Pipes, Jr., Houma, La.
Chairman Industrial Committee
Frank L. Barker, Lockport, La.
Chairman Finance Committee.
Edward J. Gay, Plaquemine, La.
Chairman Tariff Committee
H. Langdon Laws, Cinclare, La.
Chairman Legislative Committee
J. C. LeBourgeois, New Orleans, La.
Chairman Freight Rate Committee
R. H. Chadwick, Bayou Goula, La.
Chairman Membership Committee
A. H. Rosenfeld, New Orleans, La.
Chairman Publicity Committee

Members of the League desiring action on, or information, on any subject are invited to communicate with the League or with the Chairman of the Committee to which it seems to appertain.

Release of C. P. 807 and Co. 281

In accordance with established procedure, the three cooperating agencies which are working together in the development of improved sugar cane varieties for Louisiana, viz: the Office of Sugar Plants (United States Department of Agriculture), the Louisiana State University, and the American Sugar Cane League, have jointly recommended the release for commercial planting this fall of the varieties C. P. 807 and Co. 281. The official stamp of approval on these canes whose testing has been followed with great interest during the last three or four years by many of the planters, constitutes the passing of another milestone in the steady advancement of field practices.

The results of all the tests and comparisons of these varieties with the canes now commonly grown have shown conclusively their ability to materially raise the level of production attained thus far. This is, of course, due to certain superior qualities not so outstanding in the other canes. However, the Committee wishes to emphasize that even these canes are still far from the ideal demanded for the Louisiana industry, and has accordingly set down for the guidance of the planters some of their advantages and limitations to facilitate their efficient utilization in the planting program.

C. P. 807 appears particularly valuable for the heavier soils due to its tolerance of poor drainage, its hardiness, and resistance to the root disease complex. It has thus far shown complete immunity to mosaic. Its vigorous growth and good stubbling qualities should greatly reduce cultivation and weeding costs. On the other hand, its slightly higher fiber content and often crooked stalks will somewhat increase harvesting and milling expenses, which, however, will be small in comparison with the greatly increased yields obtained.

Co. 281 has given best results in the river and bayou districts, and is chiefly valuable because of its high sucrose content, straight growth, and superior yields of sugar per acre. It takes mosaic, but is apparently as tolerant as the P.O.J. varieties commonly grown. It withstands early cutting much better than P.O.J. 234, and this advantage combined with nearly equal earliness and superior yields, constitute an important advance in the development of an indispensable early milling variety. However, due to its brittleness and injury by storms, it should never occupy a large proportion of the plantings.

The distribution of its available supply of Co. 281 by the American Sugar Cane League was performed on October 11th, as advertised in the October 1st issue of the SUGAR BULLETIN. Some of this cane is still to be had however, as the amount on hand was not exhausted by the applications. Those who desire some of it should write the League without delay and their requirements will be filled in the order of their receipt. As will be seen by the front page announcement in this issue of the SUGAR BULLETIN, applications for C. P. 807 will be received by the League up to October 25th, 1930, at noon.

Expectations and Hopes
By C. J. Bourg

Washington, when Congress is not in session, is pretty much like home in September when the children have all gone back to school—quiet and relief, but you miss them just the same.

Looking to the United States Government for immediate action that will assist in establishing a fair price for sugar during the harvest of 1930, leads rather to a hope than an expectancy. At the present time in Washington it is the opinion that the agreement of the Cuban Sugar Committee to adopt the plan under consideration by the Chadbourne Committee, carries the greatest hope of immediate relief, with probable permanent good. The plan to take off 1,500,000 tons of sugar from the world market by Cuba and to limit the importations of Cuban sugar into the United States to 2,800,000 tons per annum, suggest great possibilities for the domestic sugar industry, but it is rather the assurance we need that Cuba will accordingly cease to overproduce. To be completely effective the above plan must provide for a corresponding limitation of the Cuban production of sugar, not only the amount Cuba sends into the United States market. Continued overproduction of sugar in Cuba will affect the world market, which in the end controls the price, and it is the price of sugar which actually concerns us most.

The troubled political conditions in Cuba are giving official Washington much concern. It is to be expected that in the readjustment, the sugar industry of Cuba will be placed on a basis of production and distribution more in keeping with normal times.

(Continued on page 4.)

The investigation by the Tariff Commission into the cost of refined sugars will be carried on under the new regulations, which place the "burden of proof" upon the applicant for a change in the tariff and instead of sending out field investigators for months, the various parties interested shall present their evidence and be subjected to cross-examination thereon. This will expedite the decision and the Commission believes it will be better able to secure the facts in this manner.

The Tariff Commission is not planning to inquire into raw sugar. It is not improbable, of course, that the opening of the question of refined sugar prices will bring about an inquiry into the facts concerning raw sugar. But officially there is no application for a change in the duty on raw sugar, before the Tariff Commission.

There is some encouragement to be had for the domestic sugar industry in the fact that the depression existing, is now universally recognized coupled with the feeling that something should be done about it. To the man back home, that may mean little. because he has felt this depression for so long and therefore can hardly believe anyone at all could question our right to relief. But let it be known that we are more likely to get relief, now that all branches of the industry in all parts of the world are being hurt. When all oxen are gored the indemnity will be general, at least.

It was with no small satisfaction that those interested in the success of the domestic sugar industry learned of the decision of the Treasury Department in the controversy raging over the importation of liquid sugar. No longer will it be possible for importers to have water added to their raw sugar and to "beat" the tariff rates by bringing in the mixture under the rates of duty which were intended for syrup.

The controversy over liquid sugar has been one of long standing. More than a year ago the first protests reached Washington, but at that time it was the refiners of the Eastern seaboard who led the chorus of complaint. They carried with them statistics indicating that the importation of a mixture containing water and sugar of a high degree of purity was increasing at an alarming rate. The purity of the sugar warranted the payment of the usual refined duty by the importers, but because the polariscopic readings were reduced by the introduction of water, the product paid only that duty which was prescribed for sugar of 75 degrees of purity. A vigorous effort was made to arrange the increments of the Hawley-Smoot Act to make such importations impossible, or at least unprofitable, but in the political high tension which surrounded the enactment of the schedule, Congress failed to provide a remedy.

In the meantime, and undoubtedly as a protective measure, the refiners had begun the practice of mixing raw sugar with water, reducing the polariscopic test below the 48-degree mark and clearing it through the Eastern ports at the rate which is normally paid for syrup. Each gallon of the so-called syrup contained about 2 pounds of sugar which, under the Hawley-Smoot rates, meant the payment of about an eighth of a cent a pound in duty as compared with the two cents that would have been assessed against a like amount of 96 degree sugar in undiluted form.

It is not too much to say that the Treasury Department was as vitally concerned in the settlement of the problem as the domestic sugar-makers. The import tax on sugar each year represents about one-fifth of all revenues collected at our ports, and in these days when the Government's income from other sources shows an alarming tendency to shrink, the proper administration of the sugar tariff became a matter of utmost importance. The potential difference in revenues is clearly illustrated by the test case upon which the Treasury based its decision. The disputed cargo was one brought into the United States from Cuba by the Pennsylvania Sugar Refining Company of Philadelphia. Counsel for the refiners contended that the shipment was syrup and, as such, it was not necessary to pay more than a total of $930 in duty. The Treasury took the position that the cargo was not a syrup in the strict meaning of the term and that the proper duty would be approximately $50,000. The case is now to be carried to the Supreme Court for final settlement but it requires no great courage to predict that the Treasury's decision will be upheld.

There is a general feeling among sugar men who visit Washington that the report of the Farm Board's advisory committee on sugar holds some promise of better things. It will be remembered that the most important of the recommendations of the committee was the establishment of a clearing house through which domestic sugar would be marketed with a view to elimination of cross-hauling and other wasteful practices. The beet growers' co-operative is now giving the plan a great deal of careful study, and all groups among the beet processors are lending their heartiest moral support. For the time being it must be little more than moral support for the reason that the clearing house, if it is finally formed, will be set up under conditions which seem most satisfactory to the growers. In other words, the initiative must come from the co-operatives rather than from the manufacturers of sugar. Louisiana of a certainty will have a large part in the enterprise.

If the clearing house is established and Cuba actually restricts its production as well as its exports to the United States, perhaps it is not too much to expect that there are happier days ahead.

STATEMENT OF THE OWNERSHIP, MANAGEMENT, CIR-
CULATION, ETC., REQUIRED BY THE ACT OF
CONGRESS OF AUGUST 24, 1912.

Of The Sugar Bulletin, published semi-monthly at New Orleans, La., for October 1, 1930. State of Louisiana, Parish of
Orleans.

Before me, a Notary Public in and for the State and parish
aforesaid, personally appeared Reginald Dykers, who, having
been duly sworn according to law, deposes and says that he is
the Editor of the Sugar Bulletin and that the following is, to
the best of his knowledge and belief, a true statement of the
ownership, management, etc., of the aforesaid publication for
the date shown in the above caption, required by the Act of
August 24, 1912, embodied in section 411, Postal Laws and
Regulations, printed on the reverse of this form, to-wit:

1. That the names and addresses of the publisher, editor,
managing editor, and business managers are: Publisher, The
American Sugar Cane League of the U. S. A., Inc., New Orleans,
La.; Editor, Reginald Dykers, New Orleans, La.; Managing
Editor, none; Business Manager, Andrew W. Dykers, New Or-
leans, La.

2. That the owner is The American Sugar Cane League of
the U. S. A., Inc., New Orleans, La.; C. D. Kemper, Franklin,
La., President; Percy A. Lemann, Donaldsonville, La., Vice-
President; Frank L. Barker, Lockport, La., Secretary-Treasurer.

3. That the known bondholders, mortgagees, and other
security holders owning or holding 1 per cent or more of total
amount of bonds, mortgages, or other securities are none.
                                  REGINALD DYKERS,
                                                    Editor.
Sworn to and subscribed before me this 27th day of September, 1930.
                          A. A. DE LA HOUSSAYE,
                                       Notary Public.
            (My commission expires at death.)

The Committee Rubs Its Eyes

In the minutes of the meeting of the American Sugar Cane League's "Contact Committee" with the Louisiana Experiment Station staff held Sept. 12th, 1930, and published elsewhere in this issue, appears the following statement, emanating apparently from the entomologists of the Louisiana Experiment Station:

"At the present time, from the standpoint of borer control alone, and disregarding the effects upon soil fertility, etc., it appears that the greatest degree of borer control may be secured by the thorough burning of cane trash as early in the winter as possible."

This leaves us in the same condition above the neck as we imagine a Whirling Dervish is in after he wins a Whirling Dervish endurance contest. Dr. W. C. Stubbs made the above statement apparently unequivocally as far back as 1890, or thereabouts. Since that time the scientific gentlemen entrusted with the responsibility for our entomological salvation have consumed thousands of reams of paper, of which this publication has contributed more than its share, and thousands of the hours covered by their pay checks, to convince us that we ought not to burn the trash.

The bi-annual appropriation secured by the League from the Louisiana Legislature is expended in large part for cane borer extermination work, and the League's Contact Committee which supervises this expenditure had this amazing back-fire exploded at them point blank, apparently without turning a hair. Possibly they were too flabbergasted for utterance. Can it be that all the time and money and energy expended in the past few years to put across the doctrine of the non-burning of cane trash was bet on the wrong horse and that this awful truth is now discovered?

On the subject of cane trash, we note that at the same meeting a member of the Experiment Station staff reported that he piled twelve tons of cane trash on an acre of land and found that when this amount of trash was turned under it had a depressive effect on the nitrate nitrogen in the soil and that nitrogen fertilizers ought to be applied in such a case to correct the loss occasioned by turning under the trash. This is apropos to the borer discussion because the alternative to burning the trash is to turn it under. Of course 12 tons of trash per acre is never met with in practice. It is difficult to understand why experiments were conducted based on such an amount of trash. Such experiments would seem to be academic and to have little practical value, and of course they cost as much as experiments based on prevailing conditions.

MINUTES
MEETING OF AMERICAN SUGAR CANE LEAGUE CONTACT COMMITTEE WITH LOUISIANA EXPERIMENT STATION WORKERS

Baton Rouge, La., Sept. 12, 1930.

The meeting was called to order by Chairman Wallace. There were present Messrs. A. W. Wallace, Chairman; Elliott Jones, Secretary, Stephen Munson of the Contact Committee and Messrs. W. G. Taggart, W. E. Hinds, C. W. Edgerton, E. C. Tims, E. C. Simon, G. H. Reuss, M. B. Sturgis and C. B. Gouaux of the Experiment Station Staff.

President T. F. Atkinson of the Louisiana State University and Mr. George Arceneaux of the Federal Experiment Station, were present as visitors.

A four-page mimeographed progress report was presented by Dr. Hinds of the Department of Entomology. A trip was arranged through cooperation with the Extension Service August 25 to 28, so that Dr. Hinds might learn the general field conditions as to borer infestation, Trichogramma occurrence, and also other insect species. The trip included Beggs, Opelousas, Lafayette, St. Martinsville, New Iberia, Jeanerette, Houma, Raceland, Lockport, Thibodaux, Reserve, Napoleonville, Plaquemine and Port Allen.

Sugar Cane Borer Conditions: Borer infestation was found to be extremely light. Highest infestation was at Jeanerette on Hope Plantation, where in 213 stubble approximately 10% of the stalks were bored. Six batches of eggs were taken here in 20 minutes and of the 172 eggs total all but 2 were parasitized by Trichogramma. It would appear that only from 2 to 5% of the cane stalks in an average of all varieties and fields would show borer burrows at the end of August, 1930. This percentage is remarkably low. **Soybean Caterpillar (Anticarsia gemmatilis):** This caterpillar was found at Baton Rouge by Mr. Stracener on August 18. During the trip outlined the entomologist saw no sign of soybean stripping from Baton Rouge to Melville, however, from Opelousas southward, especially in Otootan beans, the caterpillars and their moths were found in considerable numbers. Heaviest infestation appeared to be around New Iberia and Jeanerette, as in 1929. In the southern part of the cane belt, approximately 80% of the bean crop had already been harvested for hay or turned under so that the damage through this area will be comparatively small. **Blister Beetles (Epicauta vittata):** These have appeared again in large numbers in one cut of soybeans at the Sugar Station. These were controlled by a single application of barium, full-strength, fluosilicate ("Dutox," of Grasselli Chemical Co.). In 24 hours after dusting the majority of the beetles were dead or had disappeared entirely. **Trichogramma Production:** Moth production this month has been somewhat smaller than during July. Mr. Dugas' reports show a moth production of approximately 185,600 with a total egg production of 2,246,500. On account of lack of field workers and scarcity of borers at Baton Rouge it has seemed advisable to distribute the parasites produced in the heaviest known centers of borer infestation at other points in the State. On August 12 a large number of parasites were liberated on Peeble's Plantation near New Iberia. Others were sent to Mr. Gouaux and distributed by him where he felt they would do the most good. On September 5, about 100,000 were sent to Prof. W. R. Dodson at the Livestock Experiment Station, Jeanerette, for colonization in fields of soybeans where seed was desired and where moth occurrence indicated that eggs of Anticarsia gemmatilis might be abundant.

General Conclusions re Borer Control: From the results of investigational work in borer control methods, it seems clear at this time that the following plantation practices may be advisable:

1. Use the soundest, borer-free cane obtainable for seed. At Cinclare in 1929 the stand was reduced 14% where moderately infested seed cane was planted in comparison with the yield from unbored seed taken from the same field, and the weight of mill cane was 9% greater in the sound seed cut.

2. Varieties P.O.J. 36 and 36 M are so much less susceptible to borer attack than are 213 and 234 that it seems advisable to plant them generally on front cuts where borer attack is known to be most severe as a rule.

3. The method of trash disposal is still a problem and recommendations may change as further information is secured. At the present time, from the standpoint of borer control alone, and disregarding the effects upon soil fertility, etc., it appears that the greatest degree of borer control may be secured by the thorough burning of cane trash as early in the winter as possible. Experiments conducted at Cinclare in 1928-1929 showed the following results:

TRASH TREATMENT	Borer Larvae per 1,000 tops			
	Total	Alive	% Alive	Ratio of Living Larvae
Burned in January, 1929..	24	4	17	1.00
Unburned, unburied to March 1..	55	27	50	6.75
Partially buried in January	77	49	52	10.00

Department of Plant Pathology Report

A three-page mimeographed progress report was distributed by Dr. Tims. Pokkah-bong and Mosaic at the Test Fields: Counts were made between August 28th and September 4th. Five hundred stalks were counted to determine the percentages shown in the tables. The greatest increase in mosaic was found in P.O.J. 234 and 36 M. Mosaic in Co 281: From 1 to 5 plots in each of the test fields were examined. The disease is most widespread at Reserve, Glenwood and Youngsville. Mosaic in Co 290: On August 28th the disease was noted for the first time in the State at Reserve. On September 3rd a number of mosaic infected stalks were found at Glenwood. These were secondary infestations in the tops of stalks.

Root Studies

Effect of Nitrogen on Root Distribution: In early spring nitrate of soda was applied at the rate of 300 lbs. per acre to P.O.J. 213 plant and stubble cane at the Station. Nitrate was applied on one side of the row, then on the other, alternating so the roots could be examined on one side of the row where the fertilizer had been placed and on the other as a check.

Root studies were made beginning ten days after the application of the nitrate. Examinations showed no visible effect of the fertilizer on the distribution, length, or number of roots. Later a number of stools were dug up and root studies made. The differences of roots were not significant but the dry weight of the roots from the fertilized side of the stools was slightly greater.

Root Growth in Boxes: The weight of tops and roots was more than twice that of the series taken out a month ago. Greatest difference in first 6 inches of soil.

Root Excavation and Root Rot at Plaquemine: Studies were carried on at the plantation of Mr. E. J. Gay of root growth of root diseased and healthy cane. Two stools each of P.O.J. 213 plant cane affected with root disease and healthy stools were studied along with P.O.J. 36 second stubble showing poor growth and P.O.J. 36 first stubble apparently healthy. The plates were examined for Pythium. Many of the roots from the diseased stools of P.O.J. 213 showed evidence of Pythium injury while few of the roots from the healthy stools showed this type of rot. Roots from P.O.J. 36 showed very little evidence of Pythium. There was a high percentage of Pythium obtained from the P.O.J. 213 both healthy and diseased while there were very few cultures obtained from P.O.J. 36.

Mr. Sturgis' Report of the Effect of the Addition of Nitrogen Fertilizers on the Decomposition of Cane Trash in the Soil

Treatments were applied to 1/2000 acre controlled plats in the field on March 10, 1930.

Plat 1. Check; no treatment.
Plat 2. 12 tons trash plus 80# N and 40# P_2O_5 per acre.
Plat 3. 12 tons trash plus 80# N per acre.
Plat 4. 12 tons trash plus 40# N per acre.
Plat 5. 12 tons trash only per acre.

The results shown from the experimental data as listed in the tables are:

1. The turning of cane trash into soil has a marked effect in depressing the nitrate nitrogen in the soil.
2. Application of nitrogen fertilizer at the time of turning under trash will correct for the depression. An application of 40# N per acre when large amounts of trash as 12 tons per acre is turned under is barely enough nitrogen while 80# of N per acre kept the nitrate nitrogen accumulation at more than twice that in the untreated checks.
3. The addition of nitrogen fertilizers with trash stimulates the decomposition of the more resistant lignin materials in the trash.
4. The lignin fraction of cane trash is resistant in the earlier stages of decomposition and will tend to accumulate in the soil if there is a lack of aeration as

(Continued on page 10.)

1930 additions to the Users of Oliver United Cane Mud Filters ◣ ◣

CONTINUOUS cane mud filtration (using perforated brass filter medium) ... a good start was made early in 1929 when a prominent mill in Brazil installed Oliver United Cane Mud Filters and later on when a company in the Philippines followed suit.

Naturally these filters were watched closely. If they failed, it was just another attempt to solve a messy problem. If they were successful, they would be hailed as a great boon to cane sugar producers everywhere.

Were these Oliver United Cane Mud Filters successful? Did they lower costs? Did they increase recoveries?

Well, since those initial installations, Argentina, two more in Brazil, Porto Rico and two in Mexico have ordered similar units. The results obtained in Brazil and in the Philippines were strong influencing factors.

And the best part of it is that this treatment has universal application. Practically every cane sugar producer would derive equal benefits by using the Oliver United Mud Filter.

when the trash is buried, but if the trash is turned into the first 5 inches of surface soil there is no excessive accumulation of the lignin fraction.

5. The true lignin in the lignin fraction does exist in the soil as such but gradually changes, possibly as a result of oxidation, to humus material which holds a very considerable percentage of nitrogen.

6. The addition of cane trash and the resultant decomposition following from it increased the availability of phosphorus 10 to 20 lbs. per acre.

7. The addition of phosphorus with the trash had no apparent effect on the rate of decomposition. The soil was very high in available phosphorus.

8. None of the treatments showed any marked influence on the nitrogen-fixing flora of the soil and the nitrogen-fixing power as measured in the laboratory.

If cane trash is to be turned under it should be turned under lightly as soon as possible after harvest. If large amounts of trash are turned under in the spring nitrogen fertilizers may be applied with the trash to prevent the depression of nitrate nitrogen in the soil. If no correction is made for the depressive effect of the trash the crop growing on the soil will suffer from lack of available nitrogen.

General Discussions

The question came up as to what should be done about the release of the two varieties—CP 807 and Co 281. The good and bad qualities of these canes were discussed. Mr. Arceneaux stated that they have been unable to establish mosaic infection on Co 281. He stated also that he believed 281 to have more merits than any released variety. Dr. Edgerton stated that although a little mosaic has appeared on 281 in places, that this should not be taken into consideration with respect to its release because most all released varieties have mosaic.

Mr. Arceneaux says there are between three and five hundred tons of CP 807 available for release and between eight and ten hundred tons of Co 281. He does not think the Louisiana planters will go into these new canes so heavily as to hurt their crops if these varieties prove not as valuable as anticipated.

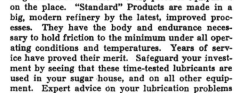

Circulation of this issue 1900 Copies

THE SUGAR BULLETIN

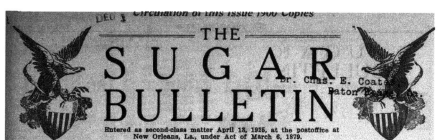

Dr. Chas. E. Coates
Baton Rouge, La.

Entered as second-class matter April 13, 1925, at the postoffice at
New Orleans, La., under Act of March 6, 1879.

We stand for the encouragement of Home Industries as against Foreign competition.

Vol. 9   NEW ORLEANS, LA., NOVEMBER 1, 1930   No. 3

League Wins Important Reduction in Intrastate Freight Rates on Raw Sugar

The American Sugar Cane League is very glad to be able to announce that the complaint filed by it with the Louisiana Public Service Commission on August 27, 1930, for the purpose of obtaining a more equitable schedule of freight rates on raw sugar from various producing points in Louisiana to New Orleans, Gramercy, Reserve and Chalmette (Three Oaks) was heard by the Commission at the St. Charles Hotel in New Orleans on September 24, 1930, and order was issued October 16, 1930, in behalf of complainant. This order became effective October 29, 1930, and is as follows:

LOUISIANA PUBLIC SERVICE COMMISSION ORDER NO. 755. NEW ORLEANS JOINT TRAFFIC BUREAU VS. LOUISIANA & ARKANSAS RAILWAY COMPANY ET AL.

In re: Rates on raw sugars, carloads, from producing points in Louisiana to New Orleans, Gramercy, Reserve and Three Oaks, Louisiana.

OPINION BY CHAIRMAN FRANCIS WILLIAMS AND COMMISSIONER DUDLEY J. LeBLANC

Complainant is a voluntary organization with its domicile in the City of New Orleans, charged with the duty of protecting and fostering the traffic and commerce of the City of New Orleans and its various constituent bodies. Among these constituent bodies is the American Sugar Cane League. This League, in turn, is composed of and represents the sugar producing and manufacturing interests of the State of Louisiana.

By complaint filed on August 27, 1930, the rates on raw sugars, carloads, from the various producing points in the State to New Orleans, Gramercy, Reserve and Three Oaks, Louisiana, are attacked. At these destination points are located sugar refineries where raw sugars are converted into a refined product.

Under proper resolution of the Commission the matter was referred to Francis Williams, Chairman, for hearing, and such hearing was had before him at New Orleans on September 24, 1930. An extensive record was there made. The findings and recommendations of Chairman Williams form the basis of this order.

While not controlling, or even of material bearing in the fixing of just and reasonable rates, it is proper to say, for it is a matter within the knowledge of all, that the sugar industry is at this time in the midst of one of the gravest crises in its history. The condition is not peculiar to Louisiana producers, but it is worldwide. To the extent that relief, in some measure, may

be afforded the industry, by a readjustment of the rates on raw sugars moving to the refining points, consistent with a reasonable basis of earnings to the carriers for the service performed, we think the prevailing conditions should be accorded some consideration in a proper disposition of this case.

The great bulk of sugar production in the State of Louisiana is west of the Mississippi River, the tonnage originating east of the river being negligible—so small, in fact, that the east side lines did not participate in the case.

A review of the various exhibits filed by both the complainant and the defendants indicates a striking lack of uniformity in the rates for comparable distances. It is shown that for a haul of 86.5 miles on the Texas & New Orleans Railroad, from Southdown to New Orleans, a rate of 17 cents is assessed. For a haul of 86.6 miles, from McCall to New Orleans, the Texas and Pacific rate is 11.5 cents. There are numerous instances where the discrepancy is even greater, but we think it unnecessary to deal with the case at any length from that standpoint.

The scale proposed by the complainant is blanketed for all hauls in excess of 210 miles, since that distance is generally the maximum haul accorded raw sugars moving within the State.

In our opinion the car mile revenue figures placed in evidence by witness Moulton for the complainant as respects raw sugar on the one hand and refined sugar and various other commodities on the other hand, conclusively demonstrate the inherent unreasonableness of the present bases. It is true that as to some of the commodities the minimum weights are lower than those proposed for raw sugars, but this is largely offset by the fact that the hauls on the raw sugars are, because of the peculiar character of the traffic, usually shorter. It is shown that for the 1929-1930 season the average weight per car was approximately 74,000 pounds. It is not contended by the carriers that any unusual service is accorded these raw sugars, other than that the spurs leading to some of the mills are somewhat in excess of the average length of spur tracks; nor is it shown that the heavy loading of raw sugars has in any instances resulted in gross train tonnage in excess of the rating of the locomotive assigned to the handling of such train. The disparity in minimum weights, therefore, becomes of minor importance.

A few comparisons of the car mile revenues under the present and proposed rates on raw sugars with similar movements of refined sugar are most convincing. According to Moulton's Exhibit 3 for an average haul of 96.5 miles the proposed rates will yield car mile earn-

THE

SUGAR
BULLETIN

407 Carondelet St., New Orleans

Issued on the 1st and 15th of each month. Official Organ of the American
Sugar Cane League of the U. S. A., in which are consolidated
The Louisiana Sugar Planters' Assn.
The American Cane Growers' Assn.
The Producers & Mfgrs. Protective Assn.
Subscription Price, 50 Cents Per Year.

Reginald Dykers, General Manager & Editor of the Bulletin
301 Nola Bldg., New Orleans

Frank L. Barker, Secretary and Treasurer
Lockport, La.

C. J. Bourg, Manager Washington Office
810 Union Trust Building

CHAIRMEN OF COMMITTEES:

C. D. Kemper, Franklin, La.
President of the League and Ex-Officio Chairman of Executive Committee

Andrew H. Gay, Plaquemine, La.
Chairman Agricultural Committee

David W. Pipes, Jr., Houma, La.
Chairman Industrial Committee

Frank L. Barker, Lockport, La.
Chairman Finance Committee.

Edward J. Gay, Plaquemine, La.
Chairman Tariff Committee

H. Langdon Laws, Cinclare, La.
Chairman Legislative Committee

J. C. LeBourgeois, New Orleans, La.
Chairman Freight Rate Committee

R. H. Chadwick, Bayou Goula, La.
Chairman Membership Committee

A. H. Rosenfeld, New Orleans, La.
Chairman Publicity Committee

Members of the League desiring action on, or information on, any subject are invited to communicate with the League or with the Chairman of the Committee to which it seems to appertain.

ings of 97.9 cents on a minimum of 80,000 pounds and 108.8 cents on a loading of 75,000 pounds. On refined sugar, at loadings of 40,000 and 45,000 pounds, respectively, the statement reflects car mile revenues of 102.4 cents and 115.2 cents. These figures are based on actual movements in 19 producing points on the Texas and Pacific. Actual movements from 22 producing points on the Texas and New Orleans Railroad, for an average haul of 119.1 miles produce similar results, as is the case with exhibits showing movements from producing points on other defendant lines.

We think these figures in and of themselves clearly justify a basis of rates which will reflect a more reasonable relationship as between the raw and refined products.

Several witnesses were offered by the carriers who presented statistical data as to earnings and operating and other expenses within the State of Louisiana as compared to system returns. These witnesses made no attempt to segregate or present cost studies as to the movement of raw sugars, and this failure, considered in connection with the arbitrary methods followed in allocating certain charges to the capital and operating accounts of the carriers to their Louisiana business, warrant us in disregarding their testimony.

In our opinion the record amply sustains the allegations of unreasonableness of the current rates as complained of in the petition and the reasonableness of the proposed scales, and an order will accordingly issue. It is

ORDERED, that for the transportation of raw sugars, carloads, from producing points in Louisiana west of the Mississippi River on the lines of the Texas and Pacific Railway Company, the Texas and New Orleans Railroad Company, the New Orleans, Texas and Mexico Railway Company, and the New Iberia and Northern Railroad Company, to New Orleans, La., points within the New Orleans District, Three Oaks, La., the following rates, rules and minimum weights shall apply:

RAW SUGAR, CARLOADS
Rates in cents per 100 pounds

Distance of	Scale A Note 1	Scale B Note 2
85 miles and less..............	9	11
110 miles and over 85	11½	13½
130 miles and over 110............	13	15
150 miles and over 130............	14½	16½
170 miles and over 150............	16	18
190 miles and over 170............	17½	19½
210 miles and over 190............	19	21
Over 210 miles..............	21	23

Note 1—Minimum weight 80,000 pounds, except when capacity of the car is less in which case capacity of the car will govern, minimum weight in no case to be less than 60,000 pounds.

Note 2—Minimum weight 60,000 pounds, except when capacity of the car is less in which case capacity of the car will govern, minimum weight in no case to be less than 50,000 pounds.

It is further

ORDERED, that on movements of raw sugars, carloads, from producing points on the lines of The Texas and Pacific Railway Company and the Texas and New Orleans Railroad Company to Gramercy and Reserve, Louisiana, the rates shall be the rates hereinabove prescribed to New Orleans, Louisiana, plus 2½ cents per 100 pounds; and that from producing points on the lines of the New Orleans, Texas and Mexico Railway Company and the New Iberia and Northern Railroad Company to Gramercy and Reserve, Louisiana, rates shall be the same as are prescribed herein from the same points to New Orleans, Louisiana; that in computing distances the shortest routes over which carload traffic can be moved without transfer of lading shall be used; that where a crossing of the Mississippi River is involved twenty (20) constructive miles shall be added to the mileage; that alternate use shall be made of the scales prescribed under Scale "A" and Note 1 and Scale "B" and Note 2, the lowest per car charge to apply; and it is further

ORDERED, that the Louisiana Public Service Commission shall and it hereby does retain jurisdiction over the subject matter of this order, reserving the right to amend, alter, modify or annul the rates, rules and minimum weights herein prescribed, either on its own motion or on the motion of any party at interest; and that all rates, rules, tariffs, authorities and regulations in conflict herewith shall be cancelled and annulled when this order becomes effective.

This order shall become effective October 29th, 1930.
BY ORDER OF THE COMMISSION
Baton Rouge, Louisiana.
October 16, 1930.
(SEAL)
(Sgd.) HENRY JASTREMSKI,
Secretary.
Attest: A TRUE COPY:
(Sgd.) HENRY JASTREMSKI,
Secretary.
(Signed) FRANCIS WILLIAMS,
Chairman.
(Signed) DUDLEY J. LeBLANC,
Commissioner.
(Signed) H. G. FIELDS,
Commissioner.

A very important saving to Louisiana shippers of raw sugar will result from this order of the Louisiana Public Service Commission. The decision to file the complaint was arrived at by the Freight Rate Committee of the American Sugar Cane League after several meetings and several conferences with the experts of the New Orleans Joint Traffic Bureau of which the League is a constituent member. Of course, the few factories that have refused to pay dues to the League will share in the benefit of the reduction in rates just as much as the League members. This cannot be helped, but there is something so radically unfair about it that it would seem as though the most confirmed individualist would realize that his course is not only unbecoming but, in the long run, destined to be less profitable to him than he now imagines.

Clarification of Louisiana Cane Juices

By C. F. WALTON, JR., and C. A. FORT,
Carbohydrate Division, Bureau of Chemistry and Soils,
U. S. Department of Agriculture

Two distinct lines of work are under way at the Bureau of Chemistry and Soils field station, near Houma, Louisiana, one being conducted by the Soil Fertility Division and the other by the Carbohydrate Division. The work of the Carbohydrate Division consists of chemical and technological research with the object of improving sugar production methods in general, and in particular studying clarification of the juice for the purpose of assisting in the production of improved and more uniform grades of sugars, sirups, and molasses.

During the early part of the grinding season in 1929, before the cane had been badly injured by the freeze, a comprehensive study of juice clarification was begun, the underlying thought being that further information should be obtained on the clarifying properties of the juices of Louisiana P.O.J. canes, and that the problem of producing white sugar in Louisiana should be reinvestigated along the lines suggested by changing economic conditions and by recent scientific developments.

By the acid sulphitation process, it is relatively easy to make 100 to 125 pounds of good quality plantation granulated sugar per ton of cane and to let the remainder of the sucrose go out, regardless of excessive inversion, in the form of high purity molasses. This is a comparatively simple process and has long been in favor in Louisiana, especially in those years when high purity molasses has brought a good price.

Market conditions often make it advisable to produce a greater proportion of white sugar by use of a somewhat different clarification process, putting all sugar possible "into the bag" by minimizing inversion losses, and making blackstrap molasses instead of high purity commercial molasses. This process is considered more difficult in some respects than the strongly acid sulphitation process, and consequently was investigated further during the 1929 grinding season.

The results of the first year's work (1929) are regarded as preliminary and will not be published at this time in complete form. The following summary, however, is given to indicate the nature of the investigations, and to call attention to certain findings that are judged to be important.

In order to have experimental results as comparable as possible with factory practice, all juices were obtained from the modern 16-roll tandem at Southdown, which in 1929 gave 93 to 94 per cent sucrose extraction. The samples are designated in this report as "double crusher and first mill" or "higher purity" juice, and as "2nd and 3rd mill" or "lower purity" juice, depending upon the part of the tandem from which the juices were taken.

RESULTS IN 1929—SUMMARY AND CONCLUSIONS

Several factory samples of plantation granulated sugar were carefully compared in the laboratory. The color of the sugars, the pH, and the turbidity of the 50-degree brix solutions varied greatly. It is obvi ously desirable to secure better quality, greater uniformity and more ready marketability in this type of sugar.

The degree of sulphuring required for good clarification of juice from P.O.J. canes was found to vary considerably. In general, it is concluded that a degree of sulphuring somewhat higher than that commonly practiced in the larger factories gives an improved clarification for white sugar. This tentative conclusion is based on small-scale clarification and sugar-boiling experiments. After sulphuring the juice to the customary degree of titrated acidity and sulphuring a corresponding sample to a greater acidity, defecating the juices to the same clarified acidity and pH values, and evaporating to sirup in a small vacuum pan, the samples were boiled to sugar, also in a vacuum pan, under strictly comparable conditions. The standardized method of sugar boiling was based upon the data of Thieme, and use was made of a graph showing the sucrose saturation of cane sirups at different purities and at varying temperatures and pressures. Both the sirup and the sugar produced from the more highly sulphured juice were better, having less turbidity, color, colloids and ash that the sugar and sirup from the best highly sulphured juice.

It was found that the combined double crusher and first mill juice from the tandem at Southdown required much less sulphuring than was necessary for the lower purity, combined 2d and 3d mill juices from the same cane. On an equal brix basis, the higher purity juice requires only about half as much sulphuring as the combined 2d and 3d mill juices. In these experiments also, the sirup samples were boiled to grain, and the sugars were compared as to quality. In handling juices from a mill giving relatively high extraction, it is evident that there is need for a higher degree of sulphuring than that now practiced at smaller factories whose mills give lower extraction.

In order to obtain the maximum yield of sugar, the sulphured juice must necessarily be limed to a relatively low degree of residual acidity, or to as high a pH as possible, approaching neutrality. The question whether a more nearly neutral clarification, accurately controlled, will produce a sugar of satisfactory quality was one of the principal considerations in this investigation. The experiments on liming sulphured juices to varying degrees of acidity, boiling the sirups to sugar, centrifuging, drying, and testing the sugars indicated that the sirup strike of sugar (1st sugar) is likely to be not only as good but probably better by liming to the higher pH value. An acidity of 0.4 cc. after liming, corresponding to a pH of about 6.8 of the clarified juice, was found to represent a satisfactory degree of liming.

Owing to the difficulty experienced in making a satisfactory grade of sugar from the lower purity juices, small scale tests were conducted in which the juice was subjected to much more drastic treatment than is customary. Juice from the 2d and 3d mills was sulphured excessively high and the flocculated material removed before liming and heating; in other experiments it was overlimed in the cold and the flocculated material removed by centrifuging before either sulphuring or adding phosphoric acid. The possible benefits of using other clarifying agents, such as "light" and "heavy" aluminum oxide of good commercial grade, bleaching powder, and decolorizing carbon, were also investigated. The results of this

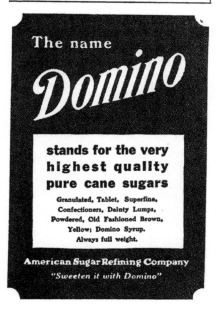

work, and of the sugar boiling experiments especially, strongly indicate that it is impracticable to produce a suitable white sugar direct from the 2d and 3d mill juices of a tandem giving relatively high (93%) sucrose extraction. The inclusion of this juice with the double crusher and 1st mill juice must make it correspondingly more difficult to produce white sugar of acceptable grade from whole mill juice. Furthermore, as is well known, in white sugar manufacture the working of juices from immature canes in Louisiana, and of juices which are of low purity for any other reason, is considerably more difficult than is the handling of juices from more mature, higher-purity canes.

The clarification of juices from frozen and deteriorated canes is even more of a problem in making white sugar of satisfactory quality. For these various reasons, it is suggested that a better plan, for the larger factories, would be to separate the mill juices, using the double crusher and first mill juice, or its equivalent, for producing a first strike of white sugar, and using the remainder of the juice from the tandem, clarified separately, for raw sugar manufacture. The molasses from the white sugar sirup strike could be combined with the sirup from the lower purity juice for raw sugar and blackstrap production.

The advantage in clarification of using lime in a relatively fine state of subdivision, and the desirability of rapid and adequate mixing to minimize the danger of local overliming, have been much investigated and discussed in recent years. Some preliminary work was done along this line, comparing the use of dry lime, thin milk of lime, heavy milk of lime, and lime sucrate. The use of sucrate, both in the cold and in the hot, was investigated. The use of sucrate in place of milk of lime in the sulphitation process was likewise studied. However, owing to the other work that was undertaken, too few experiments of this kind could be made during the season to justify final conclusions. The subject will be further investigated during the season of 1930. In general, we hope, from a continuation of the research on clarification, to be able to contribute improvements both in the sulphuring and in the liming procedures.

The part played by phosphoric acid in juice clarification was first studied in Hawaii, and a deficiency of phosphoric acid in the juice was found to be correlated with poor clarification by lime. The minimum amount of phosphate (calculated as P_2O_5) required for good clarification was reported to be 0.03 gram per 100 cc. of juice. It therefore seemed desirable in connection with the investigation of the clarification of Louisiana P.O.J. cane juices to determine the phosphate content of as many juice samples as possible, and at the same time to ascertain the extent to which an increased application of phosphate to the soil may be reflected in an increased phosphate content of the juice. This work was done in cooperation with the Soil Fertility Division of the Bureau. The analytical data, although limited in scope, indicate that normal Louisiana juices for the most part contain sufficient phosphoric acid for satisfactory clarification, the total P_2O_5 in canes grown near Southdown ranging from 0.04 to 0.08 gram per 100 cc. of juice. A portion of the total phosphorus, however, is not present in the juice in a form that is reactive with lime, and additional work on the subject is necessary to develop an analytical method for differentiating between total phosphorus and that which is present in available or reactive form. The percentage of total phosphorus in the juices from canes that received different fertilizer treatment did not vary sufficiently to warrant a definite conclusion that the phosphorus content of the juice may be increased by an increased application of phosphate to the soil.

The results of work done during the season of 1929 on the clarification of juices from frozen and deteriorated cane, and on the identification of certain fermentation products that caused trouble in factory operation will be summarized in the next issue of THE SUGAR BULLETIN.

Two Essentials for Successful Early Cropping

By ARTHUR H. ROSENFELD,
Consulting Technologist of the American Sugar Cane League

The warm, rainy, "growing" weather of September was responsible for very evident cane tonnage increases in our crop estimates, but, at the same time, considerably retarded the ripening up of the cane, as indicated by analyses from all over the State. These analyses are anything but encouraging for an early start, but, in view of the large amount of cane in sight, it seems unwise to postpone turning over the mills late enough to risk incurring serious losses through freezes. Under these conditions, planters will have to do two things very efficiently if the cane settlements and manufacturing results are to be at all worth while:

First: At this low stage of maturity, it is absolutely essential that the cane be taken to the mill with the minimum of delay possible after cutting, as inversion is extremely rapid now, and, with the present low sugar content and purity, the cane cannot drop very far before it becomes practically unmanufacturable and suffers a severe discount in price to the grower; and

Second: All growers for the first few weeks, at least, should top very drastically—taking off two or three joints more than normally and forgetting for the present the question of tonnage per acre. This will not only add to recovery per ton in the mills, but keep the cane in the higher price brackets for the grower.

In this connection a copy of a report to be presented at the meeting of the Association of Hawaiian Sugar Cane Technologists this week entitled "Effects of Cane Tops on Sugar Recovery" is produced below. The figures therein show most graphically that, even with the high sucrose cane in Hawaii, more sugar per acre can actually be produced by topping some 10 per cent additional over what is usually done, particularly in the early part of their season, and on a sucrose payment basis the better price of the low-topped cane would more than compensate the reduced tonnage per acre.

These may seem almost elementary precautions but their observance may signify the difference between a profit or a loss with present low sugar prices.

The following experiments illustrate the loss caused by the delivery to the mill of improperly topped canes:

Canes with green tops were selected from trucks in the factory yard; the tops were cut off at the base of the sheath. Canes and tops were ground in the laboratory cane mill and analyzed separately. The analysis of the whole cane, as given below, was calculated from these separate analyses (average of three tests):

	Tops Only	Topped Canes	Whole Canes
Sucrose per cent	4.17	12.71	11.65
Juice—Brix	12.23	18.20	17.50
Sucrose	5.43	15.38	14.39
Purity	44.39	84.50	82.22
Weight per cent	11.84	88.16	100.00

A lower sucrose extraction was obtained from the tops than from the remaining portion of the cane. Allowing for this, but otherwise using figures representing normal factory conditions, it was found that the tonnage of cane required to produce a ton of sugar worked out as follows:

Canes free from tops...................................... 8.72 tons
Canes with tops.. 10.34 tons

The tops representing 11.84 per cent of the weight of the cane, were responsible for an increase of 18.42 per cent in the tonnage of cane required to produce a given quantity of sugar.

It is, therefore, evident that the tops, while producing no sugar, cause an appreciable loss of the available sugar contained in the richer portion of the cane.

Cutting Cane by the Ton

The rapidly increasing interest in the practice of cutting cane by the ton leads us to publish below a table prepared for use in this connection by Mr. Robert E. LeBlanc, President and Manager of the Westfield Plantation in Assumption Parish. On all of the properties under Mr. LeBlanc's supervision the method of cutting cane by the ton has been adopted with entirely satisfactory results, and with one-third less cutters than last year he is getting the same amount of cane cut. In cane running 22 tons to the acre Mr. LeBlanc finds that good cutters are cutting very nearly three tons per day each, and although at first there was a little trouble getting the cutters to understand the principle on which they were being paid they are now getting along very well. Women cutters average about $1.50 per day. Mr. LeBlanc's cane cutting schedule is calculated per compass (6 feet) and is based on a price of 65 cents per ton. When cutting cane that yields under twelve tons per acre the new plan is not used and ordinary day wages are paid.

(Continued on page 10.)

CANE CUTTING SCHEDULE OF
THE DUGAS & LE BLANC CO., LIMITED

Cost of cutting cane per compass (6 Feet) based on a price of 65 cents per

Tons per Acre	Cost per A. @ 65c	Cost per compass	Cost per row 35 comp. long	PAY AS FOLLOWS	
				Yield tons per acre	Price per one acre
12	$7.80	$ .006446	$ .22561	12–13	23c
15	9.75	.008057	.281995	14–15–16	28c
18	11.70	.009669	.338415	17–18	34c
20	13.00	.0107438	.376033	19–20	38c
22	14.30	.0118181	.4136335	21–22–23	41c
25	16.25	.0134297	.4700396	24–25–26	47c
28	18.20	.0150414	.526449	27–28	53c
30	19.50	.0161157	.5640495	29–30–31	56c

The overseers are required to insist that cane
cut properly and they make the tonnage basis as
curate as possible. Any cane cutter who is caug
butchering cane to make time is notified that
practice must cease, and, if this warning does
bring results, the offender is dismissed. We und
stand that in cases where the cane is burned bef
cutting the schedule given herein is reduced abo
30 per cent.

Operation of Field Cane Loaders i
Louisiana

By G. H. Reuss

For years the field loading of cane in Louisia
was carried on by hand labor. In spite of the c
velopment and improvement of loading equipme
much of the cane on small sized farms is loaded
this method at the present time. The movable fi
loading machine has come into use in recent ye
and is being quite widely adopted by the larger pl
tations throughout the cane belt. During the 19
season details on the operation of these machir
were secured with the view of determining costs a
outlays of loader operation on farms of various si
and the conditions which are necessary in obtaini
operating efficiency.

The machines studied were mounted with four
six horse power engines for the operation of the loa
ing mechanism and under ordinary conditions we
drawn by four mules. A crew of five men was
quired. As an average performance these machin
loaded 115 tons per day at a cost of 13.3 cents p
ton of which 11.7 cents was actual cash expenditur
and 1.6 cents overhead charges of depreciation a
interest. This represents a large reduction in loadi
outlays over those necessarily incurred by the ha
loading method. Assuming eight tons per man as
day's work the outlay would be 18¾ cents per t
at $1.50 per day or 21.9 cents at a wage rate
$1.75.   *(Continued on next page.)*

TABLE A
AVERAGE OUTLAYS NECESSARY IN THE OPERATION OF FIELD CANE LOADERS, LOUISIANA, 1929

ITEMS	Per Ton	Per 10-Hr. Day
	Cents	Dollars
Gasoline	.9	1.02
Oil	----	.15
Grease	---	.01
Repairs	.2	.02
Man Labor	6.9	7.97
Mule Power	3.7	4.30
Total Operating	11.7	13.47
Depreciation	1.0	1.16
Interest	.6	.69
Total Outlay	13.3	15.32
Tons Loaded	----	115
Crew:		
Men	----	5
Mules	----	4
Gasoline	----	4.5 gal.
Oil	----	1.0 qts.

The outlay per ton varied quite widely between individual plantations, however. In order to determine the causes of this variation a more detailed comparison was made between two groups of machines, one composed of the three loaders having the lowest outlays and the other of the three having the highest outlays per ton. A wide variation in the acreage loaded and the tonnage handled during the season occurs between these two groups. These differences result in an overhead charge of .9 cents per ton for the low cost group in which each machine loads over 10,000 tons per season as compared with 4.1 cents for the high cost machines handling only 2,770 tons each.

TABLE B
COMPARISON OF THE OPERATION OF CANE LOADERS IN THE HIGH AND LOW COST GROUPS, LOUISIANA, 1929

ITEMS	High Cost Group	Low Cost Group
Operating Outlays per Ton	18.4 Cents	8.5 Cents
Overhead Outlays per Ton	4.1 Cents	.9 Cents
Total Outlays per Ton	22.5 Cents	9.4 Cents
Acres Handled per Machine	118.3 Acres	590.3 Acres
Days Used	39.1 Days	67.3 Days
Tons Handled per Season	2768.0 Tons	10430.0 Tons
Tons Handled per Day	62¼ Tons	155 Tons

Operating outlays are not necessarily affected by the total tons handled each year but are influenced by the amount of work done each day. The low cost loaders handled 155 tons per day and the high cost group 62¼ tons. Operating outlays were 8.5 and 18.4 cents per ton respectively.

Maximum loading efficiency is evidently obtained when each loader handles approximately 10,000 tons per year and when the cutting crew and hauling facilities are such that the loader will work at capacity each day, that is about 150 tons a day. The difference between the costs incurred under such conditions and those of performing the operation by hand is so great, however, that loaders may be profitably operated with less than capacity usage. The minimum sized unit which can employ this machine at a saving over hand loading can not be determined definitely for factors such as wage rates, and management influences it. From the data available it seems that the minimum size of farm which will justify the use of the machine method is approximately 175 acres of cane or 3,500 tons. All machines studied which handled less than this amount of cane were operated at a cost greater than that of loading by hand.

Mr. Hegenbarth Goes to Mexico

Mr. F. Hegenbarth, local representative of the Fulton Iron Works who has been active in the rehabilitation of the local sugar industry for the past three years, has asked us to tell his many friends in Louisiana that he will be absent from the State for about six months while in charge of the construction of a 1500-ton cane sugar factory and refinery at El Mante, Tamaulipas, Mexico, which is being erected by the Fulton Iron Works. Mr. Hegenbarth sailed from New Orleans on October 10th. The office of the Fulton Iron Works which has been located at 505 New Orleans Bank Building, has been moved to room No. 904 of the same building and will be in charge of Mrs. H. Byrne in Mr. Hegenbarth's absence. Any engineering problems will be promptly forwarded by Mrs. Byrne to the St. Louis office of the Fulton Iron Works which, Mr. Hegenbarth states, will continue to render its usual efficient service to the Louisiana sugar industry.

THE
SUGAR
La. State University.
Baton Rouge, La.
BULLETIN

Entered as second-class matter April 13, 1925, at the postoffice at
New Orleans, La., under Act of March 6, 1879.

We stand for the encouragement of Home Industries as against Foreign competition.

| Vol. 9 | NEW ORLEANS, LA., NOVEMBER 15, 1930 | No. 4 |

Co-ordinators Meet

Dr. E. W. Brandes, Principal Pathologist in Charge, Sugar Plant Division, United States Department of Agriculture, arrived in Louisiana on November 14th for the purpose of attending a meeting of the Co-ordination Committee which is composed of the various heads of departments in Washington and the Director of the Louisiana Experiment Station and the members of a Committee especially appointed from the American Sugar Cane League headed by Mr. David W. Pipes, Jr. The purpose of the Co-ordination Committee is to reconcile and synchronize the work done by the various Bureaus of the United States Department of Agriculture in connection with sugar cane in Louisiana. The functions of the Committee are of great importance. Dr. Oswald Schreiner accompanied Dr. Brandes as the representative of Dr. Henry G. Knight, Chief of the Bureau of Chemistry and Soils.

Dr. Brandes brought with him seven moving picture reels showing various scenes connected with the New Guinea expedition which was conducted about two years ago, and headed by him, for the purpose of obtaining new varieties of sugar cane from the unknown regions in the interior of New Guinea. These reels were shown on the evening of November 14th at the Terrebonne Parish High School in Houma, the use of which was donated by the Parish School Board for the occasion. There was no admission fee charged and interested people from far and near came to see these extraordinary moving pictures, which possess exceptional interest for Louisiana sugar planters inasmuch as they depict the far-flung activities of the United States Government in its efforts to radically improve the type of sugar cane grown in Louisiana and find and develop a species of sugar cane that will be especially well suited to our Louisiana conditions. Accompanying the display of the moving pictures there were short talks by authorities on sugar cane work in Louisiana, and Dr. Brandes acted as lecturer, explaining the pictures as they were shown.

Heading a small party of Dutch and American scientists, Dr. Brandes explored the wilds of New Guinea by seaplane seeking new varieties of sugar cane. The expedition was highly successful resulting in the collection of over 170 absolutely new varieties of sugar cane which were safely brought back to the United States. Some of these varieties are expected to prove valuable to Louisiana directly, or as parent canes in breeding work. In collecting these canes, Dr. Brandes had the unusual opportunity of seeing native life never before seen by white men, head hunters using bows and arrows and the crudest of farm implements. He took moving pictures of these wild scenes, and it is this remarkable collection of films that he exhibited at Houma.

===THE===
SUGAR
BULLETIN

407 Carondelet St., New Orleans

Issued on the 1st and 15th of each month. Official Organ of the American
Sugar Cane League of the U. S. A., in which are consolidated
The Louisiana Sugar Planters' Assn.
The American Cane Growers' Assn.
The Producers & Mfgrs. Protective Assn.
Subscription Price, 50 Cents Per Year.

Reginald Dykers, General Manager & Editor of the Bulletin
301 Nola Bldg., New Orleans
Frank L. Barker, Secretary and Treasurer
Lockport, La.
C. J. Bourg, Manager Washington Office
810 Union Trust Building

CHAIRMEN OF COMMITTEES:
C. D. Kemper, Franklin, La.
President of the League and Ex-Officio Chairman of Executive Committee
Andrew H. Gay, Plaquemine, La,
Chairman Agricultural Committee
David W. Pipes, Jr., Houma, La.
Chairman Industrial Committee
Frank L. Barker, Lockport, La.
Chairman Finance Committee.
Edward J. Gay, Plaquemine, La.
Chairman Tariff Committee
H. Langdon Laws, Cinclare, La.
Chairman Legislative Committee
J. C. LeBourgeois, New Orleans, La.
Chairman Freight Rate Committee
R. H. Chadwick, Bayou Goula, La.
Chairman Membership Committee
A. H. Rosenfeld, New Orleans, La.
Chairman Publicity Committee

Members of the League desiring action on, or information on, any subject are invited to communicate with
the League or with the Chairman of the Committee
to which it seems to appertain.

Clarification of Juices from Frozen and Deteriorated Cane

By C. F. Walton, Jr., and C. A. Fort,
Carbohydrate Division, Bureau of Chemistry and
Soils, U. S. Department of Agriculture.

The experimental work on clarification summarized
in the previous issue of the SUGAR BULLETIN was conducted on the various mill juices during a period
when the initial juice acidity was not more than 2.5
cc. (0.1 N sodium hydroxide per 10 cc. of juice).
After the severe freeze (1929), deterioration of the
cane had occurred in some cases, but by careful selection of the juices at the mill and by accepting juice
only from reasonably good cane it was possible to obtain juice for experimental purposes with an acidity
which did not exceed the figure just given. A point
was reached, however, about January 1st, when, even
with careful selection, it was no longer possible to obtain a juice of sufficiently low acidity. As it is un-
likely that direct-consumption white sugar of the best
grade can be made profitably from juice having an
initial acidity materially over 3.0 cc., and as the
frozen cane problem will always have to be contended
with in Louisiana, it seemed advisable at this time
to do as much work as possible on the clarification
of juices from frozen and deteriorated canes for raw
sugar manufacture. Consideration of the frozen cane
problem is an integral part of any program of "saving the crop."

The opportunity for this preliminary investigation
was brief, hence the results are published at this time
in the form of only a summary.

Light Liming Versus Heavy Liming

In comparing the light liming and the heavy liming
of acid juices (initial acidity over 2.5 cc.), it was
found that heavier liming, i. e., liming to a higher
pH of clarified juice, is apparently advantageous a
times in raw sugar production, but this is not always
the case with all juices irrespective of the degree o
deterioration. For example, juice having an initial
acidity of 3.85 cc. was divided into two portions, one
of which was limed to 1.3 cc. acidity, or to a pH o
5.4 of the clarified juice, whereas the other was limed
to 0.25 cc. acidity, corresponding to a pH of 6.7 o
the clarified juice. The clarified juices were evaporated in a small vacuum pan to the density of effec
sirup, and various tests were then made on the sirup
before the sugar-boiling experiments were started
The results of these tests are as follows:

Tests on Sirups	Light Liming	Heavy Liming
Acidity at 15° Brix	1.1 cc.	0.3 cc.
pH at 15° Brix	5.32	6.45
Turbidity Number at 15° Brix	707	417 (better)
% Suspended Solids	0.27	0.20
% Gums (calculated on solids)	1.67	1.46
% Invert Sugar (calculated on solids)	12.82	12.32
Dye Number (approximate measure of colloidal material)	1180	1070 (better)
Engler Viscosity at 50° Brix	106 seconds	103 seconds
Color Number at 50° Brix	97 (better)	121
Color Number at pH 7.0	133 (better)	146
% Ash (calculated on solids)	3.06	3.18
True Purity	74.2	74.6
Yield of 1st Sugar	340 grams	430 grams
Color of Sugar (50° Brix sirup)	20 (better)	34

Very closely comparable results were obtained in
a second experiment, similar to the above, with
juice having an initial acidity of 3.8 cc. The more
heavily limed samples in both experiments were clear-
er without showing a material increase in total ash.
With higher liming, there was slightly less inversion,
as indicated by the percentage of reducing sugars
(calculated as invert sugar) and the true purity. As
well as could be observed on a small scale, the boiling characteristics of the lightly limed and heavily
limed samples were nearly equal. The sugar produced by liming more heavily was somewhat darker
in color, and a quantity of elongated sucrose crystals
were observed when this sample was boiled, whereas
needle-shaped grain did not appear in the lightly-
limed sample.

A similar comparison was made with juice that had
an initial acidity of 7.2 cc. The results obtained
are as follows:

Tests on Sirups	Light Liming	Heavy Liming
Acidity at 15° Brix	2.1 cc.	0.5 cc.
pH at 15° Brix	4.9	6.3
Turbidity Number at 15° Brix	1116	306 (better)
% Suspended Solids	0.46	0.14
% Gums (calculated on solids)	1.24	1.16
% Invert Sugar (calculated on solids)	19.13	15.97
Dye Number (approximate measure of colloidal material)	1630	1370 (better)
Engler Viscosity at 50° Brix	100 seconds	108 seconds
Color Number at 50° Brix	100 (better)	646
Color Number at pH 7.0	293 (better)	1067
% Ash (calculated on Solids)	3.34	3.82
Apparent Purity	62	65

When the acidity was as high and the purity as
low as in the above mentioned examples, sugar boiling was exceedingly slow and growth of the grain
(Continued on page 4)

was obtained with difficulty so that, although the
massecuite appeared well crystallized, the sugar was
not retained by the centrifuge screen. Even when the
massecuites were remelted and reboiled, and 50 per
cent additional time was taken for the strike, the size
of the crystals was not large enough for centrifuging
This was true of both the lightly limed and heavily
limed samples.

The practical question is, at just what degree of
deterioration does it become inadvisable to put cane
through the factory, and what analytical method can
best be used in the control laboratory to indicate in
advance how the canes being received will behave in
the factory? Also, can the method of clarification be
improved in any way to make possible more efficien
handling of those "slow working" juices?

There does not appear to be any striking advantage
in either light or heavy liming of acid juices. Heavie
liming, although it increases the volume of muds to
be handled, reduces the danger of inversion and
would seem to be the better practice—at least up to
the point when difficulty in sugar boiling begins
Further work will be done on this problem whenever
juice from frozen and deteriorated cane is available

Use of Other Clarifying Agents

In other experiments, attempts were made to im
prove the quality of highly acid juice by the use of
various clarifying agents. The usual defecation with
milk of lime was contrasted with the sulphitation
process. Sulphuring the cold juice was compared
with sulphuring hot juice. Lime sucrate was used
being added both to the cold and the hot juice. In
another experiment, cold juice was purposely over
limed, phosphoric acid was added until the juice wa
neutral, and after defecation the juice was sulphured
Some of these samples were evaporated to sirup, bu
in most cases no attempt was made to boil suga
from them.

Several other clarifying agents were studied briefly
Sodium carbonate was used to replace part of the
lime required in the ordinary lime defecation, bu
the limited data obtained did not substantiate the
advantage that has been claimed for this practice
The only special re-agents tested which appeared to
have possible value were sodium fluoride and am
monium fluoride. The degree of flocculation in the
cold obtained by the use of fluorides was exceptiona
but this process, on the whole, cannot be recommend
ed at present. Further experiments are planned fo
the season of 1930.

Composition of Juice from Frozen and Badly Deteriorated Cane

At the very end of the season, when the cane wa
of such poor quality that it no longer really paid to
put it through the factory, the molasses in magma
at a near-by factory seemed to solidify or "set," so
that difficulty was experienced in pumping it out of
tank cars; and about the same time a similar produc
was obtained at the Station by evaporating exces
sively acid juice to a density of about 70° Brix. Thi
"setting" occurred on allowing the sirup to stan
over night, and took place regardless of whether the
juice had been clarified by use of lime or by hea
alone without any lime. Samples of the product wer
sent to Washington for further investigation. A tech
nical paper on this subject was read at the Cincin
nati meeting of the American Chemical Society (Sep

tember 9-12, 1930), and will be published in full at an early date.

Briefly stated, a quantity of needle-shaped crystals, amounting to about 7 per cent based on total solids, was separated from the 70° Brix laboratory samples. This substance was recrystallized and identified as the sugar-alcohol "mannite" (d-mannitol). About 4 per cent of colloidal material was also separated from the product. After filtration, this had a specific rotation of +157° indicating that this material consists largely of dextrorotatory gum. Approximately half the acid originally in the juice had been removed when the juice was evaporated to sirup. This volatile acid was found to consist entirely of acetic acid.

Although mannite has previously been reported as a fermentation product in frozen cane, the thought does not appear to have been advanced that it may occur in such quantity as to cause factory operating trouble. Owing to its limited solubility and its property of crystallizing in a web-like mass of interlacing needles, mannite is regarded as the principal cause of the "setting" and difficult handling of this type of molasses.

Mannite is not optically active under the customary conditions for polarizing samples in the control laboratory. The gums, being dextrorotatory, may introduce an analytical error. The gums cause an increase in viscosity, and are very likely responsible to some degree for the slow boiling of products from the juice of deteriorated cane. Both mannite and the gums reduce the true purity, particularly if they are present in considerable quantities, thereby necessitating a higher density in order to obtain the required sucrose saturation and contributing to poor circulation in the pans in boiling sugar.

Preliminary work has also been done to develop a laboratory analytical method for determining mannite in juices from deteriorated cane. Such a method (in conjunction with the acidity, gum and purity determination) would be of considerable use in appraising the value of deteriorated cane.

During the season of 1930, it is planned to continue the investigation of clarification for white sugar production, working principally on the higher purity juices and attempting to ascertain by repeated trials the most efficient method of clarification for producing maximum yield and satisfactory quality. Experimental work on the clarification and subsequent handling of juices from frozen and deteriorated canes will be continued whenever juices of this nature are available.

A detailed record of all investigations will be kept at the Station at Houma, La., where visitors are welcome at all times.

C. P. 807

In the United States Daily (Washington, D. C.) of October 30th, 1930, Dr. E. W. Brandes has considerable to say about the variety of cane known as C.P. 807, recently released for commercial planting through the American Sugar Cane League. Dr. Brandes gives the pedigree of C.P. 807 and points out that it is from seed produced during the winter of 1924-25 by the variety U.S. 1643, which was in turn grown from seed of P.O.J. 213 received from Coimbatore, India, in 1921. The seedling U.S. 1643 was thus one of the first produced at the Canal Point station and has an unusual and interesting history. The letters "C.

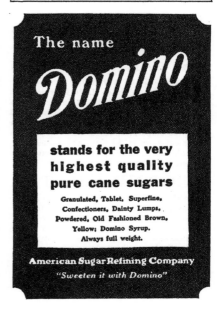

Warming Raw Juice
=== *By* ===

STEAM INJECTION

is the title of a recently published report from a Dutch factory, which you should read carefully. It fully confirms the claim made for the Corne Heater, that in spite of the higher percentage of water to be evaporated, the time for evaporation is cut down to the point where a considerable fuel saving is obtained, operation permitting to reduce labor personnel. The

CORNE HEATER

will enable you to operate at a profit during periods of low sugar prices. Inexpensive and extremely simple, readily installed, induces rapid settling, reduced boiling time and facility of drying in centrifugals. Particulars without obligation.

CHAS. CORNE
LAFAYETTE, LA.

P." stand for Canal Point, Florida, where the Federal sugar cane station for breeding new varieties of cane is located. Dr. Brandes then goes on as follows "Sugar cane seeds are, generally speaking, very short lived—that is they retain their viability for only a few days to a few weeks. In the case of P.O.J. 21: seed from India, which was carefully dried and packed in hermetically sealed packages, a large per centage of the seeds germinated here and after a journey requiring more than two months".

"The variety P.O.J. 213 did not originate in India but at the Experiment Station of the Dutch Suga Syndicate at Pasoeroean, Java. It is a species hybrid resulting from a cross between Saccharum officinarun (Var. Zwart Cheribon and Saccharum barberi) (Var Chunee) in the year 1899.

"C.P. 807 has been consistently superior in yield of sugar per acre. Compared with P.O.J. 213, th highest yielding of the P.O.J. varieties, C.P. 807 ha made an impressive record. In tests at Houma, La in 1928 the yield of sugar per acre from P.O.J. 21 was 4,865 pounds, and from the new seedling 6,48 pounds. In 1929 the average yield in four field test in various parts of the State was 4,983 pounds b P.O.J. 213 and 6,725 pounds by the seedling. Th seedling is disease-resistant to a high degree. Stub bling qualities of the new variety are quite accepta ble, as evidenced by the yield obtained, 7,003 pound of sugar per acre, in one small-scale field of firs stubble at Houma last year. The average of all can experiments in Louisiana indicates that C.P. 807 lead its nearest rival P.O.J. 213, by nearly a ton of suga per acre, or. about 35 per cent more than the best o the sugar canes now grown there. Analysis shows i to be slightly higher in fiber content than P.O.J. 21 but with modern milling equipment this presents n difficulty."

A Sugar Co-operative Almost Formed

The American Sugar Cane League has, at its offic No. 407 Carondelet Street, New Orleans, a charte for a sugar co-operative association, the formation c which is essential if any of the benefits obtainabl through the Federal Farm Board are to be secured b the cane growers and sugar producers in Louisiana The form of charter required under the law is ver simple and there are special provisions through whic it is possible to legally promulgate it at a nomina cost. In fact, while the Federal Farm Board insist that it will deal with farmers only through a cc operative association, everything possible has bee done to make the formation of such an associatio easy and inexpensive.

The charter at the League's office has already bee signed by Sterling Sugars, Inc., Shadyside Co., Inc Percy A. Lemann, The J. M. Burguieres Co., Ltd Clotilda Plantation, Inc., Valentine Sugars, Inc., an David W. Pipes, Jr. A minimum of ten signature is required and the League invites those desiring t sign to call and do so.

The Federal Farm Board is lending financial ai to cotton growers, wheat growers and growers of va rious other commodities to the tune of millions o dollars, and it has done this through the co-operative representing the producers of cotton, wheat and othe commodities. The sugar cane growers and can
(Continued on page 8.)

sugar producers ought to get their co-operative organized. When that is done, and not until that is done, they can find out what the Federal Farm Board can do for them.

In order that all interested may see how the charter reads we publish it in full below and we urge the prompt addition of many more signatures.

UNITED STATES OF AMERICA
STATE OF LOUISIANA
PARISH OF ....

The undersigned persons whose names and postoffice addresses are hereinafter set out, all of the full age of majority and engaged in the production of sugar cane, now severally and jointly declare that availing themselves of the provisions of the Laws of the State of Louisiana relative to the formation of associations and particularly of Act No. 57 of the Legislature of Louisiana regular session of 1922 and all amendments thereto, they do by these presents form and organize themselves into a non-profit co-operative association without capital stock, for the objects and purposes and under the stipulations and agreements hereinafter set forth, which they adopt as the charter of said association, to-wit:

ARTICLE I

The name of the Association shall be .... and the place of its principal business shall be ....

ARTICLE II

The purposes for which this association is formed are:

(a) To aid and assist the growers of sugar cane in the successful and profitable production, harvesting and marketing of sugar cane.

(b) To engage in any activity in connection with the harvesting, processing, manufacturing, marketing, storing or utilization of sugar cane produced or delivered to it by its members, or of the by-products thereof, or with the purchase, hiring or use by its members of supplies, machinery or equipment, or in the financing of any such activities.

(c) To establish weighing or testing services for its members.

(d) To borrow money without limitation as to amount of corporate indebtedness or liability; to pledge any of its property as security therefor; and to make advance payments and advances to members.

(e) To act as agent or representative of any member or members in any such activities, and to that end to enter into contracts with its members for the exclusive and irrevocable right to market their sugar cane.

(f) To buy, lease, hold and exercise all privileges of ownership, over such real or personal property as may be necessary or convenient for the conduct and operation of the business of the association, or incidental thereto.

(g) To buy and sell sugar cane and its by-products and contract therefor.

(h) To establish reserves and to invest the funds thereof in bonds or other securities.

(i) To draw, make, accept, endorse, guarantee, execute, and issue promissory notes, bills of exchange, drafts, warrants, certificates and all kinds of obligations and negotiable or transferable instruments for any purpose that is deemed necessary to further the objects for which this association is formed, and to pledge any of its property as security therefor.

(j) To establish, secure, own and develop patents, trade-marks and copyrights.

(k) To co-operate with its members in conducting educational work concerning the value of co-operative marketing, the adjustment of production to prospective demand, and for all other purposes pertaining to co-operation.

(l) To co-operate with other similar associations in creating central, regional, or national co-operative agencies, for any of the purposes for which this association is formed, and/or to become a member of such agencies as now are or hereafter may be in existence.

(m) To have and exercise all powers, privileges and rights authorized by the Laws of Louisiana and all powers and rights incident thereto, except such as are inconsistent with the express provisions of this charter.

(n) To do anything that is conducive to carrying out
(Continued on page 12.)

...In Louisiana's Sugar Bowl
1929 — 64 Users
1930 — 101 Users

The consistent performance of Cyanamid year after year explains the decided preference which it enjoys throughout Louisiana's "Sugar Bowl".

Another factor is its adaptability to the extensive planting operations typical of the Louisiana sugar plantation. The high analysis of Cyanamid — 21 per cent nitrogen — means that less fertilizer need be handled to supply any desired amount of actual plant-food. Its excellent mechanical condition and its convenient, "one man" 100-pound package contribute to ease and economy in application.

Cyanamid supplies in addition to nitrogen, 75 per cent of pure hydrated lime equivalent—and its continued use year after year is thus a constructive factor in maintaining permanent soil sweetness, tilth, and productivity. Cyanamid feeds the crop evenly, steadily—sustains the plant throughout the long growing season. It gives substantial increases in cane yields without lowering the sucrose or purity of the juices.

Each year offers additional proof of the ability of Cyanamid to perform consistently and well.

Your inquiries will be welcome
For further information, write

American Cyanamid Company
Pioneer Producers of Air-Nitrogen Products in America
535 FIFTH AVENUE, NEW YORK

P.O.J. 2878 Genealogy and Generalities

By Arthur H. Rosenfeld, Consulting Technologist, American Sugar Cane League

P.O.J. 2878—Which has come to be known as "the wonder cane" of Java—is now planted on that island to the extent of around 95% of its cane acreage. So many inquiries have been received regarding the parentage of this variety and its possibilities in Louisiana, that the writer has thought it well to give a short history of the production of this variety and its remarkably rapid replacement of almost all other varieties cultivated in Java.

In this connection a few remarks regarding the beginnings of cane breeding and the parentage of the predecessors in Java of its "wonder cane" may be in order. As is rather well known, up until 1887 there was a general acceptation amongst sugar cane workers of the fallacy that all sugar cane was sterile and that attempts to obtain improved strains by means of sexual variation were hopeless. This despite the fact that a Dutch botanist by the name of Rumph definitely stated the contrary as far back as the seventeenth century; and in 1858 in Barbados, in 1862 in Java itself and in 1871 on the French Island of Reunion, cane seedlings were actually produced and grown, and the statements regarding these seedlings reported in serious publications of the day. Despite these recorded facts, when the fertility of sugar cane was again announced in 1887 by Soltwedel in Java and by Harrison and Bovell in 1889, their statements were received with considerable skepticism and doubt. As far as Java was concerned, this rediscovery of the possibility of obtaining sugar cane seedlings came at a peculiarly opportune time, as it was just then that the notorious *sereh* disease was becoming extremely serious in Java.

Kobus, the father of the three P.O.J. canes which are now generally cultivated in Louisiana, seized upon this new information with avidity and immediately initiated a system of controlled hybridization—a distinct method from that followed by his West Indian confreres who knew only the female parent of their early seedlings, using a system of mass production and only noble canes for parents. Amongst these earlier canes produced by Harrison and Bovell were the D-74 and D-95 so extensively used for a generation in Louisiana.

Kobus, by selecting the more difficult task of controlled breeding, laid upon himself the work of making detailed studies of the cane flower, the separation of the different varieties into those which had fertile and unfertile pollen, etc. Inasmuch as resistance or immunity to *sereh* was one of his main problems, it was necessary for him also to select as one of the parents for his new strain a variety which had been observed to be immune to the *sereh* disease. This was the North Indian cane, *Chunnee*, which later research has indicated to be a natural hybrid of the wild cane, *Saccharum spontaneum*, and a noble cane, *S. Officinarum*. Using *Chunnee* as the male parent, a series of cane practically immune to *sereh* disease was obtained, P.O.J. 36, 213 and 234 being included in this series.

These, however, did not possess good cultural characteristics for Javanese conditions, and the *Chunnee* strain was eventually abandoned and breeding from the noble canes adopted. The two outstanding canes of this period were P.O.J. 100 and 247-B, which for

a decade and a half occupied most of the Javanese cane area. Following them came the series of canes represented by EK-28 and DI-52, which were the dominant canes in Java until the advent of P.O.J. 2878, the production of which represents a very decided move in quite another direction through the re-introduction of wild blood, which was begun by Jeswiet some 15 years ago.

Jeswiet used both as male and female parents the semi-wild *Kassoer* cane which was found growing practically wild in Java and which Jeswiet as early as 1916 considered to be a natural hybrid of the wild *Glagah* and the *Black Cheribon*, corresponding to our *Purple* cane, the latter incidentally having been almost the only cane cultivated in Java prior to 1900. Bremer, it is interesting to note, by most involved cytological research afterwards definitely confirmed Dr. Jeswiet's presumption as to the parentage of *Kassoer*. The wild blood obtained thru *Kassoer* is now considered by the Java cane breeders as essential in the parentage of the newer sexual variants because of the disease resistance or immunity transmitted thereby.

P.O.J. 2878 is really a sister cane of, that is, it has the same parentage as P.O.J. 2725, although not produced at the same time; the latter was bred in 1917 and the 2878 in 1921. To obtain this series of canes, *Kassoer* was crossed with the noble P.O.J. 100, the resultant P.O.J. 2364 thus having but one-fourth wild blood. This was again "nobleized" by crossing with the noble cane EK-28, the resultant P.O.J. 2725 and 2878 having but one-eighth wild blood, which seemed sufficient, however, in these cases, to make the cane highly resistant to disease and with a deep root system characteristic of the wild canes.

It is interesting to note the average sugar production per acre obtained through the different phases of cane breeding and the accepted varieties for distinct periods. Up to about 1900, when the *Black Cheribon* or *Louisiana Purple* cane was almost exclusively planted in Java, the average yield of sugar per acre was just about three tons. During the 15 years when the P.O.J. 100 and the 247-B was extensively grown, this average was raised to four and three-tenths tons of sugar per acre, and during the predominance of the noble crosses EK-28 and DI-52, the average was raised to four and eight-tenths tons per acre. In 1925 commercial production of 2878 was commenced and by 1927 12½% of the cane area was planted in this variety. In 1928 66% was planted, and in the crop of 1929 93% of the cane harvested in Java was of this variety. The average production per acre reached almost seven tons of sugar.

Now as regards the possibilities of this wonderful cane under our short growing season conditions in Louisiana, we must not form any illusions as to its adaptability here. It has been found in Java that this variety requires from 14 to 15 months for proper maturity and must be growing at least one month longer than the canes formerly employed there to reach the proper sugar content. With this in mind it is not difficult to understand why the trials of this variety, both at the Federal Station at Houma and at the State's Station at Baton Rouge, have shown very little indication of any possible adaptation of the P.O.J. 2878 to Louisiana's climatic conditions.

WHOLESALE AND RETAIL DEALERS IN
HORSES AND MULES
CABLE ADDRESS "WHILDEN"

CITY OFFICE
WHITNEY BUILDING
RAymond 2244

SALE STABLES
CARROLLTON AVE. & BIENVILLE ST.
GAlvez 1053

NEW ORLEANS, U. S. A.

BRANCH STABLES
THIBODAUX, LA.
DONALDSONVILLE, LA.

WITH CITY OFFICES IN THE WHITNEY BANK BUILDING AND SALE STABLES AT CARROLLTON AVENUE AND BIENVILLE STREETS, NEW ORLEANS, AND BRANCH STABLES AT THIBODAUX AND DONALDSONVILLE, LA. THE AFORESAID FIRM ARE WHOLESALERS, RETAILERS AND EXPORTERS OF HORSES, MULES, CATTLE, SHEEP AND HOGS. THEY TRANSACT A WORLD WIDE BUSINESS AND ARE INSTRUMENTAL IN FURNISHING SUGAR PLANTERS IN LOUISIANA, PLANTATION OWNERS THROUGH-OUT THE SOUTHERN STATES, AND FOREIGN COUNTRIES WITH MULES TO CON-DUCT EXTENSIVE FARM OPERATIONS.

THE FIRM OF MATTINGLY & WHILDEN, INC., IS UNDER THE DIRECTION OF MEN WHO HAVE HAD 25 YEARS' EXPERIENCE IN THE LIVESTOCK BUSINESS. OVER THIS PERIOD OF TIME THEY HAVE NEVER FAILED TO SUPPLY THEIR MANY BUY-ERS WITH MULES WHENEVER AND WHEREVER NEEDED AT SATISFACTORY PRICES, NOR HAVE THEY EVER FAILED TO LIVE UP TO THEIR GUARANTEE, WHICH THEY GIVE WITH EVERY MULE SOLD. THEY HAVE WON THE CONFIDENCE OF FARMERS THROUGHOUT THE SOUTHERN STATES AND OF FOREIGN BUYERS BY SERVING THEM IN A CONSCIENTIOUS AND HONEST WAY. THEY WILL SELL ONE MULE, A PAIR OF MULES, ONE CARLOAD, A TRAINLOAD OR A SHIPLOAD. SERVICE AND SATISFACTION IS THEIR SLOGAN.

THEY BRING MUCH TRADE ACTIVITY AND BUSINESS TO THE PORT OF NEW OR-LEANS.

OFFICERS OF THE FIRM OF MATTINGLY & WHILDEN, INC., ARE, OSCAR R. WHIL-DEN, PRESIDENT; CAMBRON C. MATTINGLY, VICE-PRESIDENT, AND JACOB C. WHILDEN, SECRETARY-TREASURER.

the policy of the Congress of the United States of America stated in the Agricultural Marketing Act, approved June 15, 1929.

ARTICLE III

This association shall enjoy a corporate existence for a period of fifty (50) years from the date hereof.

ARTICLE IV

Section I. The business affairs of this association shall be managed by a Board of Directors who shall have the power to elect the officers of the Association, and to employ and discharge all employees of the association.

Section II. The number of the Directors of the Association shall be five who shall serve for a term of one year or until their successors are elected, and the first Board of Directors shall be elected at a meeting of members in good standing to be held at the principal place of business of the association within thirty days hereof.

Section III. The officers of the association shall be a President, Vice-President, Secretary and Treasurer, upon whom citation may be served. The duties of these officers shall be determined by the Board of Directors who shall adopt suitable by-laws.

ARTICLE V

This association shall be organized without capital stock and the property rights of each member shall be equal and to each member shall be issued a certificate of membership conditioned upon the payment of dues and such other requirements as may be provided in the by-laws of this association.

ARTICLE VI

This association is formed to function as a marketing association on a cooperative basis for the mutual benefit of its members each of whom must be a producer of sugar cane and each member shall have one vote only.

ARTICLE VII

The names and postoffice addresses of the subscribers of these Articles of Incorporation are hereinbelow stated, with their relative signatures hereto affixed.

Cutting Crooked Canes— A Suggestion

By Arthur H. Rosenfeld

Now that most of the planters can begin to visualize the finish of the harvesting of their stubble canes, the question of the proper selection of the first plant cane for harvesting presents itself. Were it not for the fact that we must always bear in mind at this season of the year the probability of bad hauling weather and killing freezes, the logical thing to do would appear to be to start harvesting the cane with the highest sugar content, that is, the P.O.J. 234.

However, the very fact that this higher sucrose content means that this cane can be windrowed for a longer time than lower sucrose canes, and, as little of the P.O.J. 234 has fallen this year and will therefore be easily handled mechanically for windrowing purposes, it would appear that our procedure should be just the opposite from what would be the case in a tropical country where likelihood of freezes does not enter into cropping calculations. Another advantage of leaving the 234 until later on in the season is that this variety suffers most from early cropping and its being left standing for two or three weeks longer may mean the difference between a good and an unsatisfactory stubble crop.

Of course, where fields of 234 plant cane are located at the back of a plantation where bad roads might prevent its later economical hauling, this factor of transportation is to also be seriously weighed against the other advantages already mentioned. Fortunately, however, on the back lands there is a larger proportion of P.O.J. 213 than of either 234 or 36, and it is also the case that the 213 is the most recumbent type of cane grown and is the only variety this year showing any large proportion of fallen cane which it would be practically impossible to windrow in a satisfactory manner.

The writer would therefore suggest most earnestly that where the question of eventual transportation does not intervene too strongly, the fallen and twisted P.O.J. 213 cane be harvested first wherever the 213 plant shows even a fairly satisfactory sugar content. If this twisted, unwindrowable cane can be disposed of before the advent of genuine killing freezes, the windrowing of the 234 and 36 will be a comparatively simple proposition.

Once the 213 has been brought in, the question of convenience of loading will determine whether the P.O.J. 36 or the 234 will next be harvested, but the planters should bear in mind always that the P.O.J. 36 is the most resistant to cold of the three varieties and can often be left standing after a freeze which would make it necessary to windrow the 234. Where the location of the P.O.J. 36 is such as to permit reasonably sure transportation to derricks, the writer would suggest leaving this variety to cut the last of all.

The International Status of Sugar

By C. J. Bourg

The fate of the sugar world seems to be very much dependent upon the fortunes of the Chadbourne Committee. The price of sugar improves steadily when the Committee is active and marks time when these activities meet with postponements. Naturally, during the grinding season, any influence upon the sugar market and particularly one which holds out hope of better prices, commands the attention of all sugar people. But the progress of the Chadbourne Committee has become important and interesting well beyond the circle of those directly interested in the domestic sugar industry. It has assumed an international status and its progression is being watched by governmental and industrial agencies of many countries.

It is a real stimulant in these times of well-advertised depression, to be convinced of the success that has already attended the plans of the Committee. Although sugar meets setbacks in any Congress, American or Cuban, President Machado has gone right ahead cooperating with the Committee by presidential mandate and the elimination of the favorite "manana."

Now the Chadbourne Committee is departing for Holland, where they will meet with the representatives of the sugar industry of Java, in the hope of securing an agreement with them looking to the stabilization of the world sugar market. There has been some uncertainty as to the exact attitude of the Javanese in this regard, although they have agreed to the conference. But it is encouraging to learn from authoritative sources that at least five Javan companies are already restricting their sugar cane plantings for

next year, which means an important crop restriction that will certainly help the future of the industry.

Now from the Philippine Islands comes the refreshing news that the Legislature has passed a resolution recommending the restriction of sugar cane plantings to presently cultivated lands. This action has been interpreted as a serious determination by some and as merely a gesture by others. Nevertheless it carries the realization that this is not the time for expansion of sugar territory, which is mighty important just now.

The Treasury Department has rendered a decision of importance by which all mixtures of sugar and water entering the United States since the Tariff Act of 1930 and up to October 25th, shall be subject only to a duty of one-fourth of one cent per gallon, which is the syrup rate. Entries since October 25th will pay the full sugar duty according to the polariscopic test. The question of the proper rate for liquid sugar under the Tariff Act of 1930 will now be submitted to the United States Courts for decision, unless Congress should determine to remove the ambiguity by corrective legislation this winter.

There is little prospect of any action by the Tariff Commission on sugar rates this year. It will be remembered that Senator Copeland of New York introduced a resolution in the closing hours of the past session of Congress, asking for an investigation into the difference in the cost of production between domestic refined sugar and foreign refined sugar. The investigation has not yet been ordered by the Commission and it has not yet been determined whether such investigation will include an inquiry into the entire costs of producing refined sugar, or merely be restricted to the actual cost of refining sugar.

Refining costs are easily and immediately obtainable. The Hershey Corporation has its main office in the United States, even though its refinery is in Cuba, and its books will be as open to the inspection of the Tariff Commission as any refiner's in America. To go beyond the refining costs would open the entire question of the production costs of sugar cane, raw sugar and refined sugar.

Many hearings upon articles of import have been ordered by the Tariff Commission, but action has evi-

dently been postponed upon that part of the Copeland resolution which relates to sugar. This postponement will in all likelihood extend into the next session of Congress, when Senator Copeland may amplify his resolution with positive instructions to the Commission regarding the refined sugar investigation.

An interesting view of the European idea regarding the production of sugar domestically, is to be found in the French publication "La Betterave" for August, 1930. They take cognizance of the fact that beet sugar production in France is on the increase, but the consumption of sugar is not increasing in the same proportion. They anticipate that unless something is done, the French producer will face the "unpleasant necessity" of exporting his sugar. This problem is regarded so seriously there that they have offered a prize of one thousand francs for the best pamphlet describing the benefits of sugar as a food and the uses to which it can be put. Slogans are being sought to facilitate the work of increasing sugar consumption in France.

The recent national elections have given rise to any number of speculations concerning political activities, which may be anticipated when the Seventy-Second Congress assembles in December, 1931. Not the least important is the prospect of a change in tariff rates towards lower levels.

The low tariff advocates are looking to the more controverted items of the Hawley-Smoot Act and propose in newspaper interviews to accomplish their ends without opening the whole tariff act. Rather they would indulge in what has been known in Washington as "pop-gun" tactics. They would attack the act at specific points, proposing the amendments which they think necessary and then direct their greatest attention to the supposedly vulnerable sections. The principal assaults undoubtedly would be made on those items of the tariff law always so popular—sugar, cement, lumber and leather.

That such a program is being seriously considered is evident from the similarity of the interviews given by Democratic leaders of the Senate and House of Representatives. These leaders realize that the public does not want another general revision of the tariff to unsettle the business conditions. Nevertheless these same statesmen feel that they must justify the assaults they have made on the tariff policies of the Administration, and it will be highly effective to do this bit by bit. They claim that this procedure will eliminate the attractiveness of "log-rolling" and "trading," which causes them so much horror.

There is plenty of precedent for this pop-gunning. The Cleveland Administration had some and President Taft was made to veto some specific changes in the Payne Aldrich Act. Comparatively recent history gives the instance of the attempt to reduce the duty on sugar almost as soon as President Wilson was inaugurated. The bill did not pass, as the general revision of the tariff was later taken up instead.

It must be understood that we do not feel any immediate anxiety about the Seventy-Second Congress. Much will happen before it organizes. A Republican Ways and Means Committee will hardly start any tariff legislation of any variety. The appeal for coalition control will not be so strong and the best politi-

cal guessers in Washington are convinced that the Progressive group will establish a much closer relationship with the more regular Republicans. Like prodigal sons, they are wont to come home when presidential election time rolls around.

And now into the court of public opinion comes the Democratic party, through its undersigned seven leaders, and declare that despite and notwithstanding all that they have said, which the American people evidently believed for they so voted, there is nothing but harmony in Congress and all partisans must realize that now is the time for all good parties to come to the aid of their country. As long as this ecstacy of patriotism prevails, there is nothing to fear. As Monsieur Coolidge states very sagely "The country will survive." But how long will the armistice last?

More Trash

We have in type an interview very kindly granted us at our request by Dr. T. E. Holloway on the subject of the burning versus the burying of cane trash, but at the last moment we find it has to be crowded out by other material, especially our important Washington article which arrived at the last moment and is longer than expected. We shall print Dr. Holloway's interview in our next issue. He maintains his position on the much disputed topic in his usual patient and courteous way.

With reference to the test conducted at the Louisiana Experiment Station in which 12 tons of trash per

acre was used to demonstrate the depressive effect of this amount of trash on the nitrate nitrogen in the soil when turned under, and which we mildly criticized in the SUGAR BULLETIN of October 15th on the ground that such an amount of trash was too great to result in a practical demonstration, we are advised that the scientists conducting the test used this amount of trash advisedly because of various compensating factors involved. The investigators carefully calculated all these factors, as existent or non-existent in the particular plot of ground on which the experiment was conducted, and decided on 12 tons of trash as being the right and proper quantity to use in carrying out the experiment.

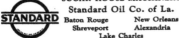

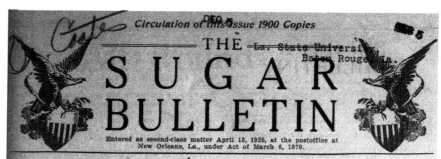

Circulation of this issue 1900 Copies

THE
La. State University,
Baton Rouge, La.

SUGAR
BULLETIN

Entered as second-class matter April 13, 1925, at the postoffice at
New Orleans, La., under Act of March 6, 1879.

We stand for the encouragement of Home Industries as against Foreign Competition.

| Vol. 9 | NEW ORLEANS, LA., DECEMBER 1, 1930 | No. 5 |

Value of Co. 281 Not Realized

As long ago as October 1st, 1930, an official announcement was published in the SUGAR BUL-LETIN to the effect that the variety of cane known as Co. 281 had been released for general planting, October 11th, 1930, being set as the date on which the supply of this cane would be allotted or parcelled out among applicants.

The demand for this cane has proved to be singularly lax and quite in contrast to the demand for the variety known as C.P. 807 which was released two weeks later; in fact we find now, two months after the date of release, that something like 150 tons of Co. 281 is still available.

We are entering on the season when a killing freeze may daily be expected and that a single stalk of this very valuable variety of cane remains still above ground is a reflection on our planting fraternity. Co. 281 is a cane that is especially well adapted to our river and bayou districts. It is recommended by the United States Department of Agriculture because of its high sucrose content, straight habit of growth, and its high yields of sugar per acre. A valuable characteristic of Co. 281 is that while it is almost as early as P.O.J. 234 in ripening, it stands early cutting better than P.O.J. 234, that is to say, it produces better stubble when cut early than P.O.J. 234 does. As a variety adapted for milling at the outset of grinding it ranks ahead of any other cane we have. A certain amount of it should be on every plantation.

If a new variety of cane suitable for Louisiana is developed by the Office of Sugar Plants of the United States Department of Agriculture and is not the object of sufficient interest to insure the immediate absorption of the limited amount usually available when the release is authorized it may be construed by the Federal authorities as indicative that we are becoming apathetic towards varietal work. No such misapprehension should be permitted.

The price of the small residue of Co. 281 now on hand is $6.50 per ton, cut and loaded. The plantation growing it receives out of this sum the price of mill cane and the remainder pays for the task of handling and distribution. A small margin is left, which goes into the League's treasury and is being used to help finance the erection of Laboratory Building No. 3 at Houma, for the use of the scientists connected with the United States Bureau of Entomology and Good Roads who are down here working on our Louisiana insect problems, including the cane borer, and certain drainage problems.

The remainder of the supply of Co. 281 is all in the vicinity of Houma and it can be shipped in carload lots, or delivered in small lots to those who will send trucks for it. The American Sugar Cane League will be glad to hear immediately from those who want it.

=======THE=======

SUGAR
BULLETIN

407 Carondelet St., New Orleans

Issued on the 1st and 15th of each month. Official Organ of the American
Sugar Cane League of the U. S. A., in which are consolidated
The Louisiana Sugar Planters' Assn.
The American Cane Growers' Assn.
The Producers & Mfgrs. Protective Assn.
Subscription Price. 50 Cents Per Year.

Reginald Dykers, General Manager & Editor of the Bulletin
301 Nola Bldg., New Orleans
Frank L. Barker, Secretary and Treasurer
Lockport, La.
C. J. Bourg, Manager Washington Office
810 Union Trust Building

CHAIRMEN OF COMMITTEES:
C. D. Kemper, Franklin, La.
President of the League and Ex-Officio Chairman of Executive Committee
Andrew H. Gay, Plaquemine, La,
Chairman Agricultural Committee
David W. Pipes, Jr., Houma, La.
Chairman Industrial Committee
Frank L. Barker, Lockport, La.
Chairman Finance Committee.
Edward J. Gay, Plaquemine, La.
Chairman Tariff Committee
H. Langdon Laws, Cinclare, La.
Chairman Legislative Committee
J. C. LeBourgeois, New Orleans, La.
Chairman Freight Rate Committee
R. H. Chadwick, Bayou Goula, La.
Chairman Membership Committee
A. H. Rosenfeld, New Orleans, La.
Chairman Publicity Committee

Members of the League desiring action on, or information, on any subject are invited to communicate with the League or with the Chairman of the Committee to which it seems to appertain.

Chadbourne Over There—Congress Here

(By C. J. Bourg)

Washington, D. C., Nov. 26, 1930.
The dominant factor in the sugar market is still the Chadbourne Committee. The details of its work are being watched with tremendous interest by sugar men, and the market, in its present position, seems poised so delicately as to register every encouraging and every disappointing note.

Since the last issue of THE SUGAR BULLETIN was published, the Chadbourne Plan has been enacted in full by the Senate and House of Representatives of Cuba, and President Machado has issued the decree giving it the force of law. If the terms of the plan are faithfully carried out, the exports of sugar from Cuba to the United States next year will be restricted to 2,800,000 tons, and 1,500,000 tons of the present surplus will be segregated to be sold in other markets than ours over a period of five years.

Their work in Cuba completed, Mr. Chadbourne and his colleagues are now in Amsterdam for conferences with members of the Dutch syndicate which controls ninety per cent of production in Java. In recent days it has been reported that the Dutch interests have shown a great deal of "anxiety" for the conference, and the prospects that they will agree to a program of restriction probably are better than at any time in the past. Precisely what terms will be offered to the syndicate remains a matter of some doubt. In some well-informed sources the opinion is that the Javanese will be asked to segregate 750,-000 tons from their current crop, and then to place a policy of restriction in effect for the 1932 planting. Undoubtedly this would have the effect of increasing raw sugar prices unless, of course, the success of the conference has already been discounted.

All this sounds highly encouraging to those of us who are concerned with a prosperous sugar industry within continental United States. Perhaps, indeed, it is altogether too bullish. As a whole, sugar brokers in New York are looking upon the situation with satisfaction, and many of them are confident that better prices will rule during the coming year. Nevertheless, there have been some indications that the time has not yet arrived at which the industry can decide that its troubles are over. The better plan is to hope for the best and be prepared against disappointment.

In the first place, deliveries to the pool of 1,500,000 tons to be segregated by the Cubans have not yet begun. In case the conference with the Javanese is successful, it is highly probable that the deliveries will be made expeditiously. If the conference is a failure, what then? Members of the Chadbourne Committee have indicated that come what may, Cuba will string along on its program of restriction. Yet it would not be entirely remarkable if the island producers came to the conclusion that Cuba, by restricting its crops without regard to overproduction in other parts of the world, would stand to lose more than it might gain. If Java restricts and the market advances, the Dutch syndicate undoubtedly would take advantage of the situation by finding markets outside the Orient. A better price might also encourage the release of large quantities of Philippine sugar.

The importations of liquid sugar, in one form or another, continue to be a source of worry to the Treasury Department. Early this week reports were circulated in Washington that the Department was ready to hand down a decision permitting the importation of refined sugar in a liquid state at reduced rates of duty, even though it had previously ruled against liquid raw sugar which was being brought in at syrup rates.

The truth of the matter is that certain importers, having been denied the privilege of bringing in liquid raw sugar at reduced rates, hit upon the idea of importing invert sugar which could not be crystallized after evaporation. Such a product might find uses in the manufacture of commercial products, but since it could not be crystallized it would overcome the complaint of the Treasury that it was losing revenue which properly belonged to it.

None can hazard a guess as to the outcome of this latest development. Perhaps a revision of the syrup schedule of the tariff act will be required to clarify the situation.

The third session of the 71st Congress which meets on December 1st at Washington has given promise of considerable parliamentary gymnastics, since the recent national elections. But as the time of convening approaches, there seems to prevail a feeling of conciliation.

First, the Democratic leaders made offers of peace and co-operation to the Republican Administration,

(Continued on page 4.)

which were hurriedly accepted. Next the Progressives announced boisterously their intention to insist upon the adoption of certain measures known as the Progressive program. As usual, farm relief headed the list. Now, the Republican leaders have come forward with the suggestion that their only interest during the present session will be to pass all appropriation bills for conducting the Government and to legislate for the relief of the unemployed; adding that they will be quite willing to permit the consideration of a reasonable number of Progressive measures, provided said appropriation and unemployment measures are passed without unreasonable delay. Naturally, the purpose of the Republican leaders now will be to limit the number of so-called Progressive measures to several of the most important.

It is expected that as a result of meetings held by the Senate Committee on Agriculture with officials of farmers' organizations, there will be considered a bill or bills regulating the Cotton and Grain Exchanges with a view to curbing short selling. The Federal Farm Board will be given additional appropriations to carry out its stabilization programs. Relief for the farmer in the drouth stricken areas will be provided in a measure that is being prepared by Congressman Aswell of Louisiana, who is collaborating with the Secretary of Agriculture and other Administration leaders.

The nominations which President Hoover will send to the Senate for confirmation will furnish the opening battle grounds. Senator Watson of Indiana as the Republican floor leader, is anxious that these nominations be considered immediately in the hope that they will all be passed upon before the Christmas holidays. Advance information on Capitol Hill indicates that fights will be made against the appointees to the Tariff Commission, with particular attention being paid to Chairman Fletcher and Commissioner Brossard. These fights will renew the flames caused by the flexible provisions in the Tariff Act. The members of the Federal Power Commission are expected to have their day in court. Not only is Louisiana interested in the fights that will be made on these appointments, but it is reasonable to expect that the results which the opposition is able to secure, will have their effect upon the attitude of the Senators during the balance of the session. At the present time it is not believed that the opposition will be able to overthrow any of the appointments made by President Hoover, but after the experience of Judge Parker last year, it is wise not to anticipate.

The bill providing the operation of Muscle Shoals by the Government as a power and nitrate producing plant is one of the measures that the Progressives will insist upon. This question has been before the American public for many years and is of special importance to the South and to all farmers. Its final passage or defeat will be a relief in itself.

A vigorous fight will be made to pass labor legislation centered around the anti-injunction measure and the outlawing of the yellow dog contracts.

The debenture will again be offered for the benefit of the American farmer and if permitted to come to a vote will undoubtedly be passed.

It must be well understood that while the Republican leaders are agreeing to permit some of these measures to be considered they are in no way agreeing to their enactment into law. The Administration will certainly oppose some of the Progressive program and there are some Republican leaders who will oppose all of it. The only reason for the concessions made by the Republican leaders is that they want to avoid for President Hoover the necessity of calling a special session, which would be necessary if the Insurgent Senators prevented the passage of any of the necessary appropriation bills, until March 4th when the session will end.

The Treasury Department has invoked Section 307 of the Tariff Act of 1930 against imports from Russia. This section provides that all goods wholly or in part produced or manufactured by convict labor shall not be entitled to entry at any of the ports of the United States. Since all opponents of the recognition by the United States of the Soviet Republic contend that Russia is building up its production of all goods through convict labor, the action of the Treasury Department will in effect be a general embargo against Russian products. This is interesting to sugar people in view of the fact that estimates by experts are that the production of sugar in Russia in 1930 will be practically double the amount produced in 1929. The Sojus Sacchar estimate the total production of all Russian sugar at 2,200,000 tons, as against 950,000 tons in 1929. However, F. O. Licht estimates this year's production at 1,760,000. It is the announced purpose of the Soviet Five Year Plan to make Russia the largest exporting country of the whole world.

The Thornton Windrowing Machine

(By A. W. Dykers)

A windrowing machine, designed by Mr. S. A. Thornton, whose name has long been connected with the invention and perfection of labor-saving devices for use in the cane sugar industry, was demonstrated by its inventor on the Georgia plantation last Wednesday, November 26th, before a gathering of some thirty or forty sugar cane planters from all sections of the Louisiana sugar district. Mr. Thornton has perfected a windrowing machine that works perfectly in straight cane. It travels up and down the rows at the rate of about three miles an hour and presents a very pretty sight as the canes seem to disappear before it. Two rows of cane are cut and laid neatly in the windrow as the machine travels at its three miles an hour gait and it seemed to be the general opinion of all those in attendance that the job could not have been done better by hand. The machine is a rather big affair. It consists of a frame mounted on crawler type tractor wheels which straddles two rows of cane. Revolving discs very similar to those used on stubble shaving machines cut the canes at the ground level and steel plates direct the cut canes into the middle windrow. Long arms which look like "feelers" which are in front of the machine help to keep it in the rows and guide the cane stalks into the discs. A forty horse-power gasoline motor supplies the power. Three men are necessary to operate it, one apiece to raise and lower each disc and one to steer it. During the demonstration two negroes were handling the discs and a white mechanic the power and steering operations. As stated above the machine works perfectly in straight canes and will windrow, according to estimates, from three to five

acres of cane an hour. It does not work well i
crooked canes. At the present time, with so muc
P.O.J. 213 cane being grown in Louisiana, this is
decided disadvantage, but it is generally agreed tha
P.O.J. 213 canes are very hard to windrow satisfa
torily in any way and the cane planters will probabl
plant the straighter varieties more largely hereafter. I
short, it appears that Mr. Thornton has perfected
windrowing machine that does its work as well as
could be done by hand and, of course, at far greate
speed. He states that he is not ready to market th
machines at the present time.

Switching Charges Levied by Texa
and Pacific Railway

Information reaches us that since the recent dec
sion by the Louisiana Public Service Commission r
ducing the rates on raw sugar from various Louisiar
points of origin to New Orleans and Three Oaks, th
Texas & Pacific Railway has discontinued the absor
tion of switching charges on shipments consigned
Three Oaks, Henderson's Refinery and the Dunb
Molasses and Syrup Company at New Orleans. I
other words, the railroad takes the position that th
recently revised rates not only supersede rates whic
were formerly in effect but also all routes and reg
lations that applied in connection with those rate
The American Sugar Cane League has referred th
matter to the New Orleans Joint Traffic Bureau an
has been advised by the Bureau that these switchir
charges should not be paid pending the outcome
negotiations between the Bureau and the Texas
Pacific Railway in regard thereto.

Behavior of P. O. J. 234 After
Cutting

Mr. C. G. Robinson, Union Indemnity Buildin
New Orleans, who owns a piece of sugar cane pro
erty near Whitecastle, La., writes us as follows:

November 26, 1930.

American Sugar Cane League,
New Orleans, La.

Dear Sir:

For your information, on my place at Whitecastl
La., I had some P.O.J. 234 cane which had been c
twenty days and during that period we had about seve
or eight days of very warm weather and it rained c
the cane. When I first hauled some of this cane it ha
been cut about ten or twelve days and the sucrose wa
slightly over nine. However, the cane hauled late
which had been lying in the field cut for twenty day
tested from 13.40 to 13.60 and some tests went over 1
The cane was shipped to the Cedar Grove Mill at Whit
castle and tested by the chemist there and they do n
understand what caused this and I would like to kno
what caused it myself for the reason I was under th
impression that all of this P.O.J. cane, if you did n
get it to the mill rather quickly, would lose a larg
amount of its sucrose. The facts in regard to the abov
cane can be verified should you desire.

Yours very truly,

(Signed)   C. G. ROBINSON.

The SUGAR BULLETIN will appreciate comments o
the above from those who feel qualified to mak
them.

As to High-Sucrose Canes

By ARTHUR H. ROSENFELD

With considerable frequency the attention of the writer is called by some of our planter friends to the fact that canes which are reported upon here in Louisiana as being unsuitable for our conditions on account of low sucrose content at *our* crop time have shown excellent sucrose and purity in Cuba, Porto Rico or some other tropical country. It must not be forgotten that these results are obtained from canes *growing* for from twelve to eighteen months and, hence, allowed to become fully mature—something impossible with a seven or at most eight months' growing season such as ours. What we must have here is not so much a "high-sucrose" as an early-maturing variety.

In fact it is the opinion of the writer that in only a very few instances are there any "low sucrose canes"; in other words, most canes will attain a high degree of ripeness if allowed to go the proper length of time needed for full maturity. What we need here in Louisiana, however, as stated above, is not so much a high-sucrose variety as one that will give satisfactory sucrose yields in an abnormally short growing season, such as that with which we have to contend. Tropical figures only bear out our observations that P.O.J. 234, 213 and 36 normally do this quite satisfactorily in the order mentioned and that P.O.J. 228, while a very high-sucrose cane, once it reaches fourteen to eighteen months' growth, shows up far behind these other three for the early cuttings we are forced to make.

All of this illustrates once more how entirely distinct are the factors which must be considered in judging the value of the same canes under distinctly different conditions.

A Riddle for the Sphinx

Having fallen into the perhaps useless habit of contributing space to the perennial discussion of the burning or non-burning of cane trash, THE SUGAR BULLETIN has asked Mr. T. E. Holloway, of the United States Department of Agriculture, who for years has advocated the non-burning of the trash, what he thinks about the apparent decision of the Louisiana Experiment Station's entomologists to advocate the burning of the trash. Mr. Holloway said:

"I doubt whether agricultural science is best served by controversy, and I do not desire to enter into a

dispute with anyone concerning the burning or the non-burning of cane trash. Everyone is entitled to his own opinion, as far as I am concerned. However, it might be worth while to review the work which has been done in the past.

"The little egg parasite, *Trichogramma*, was first found to attack the cane borer in Louisiana in 1912. I had been in the State for only a few months at the time, but it soon occurred to me that we ought to do something to protect this friend of the sugar planter. Of course, I assumed that the trash fires destroy many parasites. With the co-operation of the Sugar Experiment Station, then at Audubon Park, and with the active interest of Mr. W. G. Taggart, then Assistant Director, an experiment in not burning cane trash was outlined and in 1912-13 it was conducted on the grounds of the station. Good results were obtained, and they were reported in *The Louisiana Planter* for December 20, 1913. The experimental work was afterwards carried out to the plantations, where it could be conducted on a larger scale. It was found in the course of time that large areas on the plantations had to be considered as an experimental unit, owing to the apparent interchange of borer moths and parasites from field to field. This complication had not been encountered at Audubon Park, owing to the isolation of the fields there. When this factor, which was pointed out by Mr. Taggart, was taken into consideration good results were obtained in the plantation experiments. The results were published in *The Planter* from time to time. In 1919 Mr. U. C. Loftin and I published U. S. Department of Agriculture Bulletin 746, giving all the information then available. The directions for turning under trash given in that bulletin were very kindly prepared by Mr. Taggart, due credit being given to him. The bulletin was revised and reissued in 1928 as Technical Bulletin 41, again with Mr. Taggart's directions. Mr. Taggart at one time estimated that borer damage at Audubon Park was reduced year after year by about two-thirds by not burning the cane trash.

OSCAR R. WHILDEN
President

CAMBRON C. MATTINGLY
Vice-President

JACOB C. WHILDEN
Secretary-Treasurer

WHOLESALE AND RETAIL DEALERS IN

HORSES AND MULES

CABLE ADDRESS "WHILDEN"

CITY OFFICE
WHITNEY BUILDING
RAymond 2244
SALE STABLES
CARROLLTON AVE. & BIENVILLE ST.
GAlvez 1058

NEW ORLEANS, U. S. A.

BRANCH STABLES
THIBODAUX, LA.
DONALDSONVILLE, LA.

WITH CITY OFFICES IN THE WHITNEY BANK BUILDING AND SALE STABLES AT CARROLLTON AVENUE AND BIENVILLE STREETS, NEW ORLEANS, AND BRANCH STABLES AT THIBODAUX AND DONALDSONVILLE, LA. THE AFORESAID FIRM ARE WHOLESALERS, RETAILERS AND EXPORTERS OF HORSES, MULES, CATTLE, SHEEP AND HOGS. THEY TRANSACT A WORLD WIDE BUSINESS AND ARE INSTRUMENTAL IN FURNISHING SUGAR PLANTERS IN LOUISIANA, PLANTATION OWNERS THROUGHOUT THE SOUTHERN STATES, AND FOREIGN COUNTRIES WITH MULES TO CONDUCT EXTENSIVE FARM OPERATIONS.

THE FIRM OF MATTINGLY & WHILDEN, INC., IS UNDER THE DIRECTION OF MEN WHO HAVE HAD 25 YEARS' EXPERIENCE IN THE LIVESTOCK BUSINESS. OVER THIS PERIOD OF TIME THEY HAVE NEVER FAILED TO SUPPLY THEIR MANY BUYERS WITH MULES WHENEVER AND WHEREVER NEEDED AT SATISFACTORY PRICES, NOR HAVE THEY EVER FAILED TO LIVE UP TO THEIR GUARANTEE, WHICH THEY GIVE WITH EVERY MULE SOLD. THEY HAVE WON THE CONFIDENCE OF FARMERS THROUGHOUT THE SOUTHERN STATES AND OF FOREIGN BUYERS BY SERVING THEM IN A CONSCIENTIOUS AND HONEST WAY. THEY WILL SELL ONE MULE, A PAIR OF MULES, ONE CARLOAD, A TRAINLOAD OR A SHIPLOAD. SERVICE AND SATISFACTION IS THEIR SLOGAN.

THEY BRING MUCH TRADE ACTIVITY AND BUSINESS TO THE PORT OF NEW ORLEANS.

Ninety-Three Fulton Double Crushers

In the past thirteen years, 93 Fulton Patented Double Crushers have been installed in the large cane-growing countries of the world: Argentina, S. A., Brazil, S. A., British Guiana, S. A., Colombia, S. A., Peru, S. A., Dominican Republic, Java, Mexico, Philippine Islands, Porto Rico, Africa, Louisiana, U. S. A., and Cuba. In Cuba alone, Fulton Double Crushers were used in over 86 percent of the mills with an annual production of 400,000 bags (65,000 tons) or over during the 1926-27 season.

Increased profits automatically result from the increased capacity of your tandems—made possible by the installation of Fulton Patented Double Crushers, combined with Fulton Patented Step-Down Grooving.

Fulton offers a complete co-operative mill engineering, designing and construction service * * * from car dump to bagasse carrier. Full descriptive literature on request.

FULTON IRON WORKS CO., ST. LOUIS, U.S.A.

BRANCH OFFICE
505 New Orleans Bank Bldg.

NEW ORLEANS, LA.   PHONE RA. 3414

Circulation of this Issue 1900 Copies

THE
SUGAR

BULLETIN

Entered as second-class matter April 13, 1925, at the postoffice at
New Orleans, La., under Act of March 6, 1879.

*We stand for the encouragement of Home
Industries as against Foreign competition.*

| Vol. 9 | NEW ORLEANS, LA., DECEMBER 15, 1930 | No. 6 |

History of C. P. 807

By G. B. Sartoris, Pathologist,
Office of Sugar Plant Investigations, Bureau of Plant Industry.

The parentage of C.P. 807 was briefly mentioned in a short article in the Sugar Bulletin of November 15, 1930, but it is believed that the Louisiana sugar planters, who are thoroughly acquainted with its grandparent and with one of its great-grandparents, may be interested in a more detailed account of its history. Two of its ancestors stand out very prominently in Louisiana: Black Cheribon, known in Louisiana as Louisiana Purple, and P.O.J. 213. P.O. J. 213 was produced at the experiment station ("Prœfstation Oost Java") of the Java Sugar Syndicate at Pascœrœan, Java, by crossing Black Cheribon (female) with Chunnee (male). Black Cheribon (Louisiana Purple) was the standard cane in the sugar cane growing sections of the United States for many years and, in fact, it may be said that the sugar cane industry of the United States was founded upon it. For nearly a century it was productive of wealth for the state, but during recent years the yields of Black Cheribon and the other "noble" varieties which had long been grown declined rapidly as a result of the attack of the mosaic disease and by 1926 these varieties were no longer capable of producing profitable yields. The planters are familiar with the P.O.J. varieties which were introduced at that time and with the rapid revival of the industry as a result of the cultivation of these varieties, but it may not have occurred to them that P.O.J. 213, which soon became the leading variety, largely took the place of its parent variety Black Cheribon. It is remarkable that P.O.J. 213 is tolerant of the mosaic disease because both of its parents are susceptible to this disease.

The lineage of C.P. 807 is as follows:

(female) Black Cheribon X Chunnee (male)

Self fertilized (?)	P.O.J. 213
Self fertilized	U.S. 1643
	C.P.807

On March 17, 1921, seed from P.O.J. 213 which had been grown in India was received from Coimbatore, India. The complete history of this seed is not available, and it is possible that it may have resulted from a crossing of P.O.J. 213 with an unknown male parent. The seed was sown on March 24 at the United States Sugar Cane Field Station, Canal Point, Florida, and the seedlings obtained were planted out in July, 1921. In February, 1922, one of the seedlings of this progeny was given the number U.S. 1643. Its habit of growth was described as, "reclining to erect, very prolific, 9½ feet tall, stalks 1½ inches in diameter, nodes 6 to 8 inches long, pale green to yellow, semi-clean, leaves average width." Trials of U.S. 1643 showed that it was not suitable for commercial culture in the United States.

In 1924 self fertilized seed was obtained from U.S. 1643. The seed was planted in the spring of 1925 and the seedlings obtained were planted out during the summer. A certain seedling of this progeny was selected and given the number C.P. 807. Cuttings of C.P. 807 were sent to the United States Sugar Plant Field Station, Houma, Louisiana, and the Louisiana State Agricultural Experiment Station, Baton Rouge, Louisiana, on February 11, 1926. The valuable characteristics of this variety, including tolerance to disease and yields of cane and sugar greatly exceeding the yields afforded by P.O.J. 213 and the other P.O.J. varieties grown in Louisiana, were prov-

THE

SUGAR
BULLETIN

407 Carondelet St., New Orleans

Issued on the 1st and 15th of each month. Official Organ of the American Sugar Cane League of the U. S. A., in which are consolidated
The Louisiana Sugar Planters' Assn.
The American Cane Growers' Assn.
The Producers & Mfgrs. Protective Assn.
Subscription Price, 50 Cents Per Year.

Reginald Dykers, General Manager & Editor of the Bulletin
301 Nola Bldg., New Orleans
Frank L. Barker, Secretary and Treasurer
Lockport, La.
C. J. Bourg, Manager Washington Office
810 Union Trust Building

CHAIRMEN OF COMMITTEES:

C. D. Kemper, Franklin, La.
President of the League and Ex-Officio Chairman of Executive Committee
Andrew H. Gay, Plaquemine, La,
Chairman Agricultural Committee
David W. Pipes, Jr., Houma, La.
Chairman Industrial Committee
Frank L. Barker, Lockport, La.
Chairman Finance Committee.
Edward J. Gay, Plaquemine, La.
Chairman Tariff Committee
H. Langdon Laws, Cinclare, La.
Chairman Legislative Committee
J. C. LeBourgeois, New Orleans, La.
Chairman Freight Rate Committee
R. H. Chadwick, Bayou Goula, La.
Chairman Membership Committee
A. H. Rosenfeld, New Orleans, La.
Chairman Publicity Committee

Members of the League desiring action on, or information on, any subject are invited to communicate with the League or with the Chairman of the Committee to which it seems to appertain.

en by trials carried on during the period 1926 to 1930, and it was released in October, 1930, for commercial culture in the state.

C.P. 807 is the first sugar cane variety of commercial value which has been produced in the United States. It represents ten years of work, and the first five years of this work was performed by Dr. E. W. Brandes and the late Mr. Peter Klaphaak under the most trying conditions. To have obtained a variety of sugar cane possessing such valuable characteristics in so short a time is a noteworthy achievement, and presents ample encouragement that other varieties possessing the good characteristics of C.P. 807 and fewer of its faults will be produced.

The Art of Propaganda

Readers of the leading American magazines and of the Sunday supplements in the American newspapers can hardly fail to have noticed an eruption of material recently which relates to Cuba, our obligations to the Island, the sacrifices in our behalf made by the Cubans, the value of our trade with Cuba, and the advisability of increasing the ties that now bind us to the Pearl of the Antilles. That these articles have not appeared by chance, but are part of a propaganda program, can hardly be doubted. The latest one to come to our attention appeared in the *Atlantic Monthly* for December and was written by Professor Cyrus French Wicker of the University of Miami, Florida. In it he advocates free trade with Cuba and

his article is written along lines that identify him a: a special pleader in behalf of Cuba and its welfare Why he assumed this role we of course do not know but it seems to us to run close to a violation of th(Code of Ethics of the American Association of Uni versity Professors adopted by that organization las summer because of the widespread participation o university professors in the discussion of matters o public policy that are of a controversial nature. A letter of protest to the Editor of the *Atlantic Monthl:* by the General Manager of the American Sugar Can(League elicited the following reply:

THE ATLANTIC MONTHLY
Boston, Mass.,
4 December, 1930.

Dear Mr. Dykers:

Thank you for your interesting letter. We believe tha public opinion in the United States sustains the bargai: we made with Cuba, and takes cognizance of the fac that the Cuban sugar business antedates the develop ment in the United States, to which your letter refers And, further, that sugar being Cuba's sole support, w(must frankly face a situation which means that she mus either sell sugar or face revolution.

Yours faithfully,
(Signed) THE EDITOR.

Reginald Dykers, Esquire,
American Sugar Cane League of the U. S. A., Inc.,
New Orleans,
Louisiana.

We offer the above as an example of how much falsity and fatuity can be condensed into a half dozen lines. Perhaps the Editor of the *Atlantic Monthly* means to be merely facetious when he implies that thousands of the best class of American citizens, most of them farmers in moderate circumstances, should be required to lay their all on the sacrificial block because otherwise politicians in a West Indian island might goad their followers into spilling each other's more or less worthless blood. Benedict Arnold himself would hardly have endorsed so un-American a sentiment.

The attitude of some of the great magazines published on the North Atlantic seaboard seems for some reason to be remarkably sympathetic to Cuba. It is not impossible that this attitude may be accounted for by the supposition that the stock and bond paper of Cuban sugar enterprises is so thickly sprinkled over all that part of the United States that those whc control the policies of the magazines have more ol less of it in their safe deposit boxes. Instead of using their surplus money to give employment to American working men in the United States and thus indirectly foster the building of homes, schools and churches ir this country, they may have elected to send it tc Cuba and pay it to cheap black and mixed breed labor there on the theory that such a course would mean larger returns. That this policy has led tc such an overproduction of sugar in Cuba as to jeo pardize all the investments made in sugar property in the Island is the irony of Fate, but such an out, come has simply made these investors frantic and illogical in defense of their ill-starred and unpatriotic venture.

It is interesting to note in this connection the al leged existence of a so-called "propaganda mill" ir behalf of Cuba, as described in *"The Editor and Publisher,"* New York, in its issue of November 29, 1930 *"The Editor and Publisher"* claims to have had th(full text of the plan placed in its hands, the manag ing head of the proposed "propaganda mill," it i:

id, being Carl Byoir, Chairman of the Board of irectors of the *Havana Post*, an English language iily published in Havana, but having offices, in large of Mr. Byoir, at 10 East 40th Street, New ork. The plan, as quoted by the *"Editor and ublisher"* embraces a proposal for the establishment 1 New York of an office to take care of the distribu-.on of news articles and items to 1700 daily news-apers and 250 weekly and monthly magazines. It is vident from the text, however, that this plan has ad its inception in Cuban politics, and that its nb-:ctive is to boost the administration of President achado in American minds, probably with the lought that should revolution break out in Cuba, merican public opinion, if properly educated, will rce the United States Government to intervene in :half of the Machado faction. Once organized, how-/er, the machinery of such a publicity bureau could : easily utilized for purposes inimical to our domes-c sugar interests, and that it would be so used ad-its of little doubt.

How to counteract all this is something of a prob-lem, because such activities cost a large amount of money, and any countervailing activity along pub-licity lines would cost as much or more. Mr. Byoir's plan is said to include "the employment of a corps of experienced newspaper men who would daily transmit to all North American papers information and special articles for Sunday editions. Contracts would be made with the best known magazine writers to pre-pare articles covering the various points we may wish to impress on the North American public."

How much of the recent plethora of magazine arti-cles favorable to Cuba is due to some such systema-tized propaganda mill as that attributed to Mr. Byoir it is hard to say. Perhaps the Board of Trustees of the University of Miami could find out from Profes-sor Cyrus French Wicker why he rushed into print. He advocated in the December *Atlantic* a policy that would wipe out the sugar industry of the United States, including that of Florida, overnight, which would not be a laughing matter.

Russia

We have recently had occasion to comment on the importation of manganese ore from Soviet Russia, which was laid down at United States ports at prices so low that the American producers of manganese ore could not compete with it. Before the World War Russia was an immense producer of beet sugar. In-vestigations at the United States Department of Com-merce at Washington fail to show any importations of sugar into the United States from Soviet Russia, but that country has been sending in candy in limited amounts, the statistics for recent years being as follows:

1928	127,554 lbs. valued at $ 21,217	
1929	321,118 lbs. valued at $ 45,037	
1930 (10 mos.)	715,502 lbs. valued at $ 62,735	

It will be noticed that the 1928 importations were valued at 17c a pound, the 1929 importations at 14c a pound and the 1929 importations at 9c a pound. The United States Department of Commerce declares that the grade of candy imported in 1930 at a valua-tion of 9c a pound cannot be produced in this country for less than 26c a pound. This is indicative of what may be in store for us if the Soviet 5-year program should include the export of large amounts of sugar.

Senator Tasker L. Oddie of Nevada has introduced a bill in the Senate to prohibit the importation of any article or merchandise of any description from the Russian Soviet Union. The bill is very brief and reads as follows:

"Be it enacted by the Senate and House of Repre-sentatives of the United States of America in Con-gress assembled, That the transportation into the United States, or any territory subject to the jurisdic-tion thereof, of any article or merchandise (1) from any territory subject to the jurisdiction or control of the Government of the Union of Soviet Socialist Re-publics, (2) mined, produced, or manufactured wholly or in part in any such territory, or (3) produced or manufactured from materials, any of which have been mined, produced or manufactured in any such terri-tory, is prohibited. The Secretary of the Treasury is authorized and directed to prescribe such regula-tions as may be necessary for the enforcement of this Act."

The *Washington Post* in its issue of December 6, 1930, strongly endorses Senator Oddie's bill and pre-dicts the demoralization and destruction of numerous American industries unless some such measure is passed.

The representatives in Congress of Louisiana and the beet sugar states should carefully study this mat-ter. It may prove to be one of vital importance, for while Cuba's policy of giving away her 20% prefer-ential has served to keep all other foreign sugar out of this market Russia may be able to override this barrier by means of her communistic labor system which has already demonstrated its efficacy in the way of low cost production in the case of manganese ore and apparently also in the case of candy.

Doubtless some legislators who will at once agree that goods made by compulsory labor in Soviet Rus-sia ought not to be allowed to enter the United States at all, because that would be unjust to our home labor, will continue to contend that a tariff on goods made by ill-paid and half-starved foreign labor in other places, not Sovietized but occupying a similar low level of existence, is all wrong. One can be just as harmful as the other, and both should be barred.

Investigation of Refined Sugar Cost Dismissed

Hon. Sidney Morgan, Secretary of the United States Tariff Commission, has sent to the SUGAR BUL-LETIN the following "Public Notice" declaring that the investigation of the cost of producing refined sugars instituted in accordance with Senate resolutions 309 and 325 adopted last July, has been discontinued and dismissed. The official statement reads:

"It is hereby ordered by the United States Tariff Commission on this 5th day of December, 1930, pur-suant to provisions of Senate Resolution No. 348, 71st Congress, 3d Session, that the investigation here-tofore, on the 3d and 22d days of July, 1930, insti-tuted, in accordance with Senate Resolutions Nos. 309 and 325, 71st Congress, 2d Session, for the pur-poses of Section 336 of Title III of the Tariff Act of 1930, with respect to the differences in costs of pro-duction of, and of all other facts and conditions enum-erated in said section with respect to, the articles described in paragraph 501 of Title I of said tariff act: namely,

Sugars, including the sugar content of mixtures containing sugar and water, testing by the polariscope above 96 sugar degrees,

being wholly or in part, the growth or product of the United States, and of and with respect to like or similar articles wholly or in part the growth or product of competing foreign countries, be, and the same is hereby, discontinued and dismissed, without prejudice.

"Ordered further, that public notice of this order shall be given by posting a copy thereof for thirty days at the principal office of the Commission in the City of Washington, D. C., and at the office of the Commission at the Port of New York, and by publishing a copy of this order in "Treasury Reports" published by the Department of Commerce.

"By order of the United States Tariff Commission this 5th day of December, 1930.

"Sidney Morgan,
"Secretary."

Keeping Qualities of P. O. J. Cane

Mr. Lewis E. Murrell, of the Geo. M. Murrell P. & M. Co. of Bayou Goula, sends us the following "observations" on the keeping qualities of P.O.J. cane this year made by his chemist, Mr. Thomas Hale.

We have submitted Mr. Hale's figures, as well as those appearing in our last issue from Mr. C. G. Robinson of White Castle, to Mr. C. F. Walton, Jr., Research Chemist of the United States Sugar Plant Field Station at Houma, and to Dr. Charles E. Coates, Dean of the Audubon Sugar School at Baton Rouge, with a request for their comments, but neither of these gentlemen has replied. Mr. Hale's statement is as follows:

Bayou Goula, La., Dec. 3, 1930.
Tally Ho Plantation,
1930 Crop.
Observation on keeping qualities of P.O.J. 213 cane (Augusta Plantation) from Nov. 9th to 13th, inclusive, P.O.J. 213 from a certain 13-acre plot averaged:

13.65 Bx.   Yield: 142.8# Rec. 96 Sugar
10.51 Suc.   5.4 Gals. Molasses
77.00 Pur.

From the 14th to the 26th due to constant rain and the condition of the roads, this cane (13 acres of cut 213) lay in the field exposed to rain and high temperatures (as high as 90 deg. F.).

On the 26th (a period of two weeks) milling was resumed of this cane, and practically all was ground by the 29th, inc. This juice analyzed:

14.86 Bx.   Yield: 151# 96 sugar
11.24 Suc.   6.4 Gals. Molasses
75.63 Pur.

Conclusion: Apparently at the expense of loss of weight (the weight was not determined) due to evaporation, we have had a concentration of solids in the cane. But structurally the sucrose broke down faster than the non-sucrose solids, because we have a fall in purity, however, this structural decomposition was very slow; but 1.37 points in two weeks. Due to this purity drop, though after two weeks we had a 6.94% increase in sucrose, the increased recoverable 96 sugar content was but 5.74%. This, because recovery is a function of the percentage of non-sucrose solids (purity) present.

The poor keeping qualities of last year's P.O.J. cane, the good keeping qualities of this year's P.O.J.

(Continued on page 6.)

appear to substantiate the theory that the keeping properties of this cane is a variable quality depending upon the meteriological conditions at its growth. Apparently land is a minor factor because last year over the whole sugar belt the cane kept badly.

This observation gives no light what influence the state and age of the cane when cut has upon its keeping qualities. Certain, however, this cane was very green.

THOS. HALE, Chemist.

Address of Mr. David W. Pipes, Jr.

(Delivered at Meeting of Co-ordination Committee, Houma, La., November 14th, 1930.)

On behalf of the American Sugar Cane League, the organization which represents the sugar cane interests of Louisiana and the United States in general, I wish to express thanks and appreciation to the Federal and State research and experimental workers who have made this meeting possible.

There was held in Houma this morning a conference which is symbolical of the thought and methods prevailing today in the Louisiana Sugar Cane Belt. The conference referred to was a joint committee meeting of various agencies working on U. S. cane problems and particularly those of Louisiana, composed of representatives of the various bureaus of the United States Department of Agriculture, doing research work, the staff of the Louisiana State University and the planters all joining together and planning a co-operative attack on the most vital problems confronting the industry. It is the third such meeting held in the last few years and the first ever held in the Cane Belt of Louisiana. The meeting is typical of the new agricultural thought. Results obtained to date illustrate the fruitful possibilities of such endeavor.

Sugar cane raising has existed commercially in Louisiana since 1795. Through generations it has been the backbone money crop of South Louisiana. The livelihood of hundreds of thousands of people has depended largely on its welfare. The soil is wonderfully rich and the people frugal and industrious. However, the climatic conditions and investments in machinery and equipment are such that the crop is vital to South Louisiana and under present conditions almost impossible to replace profitably.

Like many other branches of agriculture the industry got out of step with modern scientific knowledge and economic development. Each planter was a law unto himself. There was too little comprehension of the light which modern science could throw on our problems. In extenuation I take the liberty of saying scientific research work in agriculture is a relatively new development, and too little used in the solving of one of the nation's biggest problems.

Starting about 1916 Louisiana was stricken by the serious Mosaic cane disease. Almost before planters realized what had happened, the crops were cut into halves, then into quarters and less. I will not dwell on the suffering of many during the years from 1920 to date. The effect of the disease in crop failure has been intensified, by lowering prices for our products due to past war adjustments, and very unusual climatic conditions of the last few years, including the worst flood in history.

Suffice it to say that thousands of as good men as ever trod shoe leather, planters and business men, lost their savings and their homes, largely from conditions beyond reasonable control. Without doubt the Mosaic disease was the chief cause of a monetary loss to South Louisiana of over one hundred and fifty millions of dollars, and the effects of which will be suffered for years to come.

From the calamity, there has developed two great redeeming features. First, a keen realization has come to many of the remnant of planters left in the industry of the necessity of team work. Secondly, under our great government fortunately there is means of giving relief formerly undreamed of—namely, making available modern scientific agricultural knowledge. Louisiana can never equal the length of sunshine and cheap labor of the tropics. Undoubtedly, though with reasonable tariff protection, with full utilization of American brains, manufacturing ingenuity and quicker access to markets she can and will build a sound livelihood for her people. Scientific research is coming into the Sugar Belt as never before. The best and safest foundations to insure this livelihood are being laid.

It may be in order to sketch some of the developments of the recent years.

In 1918 Dr. E. W. Brandes, an eminent scientist and one of our guests tonight, called attention to Mosaic disease in Louisiana and its possible ravages—Bulletin 829. His warning was then unheeded.

In 1922 and 1923 a few stalks of P.O.J. 234, 213 and 36 cane, resistant to Mosaic disease, was given by Dr. Brandes, Office of Sugar Plant Investigations, Bureau of Plant Industry, U. S. Department of Agriculture, to the estate of H. C. Minor, "Southdown." The request for the original P.O.J. 234 being made through Mr. Elliott Jones, General Field Manager at Southdown. I think in 1923 the breeding station was erected at Canal Point, Fla., by United States Department of Agriculture. In 1924 wide distribution of new varieties was made over the State by the American Sugar Cane League. In 1925 the League erected near Houma a field laboratory to further research work and secured acreage for test work.

Extra appropriations were made in 1926 by Louisiana State Legislature to study cane problems at the State University Cane Experiment Station. During 1928 another Federal laboratory unit was erected and in that year was formed the co-ordinating committee to make more effective the work of all agencies, Federal, State and planters. During 1930 provision was made for a third laboratory building near Houma.

In the meanwhile many other facilities of both the State and the Federal government have been brought into use. Intensive studies have been made of soils and fertilizers, diseases, water levels, drainage, harmful insects, importation of parasites to control cane borers and studies of chemical problems in sugar factories.

Possibly one of the most striking statements that can be made is that in one hundred years Louisiana had four commercial varieties of cane. Today there is being bred and imported for Louisiana use and for syrup cane production throughout the South over a hundred thousand new varieties per year to be

INVALUABLE TO EVERY CANE SUGAR FACTORY

...Continuous, Clean *and* Single-Stage Handling of CANE MUDS.

CONTINUOUS, clean and single-stage ... three important features of the new Oliver United method of handling cane muds.

And then add to these three the following:

Use of perforated metal plate instead of cotton filter cloth.

Reduction in inversion and mechanical losses.

Reduction in load on the evaporators due to minimum amount of wash water.

Advantages such as these are what make the new Oliver United Cane Mud handling invaluable to raw sugar producers. The several operators already using this handling will back up this claim.

tested in every conceivable way to secure canes of more productivity and value.

There is now going on an intensive study of cane deterioration to find ways and means of protecting and storing cane and operating factories during bad weather with consequent elimination of lost time and lowering of expense.

Most of the funds to carry on this work are properly secured from State and Federal appropriations and the need and benefit of the work can best be pointed out by an organized body. Through their organization to aid this and other work, the planters and allied interests have taxed themselves annually tens of thousands of dollars. The building equipment alone at the Federal station in Terrebonne Parish represents now an investment of twenty odd thousands of dollars.

This may sound like a big program, and in a way it is, but it is only a beginning. Better and higher yielding canes and improvement in cultural methods must be secured. Mechanical harvesting is needed. We make too little use of our by-products and know too little of their potential values. More efficient men and machinery, new capital and profits can only come into being by overcoming more of these difficulties. Sugar from sugar cane and sugar beets is one of the few crops in the United States of which there is unlimited room for expansion. The continental United States produces about one-sixth of its consumption and acreage devoted to sugar culture will aid in enabling other farmers to abandon over-produced crops of cotton and grain.

The American Sugar Cane League maintains that research work done in Louisiana on sugar cane is not for Louisiana benefit alone. Men and machinery can be put here for a fraction of the cost it takes to place them in the tropics. Such work will aid the whole South in the development of cane, the juice of which, easily made into syrup, is a wholesome, palatable food of high nutritive value. This research work will help improve sugar cane production methods in our tropical territories and possessions—the Philippines, Porto Rico, Hawaii and its benefits will undoubtedly spread to Cuba. Properly directed, it will lead to more and more knowledge—safer, sounder, more efficient and more profitable production in Louisiana and carry with its fulfillment a cheaper price to the consumer.

We know full well the crushing burden of heavy debts. Progress in agriculture at best takes time and a community suffering such as ours cannot but grow impatient for relief, but today as accomplishment there are several hundreds of thousands of acres and millions of new canes from the warning of 1918 and the few stalks of 1922. A good many millions of dollars has been added to the producing power of Louisiana and above all, is the increasing knowledge that the foundations are being laid, largely through cooperative effort, research, careful testing and experimentation, which will give our rich lands, with reasonable care, opportunity to provide again a livelihood to the workers thereon.

Gentlemen of the United States Department of Agriculture and the Louisiana State University, it is my honor and privilege to welcome and express to you again keen appreciation of your interest and work in our behalf.

The Mighty Mississippi

The Editor of the SUGAR BULLETIN has received a opy of a very valuable historical paper prepared by on. Harry D. Wilson, Louisiana Commissioner of griculture and Immigration, and entitled "Louisia's 100-Year Struggle With the Mighty Mississppi."

In this document, which has been printed by the :ate of Louisiana in pamphlet form, Commissioner ilson has sought to give a comprehensive outline of ie important part played by the various parishes in ouisiana which have been affected by the recent ational flood control projects, and he has divided iem into two sections, those affected by the Atchafaya floodway and those affected by the Bœuf flooday. The author goes back into the early history of ouisiana for much of his data and he carries the hisiry of the parishes referred to from their creation, hich in some cases occurred before Louisiana beame a part of the United States in 1803, up to now. tatistics are given as to crops produced in these arishes, their population, their property values and heir industrial enterprises, the development of all hese features being traced decade by decade up to he present.

Commissioner Wilson's researches along these lines ave provided a very powerful argument against the acrifice of the territory comprised in the floodway rojects that are included in the so-called Jadwin lan of Flood Control on the Lower Mississippi. The ommissioner has handled the whole matter with his customary thoroughness.

Cane Molasses as Anti-Anemia Insurance

By Arthur H. Rosenfeld, Consulting Technologist, American Sugar Cane League.

Those who have followed recent nutritional studies know that young rats fed on exclusive milk diet soon develop anemia and die, the explanation given by the nutritional expert being that milk does not contain a sufficient quantity of iron and copper, two substances which have been found essential for the production of hemoglobin, the red-coloring matter of the blood.

Dr. W. E. Krauss of the Ohio Agricultural Experiment Station has been for some time searching for various foods which would properly supplement milk, and one of those tried was cane molasses. He obtained a remarkable response, both in the prevention and curing of anemia, through the use of cane molasses, which result naturally suggested the question as to whether beet molasses would have a similar effect.

In the bi-monthly bulletin of the Ohio Agricultural Experiment Station, No. 147, Dr. Krauss now discusses these latest experiments. White rats recently weaned were allowed access to all of the whole milk they could drink. To one group one-half of a gram of cane molasses was fed. In a separate dish each day and to a comparable group, a half-gram of beet molasses was fed in the same manner. Still another group was maintained on milk alone until anemia developed. Then half of this latter group were fed, in addition to milk, one-half gram of cane molasses daily, and the other half, half a gram of beet molasses daily.

The presence or absence of anemia can be simply detected by determining the amount of hemoglobin in the blood, and such determinations were frequently made of each rat during this experiment. As to the result, we will quote from the report of Dr. Krauss in summing up his observations:

"It is very obvious from the curves that the combination of milk and cane molasses allowed excellent growth and maintained the hemoglobin content of the blood at a high level. When cane molasses was added after severe anemia had developed, hemoglobin regeneration was restored, and the blood was soon normal. On the other hand the combination of milk and beet molasses resulted in retarded growth and did not prevent the development of anemia; also, the addition of beet molasses to the diet of rats suffering from nutritional anemia had no beneficial effect.

"To explain these results, chemical analyses of the ash or mineral matter in the two kinds of molasses were made. It was found that the cane molasses contained much more iron and copper than did beet molasses. Since these two elements had previously been shown to be essential for hemoglobin regeneration, it was concluded that the superiority of the cane molasses was due to its high iron and copper content."

Yet the price of Louisiana blackstrap is 5½ cents!

Lost Motion

The attention of the SUGAR BULLETIN has been called to the fact that the post of research chemist at the Louisiana Experiment Station has been vacant ever since the resignation of Dr. J. F. Brewster, some two or three years ago. It is our impression that something like $150,000 was spent in creating a chemical laboratory, second to none, at Baton Rouge, and if it be true that this investment is not being utilized something ought to be done about it. It is quite possible that there are good and sufficient reasons why Dr. Brewster's former post has been allowed to remain vacant and the magnificent equipment stands unproductive. We shall be glad to print any statements on the subject that are pertinent and authoritative.

Look At This!

CASTAGNOS GEARED STUBBLE SHAVER

Your attention is called to the accompanying photograph of this new, heavily constructed, positively driven and tractor-drawn stubble shaver, which we believe, constitutes a decided step forward in the efficient handling of this phase of our agricultural work.

We are sure that you will at once appreciate the great advantage of having a positive drive for the shaving discs as against the friction drive formerly employed, the efficiency of which depended entirely upon a clean, even off-bar. You well know that when the off-bar was not clean-cut and narrow, or where rains had washed a part of the ridge down, the discs of the old stubble shaver had friction on both sides, did not revolve in certain areas and hence split or pulled out the stools.

No such bad results are possible with the New Geared Stubble Shaver. The turning of the discs is assured and also the higher disc speed necessary for most efficient cutting and least splitting of stools is obtained by its use with a tractor.

This new shaver was used very successfully in shaving all the stubble this year at the plantations of E. G. Robichaux Co. (Cedar Grove) and Lewis Murrell (Tally Ho). Both of the above reported this shaver giving excellent results, and were able to shave from 20 to 23 acres per day.

The shaver, you will notice, is very strongly constructed and well adapted to the hard use given a tool for the shaving of the new type canes.

THE REVOLVING KNIVES ARE 30 INCHES IN DIAMETER, MADE OF HIGH TEMPERED STEEL, AND ARE SO DESIGNED AS TO PERMIT A 10-INCH VERTICAL SHIFT OF THE KNIVES, WITH A POSITIVE SET POSITION OF SAME. THIS REMOVES THE UNSATISFACTORY FEATURE OF EVERY STUBBLE SHAVER HITHERTO IN USE. IT ENABLES THE PLANTER TO DO STUBBLE SHAVING AS IT OUGHT TO BE DONE, AND AS IT MUST BE DONE TO SECURE THE RESULTS THAT STUBBLE SHAVING IS INTENDED TO PRODUCE.

For destroying stubble we have designed an attachment for the forward portion of the frame on which two disc coulters can be placed, thus cutting the stubble into three portions.

Orders for these machines should be in our hands in ample time to permit of their being manufactured and delivered before the normal season for stubble shaving.

CASTAGNOS CANE LOADER CO.

DONALDSONVILLE, LA., or

CHAS. WIGGIN,
MARITIME BLDG., NEW ORLEANS

THE La. State University, Baton Rouge, La.
SUGAR
BULLETIN

Entered as second-class matter April 13, 1925, at the postoffice at
New Orleans, La., under Act of March 6, 1879.

We stand for the encouragement of Home Industries as against Foreign Competition.

Vol. 9   NEW ORLEANS, LA., JANUARY 1, 1931   No. 7

The Year's End

The sugar planters of Louisiana are engaged in a business that takes more than a calendar year to complete its cycle. They begin preparing their fields for planting in the late summer and reap their crops in the fall and winter of the following year. Nevertheless we are accustomed to visualize our industry by years. This being the case, what sort of a picture is presented by 1930?

Looked at from a weather standpoint it was a decidedly unfavorable year for growing a crop of sugar cane. It was cold up to the middle of June, when the temperature suddenly became unseasonably hot, attended by drought, and it was not until September that enough rainfall was secured to make the crop take on a normal rate of growth, and that at a time when it should have been ripening instead of making more tonnage. In the face of this we find that the P.O.J. canes fought their way to almost a normal degree of weight and sucrose, measured by pre-mosaic standards. The opinion seems to be universal that they gave a wonderful exhibition of vitality and hardihood during the cold spring and the dry summer, and speculation is rife as to what the crop would have been if the spring had been spring-like and the summer had brought those alternations of heat and rainfall that characterize our summer weather as a rule. More cane than existing mills could have ground would doubtless have resulted. The grinding season was, on the whole, favorable, and in marked contrast to that of the previous year, which was one of the most unfavorable on record. There were no losses from frozen cane, and a minimum of time was lost from wet weather. Prices, unfortunately, were distressingly low.

We think it is reasonable and right to say, as the year 1930 ends, that it subjected the Louisiana sugar industry, as yet only convalescent from the mosaic disease, to an extraordinary strain, in both weather and price, and that the industry stood it without quailing. It gave substantial evidence that it now has behind it the reserve strength, not financial, unfortunately, but in every other respect, to hold its own in bad seasons and much more than hold its own in good ones. Such being the case, there is ample cause for congratulations and rejoicing.

===== THE =====
SUGAR BULLETIN

407 Carondelet St., New Orleans

Issued on the 1st and 15th of each month. Official Organ of the American Sugar Cane League of the U. S. A., in which are consolidated The Louisiana Sugar Planters' Assn. The American Cane Growers' Assn. The Producers & Mfgrs. Protective Assn. Subscription Price 50 Cents Per Year

Reginald Dykers, General Manager & Editor of the Bulletin 301 Nola Bldg., New Orleans

Frank L. Barker, Secretary and Treasurer Lockport, La.

C. J. Bourg, Manager Washington Office 810 Union Trust Building

CHAIRMEN OF COMMITTEES:

C. D. Kemper, Franklin, La.
President of the League and Ex-Officio Chairman of Executive Committee

Andrew H. Gay, Plaquemine, La,
Chairman Agricultural Committee

David W. Pipes, Jr., Houma, La.
Chairman Industrial Committee

Frank L. Barker, Lockport, La.
Chairman Finance Committee.

Edward J. Gay, Plaquemine, La.
Chairman Tariff Committee

H. Langdon Laws, Cinclare, La.
Chairman Legislative Committee

J. C. LeBourgeois, New Orleans, La.
Chairman Freight Rate Committee

R. H. Chadwick, Bayou Goula, La.
Chairman Membership Committee

A. H. Rosenfeld, New Orleans, La.
Chairman Publicity Committee

Members of the League desiring action on, or information on, any subject are invited to communicate with the League or with the Chairman of the Committee to which it seems to appertain.

Let's Have a Happy New Year!

By C. J. Bourg

There are so many sources of propaganda regarding the Chadbourne plan that it is difficult for persons not on the inside to interpret the present status. We are certain that Cuba, Java, Belgium, Czechoslovakia, Hungary and Poland have accepted in principle the terms of the Chadbourne plan and have signed a tentative accord. But the Germans have lived up to their record of "boche" hard headedness.

It is the opinion of men who are accustomed to dissecting publicity, that the cable dispatches from Mr. Carlisle McDonald who is the representative of the New York Times in Europe and who attended both the Amsterdam and Brussels meetings, give the most accurate report of the situation. His latest dispatches indicate he has direct information that the Germans are going to drive the very hardest bargain that they can get, but eventually they will reach an agreement that will bring about their signature to the international agreement. The Germans know that no plan such as is proposed can be successful without the agreement of all important sugar producing nations. They also know that the American and Dutch banks will assist them, if necessary to secure their signature. Therefore they are playing the game for all it is worth with the purpose of making a last minute decision to the best advantage.

That the Chadbourne plan is due for a great many difficulties must be expected, for it has ever been a most precarious venture for any world industry to seek to control distribution and production by common agreement. It has been tried before although the circumstances have not been entirely the same. The efforts in recent years of the rubber industry and the coffee industry to establish international control have not resulted in accordance with their plan. We mention this not because we believe that there is no probability of success but rather that it will require the utmost good faith and the master strategy of such men as Thomas L. Chadbourne has already proven himself to be. But Mr. Chadbourne himself is in Paris in the care of physicians, recovering from the exhaustion of six months of strenuous and continuous effort in behalf of a world sugar curtailment agreement.

The Clearing House

Another effort of considerable proportions is being made for the benefit of the sugar producers in the United States. This is the establishment of a National Clearing House seeking to eliminate the brutal competition now existing and especially the costly cross-hauling of sugar. The plan to have a corps of traffic experts determine the cheapest market for the output of each factory in the United States will serve as the basis of a common sense agreement by which sugar will be distributed to the consumption centers from the nearest points of production. Progress has been made in this regard by the Cooperative Committee appointed from the domestic sugar industry by the Federal Farm Board. This plan should be ready for adoption by Spring.

The Appropriations Bill for the Department of Agriculture which has just passed the House of Representatives continues all appropriations which were made last year and in addition there are several of special interest to the Louisiana sugar cane industry. An appropriation of seventy-five thousand dollars has been made for research looking to the commercial use of farm wastes, with special mention being made of bagasse, corn stalks and rice hulls. It is the opinion of the heads of scientific work in the Department of Agriculture that the sugar industry should be able to take care of its overhead by commercializing by-products. An additional appropriation of five thousand dollars has been authorized for experiments relative to the deterioration of sugar cane. It is expected that these experiments will lead to the protection of sugar cane from freezes or at least the reduction of the losses to a minimum.

The Bureau of Agricultural Engineering will receive an additional ten thousand dollars for the purpose of making an investigation of all existing sugar cane harvesters and looking to the improvement of one which can serve to lower the cost of production and to make more efficient the harvesting of sugar cane.

Full recognition and appreciation must be accorded Congressman Numa F. Montet and Congressman John D. Sandlin of Louisiana who are responsible for these increases which mean so much to the future of our industry. Mr. Montet, in cooperation with our Washington office formed a very effective liaison between the Department of Agriculture and Congress, furnishing them with all information and appearing before the Committee in support of the recommendations of the experts from the Department of Agricul-

(Continued on page 4)

Friends of Cyanamid ⌄ ⌄

Perhaps no other single factor is more responsible for the general acceptance of Cyanamid in Louisiana's "Sugar Bowl," than the fact that it "performs consistently and well" in good seasons and in bad. It is dependable. Cyanamid made many new friends for itself in the dry season just past. And it has a great many "old friends." More than a hundred Louisiana cane planters used Cyanamid last year—thirty-seven more than the number using it the year before. Repeat-purchasers bought more Cyanamid per plantation.

The reasons for this leadership of Cyanamid go much further than its obvious attraction of economy. Its high-analysis, free-drilling qualities, convenient, clean "one-man" package contribute much to ease and economy in application—important considerations to the planter operating extensive properties largely with unskilled labor.

In addition to its 21 per cent of nitrogen, Cyanamid contains 75 per cent of hydrated lime-equivalent. The continued use of Cyanamid year after year builds up the calcium content of the soil, promoting good tilth, counteracting acidity and toxic plant residues, and favoring beneficial bacterial activity.

The progressive availability of Cyanamid results in even, sustained feeding of the cane. Sucrose and purity percentages are maintained and substantial increases in yield are economically produced.

Your investigation of the record of Cyanamid performance in your neighborhood is invited. We will gladly supply additional facts and data.

For further information, write

American Cyanamid Company

Pioneer Producers of Air-Nitrogen Products in America

535 FIFTH AVENUE, NEW YORK
1820 JEFFERSON AVENUE   NEW ORLEANS

ture. Congressman Sandlin as a member of the Committee on Appropriations was our very successful champion in Committee. Our hope now is that the Senate will act quickly on this important Supply Bill before the Senate gets into a snarl at the end of the present session, as there is every indication that there will be great bitterness existing before March 4th, involving the White House, and an Insurgent movement within the Republican Party of disturbing proportions. A special session is no longer improbable.

Cooperation

The Domestic Sugar Producers' Association held a meeting at Chicago this month to adopt a program for the new year and to discuss the various legislative and governmental developments. The policies of the various members, which include the beet sugar people of the West, the Hawaiians, the Porto Ricans, the corn sugar producers and the sugar cane growers of Louisiana and Florida, appeared to be in entire accord and a united front will be maintained. Questions concerning the securing of a higher refined differential, legislation against the importation of liquid sugar at syrup rates and the adoption of a publicity program, were the subjects of detailed discussions and the representatives at Washington were instructed to keep the closest possible contact.

The United States Tariff Commission has made a report to the Ways and Means Committee recognizing that the refined differential was not sufficient protection. However, Chairman Hawley of the Ways and Means Committee immediately issued a statement that no legislation is planned on this matter during the present session, because he and other Congressional leaders fear that the opening of any one schedule of the Tariff Bill would immediately lead to the re-opening of many other schedules by Congress. Mr. Hawley suggested that the Flexible Provisions of the Tariff Act were intended to take care of such situations, which amounts to a suggestion from him that if the refiners are not satisfied with the present provisions of the law, they may avail themselves of a Tariff Commission investigation.

On liquid sugar, a protest has been filed by the Savannah Sugar Refining Company with the Collector of Customs, against the Treasury decision which refuses to permit the entry of liquid sugar under the molasses and syrup rate of one-fourth of one cent per gallon. This undoubtedly means that the question will be carried through the courts and we are informed that the Treasury Department is sufficiently concerned about this matter which involves some one hundred and forty million dollars of revenue from the sugar tariff, to be preparing an official request that Congress clear the language of the sugar schedule, so there will be no doubt as to its meaning that sugar in any form shall pay the same rate of duty. We believe that Congress is having too much trouble finding money to take care of extra appropriations to disregard such a request.

A Wish

The New Year holds so many possibilities of hope, that the writer takes this occasion to wish for the sugar industry in Louisiana and Florida, the turning point upward in the cycle that has gone beyond the ancient seven years. May Chadbourne succeed and the tariff for which we fought and bled become effective to its full extent, even against Cuba!

A Note on the Ripening of the P. O. J. Canes

(1) P.O.J. 234
(2) P.O.J. 213
(3) P.O.J. 36

The above represents in general the chronological
ening periods of the three P.O.J.'s. The 234, while
s resistant to cold than the other two, still has
o or three degrees margin over the D-74 and Na-
e. It ripens surprisingly early and is followed by
2 213 in about two weeks, with the 36 reaching a
rity comparable to the 234 about a month later as
rule. Of course, as stubble each of these will ripen
out fifteen to twenty days earlier than the plant.
The writer thinks we can safely plan to extend our
inding season a bit by employing P.O.J. 36 for the
it grinding. With this in mind the 36 should al-
iys be planted on lands as near as possible to the
rricks, so that it can be most conveniently hauled
ring the bad weather that we are likely to run
:o if the crop is materially extended after Christmas.

*Arthur H. Rosenfeld, Consulting Technologist,
American Sugar Cane League.*

eeping Qualities of P. O. J. Canes

Baton Rouge, La., December 18, 1930.

ditor Sugar Bulletin:

I have read the clipping from the recent number
f the SUGAR BULLETIN relative to analyses of some
.O.J. cane near White Castle.

This cane was analyzed before cutting, and after
ying in the field about two weeks. Inasmuch as
t would naturally lose in weight, the percentage of
ucrose would of course be higher after keeping, pro-
ided there was no inversion and the test for inver-
ion would not be sucrose, but purity. In this case
he purity fell from 77 to 75.6 over a period of two
ir three weeks, that is, the cut cane deteriorated
inly to this extent. According to my experience, this
s a very small deterioration. Normally I believe
he deterioration would be much greater, probably
bout five points or over. Why this particular cane
:ept so well, I do not know, but I feel quite sure
t would not be safe to cut cane under the assump-
ion that another lot would do as well.

A little later in the season, with the temperature
n the neighborhood of 40° F., P.O.J. cane, after
ieing cut several weeks may show comparatively little
oss in purity, but for the most part, at least, Java
anes should be ground as soon as possible after cuting. The time they will last undamaged after cuting is perhaps not definitely determined, but in
aany canes, with a temperature of from 50 to 60°
'. the deterioration has been very considerable, as I
aid before, at least five points, and sometimes more.
am inclined to think this is primarily a question of
emperature.

The following experiments run in 1928 by Mr. J.
A. Webre and myself might be of interest.

About one hundred (100) pounds each of P.O.J.
ane, Nos. 234, 213, and 36 was kept protected from
he weather, and analyzed at intervals. For each
nalysis, about ten canes were cut into tops, middles
nd bottoms which were analyzed separately. . The
xtraction was about 64 in each case.

(Continued on page 6.)

P. O. J. 36	November 15th				November 17th				November 19th				November 21st				November 23d				P_ Dr_
	Suc.	Gluc.	Acid	Pur.	Suc.	Gluc.	Acid	Pur.	Suc.	Gluc.	Acid	Pur.	Suc.	Gluc.	Acid	Pur.	Suc.	Gluc.	Acid	Pur.	
Tops	7.3	2.1	2.9	57.7	6.7	3.3	2.8	50.9	5.8	3.8	2.8	46.4	6.6	3.8	2.9	48.1	5.4	4.0	2.9	37.3	2
Middle	11.1	1.7	2.6	73.1	10.7	2.9	2.5	71.1	10.1	3.0	2.6	68.2	9.9	3.2	2.7	66.3	8.5	3.5	2.8	54.2	1
Bottom	12.9	0.8	1.4	81.1	12.5	2.2	2.0	78.8	11.9	2.0	2.1	76.7	11.0	2.2	2.1	70.0	10.4	2.5	2.0	65.6	1
Average	10.5	1.5	2.2	71.9	10.1	2.8	2.4	68.0	9.4	2.9	2.5	65.6	9.2	3.0	2.5	58.2	8.4	3.4	2.5	61.8	
P. O. J. 234																					
Tops	12.9	1.7	2.9	77.9	10.9	1.4	2.8	70.6	10.1	2.0	2.7	64.4	10.2	2.8	2.3	61.7	9.8	3.5	2.7	56.1	2
Middle	14.5	0.8	2.5	81.1	14.2	0.6	2.8	81.9	14.4	1.0	2.5	79.9	13.5	1.7	2.2	80.7	13.3	1.8	2.5	72.3	
Bottom	14.0	1.2	2.3	82.5	13.7	0.5	2.0	81.7	15.0	.66	2.1	82.6	14.1	1.1	1.6	79.1	13.5	1.7	1.7	74.3	
Average	13.9	1.2	2.5	80.7	12.5	0.7	2.4	78.6	13.0		2.3	77.3	12.4	1.6	1.9	75.8	11.9	2.1	2.1	68.6	1
P. O. J. 213																					
Tops	8.8	3.2	2.3	68.4	9.2	3.4	2.3	67.4	11.2	2.3	2.0	76.3	11.2	2.9	2.0	74.1	10.3	3.0	2.5	71.4	+
Middle	12.9	1.8	2.2	80.7	13.1	1.9	2.3	81.8	14.5	1.6	1.5	86.9	13.1	2.1	1.8	80.9	12.4	2.8	2.0	76.7	
Bottom	13.8	1.6	1.8	86.1	13.0	1.7	1.8	82.5	13.3	1.8	1.7	84.5	14.8	1.6	1.4	86.4	12.8	2.7	2.3	77.5	
Average	11.8	2.2	2.1	78.4	11.8	2.3	2.1	77.2	13.0	1.9	1.7	82.6	13.1	2.2	1.7	80.5	11.8	2.8	2.3	75.2	

Loss by evaporation slightly over 4% for period November 15th-23d for all varieties.

8:00 A. M.	73.4	73.4	61.7	
11:30 A. M.	75.2	75.2	61.7	48.2
4:00 P. M.	78.8	78.8	63.5	50. 54.2

These samples were under cover and therefore protected also from sunlight. It is of course quite difficult to get fair samples in matters of this sort, but the results are fairly significant.

There was comparatively little change in acidity throughout, and such change as did occur was evidently not the cause of the loss in purity. This loss was obviously due to the presence of an inverting enzyme which is most active at temperatures over 50° F. The very considerable drop in purity of the tops as opposed to the bottoms would indicate the comparative need of grinding the cane shortly after cutting or else of retopping in case undue time h elapsed between cutting and milling.

In the case of P.O.J. 36, after a lapse of five da the purity of the tops had fallen from 57 to 37, it is evident that a sugar juice with a purity of 37 an absolute loss if introduced into a sugar house.

The analytical work on these experiments was do by some graduate students of the Audubon Sug School and is probably more accurate than most the work done at the average sugar house.

Yours sincerely,
CHARLES E. COATES.

Drying Cane Tops for Feed

So much interest attaches to the possibility of usi cane tops for stock feed that we have asked Pro Wm. Whipple, Sugar Engineering Specialist at tl Louisiana Experiment Station, to give us the resu of the trials in drying cane tops recently conduct by him with a mechanical drier at Baton Rouge.

The possibilities attached to the successful man facture of stock feed from cane tops are recogniz as being very important. If the green tops can I removed from the cane in September or early Octob and sold as stock feed at a price that will compensa for the loss of cane tonnage thus incurred, the r mainder of the stalk could be sent to the mill at th time, without waiting another month for the top join to ripen. This is all very interesting, and Prof. Whi ple writes as follows:

Baton Rouge, December 17, 1930.

Editor Sugar Bulletin:
I have received your letter of December 15th, aski me to give you the results of the trials of L. S. drier operating on cane tops.

We have dried cane tops gathered from the cane cut for the mill, as well as tops gathered from the ca sold for seed, which, of course, were cut at a high point on the stalk.

Neither of these materials gave any trouble in tl drying other than the necessity of slowing down tl speed of the fan so as to give a slower air velocity the air through the drum. With this change it is p sible to produce a feed of any desired average moistu content from 5% up. The moisture in the raw materi was slightly over 75% for the tops of cane cut for t mill as well as those cut for seed.

It was necessary to slow down the fan producing t

current of air through the drum for the reason that the blades of the leaf tend to carry the leaf through the drier before the midrib section can give up its moisture o the point that it can be safely stored without danger of heating.

Crops similar to cane tops and sorghum can be successfully dried in no other type of drier than one which has a current of air to carry out the dry particles. The Arnold dryer operated by Godchaux Sugars at Reserve, and by the J. M. Burguieres Co. at Cypremort, as well as the Koon-Munch dryer at La Place operate on this rinciple and have successfully dried cane tops.

In these driers as well as the one at L. S. U. the material is dried at a low temperature, which does not estroy the carbohydrates, so that the final product has ll the feed value of the raw material with the moisture educed to the point where it can be safely stored. At he University we have used a corn harvester on corn nd soybeans grown together and have passed the bundles of feed direct to the ensilage cutter of the drier roducing a palatable concentrated feed containing the ars of corn, the corn stalks and the soybeans complete, f a uniform moisture content. This process is of interst because of its low cost of harvesting.

WILLIAM WHIPPLE,
Sugar Engineering Specialist.

In addition Prof. Whipple has sent us the text of n address on "Artificial Drying of Hay," presented y him at the meeting of the American Institute of :hemical Engineers held in New Orleans, December -10, 1930. The address is full of valuable data nd we publish it in full elsewhere in this issue of the SUGAR BULLETIN.

Artificial Drying of Hay

By Wm. Whipple, Professor of Steam Engineering, Louisiana State University; Sugar Engineering Specialist, Louisiana State University.

Louisiana with its high rainfall has always been able to grow heavy crops of hay, but has lost a large proportion of the crop in the curing as dry weather is required to make a good quality of hay.

Plants with large stems like soybeans and cowpeas take three or four days to cure and in ordinary field drying the loss of leaves and the damage from the sun by bleaching is very considerable. Many plants with succulent stems cannot be cured naturally at the time of greatest feed value because of the high moisture content. Some hay crops, such as corn and soybeans grown and harvested together, are difficult to cure because one part such as the soybean leaves loses its moisture much more rapidly than the stalks or grains of corn.

Rapidity of drying is important for successful curing of hay to prevent excessive losses of the carbohydrate portion of the plant by respiration and fermentation, but if exposed too long to the action of strong sunlight, the hay is damaged by bleaching.

The first attempts of artificial drying consisted of assisting the natural process by blowing heated air through haystacks.

This was followed by the hopper or tray method and afterwards by the conveyor belt method. All of these methods are of the opposite current type, both the heating medium and the material to be heated having their highest temperatures at one end and their lowest temperatures at the other.

The conveyor belt method passes the material through a tunnel and has the advantage of being a continuous process. All of these methods expose the comparatively dry leaf particles and the wet stems

nitrogen

applied right after the off-bar builds bigger profits

to the drying medium for the same length of time and result in over-drying the leaves in order to reduce the moisture in the heavier stems.

The discovery that furnace gases made a suitable drying medium eliminated the nest of steam coils which had been used for heating the air. Flue gases mixed with air were used for stack, tray and conveyor type driers, and this suggested the possibility of using higher temperatures in order to obtain greater economy of fuel.

A revolving drum drier with flights fastened to the inside of the cylinder set at an inclination toward the discharge end to make the material travel slowly through the drier, under the influence of gravity and the rotary movement, was also used with opposite current flow for the hay and hot air. As long as indirect drying with steam coils was used these driers with opposite current flow undoubtedly had advantages and for materials which are subject to damage from case hardening due to too rapid drying on the surface, the opposite current drier is used in order to warm up the material with air of relatively high moisture content before evaporating moisture.

The temperature to which air may be heated with a drier constructed for opposite current flow is limited by the highest temperature which the material will bear and the amount of moisture left in the material. If the material is completely dried, it will be heated almost to the temperature of the entering air; but if it still contains considerable moisture after drying, as is the case with hay, the temperature of the outgoing material will be somewhat less than that of the incoming air.

The heated air used for drying must first heat the wet material, then give to it the heat necessary to evaporate the water and still be hot enough to retai the evaporated water together with its original moi ture without being saturated.

The moisture carrying capacity of air increas rapidly with the temperature so it is important have the air leave the drier at the highest feasib temperature. This same quantity of air, howeve must be so much hotter when it enters the drier th its cooling to the temperature of exit is enough heat the wet material and evaporate the containe water.

If we heat air containing 90 grains of moisture the pound corresponding to 80° F., 60 per cent rel. tive humidity to a temperature of 240° F. and allo it to cool by evaporation until its relative humidi is 70 per cent, its temperature would then be 11! F., and it would carry 300 grains of moisture to t pound. It would then require $\frac{7000}{300-90}$ — 33 poun of air for each pound of moisture removed from t wet material, and the fan would have to be plac at the most unfavorable spot where the temperatu and volumes are highest.

A single drum type rotary drier with drum 6 diameter, 40 feet long, has been built at Louisiar State University in which the wet hay material brought into direct contact with furnace gases at temperature of 1500° to 1600° F., after being c into 3/16 in. lengths by an ensilage cutter.

An induced draft fan draws out gases after bei cooled by furnishing heat for the necessary evapor tion at a temperature of about 160° F. and mai tains in the drum a current of air sufficient to car out of the hot zone all particles of low density a therefore all particles of low moisture content. Tv semi-circular baffles near the discharge end of t drum retard the movement of the hay through t coolest part of the drying medium, thereby helpi to give a uniform moisture content to all of t product.

By varying the temperature of the exit gases, t moisture in the cured hay can be maintained at a desired point, and the moisture content will rema constant as long as this temperature does not var This drier operates on parallel current flow.

Air at 160° F. will carry 2150 grains of moistu per pound and at 85 per cent saturation will car 1840 grains of moisture, so that it will requi $\frac{7000}{1840-90}$ — 4 lbs. flue gases to carry off each pou of water evaporated from the hay.

(Continued on page 1

The following firms wish to congratulate the Louisiana sugar producers upon the completion of a successful campaign in the face of many obstacles and are confidently looking forward with them to a bigger and better cane crop during 1931.

The fuel used can be natural gas, oil, coke, coal or any other that can be burned without smoke.

When burning fuel oil, the evaporation obtained is between 10 and 11 pounds per pound of oil so that the pound of oil must be burned with 39 pounds of air in the first case, and with 43 pounds of air in the second case to make 40 and 44 pounds of flue gases, respectively, to carry off the evaporated water. Fourteen pounds of air is required for complete combustion so that these figures correspond to 180 per cent and 200 per cent of excess air. If we figure the theoretical furnace temperature for 40 lbs. of flue gas, using .237 for specific heat, we find that the pound of oil at 18,500 B.T.U. will raise the temperature 1950° above the atmosphere giving 2030° F. as the furnace temperature. The furnace temperature is, of course, reduced below this theoretical figure because of the heat radiated to the entering hay as well as to the shell and the furnace walls, but the temperatures of 1600° to 1500° obtained are close to the temperature to be expected with these air mixtures.

This parallel current drier has the distinct advantage of drying all particles to about the same moisture content regardless of variations in the raw material. The velocity of the flue gases carries the lighter leaf portions through the drum in a few seconds while the heavier stalks are picked up and dropped through the path of the hot gases until they lose their moisture. The entire drum is under a vacuum of about ½ in. static water pressure maintained by the ventilating fan which helps to keep down the maximum temperature of the material as well as to reduce the amount of heat required for the evaporation.

It is indeed a fact that at entrance to the drum the small particles of hay receive considerable heat by radiation from flame and from the incandescent brick work so that the temperature of the material would be considerably higher than the wet bulb temperature of the flue gases and the rate of vaporization increased above what it would be if shielded from such direct radiation. However, the moist particles are surrounded by hot gases containing very little moisture and the vapor ,although at the same temperature as the flue gases, is not at the tension or pressure proper to it at that temperature. The action in regard to the evaporation of water is exactly the same as though it were in a partial vacuum. The vapor tends to take up the offered moisture until its tension corresponds to the temperature.

This method results in drying the material with-

ut subjecting it to a temperature high enough to be
jurious. The heat which must be supplied to the
rying material can enter only through the surface
nd cutting the hay into short lengths increases the
atio of dry to wetted surface and thus speeds up the
rying rate because it exposes the greatest possible
urface to the hot gases. The high velocity of over
feet per second of the gases past the wet surface
f the material as well as the high mean tempera-
ıre difference between the heating medium and the
rying material both tend to speed up the drying
rocess and give high evaporative capacity to the
ype of drier under consideration.

Cowpeas, soybeans, alfalfa, grass, sugar cane tops
nd a mixture of corn and soybeans have all been
ried successfully in the drier, turning out products
f excellent aroma, of about the same color as the

raw material. Cows and other animals eagerly eat
the artificially cured hay. Chemical analyses show
advantages in hay so cured when cut at the stage
most favorable for sun curing. Earlier cutting for
many crops would give a higher yield of protein
per acre and a more concentrated and palatable
feed.

Artificial drying saves the loss of leaves containing
most of the protein of the plant and avoids the large
loss in carbohydrates during fermentation.

German investigators have found that artificial drying decreases the digestibility of the protein in proportion to the temperature used in drying. This
would be true of an opposite current drier operating
under high temperature where the dried hay temperature would almost reach that of the entering air, but
in a parallel current drier operating under slight

vacuum, the hay would never reach a temperature higher than 190° F. and would rapidly cool off as it gave up its moisture.

Feeding tests are being made to compare the values of the hays and so far the artificial hays compare favorably with the best of the sun-cured.

The power requirement for the drier and ensilage cutter together is 17 horse power or less than 13 kilowatts. A crew of 5 men which includes two men filling sacks can run the plant to its capacity of from 2300 to 3000 pounds of dry hay per hour, depending on its initial moisture content. The amount of moisture evaporated per hour is about 4500 pounds.

The operating cost per ton of dried hay is about $2.75. If the crops are cut a few hours before being hauled to the drier, there will be a considerable loss of moisture in the field which will cut down the fuel cost at the drier, and by increasing the output of dry hay will also reduce the labor and power costs. The dried cut hay can be blown into bins for storage where, with its low moisture content, it will keep indefinitely. It can be successfully baled in the heavy type balers used for baling sugar cane bagasse. It can be mixed with molasses without grinding or ground into meal and then mixed with molasses, both of these molasses feeds being packed into sacks.

The parallel current drier with the high mean temperature difference dries the hay in the shortest possible time and by avoiding high temperatures in the hay produces a finished product as nearly equal to the wet, green material as physically possible.

The moisture content can be reduced to the point where the hay will keep indefinitely without fermentation or danger of heating.

The drier which will accomplish this result is of such simple construction that the initial cost is low and the cost of upkeep negligible.

Louisiana's Sugar Bowl Welcomes Aid of Agricultural Scientists

Washington, D. C., Dec. 23, 1930.

Growers of sugar cane and manufacturers of cane sugar in Louisiana are cooperating intelligently in all the work the United States Department of Agriculture is doing to assist the industry and to put it on a more profitable basis, says Dr. Henry G. Knight, Chief of the Bureau of Chemistry and Soils, who bases his opinion on first hand contact with the planters and factory owners. Doctor Knight has just returned from a trip through the Louisiana sugar belt.

Doctor Knight visited the sugar factory at Southdown, La., the Sterling sugar factories at Franklin, La., and the Godchaux Sugars, Inc., factories at Reserve, La., and Raceland, La., going over the plantations upon which these factories operate and studying the method of handling sugar cane from the time it is planted until the granulated sugar is manufactured and placed in bags.

"Planters and manufacturers alike are seeking opportunities to offset the losses caused by the present low price of sugar, and are supporting the work which the department is doing to increase production per acre and per labor unit by fertilizer experiments with the new varieties of canes and by studies looking to increased factory efficiency," says Doctor Knight.

"Factory owners are keenly interested in methods recommended by the Bureau of Chemistry and Soils for clarifying the cane juice in the process of manufacture, and express their conviction that, aside from increasing the sugar-content of the cane by means of new varieties and better methods of fertilization, the best way to overcome the handicaps of the present low price of sugar is by such methods of clarification as are being recommended by the Department of Agriculture."

Other efforts of the growers to overcome the present adverse conditions of their industry in which, Doctor Knight says, the department's help is appreciated, are the attempt to increase the cane sirup business by the manufacture of a high-grade plantation product, and the endeavor to expand the utilization of sugar cane bagasse for industrial purposes. He says that some of the bagasse is now being used in the manufacture of wall board, but the greater part is still going under the boilers of the sugar factories as fuel.

Doctor Knight emphasizes that the planters are enthusiastic over the new varieties of P.O.J. cane which have been introduced by the Bureau of Plant Industry. He visited several experimental fields on different types of soil where the Bureau of Chemistry and Soils is directing fertilizer experiments intended to increase the acre yields and decrease production costs of sugar cane. He also visited the Louisiana Experiment Station at Baton Rouge where Dr. C. T. Dowell, director of the station, is planning to expand the field experiments in fertilizers and new varieties which are proving of practical benefit to the industry.

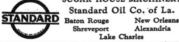

Dr. Chas. E. Coates,
Baton Rouge, La.

THE SUGAR BULLETIN

Entered as second-class matter April 13, 1925, at the postoffice at
New Orleans, La., under Act of March 6, 1879.

*We stand for the encouragement of Home
Industries as against Foreign Competition.*

Vol. 9   NEW ORLEANS, LA., JANUARY 15, 1931   No. 8

The Chadbourne Plan

Mr. Thomas L. Chadbourne appears to have successfully carried out the plan conceived by him some six months ago to bring about concert of action among the exporting sugar countries of the world for the purpose of checking the growing disparity between sugar production and sugar consumption. The excess of production over consumption in certain countries has brought all sugar producers who sell any considerable part of their output on the world's market to the verge of ruin, and the desperate situation of such producers, of which the Cubans are the most conspicuous example, has led them to force their sugar at ridiculous prices into even the protected markets, thereby demoralizing those markets as well.

The plan of Mr. Chadbourne is fundamentally sound, as affects exported sugar, and ought to work, inasmuch as it comprises a fixed agreement to restrict exports and has now been definitely agreed to by Cuba, Java, Czecho-Slovakia, Poland, Belgium, Hungary and Germany. The weakness in it, if there be one, is that the actual production of sugar may conceivably not be reduced in any of the contracting countries, with the result that a surplus will pile up within their borders which will finally become so burdensome that it will break through even the most meticulous agreement. It is believed, however, that, knowing they cannot export beyond a certain quantity of sugar, and knowing their home consumption, all the countries will realize the necessity of making less sugar and will act accordingly. There is encouraging evidence of such a determination. In any case the production will not become greater than it would be without an agreement and in all likelihood will be much less.

We who produce sugar in the United States, a country that exports no sugar of its own production, and hence has no reason to reduce its output, are interested chiefly in the feature of the Chadbourne plan which calls for the importation into the United States from Cuba of no more than 2,800,000 tons of sugar in 1931 with certain small increases for the following four years based on our increase in consumption, and the steps taken to segregate the present Cuban surplus of 1,500,000 tons, this surplus to be gradually worked off during a five-year period. Undoubtedly the existence of this surplus was the most powerful weapon in Mr. Chadbourne's arsenal. With it he could wreck the sugar world. In offering to spike this gun he tendered an almost irresistible inducement to the conferees from other countries.

The last country to sign the agreement was Germany. Her acquiescence was brought about only by allowing her to export about twice as much sugar as originally proposed and was coupled with a proviso that in no case would any situation be allowed to arise which would in the slightest degree interfere with the policy of supplying the German people from German sources with all the sugar they need. Our United States Congress might chew that cud to advantage.

As for Mr. Chadbourne himself the sugar world at large should acclaim him as possessing a

THE
SUGAR BULLETIN

407 Carondelet St., New Orleans

Issued on the 1st and 15th of each month. Official Organ of the American
Sugar Cane League of the U. S. A., in which are consolidated
The Louisiana Sugar Planters' Assn.
The American Cane Growers' Assn.
The Producers & Mfgrs. Protective Assn.
Subscription Price 50 Cents Per Year

Reginald Dykers, General Manager & Editor of the Bulletin
301 Nola Bldg., New Orleans
Frank L. Barker, Secretary and Treasurer
Lockport, La.
C. J. Bourg, Manager Washington Office
810 Union Trust Building

CHAIRMEN OF COMMITTEES:
C. D. Kemper, Franklin, La.
President of the League and Ex-Officio Chairman of Executive Committee
Andrew H. Gay, Plaquemine, La,
Chairman Agricultural Committee
David W. Pipes, Jr., Houma, La.
Chairman Industrial Committee
Frank L. Barker, Lockport, La.
Chairman Finance Committee.
Edward J. Gay, Plaquemine, La.
Chairman Tariff Committee
H. Langdon Laws, Cinclare, La.
Chairman Legislative Committee
J. C. LeBourgeois, New Orleans, La.
Chairman Freight Rate Committee
R. H. Chadwick, Bayou Goula, La.
Chairman Membership Committee
A. H. Rosenfeld, New Orleans, La.
Chairman Publicity Committee

Members of the League desiring action on, or information on, any subject are invited to communicate with
the League or with the Chairman of the Committee
to which it seems to appertain.

---

constructive intelligence of high order. Once a
Chicago policeman he rose by sheer ability to a
place of leadership at the New York bar. He is
largely interested, either personally or through
clients, in Cuban sugar production, and whether
the stupendous undertaking he has performed
in bringing about a world agreement on sugar
exports accomplishes all that is expected of it
or not its author and chief protagonist must
take rank as one of the ablest sugar men of
this generation.

Getting the Middles Out

*By Arthur H. Rosenfeld, Consulting Technologist,
American Sugar Cane League.*

To the contrary of conditions last winter, those of
this winter as well as of the harvesting season just
finished, have been particularly propitious for the
successful carrying through of stubble cane, and it is
very probable that our planters will be able to retain
a much larger than normal proportion of second year
stubble from their best fields of both P.O.J. 36 and
213 first year stubble of last year. It is, in fact, likely that a fair amount of third year stubble of these
two varieties can be profitably carried through this
season, particularly if the wrapping of middles, off-
barring and fertilizer application are performed early
in the cultivating season.

The larger indicated proportion of stubble cane fo
the crop of 1931 should more than compensate th
slightly reduced indicated plantings, and conditior
have also been extremely favorable for carryin
through the fall planting cane in excellent conditior
However, this should be insured now by the comple
tion of the getting out of the middles of the fall plar
cane, a large amount of which is still undone due t
the recent completion of crop and the absolute nece
sity of resting the mules after the almost continu
hauling during an exceptionally favorable harvestin
season.

Should rainy weather set in now before these mic
dles are out and the drainage properly established,
might largely nullify the excellent prospects for
good stand from these plantings. Hence the immed
ate rectification of the above-mentioned condition
the best crop insurance the planter can take out fo
his plant cane crop.

A New Stubble Shaver

By A. W. Dykers

The writer had the pleasure during the past weel
of seeing the new stubble shaving machine that i
being offered to the sugar planters this season b
the Castagnos Cane Loader Company and we be
lieve that it will interest the field men over the ter
ritory to know that the shaver has been pronounce
a complete success by both the Cedar Grove an
Tally Ho plantation managers who tried it out la:
season. During past seasons there has been consic
erable controversy as to the desirability of shavin
the stubble crop but we understand that this ha
been caused chiefly by the poor shaving work tha
the old slide type of shaver accomplished rather tha
by any discussion of the actual value of proper shav
ing. The slide type of shaver pulls the cane stalk
out of the ground, injures the eyes, and generall
mangles the stubble to such an extent that the yiel
is materially affected and it is probably becaus
of this that some producers consider it poor polic
to shave the stubble crop.

Figures shown the writer by Mr. John Leche, c
the Cedar Grove plantation, where stubble shavin
has been practiced for years, point to the conclusio
that the proper shaving of the stubble crop will grea
ly increase production and pay good dividends eve
when slow moving machinery is used, and it is ver
interesting to note that the stubble shaving machin
we are describing is a result of experimental work o
that plantation.

Briefly, the machine consists of a frame, mounte
on four wheels, from which two discs are suspende
at approximately the center position. These discs ar
geared directly to the back axle of the machine an
are positive-driven so that their turning is assure
as long as the machine is in motion. The discs are so de
signed as to permit an eight inch vertical shift of th
knives which allows ample adjustment for any fiel
conditions. Power is furnished by the tractor pullin
the machine, the turning of the back wheels auto
matically revolving the discs. An attachment con
sisting of two disc coulters, designed for destroyin
stubble, can be placed on the forward portion of th
frame thus creating a very thorough stubble de
stroyer. Only two men are necessary to operate th
machine, one to drive the pulling tractor and one t

handle the machine proper. Twenty-two to twenty-five acres of stubble can be covered in a day which is just about three times as fast as the old type shaver. Mr. Lewis Murrell told the writer that he used a 10-20 tractor for pulling the machine on Tally Ho and that it handled it very easily in high gear. Both he and Mr. John Leche pronounce the machine the finest for this purpose that has ever been introduced in the Louisiana sugar district.

In these times of keen competition in the sugar producing business when every effort is being made to increase the producing power of both our fields and factories we feel that it is our duty to call all new devices that point to a saving in production to the attention of our readers and that they in turn should show their appreciation of the efforts of the manufacturers by giving them the consideration that they deserve. It may be that each different device constitutes only small savings by itself but collectively a great deal of constructive work is being accomplished by the experts who are trying to create ways of speeding up work, increasing yields and bringing about cheaper production costs. According to those who have used the stubble shaver described above a substantially increased yield will be accomplished through its general adoption over the territory and for this reason we have undertaken to call it to the attention of our readers.

Hawaii Is Puzzled

Papaikou, Hawaii, T. H.
Dec. 26, 1930.

Editor Sugar Bulletin:

In your issue of December 1, 1930, an article written by C. G. Robinson of White Castle, La., on the behavior of P.O.J. 234 cane after cutting, was called to my attention.

Nine percent sucrose after being cut ten days and 13½% after laying cut twenty days is against most of the accepted theories on this subject.

The writer would like to know the percent sucrose at time of cutting and the percent sucrose after twenty days per weight of freshly cut cane.

In Hawaii cane loses weight after being cut two or three days as well as sucrose. In ten days the total losses of sugar will be around 20%. After that it deteriorates rapidly depending on weather conditions.

One solution may be that cane is like apple cider, which when frozen, the good stuff is in the center of the barrel.

Yours truly,

H. D. BEVERIDGE.

In our issue of January 1, 1931, Dr. Chas. E. Coates discusses the matter referred to by our Hawaiian subscriber and gives considerable data relative to the keeping qualities of cut cane. The idiosyncracies of the P.O.J. canes recently introduced in Louisiana are not yet thoroughly ascertained.—*Editor Sugar Bulletin.*

Turning Cane Trash Under

The *Sugar Bulletin* has received a publication issued by *Zentralblatt fur Bakteriologie, Parasitenkunde und Infektionskrankheiten,* Jena, Germany, entitled "The Effect of Plowing Under Cane Trash on the Available Nitrogen of the Soil." The treatise is written by Wm. L. Owen and W. P. Denson of the Department of Bacteriology, Louisiana Experiment Station, and, notwithstanding its place of publication, is printed in English. It is one of the ablest research articles on a Louisiana agricultural topic that it has been our good fortune to read in many years, and the fact that it was published by one of the leading units of the German scientific press is in itself a certificate of high merit.

The study of the effect of plowing under cane trash by Messrs. Owen and Denson is particularly interesting just now because of the recent expression of the experts of the Louisiana Experiment Station against the turning under of cane trash as a cane-borer preventive. Dr. T. E. Holloway, the noted Federal entomologist, and persistent advocate of burying the cane trash, will be gratified to note that the authors lean towards the advocacy of this procedure. When it comes to telling us, in so many plain words, however, whether we ought to turn the trash under or not Owen and Denson are as canny as the Pythoness of Delphi. They have chewed the sacred laurel, drunk the waters of Kassotis, seated themselves on their tripods and arrived at the following conclusions

1. The addition of fresh cane trash to soils containing nitrate causes a very rapid transformation of the nitrogen into organic forms.

2. The depressing effect of cane trash upon nitrates, diminishes at a fairly constant rate when this crop residue is in conflict with the soil, and under ordinary conditions it has perhaps lost most of its pernicious effects at the time the fertilizer is applied to cane.

3. The addition of fresh trash retards appreciably the rate of growth of corn plants, but the incorporation of trash which has been partially buried for several months, increased the yields and the initial rate of growth.

4. The addition of cane trash to soils increases their water holding capacity, and decreases their rate of drying, so that in seasons of drought this may be quite a factor in conserving the moisture of the soil.

5. The addition of cane trash to soils results in appreciable gains to total nitrogen, indicating the stimulation of the nitrogen fixing bacteria by the products resulting from the decomposition of organic matter incorporated in the soil.

6. The facts that field experiments over a period of several years at this Station, have shown no decrease in crop yield from the practice of turning under

cane trash it would appear that the nitrate nitrogen
immobilized by the presence of the organic matter
is in excess of the immediate requirements of the
growing crop. This would make the practice of turning under trash consistent with the necessity of conserving the surplus available nitrogen in the soil.

7. Whether the continued practice of incorporating
such large quantities of organic matter with a C:N ratio
of approximately 1:40 would tend to so increase the
accumulation of the more resistant constituent lignin
as to unfavorably affect the composition and the productiveness of a soil is a question, the importance of
which warrants further study.

It will be noticed that Messrs. Owen and Denson
say that several years of experiments show that no
decrease in crop yields has resulted from turning
under the cane trash. With the usual earnestness of
scientists they were evidently not content with this
bald fact, which is, after all, the principal sum and
substance of what we want to know, but they felt
it incumbent on them to find out why such a fact
should be. This they have accomplished at great
length. But we must not be too sure, or too confident or too free from care. To prevent such an attitude of mind, which would not be compatible with
scientific ethics, Messrs. Owen and Denson tell us,
in the concluding paragraph of their conclusions, that
if the turning under of cane trash be kept up indefinitely they do not know whether it will affect the
productiveness of the soil or not.

So, like almost everything else in our existence, it
is a case of wait and see. The first hundred years
are the hardest. In the meanwhile Messrs. Owen
and Denson have contributed to our sugar literature
something very elaborate and thorough in the way
of a study of the processes taking place when quantities of cane trash are buried in the soil on our Louisiana sugar plantations. They have placed our industry in their debt.

Plantation Economics

Mr. G. H. Reuss, who is a member of the staff of
the Louisiana Experiment Station, with the title of
Assistant Economist, is the author of a Bulletin entitled "An Economic Study of Factors Affecting Farm
Organization and Power Utilization on Sugar Cane
Farms." A title as comprehensive as that calls for
considerable text if the subject is to be properly covered, and Mr. Reuss has evidently done much of investigational and research work, which he describes
and summarizes in his article. If the statistics he has
gathered are correct, and he seems to have obtained
them from reliable sources, he has presented us with
a valuable compendium of information and one which
every member of the American Sugar Cane League
ought to read. There is at least one favorable aspect
to it, and that is that the author has avoided a common fault of those who prepare Experiment Station
Bulletins, the fault of forgetting that they are writing
something for the instruction and comprehension of
laymen and not something that will demonstrate
their erudition and their familiarity with technical
terms to their fellow scientists. Mr. Reuss' Bulletin
is a plain-spoken affair, purporting to give a great
deal of practical information as to the economics of
a sugar plantation in Louisiana. At the end he prints
a summary of the conclusions he has arrived at,
which are as follows:

(Continued on page 6.)

Friends of Cyanamid ↘ ↘

Perhaps no other single factor is more responsible for the general acceptance of Cyanamid in Louisiana's "Sugar Bowl," than the fact that it "performs consistently and well" in good seasons and in bad. It is dependable. Cyanamid made many new friends for itself in the dry season just past. And it has a great many "old friends." More than a hundred Louisiana cane planters used Cyanamid last year—thirty-seven more than the number using it the year before. Repeat-purchasers bought more Cyanamid per plantation.

The reasons for this leadership of Cyanamid go much further than its obvious attraction of economy. Its high-analysis, free-drilling qualities, convenient, clean "one-man" package contribute much to ease and economy in application—important considerations to the planter operating extensive properties largely with unskilled labor.

In addition to its 21 per cent of nitrogen, Cyanamid contains 75 per cent of hydrated lime-equivalent. The continued use of Cyanamid year after year builds up the calcium content of the soil, promoting good tilth, counteracting acidity and toxic plant residues, and favoring beneficial bacterial activity.

The progressive availability of Cyanamid results in even, sustained feeding of the cane. Sucrose and purity percentages are maintained and substantial increases in yield are economically produced.

Your investigation of the record of Cyanamid performance in your neighborhood is invited. We will gladly supply additional facts and data.

For further information, write

American Cyanamid Company
Pioneer Producers of Air-Nitrogen Products in America

535 FIFTH AVENUE, NEW YORK
1820 JEFFERSON AVENUE   NEW ORLEANS

AERO BRAND
CYANAMID

Oliver United
.. Continuous
CANE MUD
FILTERS

More Sugar from the *Same* Grind .. *at a Lower Unit Cost*

REDUCTION in polarization and mechanical losses are the two ways in which the Oliver United Continuous Cane Mud Filter produces more sugar from the same grind.

The mud is handled quickly, continuously and cleanly. Little wash water is needed in order to hold losses at a low figure—a point which also helps in the evaporator room.

Being entirely automatic, operating labor costs are practically eliminated.

These operating advantages mean that costs are definitely lower and the added sugar is recovered at a lower unit cost. In addition, as features that also help lower costs, there are the simplified handling and the elimination of the cotton filter cloth nuisance (long-life perforated metal plate being used instead of cloth).

Get ready now for the next crop. Ask for our recommendation for installing the Oliver United Cane Mud Filter in your mill.

1. The price of agricultural products has been relatively low when compared with the price of the commodities which farmers purchase and is only slightly higher when related to the price of all non-agricultural products.

2. When compared with a pre-war base, 1913, the prices of sugar, rice, and corn are lower than those of cotton, sweet potatoes, white potatoes, veal, and beef.

3. The man labor and mule use requirements of the various crops grown in the cane area are not largely influenced by the size of the unit operated.

4. Differences in soil types, in plantation layout and in the managerial ability of individual operators seem to be factors which account for the wide differences in labor and power requirements between individual farms.

5. Cotton, corn, sweet potatoes, white potatoes and truck crops when included in the crop organization of cane farm lend themselves to the efficient utilization of machinery. Rice, however, cannot readily be incorporated in the farm organization due the large amount of specialized machinery which requires.

6. Under a crop system of corn and cane the labor and power requirements are high during the early spring months and during harvest. These requirements can be shifted somewhat from fall spring or vice versa by regulating the time of planting cane. Any further smoothing of labor and power distribution will depend upon the efficient use power machinery for cultural operations and upon the development of efficient harvesting machines. The latter factor is the limiting one at present.

7. Under the existing scale of prices the income at present cane yields has not been sufficient to defray outlays for production.

8. The possibility of profitably increasing the amount of livestock exists on plantations having large proportion of black land and on those which do not have ready access to a sugar house.

9. Large sized plantations have an advantage in machinery utilization, in crew organization and in purchasing efficiency over small sized units.

10. Operating costs for the inter-row tractor studied amounted to $7.90 per ten hour day while straddle row or 15-30 tractors required outlays of $11.27 per day. Due to the disposition of overhead charges costs incurred on individual farms varied inversely with the amount each tractor was used per year.

11. The cost of mule maintenance varied from $161.00 per head on family sized farms to $210.00 on plantations of more than 300 crop acres operating without tractors. Increased quantities and better quality feed account for a large part of this difference.

12. Plantations using tractors had less depreciation on mules, a lower death loss, and lower veterinary charges than plantations of a similar size operating without tractors. These differences lower the

cost of mule maintenance on tractor farms by $16.00 per head.

13. Tractor farms worked twenty crop acres per mule while non-tractor farms of the same size worked sixteen crop acres.

14. The replacement of mules by tractors and the reduced cost of mule maintenance due to tractor use, was such, on the average, that the total power costs per acre, including tractor outlays, was lower on those farms employing tractors than on those using mules only. Several farms included, however, raised rather than lowered their power costs by using tractors.

15. The fact that tractors have not been able to replace mules during harvest and that no single type or size of tractor has been developed which will efficiently perform all the cultural operations on cane are the factors which limit extensive use of tractors on cane farms. Further study of larger numbers of machines and of new types of tractors will be necessary to determine more definitely the place which tractor power should occupy in the organization of sugar cane farms.

16. Field cane loaders on the farms studied were operated at a cost of 13.3 cents per ton. This is considerably below hand loading costs.

A Bouquet

The American Sugar Cane League has received the letter published below from the Interstate Trust & Banking Co. It is always very gratifying to receive encomiums, from any source, and we violate no confidence when we confess that a well considered compliment from a New Orleans bank to the organized sugar interests of Louisiana, as represented by the League, mantles our cheeks with a flush of honest pride. Here is the letter:

INTERSTATE TRUST AND BANKING CO.
New Orleans
Jan. 6th, 1931.

The American Sugar Cane League of the U. S. A.,
407 Carondelet Street,
New Orleans, Louisiana.

Gentlemen:

We beg to acknowledge receipt of your letter of January 1st. I am advised that our Auditing Department has sent you a check covering our dues to the American Sugar Cane League for 1931.

We have a very high opinion of the American Sugar Cane League and what it has accomplished for the State of Louisiana and its sugar interests. The work could not be done better. It has given this Bank great satisfaction. We are particularly interested in your work because, of course, any re-establishment, as one might say, of the sugar industry in Louisiana will be of advantage to its banking business. We wish to help you in any way that we can. Let us know whenever you want us to help you and whatever we can do we shall be glad to do.

With best wishes to the American Sugar Cane League and with great hopes for the future, I beg to remain on behalf of the President and Officers of this Bank for whom I write,

Very sincerely yours,
(SIGNED) ELIOT NORTON.

Forty Thousand Available for Sugar Work

The State Board of Liquidation has authorized the
Louisiana Experiment Station to borrow the sum o
$40,000.00 which was appropriated for sugar inves
tigation and experimentation work by the Louisian;
Legislature at its last session, at the request of the
American Sugar Cane League. It will be recalled
that the item was vetoed for fiscal reasons by Gover
nor Long, whose attitude towards it was friendly
however, and who promised to try to arrange mat
ters so that it could be borrowed through the Stat
Board of Liquidation. This has now been done.

The League's "Contact Committee," which confer
monthly with the Louisiana Experiment Station offi
cials as to how this money shall be spent, will re
sume its meetings this month, assembling at Bato:
Rouge on January 23d. The membership of the Con
tact Committee consist of Messrs. A. W. Wallace
Chairman, Andrew H. Gay, Stephen C. Munson an(
Percy Lemann. These gentlemen have resting o1
their shoulders the heavy responsibility of advisin;
with the Experiment Station authorities as to ho\
the large sum of money involved in the above
mentioned appropriation shall be spent. We have n
doubt they will be glad to receive suggestions an(
will give all such careful consideration.

News From Washington

C. J. Bourg

The prospects of an extra session of Congress to b
held this Spring, are becoming closer to certainty wit
every day's session in the Senate. No one on Capi
tol Hill questions any longer the existence of a mil
filibuster, and it is the opinion of your corresponden
that several of the appropriation bills will not b
passed by March 4th and President Hoover will b
called upon to do what he would rather avoid mor
than anything in the world, that is, issue the call fo
an extra session.

The distinct compliment which was paid to th
Louisiana Sugar Industry by Dr. Henry G. Knigh
Chief of the Bureau of Chemistry and Soils is mor
significant than the public generally realizes. It i
well known that much of the research work done b
the United States Government has not been appre
ciated and in many cases is not adopted by the pe1
sons who are intended to be the beneficiaries. A
Mr. David W. Pipes, Jr., recently pointed out we we1
ourselves guilty of this attitude when in 1918 th
warning against Mosaic Disease published by Dr. F
W. Brandes in Bulletin 829 went unheeded. But it 1
a pleasure to bear witness to the fact that the farm

ers of Louisiana have established a reputation with the Department of Agriculture as being not only co-operative but very appreciative of the efforts of this Governmental Agency to assist them with their problems. There is no doubt that this intelligent support of the work being performed by the scientists of the Department of Agriculture, is responsible in large measure for the increased enthusiasm being shown by the Director of Scientific Work in arranging his research program. The appropriation bills in Congress contain the practical result of this friendly co-operation, in the re-allocation of all funds for sugar cane and its by-products as well as additional appropriations for further extensions towards the solution of our problems.

We give a practical indication of exactly what we mean, by reproducing the tabulation or estimated cost of research on utilization of sugar cane bagasse, submitted by the Department of Agriculture Committee of which Dr. Knight is Chairman:

Sub-Committee	Salaries	Building	Equipment	Operating	Total	Projected Totals
Road building research* Paper and Board......	$27,500	$12,500	$50,000	$10,000	$100,000	$100,000
Feeds, wax, dry distillation and miscellaneous:						
1. Mixed feed ingredient						
(a) Briqueting.........	2,600	------	2,000	5,400	10,000	
(b) Feeding...........	15,000	------	5,000	5,000	25,000	
2. Sugarcane wax*......						
3. Flour for absorbents, manufacture of explosives......	------	------	3,000	2,000	5,000	------
4. Artificial silk and dry distillation.						
(a) Rayon...........	10,600	------	1,000	3,400	15,000	------
(b) Dry distillation...	10,600	5,000	2,000	3,400	21,000	76,000
TOTAL..............	$66,300	$17,500	$63,000	$29,200	$176,000	$176,000

*No additional funds required for first year.

The Chadbourne negotiations seem to be about to become a successful final agreement. With the reaching of a compromise with the Germans, Mr. Chadbourne seems to have won the last of many preliminary victories towards a complete success. Mr. Chadbourne has certainly established himself as a diplomat of great courage and persistency.

It must be significant that editors and statesmen have been slow, if not hesitant, to criticize or to discuss the Chadbourne negotiations to organize and limit the export sugar supply of the whole world. It is well known that the Department of State does not disapprove. One writer even went so far as to comment that Mr. Chadbourne is working "with the admiring and hopeful sanction of the appropriate officials of our Government." It is interesting to note the extensiveness of the plan from the following quotation of a part of the speech delivered by Mr. Chadbourne in Brussels to the assembled representatives of the sugar producing business of the world:

"All industries have transgressed good economic laws, and, as a result, there is enormous over production in practically all world commodities. What has then been the ensuing consequence? It has been an unemployment situation unheard of for generations. We are trying a bigger case than the sugar

case. The capitalistic system is on trial. If you think that the people who are running the industries of the world can by their greed produce such depressions as this and then not promptly take steps to remedy them, you are mistaken. The people who are suffering will challenge our system just as surely as the earth goes round the sun. You must set an example which may be followed by all other industries and which will establish production and consumption throughout the world on a balanced basis."

While no action has been taken yet in Congress or before the Tariff Commission looking to the correction of the sugar tariff with reference to the refiners differential and liquid sugar, representatives of the various branches of the Domestic Sugar Industry are seeking to develop the best possible plan of action which will secure relief without disturbing our present legislative situation. A decision will undoubtedly be reached during the present month.

Senator Brookhart of Iowa recently introduced a resolution calling for an investigation into the reason "why brown and unrefined sugars are higher in price than white and refined sugars, and particularly whether such conditions are a result of a combination in restraint of trade." In the course of our duties we endeavored to ascertain the reason for the resolution and the causes which aroused the suspicion of the sharpshooting Senator from the State where the tall corn grows. On information from reliable sources we now report that it seems the Madame wanted some brown sugar, so she went to the corner grocery and to her amazement she learned that they were selling brown sugar (which of course was the package sugar put up by the New York and other refiners located in the cities and not the brown sugar made on the plantation) for 9 cents a pound and white sugar for 5 cents a pound. We do not know the details of debate (which is not usually conducted under parliamentary procedure where a Senator may decline to yield), but of this we have documentary evidence: the Senator introduced the resolution and the United States Government is going to find out "how come." The full text of the resolution is as follows:

Whereas the price of whole-wheat flour is now higher than white flour; and

Whereas the price of brown and unrefined sugars is now higher than white and refined sugars: Therefore be it

Resolved, That the Committee on Agriculture and Forestry of the Senate, or a duly authorized subcommittee thereof, is authorized and directed to investigate and report to the Senate the reasons why whole-wheat flour is higher in price than white flour and why brown and unrefined sugars are higher in price than white and refined sugars, and particularly whether such conditions are a result of a combination in restraint of trade.

For the purposes of this resolution such committee or subcommittee is authorized to hold hearings and to sit and act at such times and places as it deems advisable; to employ experts and clerical, stenographic, and other assistance; to require by subpoena or otherwise the attendance of witnesses and the production of books, papers, and documents; to administer oaths and to take testimony and to make all necessary expenditures as it deems advisable.

The cost of stenographic services to report such hearings shall not be in excess of 25 cents per hundred words. The expenses of such committee, which shall not be in excess of $15,000, shall be paid from the contingent fund of the Senate.

Look At This!

CASTAGNOS GEARED STUBBLE SHAVER

Your attention is called to the accompanying photograph of this new, heavily constructed, positively driven and tractor-drawn stubble shaver, which we believe, constitutes a decided step forward in the efficient handling of this phase of our agricultural work.

We are sure that you will at once appreciate the great advantage of having a positive drive for the shaving discs as against the friction drive formerly employed, the efficiency of which depended entirely upon a clean, even off-bar. You well know that when the off-bar was not clean-cut and narrow, or where rains had washed a part of the ridge down, the discs of the old stubble shaver had friction on both sides, did not revolve in certain areas and hence split or pulled out the stools.

No such bad results are possible with the New Geared Stubble Shaver. The turning of the discs is assured and also the higher disc speed necessary for most efficient cutting and least splitting of stools is obtained by its use with a tractor.

This new shaver was used very successfully in shaving all the stubble this year at the plantations of E. G. Robichaux Co. (Cedar Grove) and Lewis Murrell (Tally Ho). Both of the above reported this shaver giving excellent results, and were able to shave from 20 to 23 acres per day.

The shaver, you will notice, is very strongly constructed and well adapted to the hard use given a tool for the shaving of the new type canes.

THE REVOLVING KNIVES ARE 30 INCHES IN DIAMETER, MADE OF HIGH TEMPERED STEEL, AND ARE SO DESIGNED AS TO PERMIT A 10-INCH VERTICAL SHIFT OF THE KNIVES, WITH A POSITIVE SET POSITION OF SAME. THIS REMOVES THE UNSATISFACTORY FEATURE OF EVERY STUBBLE SHAVER HITHERTO IN USE. IT ENABLES THE PLANTER TO DO STUBBLE SHAVING AS IT OUGHT TO BE DONE, AND AS IT MUST BE DONE TO SECURE THE RESULTS THAT STUBBLE SHAVING IS INTENDED TO PRODUCE.

For destroying stubble we have designed an attachment for the forward portion of the frame on which two disc coulters can be placed, thus cutting the stubble into three portions.

Orders for these machines should be in our hands in ample time to permit of their being manufactured and delivered before the normal season for stubble shaving.

CASTAGNOS CANE LOADER CO.

DONALDSONVILLE, LA., or

CHAS. WIGGIN,
MARITIME BLDG., NEW ORLEANS

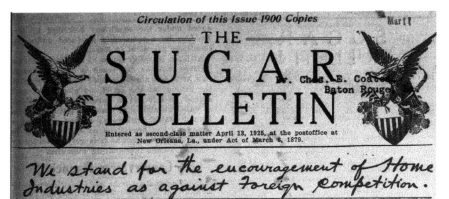

Circulation of this Issue 1900 Copies

THE
SUGAR
BULLETIN

Entered as second-class matter April 13, 1925, at the postoffice at
New Orleans, La., under Act of March 6, 1879.

We stand for the encouragement of Home Industries as against Foreign competition.

Vol. 9   NEW ORLEANS, LA., FEBRUARY 1, 1931   No. 9

Give Us This Day Our Daily Cent

Mr. Frederick W. Todd, United States Commercial Attache at Havana, Cuba, has been in New Orleans during the past ten days and has invited conferences with New Orleans business men relative to business conditions and business contacts in Cuba. He has also addressed the Young Men's Business Club along the same lines, and we believe his talks have been made in his official capacity. Because of his position as United States Commercial Attache it is his business to be familiar with the financial, industrial and economic sides of Cuban life and doubtless he is.

In the course of his address before the Young Men's Business Club which was delivered in the Gold Room of the Hotel Roosevelt on January 21st, Mr. Todd said, according to newspaper reports of the meeting, that the average rural Cuban may be compared to the Chinese coolie; that half a million people in Cuba do not pay house rent but live on the property of their employers and receive a bare subsistence for their upkeep. "As to the cost of sugar production," said Mr. Todd, "there is no such thing in Cuba. The Cuban sugar worker can live on little more than a cent a day if he is called on to do so."

Here we have a public statement made by a United States Government official which is of marked significance at the present time, when the principle of regulating the tariff by ascertaining the difference in the cost of producing an article at home and the cost of producing it abroad seems to have met with tacit acceptance from both of our great political parties. The creation of the United States Tariff Commission is the concrete result of this attitude of mind. Such a theory takes no account of the advisability of developing certain industries at home by the degree of protection needed for the purpose, which it was vitally necessary to do in the early history of our country, and is still obviously necessary in many instances. It should be put into effect, for instance, in the case of that great household necessity, sugar, for which we should not be dependent on foreign countries. On the other hand it eliminates the free trade idea, once so dangerously popular among certain elements in the Democratic party. The evidence presented by United States Commercial Attache Todd is staggering in its revelations as to the negligible cost of producing sugar in Cuba. He says there is no such thing as cost.

In every investigation that has been made of the cost of producing sugar in Cuba no data has been included except the manufacturing costs. The cost of producing cane in Cuba has never been investigated by the United States Tariff Commission. Mr. Todd implies that it is virtually non-existent and his statement is of incalculable importance in any comparison of costs, for in the United States the cost of growing cane, or beets, is by far the largest single item in the production of sugar. It is in this rural phase of sugar production, rather than in the manufacturing phase, that the economic and living conditions prevailing in Cuba are abhorrent to our standards and which, far from being overlooked, should be taken into primary account in any investigation having as its

THE
SUGAR
BULLETIN

407 Carondelet St., New Orleans

Issued on the 1st and 15th of each month. Official Organ of the American
Sugar Cane League of the U. S. A., in which are consolidated
The Louisiana Sugar Planters' Assn.
The American Cane Growers' Assn.
The Producers & Mfgrs. Protective Assn.
Subscription Price, 50 Cents Per Year.

Reginald Dykers, General Manager & Editor of the Bulletin
301 Nola Bldg., New Orleans
Frank L. Barker, Secretary and Treasurer
Lockport, La.
C. J. Bourg, Manager Washington Office
810 Union Trust Building

CHAIRMEN OF COMMITTEES:
C. D. Kemper, Franklin, La.
President of the League and Ex-Officio Chairman of Executive Committee
Andrew H. Gay, Plaquemine, La.
Chairman Agricultural Committee
David W. Pipes, Jr., Houma, La.
Chairman Industrial Committee
Frank L. Barker, Lockport. La.
Chairman Finance Committee.
Edward J. Gay, Plaquemine, La.
Chairman Tariff Committee
H. Langdon Laws, Cinclare, La.
Chairman Legislative Committee
J. C. LeBourgeois, New Orleans, La.
Chairman Freight Rate Committee
R. H. Chadwick, Bayou Goula, La.
Chairman Membership Committee
A. H. Rosenfeld, New Orleans, La.
Chairman Publicity Committee

Members of the League desiring action on, or information on, any subject are invited to communicate with the League or with the Chairman of the Committee to which it seems to appertain.

purpose the ascertainment of the cost of producing sugar in Cuba as compared with the cost of producing it in the United States. Any investigation that omits the cost of producing the cane lacks the main essential.

We have heard a great deal lately about the damage, present and prospective, to various American industries caused by the importation of commodities into the United States from Russia, at ruinously low prices, these prices on the Russian goods being possible only because labor in Russia in not paid wages, and receives from the Soviet Government only such sustenance, clothes and shelter as, in the opinion of the officials, will sustain life. The objections raised against allowing Russian goods made under such conditions to enter the United States and drive similar goods produced here out of the market are thoroughly justified. Legislation should be had to prevent it. The justification for allowing the importation of sugar produced in Cuba under the conditions outlined by Attache Todd should be measured by the same yardstick and the conditions under which it was produced should be taken into full account. Just as much damage can be done through the importation of a commodity pro-

duced under the conditions described by Mr Todd as by a commodity produced under th conditions prevalent in Russia.

At least, if the Congress of the United State believes that the difference in cost of produc tion here and abroad should be a criterion o the amount of the tariff, no element of cos should be left out in computing such differ ences. The ability of Cuba to put sugar int United States' harbors at around one cent pound as has been done so systematically i the past several months is largely explained b Attache Todd's illuminating discourse.

Conservative Finance

According to a statement made a few days ago by an official of the United States Treasury the Federa Intermediate Credit Bank at New Orleans discounted notes of 406 Louisiana cane growers for a tota amount of $1,667,498.44 on the 1930 cane crop Those through whom this credit was secured performed a service of inestimable value to our suga industry. The amount borrowed from this source however, ought to be vastly more. There were some 200,000 acres in cane in 1930 if we may accept the Federal figures and even though all cultivation costs were skimped and held down to unprecedented low levels through necessity and no field work done that could be postponed to some time in the future, it is probable that this sum represented not one-fifth of the total amount expended on actual agricultural operations in the Louisiana sugar district in the past year. This will come as something of a surprise to most of us who have rather absorbed the impression that the loans made through the Federal Intermediate Credit Bank were a more prominent factor than this in the financing of the cane crop. The total number of cane growers affected, 406, likewise bears a low ratio to the total number of cane growers in the Louisiana sugar district which has been variously estimated at from 5,000 to 10,000 and at the present time is probably nearer the former than the latter figure. Obviously most of the farmers growing cane in Louisiana get their financial requirements filled from other sources, even though some of the loans, while made to one man, were for the benefit of a number of people.

The official statement we have before us goes on to say that of the 406 farmers to whom the Federal Intermediate Credit Bank made loans, 169 furnished security in the shape of crop liens and chattel mortgages without other collateral, and 237 were required to put up collateral, in addition to the mortgage on their chattels and their crops. That nearly 60% of all the cane growers to whom loans were made were able to furnish collateral, thus safeguarding the Government over and above the security furnished by the chattel mortgage, the crop lien and the shock absorber composed of the stock of the Credit Corporation through which the loans were made, speaks well for the soundness and solvency of the borrowers as a class. It also seems to indicate that the Federal Intermediate Credit Bank carries on its business in a way which approximates in safety and security the business carried on by ordinary commercial bankers

The Advertisers in the Sugar Bulletin are contributing owards the support of the American Sugar Cane League ind should enjoy your special consideration; help them o help the Domestic Sugar Industry by doing business vith them whenever possible.

ho, notwithstanding that they have behind them no :sources but their own capital and surplus, and are ı business primarily to make money and not to aid griculture, have taken courageous risks as often as ıey properly could in all parts of the United States ɔ help the situation that has prevailed during the ast year, and, in many cases, more often than they roperly could.

Loans made by the Federal Intermediate Credit ıank in New Orleans to farmers in Louisiana other han cane farmers, in 1930, totalled $2,385,107.13 and here were 1146 such loans, of which all but 105 were ecured by collateral in addition to crop liens and hattel mortgages.

The United States Government will evidently not ɩe bankrupted by losses through its Intermediate :redit Banks unless those located elsewhere have nore of a dare-devil strain in them than the one we ɩave here.

Putting the Filipinos on the Spot

Mr. Garet Garrett has an article in the January !4th issue of the *Saturday Evening Post* about the ɔhilippines. It is a very interesting article and gives ı description of the attitude of the Filipinos towards he Americans that will be new to the majority of us. \ccording to Mr. Garrett the Americans in the Philip->ines, both business men and officials, instead of >eing top dog, as most of us have supposed, are so horoughly cowed by the Filipinos that they are .fraid to talk to each other about Governmental mat-ers unless they are shut up in a sound proof room. The Government is completely in the hands of the ʻilipinos, the American Governor General being a nere man of straw, shorn of all real power. In prac-ically every respect the Philippines are an auto-ıomous foreign country which parasitically battens ɩn the United States for everything it needs or wants ɩnd is waxing fat and prosperous through the free ːntry of its products into the United States. This s one of the most valuable perquisites it enjoys. If here be any real point to Mr. Garrett's article it is hat a situation exists in the Philippines that is so ncongruous that it cannot very well continue. There eems to be no reason why the Philippine products hould come in free except that certain users of these ɩroducts in the United States are powerful enough to naintain such a state of affairs. Their origin is as ɩtrinsically foreign as if they came from Abyssinia.

Concerning sugar imports Mr. Garrett says: "The \merican economic motive in the Philippines is un-mportant to begin with and, in any case, unprofit-ble. The United States Treasury receives not one ent of revenue from the Philippines. It taxes them or nothing. But on Philippine products sold in the

United States it waives import duties amounting to forty to fifty millions a year, and this sum is, in fact, a subsidy to Philippine industry. For example, free sugar from the Philippines does not affect the price to the American consumer, and this is so because it is a fragment of the total quantity imported. That is to say, if the quantity received from the Philippines came instead from Cuba, and paid the import duty, the price of sugar would be the same as it is to the consumer, but the American Treasury would be richer by, say, thirty million dollars annually."

He lets it go at that in this article, but he promises two more articles to follow and we are much intrigued to know whether he will return to the subject.

We suspect that the same incentive, "gangway for Cuba!", is behind Mr. Garrett's articles in the *Saturday Evening Post* that was behind Mr. Marcosson's fulsome article on Cuban sugar in the same journal some months ago, but it is being disclosed in a more subtle way. The Cubans would like to see the Filipinos given their independence legally, instead of having them merely assume it to the eye as they now do, because that would mean a United States tariff on

Philippine sugar and a better opportunity in th United States for Cuban sugar. There is plenty mil in that cocoanut.

If the *Saturday Evening Post* is following up th Marcosson massacre of the domestic sugar industr by setting the stage for a Cuban-Philippine fight w want a ring-side seat. Whether the Post has see to it that all the brass knuckles are on Cuba's fist or not, it is bound to be an entertaining spectacl(

If, as a result of Cuba's adept propaganda, the pec ple of the United States have their attention directe to the impropriety of our economic relations with th Philippines and are led to insist that Philippine prod ucts, including sugar of course, be deprived of th unjustifiable privilege of free entry into this countr that they now enjoy, it will be the first and only useful service the Pearl of the Antilles has ever performed for us since Columbus' boatswain spat upon its outlying rocks in 1492.

Fertilizer in 1931

By Arthur H. Rosenfeld

In the SUGAR BULLETIN, Vol. VIII, No. 11 (1930), pages 6 and 10, the writer published a provisional statement regarding results of co-operative fertilizer demonstrations during 1929, the detailed results of these being published in the 15th May issue of the BULLETIN. These figures showed that almost without exception applications of Nitrogen alone to stubble cane at the rate of 30 to 40 pounds per acre had resulted in a net gain over unfertilized check plots of from 6 to 10 tons of cane per acre, just as in the co-operative experiments during the two previous years. Equally consistently and with only a few notable exceptions on certain isolated border soil types on the extreme northern and western edges of the cane belt the addition of 200 pounds of Calcium Super-phosphate to the nitrogenous application again resulted in a commercial loss, i. e., the Super-phosphate failed to produce enough additional sugar per acre to pay for itself.

All data on the 1930 demonstration tests are not yet ready for publication; but as the time has arrived for the purchase of fertilizer for this year's application, it seems advisable to state at this time that the 1930 figures strongly endorse the findings of three previous years.

The results of the past four years of co-operative demonstrations have shown that an investment of $4.00 to $5.00 per acre in applying 30 to 40 pounds of Nitrogen to stubble cane has resulted in a profit of from 150% to 200% on the investment, and this year, with Nitrogen about 18% lower in price per unit than last, the proportional return should be greater. Passing 40 to 45 pounds of Nitrogen as such per acre, there seems to be a depressing effect on the sucrose content of the juice, with the result that, whereas tonnage may be increased above that from the normal application, the percentage return on the investment is much less than where from 30 to 40 pounds of Nitrogen per acre are employed. Even in the few cases where there is a small gain from the use of Phosphoric Acid, the percentage return on the investment is nowhere near that from the Nitrogen applications. Hence the writer is of the opinion that, with the exception of a very few outlying soil types, the Louisi-

(Continued on page 6.)

ana planters would receive the best return on their fertilizer investments by omitting Phosphoric Acid entirely from the 1931 fertilization program, in view of the very low sugar prices and the absolute necessity of economizing all along the line until conditions improve.

These Letters Should Be Answered

All Louisiana members of the Domestic Sugar Bureau, Chicago, and we believe practically all of the producers of direct consumption sugar in Louisiana are members, are advised that at the annual meeting of the Bureau, February 10, 1931, certain important amendments to the Code of Ethics will be proposed. As the By-Laws provide that the Code of Ethics can only be amended by a vote of nine-tenths of all the members it is very necessary that those Louisiana members who cannot attend the meeting send their proxies either to Mr. J. O. Douglas, the Executive Secretary, or to some one else whom they know will be at the meeting.

Mr. Douglas writes us that an important amendment to the Code of Ethics proposed at the last annual meeting could not be adopted because four Louisiana members, whose presence either in person or by proxy was necessary to make up the required nine-tenths of the membership, would not respond to letters or telegrams sent to them. Every member of the Domestic Sugar Bureau in Louisiana who is requested by Mr. Douglas to attend the meeting February 10, 1931, should respond, one way or another.

Washington News
By C. J. Bourg

The six members of the United States Tariff Commission appointed by President Hoover, having been confirmed by the Senate, we learn from the discussion of their qualifications that their opinions and antecedents count little, except those which have a sucrose content. The alert Mississippian who is Irish in name only, Pat Harrison, burst forth in frenzied oratory when the name of Edgar Brossard from Utah was being considered. The name sounded distinctly like South Louisiana Cajin and besides he comes from a state which produces both sugar and Smoot. But nobody would become agitated for some reason; maybe it was because the price of sugar has gone down since our neighbor prophesied the increase
(Continued on page 8)

of duty would cost the American "consumah" hu dreds of millions of dollars.

An amusing incident of the executive session which the Tariff Commissioners were considered that Senator Borah opposed the nomination of Hen Fletcher because the nominee admitted that he kno little about the tariff, while Senator Harrison cas gated Brossard because that gentleman has been co nected with the Tariff Commission for many yea and has taken part in its investigations both as economist and as a commissioner, hence he does kno something about the tariff.

Corn sugar has been a prominent news item f some weeks, as a result of Secretary Hyde's rece ruling which permits the use of corn sugar in foc products without declaration on the label. It was tl focal point of the conventions of grocers, canners an food brokers held in Chicago last week. These co ventions passed very expressive and pointed resol tions condemning the action of the Secretary of Agi culture. It is no secret that the Secretary acte against the advice of the Department scientists, b at the request of forty-three Congressmen from co states.

Your correspondent is not among those who woul view with alarm the expansion of the corn sugar i dustry. Looking at the development of this industi from the legislative standpoint, we are pleased to we come to our fold these two score or more of Congres men who will now have a greater appreciation of th *domestic sugar industry* and its direct benefit to th farmers of the United States. We sincerely believ that the United States should produce as nearly to i entire consumption of sugar as possible, and we ar ticipate that should the corn sugar production read increasing proportions, it will displace *foreign* suga and help us to become a greater American enterpris

There is one question of ethics and morals whic should have been submitted to the Wickersham Con mission. It is based upon the following facts: Cei tain distributors of sugar were concerned over sharp decline in their sales at some points. An in vestigation revealed that some of the wholesalers wei putting in larger supplies of corn sugar to replac cane and beet sugar. These wholesalers admitted growing demand for corn sugar from certain cas buyers, who didn't seem to have definite busines addresses. Now, it develops that the impression ha become more or less general that corn sugar wi make whiskey cheaper and quicker than sucros which has evidently attracted the attention of thos unknown persons who still have stills. Was this in pression created by supersalesmanship? How can on meet such competition? Of course, one never ask to what use the buyer will put pure cane sugar! Bi both Fleishmann's Yeast and Corn Products hav been indicted for conspiracy because bootleggers mad use of their goods. Would it be conspiracy to tr nd convince the unknown still public that sucrose nakes bigger and better fruit-juice *et seq.?*

As March 4th approaches, the spectre of an Extra iession looms as inescapable. There is too much anagonism between Congress and the President to hope or effective compromise. Besides, the Democrats re building the issues for 1932 right now and measires are to be considered which will take more time han is available in the remaining forty days. The ig fight will be to place the blame for the Extra iession. If the filibuster is smoked out into the open nd becomes too apparent, the Democrats will be lamed. If they can force a veto or a conference talemate, the Republicans will be blamed.

Strange as this may seem, many well-informed bservers have not yet been convinced that the Demcrats in the House of Representatives are anxious to rganize the House. The lure of Committee Chairnanships and patronage is very strong, but many ational politicians are giving no consideration to nything but the presidential election, less than two ears hence. The Democrats will have the same posibility of a coalition in the House that they have had 1 the Senate, and how it has worked!

To take control of the House, would force the Demcrats to re-open the tariff, which they are not anxous to do immediately preceding a national election. They could hardly justify the tremendous criticisms oured upon the Hawley-Smoot Act, if they controlled he Ways and Means Committee and yet left the ates where they are. Their position will be much asier to continue attacking, without responsibility.

These observations are made in demonstration of ur reasons for believing that there will be no tariff egislation for at least two years.

The Steering Committee of the Senate has anounced that the bill for Philippine Independence ill be made the unfinished business of the Senate at ome time before the end of this Session of Conress. Senators Hawes and Cutting, whose joint bill as received a favorable report from the Committee n Territories and Insular Affairs, have been pressg for action with the active assistance of Senator roussard, also a member of that Committee. The ecision to give this measure a preferred status in the enate has revived the hopes of the proponents that vote will be had upon the principle of Philippine ndependence before March 4th. The increased inrest being shown by Middle Western farmers, who ave felt the impact of competition with Philippine roducts, leads certain of us to believe that the ances are very good for a favorable vote in the enate. It is probable that this vote will be nothing ore than an expression, because there is really little ope that the House will consider the matter at all uring this Session, and we know that the present aders in the House are opposed to Philippine Indeendence. But the action of the Senate in voting faorably now will be a very helpful step forward towards favorable action in the House and Senate at the next Session.

Mr. Thomas L. Chadbourne has returned from Europe very optimistic and enthusiastic about the success of his plan. He had hardly landed before he issued a very bullish statement predicting that the prices of sugar would be two and one-half cents per pound as soon as the final agreement is signed at Cannes in about six weeks. He was decidedly of the opinion that he could induce Russia to enter into the agreement, adding that he had already started negotiations with the Russians and hoped to reach an agreement with them so that they might sign the final general agreement at Cannes.

Mr. Chadbourne plans after the agreement is signed, to have a permanent commission appointed to carry out the plan. He also will seek to organize an international research group to extend the progress of the sugar industry and to adopt a world-wide advertising campaign. Mr. Chadbourne is of the opinion that new methods can be found for reorganizing sugar marketing with more consideration given to the consumers' side. It is evident that Mr. Chadbourne is not confining his thoughts and plans to overcome present conditions, but with great foresight and an apparently thorough knowledge of the problems which the world sugar industry must solve, he is anticipating all situations from the standpoint of growers and producers in all countries of the world.

Corn Sugar

We print elsewhere in this issue a page advertisement that has been inserted in the sugar trade press throughout the United States by the Corn Products Refining Company. The purpose of the advertisement appears to be to explain the viewpoint of the producers of corn sugar in connection with the recent ruling of the Secretary of Agriculture of the United States, and it is published by the Sugar Bulletin as a paid advertisement, without comment.

Recommended Procedure Regarding Sugar Cane

(Prepared for County Agents by W. G. Taggart)

Greatest limiting factor in producing tonnage of sugar cane is time. We have from seven to nine months in which to grow a crop which in its native habitat requires twelve to twenty-four months to reach maturity. We cannot stretch our time at either end but we can accomplish the same thing by getting the maximum growth out of cane every day between germination and harvest time. Every day of the growing period in which cane fails to make progress is a shortening of our growing time. It therefore behooves us to use our intelligence to bring about conditions which are conducive to steady growth. We cannot write a recipe for growing a crop which will prove infallible, but we can lay down a set of rules based on experiment and experience which if used judiciously and altered to fit the variable weather, local conditions, and unusual happenings will help to produce a profitable crop.

1. Cane should be planted only on land suitable to the crop and not then unless that land contains sufficient organic matter to insure a reserve water supply. (Drought shortens our growing period more than any other factor.)

2. Nature tells us when spring is about to break and we should heed the call by preparing the soil to receive the benefits of the first warm weather. It is against the nature of cane to hibernate, but we force it to hibernate. While cane is a long suffering plant, it needs our help to get off to an early start. We can render this help by removing the excess soil from the seed as soon as it is safe to do so, bringing the eyes which are to germinate close to the surface and setting them on the bark for drainage and warmth.

If the stubble land has been packed and cut up by the wagon during the winter haul, countersink them before wrapping the middle. Nothing will pay better. Use the stubble shaver and the scraper but keep them razor-sharp and use them judiciously. Examine the stubble before shaving and don't make shaving a habit, but shave with a purpose. (The purpose is first to bring the benefits of the fastest germinating eyes close to the surface, and second to clean the drill.) Use the scraper as soon as you see that the cane wants to come and before many canes have come through. There is but little danger from frost damage to seed cane after the cane has begun to come up in the early spring. At that time, even thin ice will not hurt the seed cane when covered by an inch of soil. On the other hand, while most of the young cane which are broken by the scraper will germinate again, this germination will be retarded, and the plants will grow off slowly. (Marked eyes which had been broken by the scraper required two to three weeks extra for germination.) This is a condition not to be desired and one which should be avoided by early scraping.

If the weather is such that a stand of cane is insured before the scraper or the shaver, particularly the shaver, have been used, accept the situation and do not undo nature's work.

3. After securing a stand of cane, we should do all we can to keep it steadily growing. We can accomplish this by applying our fertilizers early, breaking our middles deeply, and then cultivating judiciously. (No more plowing but cultivating.) The first and sometimes the second cultivation can be done more cheaply and satisfactorily with the spring tooth attachment on a straddle row cultivator. This tool will complete a six-foot row and clean it in one trip, working so close to the young cane that hoeing is minimized. It should not be depended upon to fight bad infestations of Johnson grass. If the middles have been broken deeply at the time of applying fertilizers

and the land is in good condition, it will not be necessary to run out the middles after the first cultivation with the spring-tooth attachment. Should this tool be used for second cultivation, then the middles should be thrown out and the rows shaped immediately. This should be done in order to let the root system which at that time should be growing well out into the middles get set in permanent place. After the second cultivation, the usual tools, namely, the disc cultivator and one of the middle cultivators, should be used to finish the crop, but always the work of these implements should be so regulated that as little root pruning as possible is done. (Root pruning is second to drought in limiting our growing season.)

4. In general, we have cultivated cane too late. Lay-by always tears up the root system, and unless followed immediately by rain checks growth. We should rather anticipate the time when the crop will shade the ground, than to wait for the thing to actually happen before laying-by. Cane grows fastest after lay-by. An early growth is most liable to be rich in sugar.

Since nitrogen is the most used plant food, the following figures from the experiment station are given as a general guide. All cane growing on these plats followed one crop of corn and soybeans, with the soybeans turned under. It is clearly seen that fertilizer was not needed on the plant cane crop, and it is as clearly seen that nitrogen from any of these sources paid handsomely when applied to the stubble crop. We would advise buying your nitrogen from the one of these sources which gives you nitrogen at the cheapest price per pound.

Comparison of Nitrogenous Materials (P.O.J. 213)

| | \multicolumn{4}{c}{AVERAGE OF} | | | | |
| | \multicolumn{4}{c}{3 Years Plant Cane} | \multicolumn{4}{c}{2-Yr. 1st. Stubble Cane} |
	Tons Acre	Brix	Sucrose	Purity	Tons Acre	Brix	Sucrose	Purity
Check	36.61	14.74	11.46	77.06	24.16	15.75	12.70	80.63
Super Phosphate Potash	35.48	14.08	10.52	74.71	27.00	15.50	12.49	80.58
Cyanamid plus (PK)	37.17	14.78	11.19	75.71	31.30	14.89	11.43	76.76
Leuna Saltpeter plus (P.K.)	38.97	14.05	10.13	72.10	30.30	14.38	10.24	71.27
Nitrate Lime plus (P.K.)	37.25	14.77	11.30	76.51	32.57	14.47	10.81	74.71
Nitrate Soda plus (P.K.)	36.24	14.38	10.98	76.36	34.91	14.31	10.44	72.96
Sulphate Ammonia plus (P.K.)	35.86	14.62	11.34	77.56	33.45	15.3	11.87	78.98
Urea plus (P.K.)	36.03	14.49	11.08	76.52	30.46	14.05	10.67	75.94

Cal Nitro and Ammonium Nitrate were used in 1930 and gave as good returns as the other materials.

Ration: N. — 36 Lbs. Acre
        P. — 36 " "
        K. — 35 " "

Look At This!

CASTAGNOS GEARED STUBBLE SHAVER

Your attention is called to the accompanying photograph of this new, heavily constructed, positively driven and tractor-drawn stubble shaver, which we believe, constitutes a decided step forward in the efficient handling of this phase of our agricultural work.

We are sure that you will at once appreciate the great advantage of having a positive drive for the shaving discs as against the friction drive formerly employed, the efficiency of which depended entirely upon a clean, even off-bar. You well know that when the off-bar was not clean-cut and narrow, or where rains had washed a part of the ridge down, the discs of the old stubble shaver had friction on both sides, did not revolve in certain areas and hence split or pulled out the stools.

No such bad results are possible with the New Geared Stubble Shaver. The turning of the discs is assured and also the higher disc speed necessary for most efficient cutting and least splitting of stools is obtained by its use with a tractor.

This new shaver was used very successfully in shaving all the stubble this year at the plantations of E. G. Robichaux Co. (Cedar Grove) and Lewis Murrell (Tally Ho). Both of the above reported this shaver giving excellent results, and were able to shave from 20 to 23 acres per day.

The shaver, you will notice, is very strongly constructed and well adapted to the hard use given a tool for the shaving of the new type canes.

THE REVOLVING KNIVES ARE 30 INCHES IN DIAMETER, MADE OF HIGH TEMPERED STEEL, AND ARE SO DESIGNED AS TO PERMIT A 10-INCH VERTICAL SHIFT OF THE KNIVES, WITH A POSITIVE SET POSITION OF SAME. THIS REMOVES THE UNSATISFACTORY FEATURE OF EVERY STUBBLE SHAVER HITHERTO IN USE. IT ENABLES THE PLANTER TO DO STUBBLE SHAVING AS IT OUGHT TO BE DONE, AND AS IT MUST BE DONE TO SECURE THE RESULTS THAT STUBBLE SHAVING IS INTENDED TO PRODUCE.

For destroying stubble we have designed an attachment for the forward portion of the frame on which two disc coulters can be placed, thus cutting the stubble into three portions.

Orders for these machines should be in our hands in ample time to permit of their being manufactured and delivered before the normal season for stubble shaving.

CASTAGNOS CANE LOADER CO.

DONALDSONVILLE, LA., or

CHAS. WIGGIN,
MARITIME BLDG., NEW ORLEANS

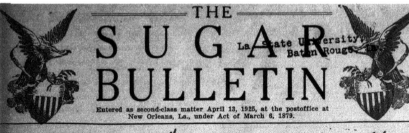

THE
SUGAR
La State University
Baton Rouge
BULLETIN

Entered as second-class matter April 13, 1925, at the postoffice at
New Orleans, La., under Act of March 6, 1879.

We stand for the encouragement of Home Industries as against Foreign competition.

| Vol. 9 | NEW ORLEANS, LA., FEBRUARY 15, 1931 | No. 10 |

How Shall We Profitably Utilize Our Blackstrap?

The abnormally low price of blackstrap molasses has revived the idea of utilizing it on the plantations as stock feed, which was discussed, studied and practiced 25 years ago and considered at that time to be a demonstrated success. In the intervening years it seems to be the case that blackstrap made on the Louisiana plantations has continued to be used to make mixed feeds for work animals and for cattle, but unfortunately these feeds have not been made by the producers of the blackstrap. They have been made in large establishments located in various parts of the United States, the owners of these establishments buying the blackstrap for a tithe of the amount they subsequently sold it for as an ingredient in their mixed feeds.

Our attention is drawn to all this at the present time through the fact that the Interstate Commerce Commission has made a ruling, to become effective April 1, 1931, which does away with the milling in transit rate on mixed feeds which contain products of other than grain origin, and the result of this ruling, if the railroads do not successfully oppose its application, will be to make it more expensive for the great centralized feed mixing establishments to assemble their non-cereal ingredients, and it will give a formidable impetus to the production of mixed feeds containing molasses right at the place where the molasses itself is produced, that is, on the Louisiana plantations. We can, and do, produce on our plantations all the ingredients it is necessary to have for mixing with the molasses. We are able to grow unlimited amounts of hays and forages and we have a great potential ingredient for mixed feeds in dried cane tops.

The fact of the matter is that after being the discoverers of the value of molasses as stock feed, which we did as far back as 1905, and after all the research work done at our Louisiana Experiment Station at that time by the distinguished Dr. W. H. Dalrymple, who not only showed that molasses was a valuable ingredient of stock feed but who prepared a number of formulas for mixing it with corn and cob meal, alfalfa hay, cotton seed meal, pea vine hay and other forages to make a balanced ration, we have allowed the actual utilization of blackstrap molasses as stock feed to be usurped by centralized feed mixing plants in other states and in many cases we have bought back our own molasses from these people at many times the price they paid us for it.

As late as 1914, just before the outbreak of the World War, molasses rations, compounded on Dr. Dalrymple's formulas, were used in the feed lot, the stable of the work stock and in the dairy of the Louisiana Experiment Station at Baton Rouge, and when farmers applied to the station for a feeding ration the station rarely supplied one that did not contain its legitimate quota of molasses, based on carefully tested formulas.

The manufacturers of mixed feeds seized on this discovery with avidity. They found that a cheap ingredient for their feeds was available which had a high nutritive value as a factor in a balanced ration. Not only that, but they got a "milling in transit" rate on it from the railroads which enabled them to ship it to their plants and then from their plants to their customers, after mixing it with other materials, all at one freight rate. It is this "milling in transit" rate that the Interstate Commerce Commission is about to do away with.

At the hearings on the Hawley-Smoot Tariff Bill before the Ways and Means Committee of Congress in 1929, some testimony was elicited from the mixed feed manufacturers which throws considerable light on the part played by molasses in stock and cattle feeding. Mr. J. H. Caldwell of the Ralston-Purina Mills in St. Louis, who is President of the Mixed Feed Manufacturers' Association, said that the mixed feed industry of the United States represented over two hundred million dollars and produced annually over ten million tons of feed, worth about $400,000,000. He said that at least three-fifths of this enormous quantity of feed contained blackstrap molasses as its

===== THE =====

SUGAR
BULLETIN

407 Carondelet St., New Orleans

Issued on the 1st and 15th of each month. Official Organ of the American
Sugar Cane League of the U. S. A., in which are consolidated
The Louisiana Sugar Planters' Assn.
The American Cane Growers' Assn.
The Producers & Mfgrs. Protective Assn.
Subscription Price, 50 Cents Per Year.

Reginald Dykers, General Manager & Editor of the Bulletin
301 Nola Bldg., New Orleans
Frank L. Barker, Secretary and Treasurer
Lockport, La.
C. J. Bourg, Manager Washington Office
810 Union Trust Building

CHAIRMEN OF COMMITTEES:
C. D. Kemper, Franklin, La.
President of the League and Ex-Officio Chairman of Executive Committee
Andrew H. Gay, Plaquemine, La,
Chairman Agricultural Committee
David W. Pipes, Jr., Houma, La.
Chairman Industrial Committee
Frank L. Barker, Lockport, La.
Chairman Finance Committee,.
Edward J. Gay, Plaquemine, La.
Chairman Tariff Committee
H. Langdon Laws, Cinclare, La.
Chairman Legislative Committee
J. C. LeBourgeois, New Orleans, La.
Chairman Freight Rate Committee
R. H. Chadwick, Bayou Goula, La.
Chairman Membership Committee
A. H. Rosenfeld, New Orleans, La.
Chairman Publicity Committee

Members of the League desiring action on, or information on, any subject are invited to communicate with
the League or with the Chairman of the Committee
to which it seems to appertain.

essential basic ingredient, all of it cane molasses.
"Generally speaking," said Mr. Caldwell, "there can
be no development of the mixed feed industry without blackstrap molasses any more than there could
be a steel industry without pig iron, an electric industry without copper, or a fertilizer industry without
potash and nitrate." Mr. Caldwell added that his
company alone uses twice as much blackstrap every
year as is produced in the whole state of Louisiana.
We reproduce below some extracts from Mr. Caldwell's testimony:

MR. RAMSEYER: Mr. Caldwell, I want to ask you this
question. How much of this blackstrap molasses do you
mix with these cattle feeds?
MR. CALDWELL: That will depend entirely on what
kind of feed you are making, for what kind of animal.
MR. RAMSEYER: I am talking about cattle—steers.
MR. CALDWELL: Feeding steers or feeding dairy
cows?
MR. RAMSEYER: Steers.
MR. CALDWELL: It will range all the way from 20 to
50 per cent of the total feed.
MR. RAMSEYER: You mean to say that in a ton of
feed, mixed feed, there will be half blackstrap?
MR. CALDWELL: In some cases.
MR. RAMSEYER: How many gallons?
MR. CALDWELL: There are 171 gallons in a ton. Half
of that would be 85 gallons.
MR. RAMSEYER: Eighty-five gallons of blackstrap to
mix a ton of feed?
MR. CALDWELL: Where it is feed for fattening
steers.
MR. RAMSEYER: And for dairy?
MR. CALDWELL: It will run about 8 or 10 per cent
of blackstrap. It is much lower for dairy cows.

MR. MARTIN: What is the price per ton of that fee
MR. CALDWELL: I do not know. I could not tell y
at this time; what it is right now.
MR. GARNER: Did I understand you to say that y
are the largest manufacturer in this country?
MR. CALDWELL: We claim that distinction.
MR. GARNER: If I understand it, your company alo
uses more blackstrap molasses than is produced
Louisiana?
MR. CALDWELL: We use practically twice as mu
as is produced in Louisiana.
MR. GARNER: And yet you can not tell this comm
tee the price of a ton of your article of feed?
MR. CALDWELL: I can not tell you the exact pric
MR. GARNER: Can you approximate it? Can you gue
within $40 of it?
MR. CALDWELL: The steer feed would be appro
mately $40 a ton.
MR. GARNER: With 50 per cent blackstrap molasse
MR. CALDWELL: Something like that.
MR. GARNER: What would the dairy feed, containir
from 8 to 10 per cent blackstrap molasses, be worth?
MR. CALDWELL: That would be worth more; qui
a bit more.
MR. GARNER: In other words, the larger the percen
age of molasses, the less the feed is worth, is that th
idea?
MR. CALDWELL: That is right.
MR. GARNER: And the more valuable it is?
MR. CALDWELL: To a certain extent, yes.
MR. RAMSEYER: What do you pay for this blac
strap?
MR. CALDWELL: At the present time it is 10½ cen
a gallon f.o.b. the Gulf.

At the present time blackstrap molasses is bringin
the producers in Louisiana about half the figure mer
tioned by Mr. Caldwell in his testimony. To sell it
such a price is both ruinous and ridiculous. Why car
not we make mixed feeds ourselves and thus get fc
our blackstrap approximately the price the mixe
feed people get when they sell the molasses in thei
feed? Mr. Caldwell says that one ton of mixed fee
for steers containing 85 gallons of molasses, whic
amount of molasses can be bought now for about $
sells for $40. To the molasses must be added a thou
sand pounds of soy bean or alfalfa hay, whole e
corn and similar provender, all of which we hav
right on our plantations. The abolition of the millir
in transit rate may open our eyes to certain va
possibilities. It is in the hope that serious and cor
structive thought may be aroused among us that th
article is written.

Raceland Wins

The Buck Horns, annually awarded by the Ame
ican Sugar Cane League to the Louisiana facto
grinding the largest amount of cane, have been w
again this year by the Raceland Factory of Godcha
Sugars, Inc. The amount of cane ground at Racelar
was 144,205 tons. The same factory won the hor
last year with a tonnage of 151,684.

Pioneer Inventor Dies

The old guard throughout the Louisiana sugar i
dustry will learn with regret that Mr. Jules Gaussir:
of Baldwin, La., passed away on January 31, 1931,
the age of 76. Mr. Gaussiran designed the windrowi
machine that bore his name and placed it on the mark
about 25 years ago. He was a very conspicuous figu
at that time at all the field days and similar occasio
and was a man of kindly and agreeable disposition
modest and retiring, and generally beloved and
spected.

r. Godchaux May Lend His Aid

We are informed that Mr. Jules Godchaux has been ked by the United States Court to serve as one of e receivers of the South Coast Company to replace r. W. K. DePass, who has requested that he be lieved of his office as one of the receivers because the demands made on his time by his private busiss. The bondholders, stockholders and creditors of e South Coast Company will be so singularly fornate if Mr. Godchaux accepts the appointment that e incident deserves comment.

No sugar enterprise in Louisiana was watched with ore intense and hopeful interest than that of the uth Coast Company. There was a feeling of loyalty it and of interest in its welfare prevalent even ong people not identified with it in any way. That series of events grouped themselves in fatalistic shion to embarrass it is a matter of sorrowful history. Mr. Godchaux is peculiarly well qualified, we be-ve, to put this vast enterprise back on its feet. He to the manner born and imbibed the atmosphere of 1e Louisiana sugar industry with his mother's milk. is familiarity with local conditions, local atmosphere, cal temperament, is exceptional. He is as indigenous the water hyacinth. So far as this particular inustry is concerned he is something over, above and yond an able executive.

Every business, everywhere in the world, is a sort witch's caldron, and it is sometimes necessary to ir into them ingredients not found in any of the ok books. When that happens the only guide is a fted nostril. Somebody must be found whose nose 1ows and we think that Mr. Jules Godchaux is that rt of a person.

Washington News

By CLARENCE J. BOURG

There is one topic in Washington just at this time hich forms part of every conversation. Will there be 1 extra session?

It has been a long time since so much outside inuence has been brought to bear upon Congress. our correspondent does not remember when national ilitical leaders have been as active as they are now both parties for one purpose. If there is anybody the United States who favors an extra session, :nator Borah excepted, he is not making it known iblicly.

The full force of the press was used last week in eking to interpret the compromise on the drouth lief as final proof that the President would not have re-convene Congress this summer. There is no reirter or editor who believed that to be true.

It is significant that Senator Norris and other Progressives have not said very much about their pro gressive program recently. They have permitted the Red Cross fight and the soldiers' bonus to be regarded as the obstacles. However, it will be remembered that Senator Norris said very definitely in December that he would insist upon disposing of measures concerning Muscle Shoals, the elimination of the lame duck congress, and the Anti-Injunction Act. None of these have been finally acted upon. Will the Senator continue to remain silent in the closing days, if no action is taken on his pet measures?

As a live issue the tariff bobs up every day in Congress. Resolutions directing the Tariff Commission to investigate the cost of production of several articles have been passed. Undoubtedly the Tariff Commision has made a favorable impression through its prompt handling of investigations affecting maple sugar, leather, straw hats and flour, on which the President has proclaimed a reduction. On wire fencing and netting an increase has been ordered, while ultra-marine blue and wool floor coverings had their rates confirmed without change. When it is considered that the present commission was organized in September, the speed with which they have been able to complete these reports has made a favorable impression.

The oil people have been very active in their effort to secure an embargo; but the Ways and Means Committee has consistently refused to bring out any amendment to the Hawley-Smoot Act. Senator Capper has atttempted to produce an embargo by means of a bill which he had referred to the Senate Commerce Committee and on which he received a favorable report. But if he is able to secure favorable consideration from the Senate it is freely prophesied that the bill will die in the House Committee, as the House of Representatives is very jealous of its prerogative to initiate all revenue bills.

There has been considerable agitation for an embargo on lumber, but no action has been taken. There is a real effort being made for an embargo against all Russian products.

The agitation in both the Senate and the House for legislation immediately to clarify the liquid sugar situation, has found the sympathetic ear of a majority in both chambers, particularly for the reason that the one hundred and forty million dollars in sugar tariff revenue for the United States Treasury seems to t in jeopardy. There would be no hesitancy on the pa of the Ways and Means Committee in presen.ing th legislation for immediate action, if there would be ar assurance that the matter would be acted upon witl out amendment. But the moment that the Ways an Means Committee breaks its rule of not reporting ar tariff legislation, there seems to be a lack of confiden(that anyone could prevent amendments from beir tied on without limit.

In the meantime the main purpose and aim in th lives of the party leaders continues to be a determin. tion to pass all the supply bills before March 4th ar to keep from allowing any other controversial legi lation being brought forward. The politics of the si uation for both parties is to adjourn and stay hom until December. No other consideration is being er tertained.

For those who watched the activities of the coalitic in the Senate last year, it is interesting to follow tl developments now going on. The gossip is that thei will be divorce. In fact, there must be a separation the Democrats hope to be able to present Democrat issues next year. It was allright to have this Sena torial mesalliance during the tariff fight between th Democrats and the Insurgent Republicans, but th Democratic party cannot go to the country on a pla form built even in part by Republicans, no matt(how little Republicanism they may represent. Th Democrats know that on the question of the organiza tion of the Senate, the Insurgents will become regula again at least for long enough to maintain themselv(as chairmen of certain Senate committees. They al: know that at least some of the Insurgents have habit of becoming regular during a Presidential can paign, no matter if they do blame it on prohibitic or farm relief. And all of these things have the effect upon the attitude of the leaders towards an mixture containing sugar and water.

Notwithstanding the Congressional action, whic may or may not come about or bear fruit, the Trea ury Department is preparing to maintain its rulir on liquid sugar before the United States Custon Court at Savannah on March 27th. If the Treasu Department ruling is maintained that sucrose, whet er in the form of raw sugar or liquid sugar must p the two-cent rate of duty, then the court action w be quite as effective as anything Congress could d There are those who believe that the situation shou not be disturbed pending the decision of the cou The question will be not so much what the intent Congress was, because everybody knows that, b whether the bill actually states the intent of Congre The Treasury Department has interpreted the inte correctly and there is no cause for concern until unless the Customs Court should decree otherwise.

Contact Committee

Minutes of a Meeting of American Sugar Cane Leag Contact Committee with Louisiana Experiment Station Workers, Held at Baton Rouge, La., January 23, 1931.

Department of Entomology Report

A five-page mimeographed progress report was p sented by Dr. Hinds.

Staff Changes: Dr. Herbert Spencer resigned to acc(an attractive offer with the U. S. Bureau of Entomolo to conduct Trichogramma breeding work at Albany, Georgia, in connection with the investigations and the control of the pecan nut case-bearer. His resignation was effective October 15, 1930. Only one student assistant was continued through the summer months and until the first week of December when information was received that the Special Cane Fund for 1930-31 was available. Since that time we have been using six other students for part-time work.

Studies of the Soybean Caterpillar: The soybean caterpillar appeared in considerable abundance during September and October, but was later in development and the damage was less than in 1929. The importance of this species to soybean growers, especially in the Cane Belt, is so great that considerable time was given to its study by Dr. Hinds and Mr. Osterberger during the past fall. A report on this work has been prepared and was presented as a paper at the meeting of the American Association of Economic Entomologists at Cleveland, Ohio, on December 31st last.

Tests as to Best Grain for Breeding Sitotroga: We have been running a series of tests to determine any particular advantages in production of grain moths. At the beginning of this work we jumped at the conclusion that a soft white corn was most favorable for that work, and so we used this in stocking the moth breeding rooms. Softer types of white dent corn was the basis of our work until this year. About the middle of October we started a series of tests with four varieties of corn, yellow creole—a rather hard flinty type of corn—two varieties of white dent, and pop corn; rough rice, head rice, brewer's grain, screenings, wheat, barley, etc., were also included in our studies. In each jar we put the same weight of corn or grain, four ounces, and on the same day and from the same source 200 newly-hatched larvae, so that all started with the same initial potential infestation. Each variety of grain had three replications, thus making 12 ounces of grain and 600 newly-hatched larvae with each of the 12 kinds of grain. This required 7200 larvae to start off the work. The corn variety used previously in our work was mostly Calhoun red cob. In this comparison of varieties of corn, Calhoun red cob produced in the first generation 167, Cocke's prolific 223, and yellow creole 345 moths. The percentage of our initial stock of larvae developing successfully to the moth stage was 27, 37 and 50.7 per cent, respectively.

The moths produced in rice are smaller in size and darker in color and develop somewhat more slowly than those produced in corn. High humidity in the breeding chamber favors rapid production but if carried too far will also favor mold development in the grain. High humidity, or a supply of drinking water for the moths, lengthens the period of activity of the moth by about a day, or at least 25 per cent, and should increase the average number of eggs deposited per female in about this proportion.

Acting upon such information, we are stocking our moth rooms principally with yellow creole corn and are arranging to maintain more uniform condition of temperature and higher relative humidity than we have been using. We hope to secure correspondingly better results in the production of moths and also of the Trichogramma parasites.

Trash Disposal Tests: Definite tests for studying the effect of various methods of trash disposal upon the hibernation of borers were started at Cinclare two years ago. This year the light borer infestation made it necessary to go as far as Plaquemine to find favorable conditions for further work in trash disposal. On Island Plantation of A. Wilbert & Sons at Plaquemine, in 213 plant cane, we found the heaviest borer infestation which

3 to 5 CROPS
From This Filter "Cloth"

we have seen or heard of in the state for 1930. In this
tract of seven acres, all well drained, we have arranged
seven plats of about one acre each for this work. During
the first week of December a total of 2,825 tops were
examined from the entire area and yielded 789 borer
stages. This meant an average of 3.6 tops per borer stage
found. In similar examinations completed January 22,
1931, among 1545 tops, 180 borer stages were found. This
is an average of 8.6 tops per borer stage. The trash on
most of the plats had been burned off before the January
examination.

Sugar Cane Beetle Work at Franklin: Damage by this
insect to sugar cane, corn and rice has been common in
Louisiana for many years past. At times the injury is
very severe and may completely destroy stands of corn
and on Anna Plantation last season, probably in combination with a severe infestation of root rot and possibly of
red rot also, the stand of cane was practically destroyed
on about 75 acres.

Last spring Mr. B. A. Osterberger, assisted by Mr.
H. H. True, started an intensive investigation of this pest
at Sterling Sugars, Franklin. A progress report on this
work was submitted last August. One of the items of investigation was to determine whether the destruction of
the mother stalk in a stool of cane would actually result
in a decrease in yields or affect the sucrose content, at
harvest time. For this test Mr. True selected during the
first week of July in P.O.J. 213 plant cane, 25 pairs of
stools. In one stool the mother stalk had been destroyed
while the other stool was uninjured. In each pair the
stools were adjacent and as closely comparable as could
be found at the time. Record was made of the number
of sprouts and the height in each stool. Continuing this
work, Mr. Osterberger found at harvest time 19 pairs of
stools which could be considered closely comparable.
Among these stools on July 4th there were in the series
without cane beetle injury 199 sprouts with an average
height of 15.9 inches, in the beetle-injured series there
were 197 sprouts with an average height of 13.5 inches.
This comparison shows considerable retardation in growth
at the beginning of the test, but not a difference in
stand. At harvest time, on December 5th, in the uninjured series for the 19 stools, 148 stalks having an average length of 79.2 inches and a weight of 289 pounds
were harvested, while from the beetle-injured series adjacent there were harvested 123 stalks, with an average
length of 69.3 inches and a total weight of 216 pounds.
Chemical analyses were secured by handmill tests and
showed an average in the uninjured stools of 13.97 sucrose, while in the injured stools the average sucrose
was 14.61 per cent.

If we carry these figures out on a per acre basis, we
find as a result of a uniform beetle infestation by which
the mother stalk in each stool was destroyed—and no
other damage done—there would result a loss of 25 per
cent, or seven tons of cane per acre. The loss in tonnage
value would be about $24.50 per acre, while the net loss
of 1,070 pounds of sugar per acre would have a value
(at 3.35 cents) of $35.85 per acre. It is quite evident that
this investigation should be continued as fast as may be
possible.

In discussions regarding the extent of cane beetle damage, Mr. Kemper stated that the beetles may cut off the
sprouts completely or injure them so as to reduce their
vitality and make them very susceptible to other unfavorable conditions—possibly to infections of red rot. Dr.
Rosenfeld confirmed the report of heavy damage at Anna
Plantation where, he stated, he saw a splendid stand at
the beginning of the season but this stand gradually died
out until the loss was complete on 75 acres and decreas-
ingly severe through some 200 acres of fall plant P.O.J.

213 particularly. Mr. Kemper stated that rather heavy applications of hydrated lime seemed to have the effect of repelling the beetles. Applications were made to only the worst infested areas where some 400 or 500 pounds of lime per acre were drilled in like fertilizer. Mr. O'Neal stated that in his study of soil types in this area at Franklin the heaviest infestation occurred regularly where the soil was light gray in color and not much infestation was found where the soils were brown or dark black in color. Professor Taggart stated that Dr. H. A. Morgan reported this beetle as hibernating in turf grass areas and suggested that Mr. Kemper see whether this is the case in his territory. Dr. Hinds suggested that if this investigation is to be continued it would be advisable to have the investigator in the field by the middle of February or so as to be present during the period of greatest activity of the beetles. Last year the beetle movement had practically ceased by May 1st.

Department of Plant Pathology Report

Dr. Edgerton presented a four-page mimeographed progress report.

Pythium Root Rot Studies in Soil Kept Free of Corn and Grass, and in Regular Rotation: Two adjoining plots on the station were used, one with cane two years and corn and soybeans one year and the other with soybeans continuously for two years and no corn. Both planted in 1930 to cane. The plot with corn showed soil a little darker in color. The comparison of roots on the two soil plots showed no great difference except with Co 290. This examination was repeated, and the same results were obtained the second time. There was a great deal more root growth on the soil that had cane two years and soybeans and corn the next year than on the soil that had soybeans without any corn. Variations were not sufficient to show any marked difference between the two plots.

Pythium in the Two Plots: Pythium was present in both plots. We did not get rid of Pythium by leaving corn off for two years, which is more or less comparable with root rot troubles of certain other crops. This shows that the rotation did not get rid of this organism where the degree of parasitism was high.

Yield Tests on Mosaic-infected as Compared with Mosaic-free Cane: There was very little difference in the yields from mosaic-infected and mosaic-free seed in P.O.J. 36M and striped. But the selected D74 gave a satisfactory increased yield over the unselected.

Red Rot Condition in Fall of 1930 as Compared with 1929: A year ago last spring injury to stands of P.O.J. 213, particularly, on account of red rot was severe. This variety of cane is more susceptible to injury by red rot than P.O.J. 36 and P.O.J. 234. This year, in most places visited, the amount of red rot was very small.

These observations indicate that the seed cane planted in 1930 was of unusually high quality and very good stands are to be expected except on the very poorest soils.

Root Rot Studies—Soil Treatment: These studies have been continued. As was noted last year, there were no consistent differences observed in any of the plots as a result of the treatment.

Cane Condition in the Field (1930-31): The condition of cane as compared to last year is based mostly on comparisons made here at Baton Rouge.

The weather conditions have been quite different from those of the preceding year, with cool weather and comparatively little rain until recently. As a result, the development of shoots and roots has been slow and in some instances, practically none at all.

There is very little development of stubble cane at the present time, particularly CP 807, Co 281 and P.O.J. 36 and P.O.J. 36M. Up until the present time there has been little decay. Some little decay of shoots of D 74, purple and P.O.J. 213 has occurred on shoots whose tops were killed by freezes. Shoot roots on early cut cane for the most part have rotted.

Report of Test Fields

A four-page mimeographed progress report was presented by Mr. Gouaux.

Test Field Plantings: The test field variety project work at the six Experiment Station test fields (Cinclare,

Glenwood, Reserve, Meeker, Sterling and Youngsville) during the latter part of September, October and early November, consisted mainly of the fall planting of sugar cane varieties under actual field conditions. In all cases the new fields are on the same soil types and adjoining or in close proximity to the stubble test fields. With the exception of Youngsville, the plantings follow a previous crop of soybeans turned under.

The checkerboard system of planting of plots was used with five replications of each variety. The varieties planted are: P.O.J. 36, 36 M, 213, 234, CP 177, CP 807, Co 281 and Co 290.

Test Field Results for 1930 Season: During the 1930 harvesting season, the main work in connection with the 16 Experiment Station sugar cane variety test fields consisted of proper harvesting and the securing of accurate field and chemical data from all of these experimental fields. The work started with the handling of the four second stubble fields on October 21st, followed by six first stubble fields and completing the last of the six plant cane fields on December 16th. The chemical data given for all varieties are based on results obtained from large-scale big mill tests. A complete tabulation of these results, comprising sixteen tables, has been prepared. This data is being completed with the expectation of publication in the near future.

Stubble Shaving

By ARTHUR H. ROSENFELD

The writer is of the opinion that, particularly where any high cutting was done last crop, light shaving can be employed to advantage if carried out early enough to avoid cutting back any material growth of the stubbles. Probably no better tonnage will be secured by shaving, but, if the light shaving is performed before any material development of the stubble, it will result in more economical work thereafter.

On the whole it appears at this time that most of the subterranean eyes of the stubble are good, with the result that this cane will stand light shaving preferably with the broad shavers, and before off-barring to avoid destroying or pulling out of stools, or with the new geared shavers after offbarring. The cane has kept remarkably dormant through the winter, and even very little red rot is in evidence. All indications, therefore, point to good stands for this year's cultivation.

Finally, follow the suggestions of Mr. Taggart* in the last issue of the SUGAR BULLETIN. Keep the shavers razor-sharp and use them judiciously. "Examine the stubble before shaving and do not make shaving a habit, but shave with a purpose (the purpose is first, to bring the fastest germinating eyes close to the surface, and, second, to clean the drill). If the weather is such that a stand is insured before the scraper has been used, accept the situation and do not undo Nature's work."

*Recommended Procedure Regarding Sugar Cane.

The Consistent Performance of Cyanamid ✎ ✎ ✎

There are at least ten good reasons why Cyanamid holds its commanding position in the regard of Louisiana sugar cane planters. But above all, is the fact that Cyanamid is dependable. It performs "consistently and well"—in good seasons and bad.

Its progressive availability results in even, *sustained* feeding of the cane. Sucrose and purity percentages are maintained, and substantial yield increases are economically produced.

The field and mill laboratory results of the past season's experiments with Cyanamid are now available. Our Agriculturist in your district will be glad to place a copy of these data at your disposal and supply you with any desired further information.

For further information, write

American Cyanamid Company
Pioneer Producers of Air-Nitrogen Products in America

535 FIFTH AVENUE, NEW YORK

1820 JEFFERSON AVENUE   **NEW ORLEANS**

AERO BRAND CYANAMID

Today's Outstanding Nitrogen Fertilizer "Buy"

Circulation of this Issue 1900 Copies

THE SUGAR BULLETIN

Library Experiment Station,
Baton Rouge.

Entered as second-class matter April 13, 1925, at the postoffice at
New Orleans, La., under Act of March 6, 1879.

We stand for the encouragement of Home Industries as against Foreign competition.

Vol. 9   NEW ORLEANS, LA., MARCH 1, 1931   No. 11

Andrew Hynes Gay

Mr. Andrew Hynes Gay, the first President of the American Sugar Cane League, died at his home in Iberville Parish, La., on February 19, 1931. He had been ill but a few days, and was in the prime of life. At his funeral there were men identified with practically every phase of Louisiana's industrial and economic existence, reflecting the wide sphere of influence which, throughout his career, Mr. Gay had exercised, and testifying to the honor, esteem and affection in which he was held by all those with whom his manifold activities had brought him in contact.

We who are engaged in the sugar industry knew him best as a sugar planter. As such, he was active, and an acknowledged leader, for a great many years, and he had behind him an ancestry distinguished in the history of the sugar industry of this State, the members of which contributed in a great measure to the making of that history and who wrote in it only honorable and brilliant chapters.

Had it not been for Mr. Andrew Gay, it is doubtful if the American Sugar Cane League would ever have been launched successfully. He put behind the efforts that were made to establish it in 1922 all of his influence and initiative, and in the search that took place at that time to find a leader in whom everybody would have implicit confidence, and who was known to possess the fair, impartial and judicial disposition necessary to inspire the faith and trust of all of the, at that time, diverse elements in our industry, the choice fell unanimously upon him. He served as President two terms, and then voluntarily retired, initiating the unwritten law that has since prevailed that the tenure of office as President of the League shall not exceed two terms of one year each. It was during President Gay's administration that the gruelling fight was made before the United States Tariff Commission over the amount of the tariff on sugar, which the producers of sugar in Cuba were endeavoring to have lowered.

This controversy, which finally resulted in our favor, continued almost two years and, because of the financial burden it placed on the League, then in its swaddling clothes, consummate ability was necessary to keep the organization from foundering on the rocks of extraordinary expenditure that cropped up unexpectedly on all sides. Mr. Gay's judgment and poise were manifest during all this trying period, and when he retired from the Presidency in September, 1924, all of the work had been done and it remained only to await the decision of President Coolidge which, when it was forthcoming, was against the petition to reduce the tariff rate on sugar.

During his term of office Mr. Gay fostered innumerable lines of activity designed to upbuild and benefit the Louisiana sugar industry. He wielded with skill, and always for good, the powerful weapon of a well-knit organization, which he himself had done so much to create, and the footprints that he leaves upon the sands of time point towards the homely virtues that are the

THE
SUGAR
BULLETIN

407 Carondelet St., New Orleans

Issued on the 1st and 15th of each month. Official Organ of the American
Sugar Cane League of the U. S. A., in which are consolidated
The Louisiana Sugar Planters' Assn.
The American Cane Growers' Assn.
The Producers & Mfgrs. Protective Assn.
Subscription Price, 50 Cents Per Year.

Reginald Dykers, General Manager & Editor of the Bulletin
301 Nola Bldg., New Orleans
Frank L. Barker, Secretary and Treasurer
Lockport, La.
C. J. Bourg, Manager Washington Office
810 Union Trust Building

CHAIRMEN OF COMMITTEES:

C. D. Kemper, Franklin, La.
President of the League and Ex-Officio Chairman of Executive Committee
Andrew H. Gay, Plaquemine, La.
Chairman Agricultural Committee
David W. Pipes, Jr., Houma, La.
Chairman Industrial Committee
Frank L. Barker, Lockport, La.
Chairman Finance Committee.
Edward J. Gay, Plaquemine, La.
Chairman Tariff Committee
H. Langdon Laws, Cinclare, La.
Chairman Legislative Committee
J. C. LeBourgeois, New Orleans, La.
Chairman Freight Rate Committee
R. H. Chadwick, Bayou Goula, La.
Chairman Membership Committee
A. H. Rosenfeld, New Orleans, La.
Chairman Publicity Committee

Members of the League desiring action on, or information on, any subject are invited to communicate with the League or with the Chairman of the Committee to which it seems to appertain.

bed-rock of our community happiness.

Words are feeble things with which to attempt to review, analyze and describe a human life. The well-spring of it all is a part of the Divine magnificence and it blazes unseen behind a screen of mortal flesh until, for some reason that we do not know, it flickers out. Nevertheless, and realizing the impotence of language, the Executive Committee of the American Sugar Cane League adopted at a meeting held February 25, 1931, the following resolutions:

WHEREAS—Mr. Andrew Hynes Gay, the first President of the American Sugar Cane League, has been taken from among us by death, thus creating the first vacancy in the ranks of those few outstanding men who have been chosen, because of their high ability, to head this organization, and

WHEREAS—It was upon the shoulders of the first President of the League, who had to guide its early footsteps, create its traditions and visualize its future progress and its policies, that there fell the heaviest burden of executive responsibility, and

WHEREAS—by bearing this burden effici-

ently, courageously and intelligently, Andrew Hynes Gay won our admiration, gratitude and respect,

THEREFORE BE IT RESOLVED—That the Executive Committee of the American Sugar Cane League, speaking for and in behalf of those engaged in the sugar industry of Louisiana, and voicing the feelings and sentiments of men engaged in every sphere of that industry, declares that when Mr. Andrew Hynes Gay died there departed from this world a gallant gentleman and a splendid citizen, a leader in every field to which he lent his energy, a man with a character that was essentially constructive; a man of foresight and ability; an upright, brilliant, tolerant and sympathetic member of that depleted but still steadfast and stalwart corps, the sugar planters of Louisiana, and be it further

RESOLVED—That we express our sorrow over his passing in this official manner so that there will be a permanent record thereof in the archives of the organization which he led and sponsored at its birth, and that these resolutions shall be spread upon the minutes of the American Sugar Cane League, published in its official bulletin, and copies sent to the widow and children of our distinguished Chief Executive, who is now no more.

Sugar Cane Insect Studies at Houma and Elsewhere

The third building provided by the American Sugar Cane League at the Houma field station has been finished. On February 1, 1931, it was turned over to the Government. This provides the Houma station with an entomological laboratory and a field office for the Division of Agricultural Engineering, Bureau of Public Roads.

It seems worthwhile to outline here the activities of the Government in connection with insect pests of sugar cane. These activities are a part of the Division of Cereal and Forage Insects, in charge of Dr. W. H. Larrimer, Washington, D. C. The principal field laboratory is at 8203 Oak Street, New Orleans, La., and in connection with this laboratory there are an insectary and field cages in Jefferson Parish. Here moth borer parasites from South America are received. The parasites of the borer are, of course, beneficial, but in arriving from South America they are often found to be destroyed by "secondary parasites," so that from the puparia or "cocoons" of the beneficial insects many "secondaries" frequently emerge. If these were released in the cane fields they would go far toward nullifying the work of the beneficial parasites which attack the borer. Precautions are taken to prevent the escape of these harmful parasites, but there is also great advantage in handling them in New Orleans, at some distance from the sugar plantations. T. E. Holloway, W. E. Haley and Mrs. Ruth E. Wood, stenographer, are stationed at New Orleans.

The Advertisers in the Sugar Bulletin are contributing towards the support of the American Sugar Cane League and should enjoy your special consideration; help them to help the Domestic Sugar Industry by doing business with them whenever possible.

The work of all the laboratories is directed from this station.

The parasites are received from Argentina and Peru. For some time, H. A. Jaynes, the entomologist in South America, was located at Tucuman, Argentina, where he had the valued cooperation of the experiment station there. As there was a scarcity of parasites in Argentina, however, he has of late been at Trujillo, Peru.

The Houma laboratory has as entomologists J. W. Ingram and E. K. Bynum. Work on soil animals injurious to sugar cane roots is being conducted in cooperation with the Bureau of Plant Industry. Parasites are received from New Orleans and released in the fields of the sugar parishes. Considerable work will be done on the moth borer and other insects.

The laboratory at Crowley, La., in charge of W. A. Douglas, is primarily for the investigation of rice insects. However, Mr. Douglas renders assistance regularly in field work on sugar cane insects in the western sections. At the Crowley laboratory it was found that the sugar cane moth borer was more injurious to rice than was the rice stalk borer.

While the laboratories, aside from the one in South America, are in Louisiana, work has been done in all the Gulf states. The sugar cane mealybug was investigated at Cairo, Georgia, for several years. A parasite from Cuba was introduced into Florida. For some years work was carried on at Brownsville, Texas, and more recently, in response to local demands, some observations were made near Beaumont, Texas. A limited amount of work has been done in Mexico and Cuba.

In addition to regular duties, very valuable cooperation has been maintained with Dr. George N. Wolcott, an entomologist of much experience in West Indian and South American countries. Correspondence has been carried on at one time or another with entomologists in nearly every sugar cane country of the world.

Gaps in Stands of Sugar Cane

By GEORGE ARCENEAUX
Office of Sugar Plants, Bureau of Plant Industry,
U. S. Department of Agriculture

A review of the various factors which tend to decrease production of sugar cane per acre in Louisiana, and to increase the cost of production, leads to the conclusion that the poor, gappy stands of cane which are almost invariably found on a portion of the acreage under cultivation on any plantation represent an important factor. In the most severe cases, these gappy areas not only give no profit, but are a burden to be carried by the remaining acreage where better stands are found. In other instances, and this ap-

plies to a much greater proportion of the acreage, fair to indifferent stands of cane occur and the yields, although fairly good, fall short of the production capacity of the soil.

The following are some of the unfavorable results of gaps in cane:

(1) Increased cost of production per ton of cane because of lowered yields.
(2) Increased per-acre cost of cultivation because of additional weeding made necessary.
(3) Uneconomic use of fertilizer. (Much of it applied in gaps either leaches out or is used by weeds.)
(4) Lowering of general level of sugar content of crop by inducing late green "suckers".
(5) Increased freeze susceptibility resulting from the reduced effectiveness of the "foliage blanket".

It is generally conceded that gaps 30 inches or more in length will have a depressing effect on cane yields, but it is probable that even shorter ones are harmful.

It goes without saying that it is much better to prevent gaps than to replant them later on. The follow-

ing are some of the most important controllable causes of poor stands:

    (1) Poor drainage.
    (2) Poorly prepared seed bed.
    (3) Inadequate quantity of seed planted. (Two "running stalks" of sound cane should give a satisfactory stand under favorable conditions.)
    (4) Badly bored or otherwise unsound seed.

Gaps originating in the plant cane, because of their long duration are the most objectionable and should therefore receive primary consideration. These become particularly undesirable in the case of varieties such as C.P. 807 and Co. 281 which promise an even greater number of profitable stubble crops than the varieties now being generally cultivated.

While the replanting of gaps in cane, which must necessarily be largely hand work, is not usually done in Louisiana, our experience has been that gaps in the plant cane can be replanted to very good advantage, provided it is done in the early spring. With fall planted cane it will generally be possible to detect gaps by the latter part of March or the first part of April. Seed-material at that time will generally be at an advanced state of germination and will have to receive careful handling in order to avoid breaking off the shoots. If much foliage has developed, it should be cut back to prevent wilting. This work will be most successful if the soil is in good tilth and should preferably be done when the ground is not too dry.

Good Work

The Executive Committee of the American Sugar Cane League, at a meeting held February 26, 1931, officially awarded the buck horns for grinding the largest tonnage of cane during the past grinding to the Raceland Factory of Godchaux Sugars, Inc., as forecast in the last issue of the SUGAR BULLETIN. While the executive management of Raceland is doubtless responsible for the magnitude of that factory's cane supply, the task of getting 144,205 tons through the mills was up to the operating officials, who were: Horace Nelson, Manager; E. C. LeBlanc, Chief Engineer; W. E. McFarland, Superintendent; John Chauvin, Assistant Superintendent; W. Bondurant, Chief Chemist. It is proverbial in the Louisiana sugar district that lost time is at a minimum at Raceland. In rain or shine or freeze or flood they manage somehow or other to crash the gates of the mill and boiling house records and come through smiling. It takes a good operating staff to do that.

Sugar Fed to Hogs

The *Honolulu Advertiser* of February 5, 1931, contains the following article relative to some experiments made at the University of Hawaii in feeding raw sugar to hogs. We have not gotten that far along here in the direction of selling our sugar "on the hoof" but the principle is the same as is involved in feeding molasses and the figures arrived at are interesting. The article says:

"A new outlet for raw sugar during times of low prices has been found by the agricultural department of the University of Hawaii, which has just completed experiments showing that the cost of fattening swine is materially reduced by the feeding of raw sugar.

"The experiment was repeated three times, using 18 pigs each time, a total of 54 swine in all. In each trial, the pigs were divided into groups of six, the groups being fed different mixtures of feed. The division was made as evenly as possible in regard to ancestry, sex, age, weight, condition and other factors.

"The first lot of pigs was fed a mixture of 88 lbs. of barley, 8 lbs. of tankage, 2 lbs. of linseed oil cake meal, 1 lb. of steamed bone meal and 1 lb. of salt. In the second lot, five pounds of sugar was substituted for an equal weight of barley and in the third lot ten pounds of barley was replaced by sugar.

"In practically all cases faster and more economical gains were secured by the addition of sugar. There were a few inconsistencies in that some experiments showed best results with the use of five per cent sugar, while others registered the greatest gain when the feed containing ten per cent sugar was used.

"Professor L. A. Henke, head of the department, explained the inconsistencies by saying, 'Obviously, these were cases where the individuality of the hogs was a bigger factor than the ration that was fed to them.'

"Henke said, 'While in the States last year, I took up the matter of raw sugar feeding with the men in charge of animal nutrition at Illinois, Iowa, Colorado, Florida, Louisiana, New York and Wisconsin universities. Practically all of them expressed themselves as being interested in our experiments but none of them seemed willing to initiate work along this line.' Henke added that unless it can be demonstrated that the feeding of raw sugar will result in a decided economy in animal production, other investigators will continue to remain disinterested.

"Professor Rosco Snapp, associate professor of animal husbandry at the University of Illinois, seemed to feel

that the matter of palatability of feeds is a factor to which we have not given sufficient weight in our studies of animal nutrition, according to Henke.

"The United States department of agriculture is doing some experimental feeding with raw sugar furnished them by the Crockett refinery.

"The University dairy herd is now being used in an experiment on molasses feeding and will not be available for use in a raw sugar test for some time."

		Lot A No Sugar	Lot B 5% Sugar	Lot C 10% Sugar
Number of pigs in experiment	Exp. I Exp. II Exp. III	6 6 6	6 6 6	6 6 6
Length of experiment	Exp. I Exp. II Exp. III	84 days 112 days 84 days	84 days 112 days 84 days	84 days 112 days 84 days
Initial average weight of pigs	Exp. I Exp. II Exp. III	44.3 lbs. 54.11 lbs. 88.8 lbs.	44.3 lbs. 52.83 lbs. 88.1 lbs.	45.3 lbs. 53.64 lbs. 89.6 lbs.
Final average weight of pigs	Exp. I Exp. II Exp. III	120.5 lbs. 163.5 lbs. 180.9 lbs.	135.3 lbs. 174.06 lbs. 179.2 lbs.	141.1 lbs. 173.06 lbs. 202.7 lbs.
Average daily gain per pig	Exp. I Exp. II Exp. III	.90 lbs. .98 lbs. 1.1 lbs.	1.08 lbs. 1.08 lbs. 1.09 lbs.	1.14 lbs. 1.07 lbs. 1.35 lbs.
Total feed cost per pound of gain	Exp. I Exp. II Exp. III	$ .147 .143 .138	$ .136 .133 .143	$ .111 .137 .118

Circumstances Alter Cases

Editor Sugar Bulletin:

An inquiry from the management of a large sugar cane plantation in the Tropics well illustrates the fallacy of attempting to apply measures of control against an insect in a certain country to those of a country having entirely distinct climatic conditions. This refers to the planting of corn adjacent to cane fields to act as a trap for cane borers.

The only reason such a measure has ever been advocated in Louisiana is due to the fact that in a subtropical country, such as this, there is a very distinct dormant period and that corn planted in the early spring will produce exuberant foliage which can attract borer moths, emerging after hibernation, away from the much less exuberant early spring growth of sugar cane. Even so, this measure may be considered as rather a two-edged sword in Louisiana, due to the fact that when the trap corn reaches a stage where it should be destroyed—about the time the first borers start to form the pupæ—this corn may not be destroyed, either through negligence on the part of the grower or through a desire to obtain a few "roasting-ears" before getting rid of the corn. In such a case, naturally, as the borers breed more rapidly in corn than in cane, we have simply furnished a preferred breeding place to the borers, in which a larger supply of moths will have been produced to oviposit in the adjacent cane fields.

In the tropics, on the contrary, cane grows continuously, hence there could be no possible advantage from such a trap crop, whereas one would be planting in close proximity to his cane fields a crop which is susceptible to almost all of the diseases and insects attacking cane. This may safely be discouraged in the Tropics.

Arthur H. Rosenfeld, Consulting Technologist,
American Sugar Cane League.

Liquid Sugar

(By C. J. BOURG)

There is nothing new under the sun. The liquid sugar controversy is hailed everywhere as a modern development and a compliment to the ingenuity of American industrial giants. Yet it was precisely ninety-nine years ago that an appeal was made to the United States Supreme Court from the State of Louisiana, known as U. S. vs. 112 Casks of Sugar, 8 Peters (33 U. S.) 275, and we find the same conflict of opinion as to when a mixture of sugar and water is a syrup and when not.

The facts were that a seizure was made in the Port of New Orleans under the Customs Act of 1799, of the casks of sweet mixture, which the importer claimed was "syrup" and the collector contended it was "sugar in a partial solution in water." The Collector of Customs was allowed under the law to seize any imports which were in his opinion fraudulently entered to defraud the revenue. It will be interesting to sugar people to read what the Tariff Act of 1832 provided, viz:

Par. 16. On brown sugar and syrup of sugar cane, in casks two and one-half cents per pound; and on white clayed sugar, three and one-third cents per pound.

Par. 17. And be it further enacted that syrup imported in casks, and all syrup for making sugar, shall be rated by weight and pay the same duty as the sugar of which it is composed would pay in its natural state; and that loaf or lump sugar, when imported in a pulverized, *liquid*, or other form, shall pay the same duty as is imposed by law on loaf or lump sugar; and all fossil and crude mineral salt shall pay fifteen per cent ad valorem.

The decision of the Supreme Court of the United States in this matter makes comments which are not without humor for the sugar barons who are still debating in the century-old fashion.

"It is difficult to say what is its true denomination. Witnesses speak of it as a new article not known to trade. None call it sugar. All seem to think it may be called sirup, in some cases, though several think it is not such, according to the understanding of the articles in trade and commerce."

The official record of the Court reports the case as U. S. vs. 112 Casks of *Sugar*, and so it is referred to today.

The Treasury Department has ruled that the im-

portation of sugar, raw or refined, by using the subterfuge of mixing water with it to the extent that
there is in the mixture less than 48 per cent total
sugars, shall be considered as falling under the provisions of Paragraph 1559, which states that "on
articles not enumerated, manufactured of two or
more materials, the duty shall be assessed at the
highest rate at which the same would be chargeable
if composed wholly of the component material thereof
of chief value."

The United States Customs Court has set March
27, 1931, on the Savannah calendar for opening the
hearing on the protest of the Savannah Sugar Refining Company against this ruling. The case will not
be closed for about thirty days and it will be about
three months before a decision is made. The decision may be appealed to the United States Court of
Customs and Patent Appeals, and this latter Court's
decision is subject to the review of the Supreme
Court of the United States on a writ of certiorari.
These various steps will require at least one year, if
all of them are resorted to. Should the court of first
instance decide that the Treasury ruling should be set
aside, a suspensive appeal may be filed immediately
and all importations will continue to come in under
the Treasury ruling and the higher rate of duty will
have to be paid (under protest) in each case until
the court action becomes absolutely final.

The always existent uncertainty of court action and
the delays which seem to be a part of the court's
dignity, have led the friends of the domestic sugar
industry and of the United States Treasury to seek
congressional action eliminating any and all ambiguity
in the Tariff Law regarding liquid sugar.

Trichogramma Egg-Parasites

On page 3 of this issue of the SUGAR BULLETIN appears an advertisement inserted by Dr. A. W. Morrill of Los Angeles, California, in which he offers to
supply Trichogramma Egg Parasites for the control
of the cane borer in any number required. This advertisement is inserted with the approval of Dr. W. E.
Hinds of the Louisiana Experiment Station, and Dr.
Morrill may therefore be communicated with without
any doubts as to the bona fide nature of his offer.

It will be recalled that some 18 months ago the
Executive Committee of the American Sugar Cane
League discussed the possibility of raising a fund by
individual subscription to carry on the propagation
of the Trichogramma egg parasite, the parasites to
be sold, just as Dr. Morrill is doing, but the money
was not subscribed and nothing was done. Dr. Morrill now offers a supply of these parasites produced
by him in his Los Angeles insectary and he ought to
receive a large number of orders.

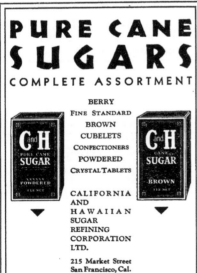

Verdict of the 1930 Season

Advantages of Cyanamid

High analysis—22% nitrogen.
Less material to handle.

Excellent Mechanical Condition
Drills freely, uniformly, accurately.

Unsurpassed Residual Effect
Built on a lime base; contains 75% hydrated-lime-equivalent to sweeten the soil and the juice.

Resistant to Leaching
Louisiana's heavy rains won't wash it out of the soil.

Progressive Availability
Feeds the crop uniformly, steadily, in proportion to its needs.

Crop-Sustaining Power
"Stays with the crop" through the critical periods of growth.

Convenient "One-Man" Package
Packed in 100-lb. sacks that do not leak.

Tested and Proved
For years, successfully used in the Louisiana Sugar Bowl. Used by 102 leading Louisiana cane planters in 1930—37 more than the number who used it the year before.

Application-Economy
Adapted for large-scale operations.

Purchase-Economy
Today's outstanding nitrogen fertilizer "buy".

The 1930 season in Louisiana's "Sugar Bowl" was a severe test for *any* fertilizer. Spring was a month late. Fertilizer application was delayed until well on in April. The long, severe Summer drought was followed by rains in September, October, and November. Cane growth was prolonged and the cane was green at harvest.

In the face of these unfavorable factors, Cyanamid gave excellent results---paid big profits. The average yield increase, produced by applications of 200 pounds of Cyanamid per acre in a dozen carefully conducted tests, was over 750 pounds of 96° sugar per acre.

One ton of Cyanamid produced nearly 4 tons of sugar. For every dollar invested in Cyanamid there was an increase of six dollars worth of sugar.

Performance like this explains the preferred position which Cyanamid enjoys in the regard of Louisiana's sugar planters. Cyanamid has performed "consistently and well"---in good seasons and in bad seasons. It is dependable, economical, profitable.

A complete, detailed report on the results of the 1930 experiments with Cyanamid will be mailed to anyone upon request. Write—

American Cyanamid Company

Pioneer Producers of Air-Nitrogen Products in America

535 FIFTH AVENUE, NEW YORK

1820 JEFFERSON AVENUE   **NEW ORLEANS**

AERO BRAND
CYANAMID

Circulation of this Issue 1900 Copies

THE
SUGAR
Dr. Chas. E. Coates,
Baton Rouge, La.
BULLETIN

Entered as second-class matter April 13, 1925, at the postoffice at
New Orleans, La., under Act of March 6, 1879.

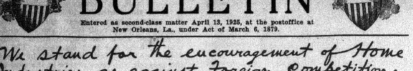

We stand for the encouragement of Home Industries as, against foreign competition.

| Vol. 9 | NEW ORLEANS, LA., MARCH 15, 1931 | No. 12 |

Liquid Sugar

The center of the stage in domestic sugar circles has been held for the past several weeks by the controversy over the importation of the so-called liquid sugar, which is a mixture of sugar and water that is claimed by its importers to be dutiable under paragraph 502 of schedule 5 of the tariff act of 1930 which refers to molasses and syrups and not under paragraph 501 of that schedule which refers to sugar. Inasmuch as the difference in the rate of import duty between the two classifications is very great there is not only a dangerous menace to the domestic sugar industry in the contentions of the importers, but also a menace to the revenues of the United States Treasury, which, if the importers succeed in getting the so-called "liquid sugar" admitted under the rates of paragraph 502, will lose upwards of a hundred million dollars a year in import duties.

Paragraph 501 of the Tariff Act of 1930 (the sugar schedule) provides a rate of duty on sugars and mixtures of sugar and water testing between 50 and 75 degrees, of 1.7125 cents per pound, with an increased rate for each sugar degree up to 100. Based on the Cuban rate, the duty on 96 degree sugar is 2.00 cents per pound, and on 100 degrees 2.12 cents.

Paragraph 502 (the molasses and sirup schedule) levies a duty of one-quarter cent per gallon on molasses and sugar sirup, not specially provided for, testing not above 48 per cent total sugars, with 275/1000 of a cent additional for each per cent above 48.

Since the passage of the Tariff Act of 1930, importers have discovered a preservative to prevent fermentation or inversion, by the use of which they can take a sugar of, say, 96 degrees or above, which ordinarily would pay a duty from 2 cents to 2.12 cents per pound, and by simply diluting it with water, reduce the sugar content of the liquid below 48 per cent and enter it under paragraph 502 at a quarter cent per gallon. After the mixture has passed through the customs house, it is a simple and inexpensive matter to evaporate the water, and then run the sugar through the refinery.

It is estimated that each gallon of liquid contains from 5 to 7 pounds of sugar, so that based on the dry substance obtained, the importer pays a duty of about 1/20 of a cent per pound instead of from 2 cents to 2.12 cents per pound.

On October 4, 1930, the Treasury Department ruled that sugar entered in liquid form should pay the rate of duty levied in paragraph 501, the sugar schedule. Since that time entries of "liquid sugar" under paragraph 502 have been stopped, but one of the importers has protested the Treasury's decision, and the matter is to be tried in the courts.

The possibility of making an attempt during the last days of the recent session of Congress to correct the verbiage of schedule 5 so as to make it impossible to evade the plain intent of the

THE
SUGAR
BULLETIN

407 Carondelet St., New Orleans

Issued on the 1st and 15th of each month. Official Organ of the American
Sugar Cane League of the U. S. A., in which are consolidated
The Louisiana Sugar Planters' Assn.
The American Cane Growers' Assn.
The Producers & Mfgrs. Protective Assn.
Subscription Price, 50 Cents Per Year.

Reginald Dykers, General Manager & Editor of the Bulletin
301 Nola Bldg., New Orleans
Frank L. Barker, Secretary and Treasurer
Lockport, La.
C. J. Bourg, Manager Washington Office
810 Union Trust Building

CHAIRMEN OF COMMITTEES:
C. D. Kemper, Franklin, La.
President of the League and Ex-Officio Chairman of Executive Committee
Andrew H. Gay, Plaquemine, La,
Chairman Agricultural Committee
David W. Pipes, Jr., Houma, La.
Chairman Industrial Committee
Frank L. Barker, Lockport, La.
Chairman Finance Committee.
Edward J. Gay, Plaquemine, La.
Chairman Tariff Committee
H. Langdon Laws, Cinclare, La.
Chairman Legislative Committee
J. C. LeBourgeois, New Orleans, La.
Chairman Freight Rate Committee
R. H. Chadwick, Bayou Goula, La.
Chairman Membership Committee
A. H. Rosenfeld, New Orleans, La.
Chairman Publicity Committee

Members of the League desiring action on, or information on, any subject are invited to communicate with
the League or with the Chairman of the Committee
to which it seems to appertain.

law was considered but the calendars of both
the House and Senate were so congested that
the plan was abandoned, and the whole matter
will consequently have to go before the courts
for decision. It seems hardly possible that such
a palpable subterfuge can succeed. Certainly
it was not the intent of Congress that importers
of either raw or refined sugar should be allowed to escape payment of the prescribed
duties by simply adding water to the imported
product.

The complaint of the Savannah Sugar Refining Corporation of Savannah, Georgia, one of
the importers of liquid sugar, will be heard
before the United States Customs Court at Savannah on March 27, 1931. The complaint seeks
to have the ruling made by the United States
Treasury Department on October 4, 1930, re-
versed. Both the United States Treasury Department and the Domestic Sugar Producers'
Association, of which the American Sugar Cane
League is a member, will oppose the plea of the
Savannah Sugar Refining Company, through
counsel, before the Customs Court.

Another case that brought forth a special
ruling by the United States Treasury Department was comprised in the importation at New
Orleans on December 16, 1930, of a quantity of
so-called "sugar syrup" from Cuba, this "sugar
syrup" being made in Cuba by boiling down a
mixture of sugar and water with an inverting
agent to make a virtually saturated solution
testing 31.98 per cent sucrose and 44.97 per cent
invert sugars, according to the Customhouse
Chemist at port of entry. The United States
Treasury Department took this case under advisement and, on February 24, 1931, ruled in
favor of the contention of the importers that
the material was a sugar syrup within the
meaning of paragraph 502 of the law and that
it differed from the "liquid sugar" importations we have just been discussing. The ruling
did not go into details, but as will be seen from
the analysis, the total sugars in the case of the
New Orleans entry were 76.95 per cent and the
material was approximately a saturated solution, although the actual sucrose content was
only 31.98 per cent. Such importations under
paragraph 502 are bound to be harmful. Many
industries can use the invert sugar as well as
the sucrose. It will all be sugar to them, for
their purposes, yet it will come in as syrup at
a nominal rate of duty. A fruit canner, for
instance, can use a syrup which has been partially or completely inverted as readily as he
can use a white sugar solution.

The Soy Bean Caterpillar

At the meeting of the League's "Contact Committee" with the Louisiana Experiment Station officials
on January 23, 1931, the fact was brought out by Dr.
W. E. Hinds that the soy bean caterpillar had appeared on our plantations in considerable numbers
in September and October, 1930. The importance of
the visitation was such that both Dr. Hinds and his
assistant, Dr. B. A. Osterberger, gave considerable
time to its study, and they prepared a report on the
pest which was presented at the meeting of the
American Association of Economic Entomologists at
Cleveland, Ohio, on the 31st of last December.

Dr. Hinds is one of the ablest, hardest working and
most conscientious scientists we have ever had at our
Louisiana Experiment Station, and we desire to say
nothing but good of him. The fact, however, that he
reported to the Contact Committee, with no doubt a
certain amount of honest pride and a perfectly satisfied conscience, that a serious caterpillar pest attacking Louisiana soy beans had been studied by himself
and his assistant and that the result of these studies,
which we will assume for the sake of argument cost
roughly about a thousand dollars of Louisiana money,
had been reported, not to the Louisiana farmers affected, but to a meeting of his fellow scientists in
Cleveland, Ohio, shows that even the best of our
Experiment Station people do not realize that their
investigations, findings and discoveries are supposed
to be for the benefit of the farmers in their own state
or locality, rather than being a means through which
they can impress the importance and scope of their
work on their fellow scientists at conventions.

The SUGAR BULLETIN confesses to a profound ig-

The Advertisers in the Sugar Bulletin are contributing towards the support of the American Sugar Cane League and should enjoy your special consideration; help them to help the Domestic Sugar Industry by doing business with them whenever possible.

norance concerning the soy bean caterpillar, his habits, innate deviltry, destructiveness and how to get rid of him. Dr. Hinds did not send us his report, or the gist of it. If he had, we would print something about it so that the Louisiana farmers who read this publication would become informed. A lot of scientific gentlemen, from perhaps all of our forty-eight states, who met in Cleveland, Ohio, last December, know all about it, but what good does that do the Louisiana farmers whose soy beans are attacked?

This is not written in any captious or fault finding spirit. It is written in sorrow and discouragement. The obsession of Experiment Station workers, not only in Louisiana but everywhere else, that they are laboring in the interest of the scientific cult rather than to help and instruct the farmers in their vicinage is hard to understand. When they do issue a bulletin or report, in nine cases out of ten it is couched in language that only a scientific man can wholly comprehend, indicating that the author, either consciously or sub-consciously, is writing for the benefit of his own scientific reputation and not much else.

If the kindly criticism implied in this article is shown to be without foundation no one will be more pleased and gratified than ourselves, and we not only invite but earnestly solicit the submission of evidence to show that we are "all wet." We ask, however, that the evidence be something more specific than a general denial.

The Capper Award

Last fall the American Sugar Cane League put forward the name of Dr. E. W. Brandes, Principal Pathologist in Charge of the Office of Sugar Plants, Bureau of Plant Industry, U. S. Department of Agriculture, as the most deserving recipient of what is known as the Capper Award, which is an annual award consisting of a medal and substantial sum in cash made possible by Senator Arthur Capper of Kansas, and bestowed for the most distinguished service rendered to agriculture during the year. The attitude of the American Sugar Cane League was of course due to the fact that Dr. Brandes was primarily responsible for saving the entire cane sugar industry of the United States from destruction by introducing the mosaic resistant P.O.J. canes.

The award for 1930, however, was not made to Dr. Brandes; it was made to Dr. Stephen Babcock, the father of the method of determining the amount of butter fat in milk. The simple apparatus by which Dr. Babcock accomplished the butter fat determination was given to the world free. He never attempted to patent it, although he could have made an enormous fortune out of it. All this took place about forty years ago, and Dr. Babcock followed it up by a long list of achievements that have distinguished him as a man seeking to benefit humanity through the discovery of various factors bearing on nutrition and food

values. In awarding the 1930 Capper prize to him the committee in charge of the award doubtless did its duty conscientiously. We still believe, however, that Dr. Brandes thoroughly deserves this distinguished recognition for the remarkable work he has accomplished in connection with the agricultural side of one of the most important domestic industries, that of cane sugar.

The Contact Committee

Minutes of Meeting of American Sugar Cane League Contact Committee with Louisiana Experiment Station Workers, Baton Rouge, La., February 13, 1931

The meeting was called to order by Mr. Percy Lemann presiding as Chairman in the absence of Mr. Wallace. Mr. Taggart received messages from Mr. Wallace stating "Regret that business is holding me away" and from Mr. Jones "Regret very much that I will be unable to meet with the Committee on Friday".

Soil Survey Report

Dr. Hurst explained by the use of a diagram which represents a triangle the "triangle arrangement" as a method of arranging and interpreting results of fertilizer experiments. The five fertilizer experiments conducted last year were at Cinclare, Belle Terre, Mandalay, Race. land and the Roy field at Lafayette. Mr. O'Neal stated that at the end of last year he and Mr. Breaux had com. pleted in a reconnaissance way quite a little study of the soils of the district. There were certain indications that they wanted to follow up and study more carefully. They are continuing this year the study of the soils of the sugar cane district as a whole. During 1929 they col. lected a large number of samples all over the district to determine if chemical reaction, acidity, could be corre. lated with certain soil types. There was a slight trend along that line but they did not have enough samples to justify definite conclusions. With the cooperation of the plantation owners in the different soil type regions, they are hoping to carry on further experiments along this line.

Dr. Dowell stated that this fertilizer report would be published in the very near future.

The subject of fertilizers was discussed, and Mr. Lem. ann stated that he found nitrogenous fertilizer on corn paid, no matter what crop had proceeded. He stated that the good stand of corn that Mr. Taggart has on the Station properties is not the general rule in the Sugar Belt.

Mr. G. H. Reuss stated that for 1930 he was just completing in the field the income-expense survey. In this survey he was getting all the cash-outlays, yields, inventories, prices received, etc., so that for each farm he will have a financial summary of operations for the year 1930.

Report on Animal Investigations

A nine-page mimeographed progress report by Dr. M. G. Snell and Mr. W. G. Taggart (Animal Industry Circular No. 2) was presented by Dr. Snell. This circular is for distribution upon request.

This experiment was started in the summer of 1929 to ascertain the cheapest and best method of feeding farm work horses and mules in Louisiana and to determine the value and extent to which molasses can replace corn in rations for farm work mules. In the first test, six teams of two mules each were divided into two lots so as to be as nearly alike as possible in weight, age, and sex, one mule from each team being placed in each lot. The mules of a team were worked together in order to equalize the amount of work done by each lot. All mules were weighed once a week on Monday morning. Water was available in the feed lot at all times. The mules were fed twice daily, noon and night. In order to secure an accurate record of feed consumption, the mules were closed in their stalls at feeding time until each mule had finished eating; then the mules were driven out, the barn closed, and any feed left in the trough weighed. Following the evening feed, the mules were left in their stalls overnight. Lot I mules received shelled corn in their feed troughs and soybean hay in the hay racks. Lot II mules received blackstrap molasses and cut soybean hay in their feed troughs and uncut soybean hay in their hay racks. These mules received one pound of molasses for every pound of shelled corn fed their mates. The molasses was mixed with rather finely chopped soybean hay at feeding time and only enough of the chopped hay was fed to take up the molasses. On days when the mules were not at work, they received only the night feed. When they were idle for several days in succession, they were turned to pasture without feed. Both lots of mules gained during the sixty-two-day feeding period, but the corn-fed mules gained 81 pounds as compared to 46.7 pounds for the molasses-fed group. All mules in each lot were from all outward appearances in good health and condition. However, toward the end of the feeding period, the molasses fed mules began to refuse part of their feed, winded easily, and were unable to do heavy, hard work during the hot summer days. From the standpoint of cost, the molasses ration was much the cheaper. The experiment was discontinued.

On May 26, 1930, molasses feeding work was resumed, the same group of mules being used as in 1929, except that another team was added making a total of seven mules to each lot. In this trial the mules were not closed in their stalls at feeding time. Instead the barn and lot space was divided so as to furnish each group of mules with comparable lot and stall space and watering facilities. The tests were run for two periods of 126 days each. At the end of this period, the rations were interchanged; Lot I mules receiving the Lot II ration, and the Lot II mules the Lot I ration. Weights were taken on three consecutive days at the beginning and end of each period and on Tuesday of each week. The mules were fed twice daily, one-third of the grain and molasses ration being fed at noon and the remainder plus the hay at night. On days when the mules were idle, only the night feed was fed. Over the period of 252 days, the mules receiving the three pounds of molasses gained on the average 3.93 pounds each, while the mules receiving double this amount or six pounds lost 9.45 pounds per mule. This difference in live weight may indicate (1) a slight difference in the feeding value of shelled corn and molasses or (2) that the extra cob and shuck in the Lot I ration had some nutritive value. In general appearance and condition, no difference could be noted. The mules in both lots worked satisfactorily even during the periods of heavy work of cane harvesting and the preparation of cane land. If molasses is fed to replace a part of the corn in a work mule's ration, the results show that molasses can be fed in place of corn grain up to six pounds per mule per day, and the replacement value of molasses is equal to that of corn grain pound for pound to this point. The feeding of the molasses in place of corn resulted in a lowering of the cost of the rations. This work is being continued.

Sugar Cane Variety Report for Season 1930-31

A ten-page mimeograph progress report was presented by Mr. Simon.

On February 27, 1930, we were sent 123 new varieties of sugar cane from the United States Breeding Station, Canal Point, Florida. These are the most promising varieties that we have yet received. Many of them were equal to our standard canes in sucrose analysis and some of them were superior as plant cane. A noticeable characteristic of these new varieties is their comparative freedom from disease, most of them being very healthy in appearance. In a few cases mosaic was noticed and, of course, some of the minor diseases showed up. Of the older varieties, CP. 807, Co. 281 and Co. 290, we now have enough of all three to give yield figures and comparisons. The variety CP. 807 seems to have the characteristics of early growth and of maturing a fair sucrose content comparatively early, increasing this content but little later on. This variety has shown great vigor ever since it has been under cultivation at the station and has given tonnages surpassing all other varieties up until 1930-31. It seems to be very healthy, showing no mosaic disease and comparatively little damage through minor troubles.

Co. 281 has given very good results at the station both in yields of cane and yields of sugar per acre, as plant cane, first stubble cane and second stubble cane. It seems to have a tendency to sucker on until late in the season. Another characteristic seems to be that this variety has a sucrose content almost comparable with P.O.J. 234. Here at the station it does not appear to be as early a maturing variety as P.O.J. It matures later on in the season, maturing fast when it does start. The erect mode of growth of this cane should make it a desirable type for some sections of Louisiana, particularly those sections to which the D-74 seemed to be best adapted and most generally planted before the advent of the P.O.J. varieties. This variety has shown a small amount of mosaic disease.

The variety Co. 290, which as yet has not been tested under all conditions throughout the state, and of which we necessarily know little except the observations here at the station, has shown itself to be the most vigorous cane at present grown on the experiment station. In tonnage per acre, last season, it ranked well ahead of CP. 807, both as plant cane and as stubble cane. In sucrose content, it ranked with P.O.J. 213.

The varieties Co. 290 and CP. 807 were both up to a stand and could have been fertilized the last week in March, whereas our standard varieties did not reach that condition until April 29.

Comparisons of Windrowed and Standing Canes, Seasons of 1929-30 and 1930-31

A fourteen-page mimeographed progress report was presented by Mr. Simon.

In the canes windrowed and standing for the two seasons, 1929-30 and 1930-31, we have a direct comparison. In each case the varieties were the same. The date of windrowing is nearly the same, there being one day's difference, the plats this season being windrowed on December 2, those last season December 3. The weather previous to the dates of windrowing was also similar, there being a rain on November 24, 25 and 26, 1929, of 2.28 inches, as against a rain on November 28, 1930, of 1.50 inches. The conditions at time of windrowing were favorable in both cases, the ground being moist and the temperature cool, the only variance being in the condition of the canes. Those of the 1929-30 season were killed much more thoroughly than those of the 1930-31 season; also the canes windrowed in the 1929-30 season were more crooked than those of the 1930-31 season, with the two exceptions, P.O.J. 36-M and Co. 281. In addition, a great many more borers were prevalent in the canes last year than this year, especially in the variety P.O.J. 213. The seasonal weather after windrowing in 1929-30 was much more severe than the weather for the corresponding time in 1930-31. The results of the two tests show some variation in the keeping qualities of some of the varieties for the two seasons.

In the season 1929-30, P.O.J. 36-M was the variety which kept best in the windrow, holding its own in purity until January 16 with slightly increasing acidity, the acidity at that time being only 2.8 cc. It then began to break, but lost purity slowly until February 3, at which date the acidity had gone above 4 cc., which point would probably mark the point of satisfactory millable cane. P.O.J. 213 came second, holding until January 6, with slightly increasing acidity, the acidity at the time being 3.3 cc. It then began to break very slowly, almost holding its own in acidity and purity until January 27, the acidity on this date being 4 cc. Co. 281 came third. It held its purity until January 9, acidity rising to 3.4 cc. After this date deterioration began and the acidity rose very fast, on January 13 being 5.9 cc.

P.O.J. 234 came fourth, holding its own well until January 6, at which time it had an acidity of 3.5 cc., breaking at this point. The analysis on January 9 showed that this variety had begun to lose in purity and

had increased very much in acidity, being 5.3 cc., by January 13. CP. 807 came last, keeping the poorest of any of the varieties. December 27 marks the date of the last normal analysis of this variety. At this time, however, the acidity had begun to show signs of rising. The acidity had gone to 4 cc. on January 9.

In the standing cane for the 1929-30 season, all varieties kept well until December 16, at which date P.O.J. 234 began to show signs of deterioration, dropping in purity. On December 20 the varieties P.O.J. 213 and CP. 807 both began to show signs of decreasing in purity. The varieties P.O.J. 36-M and Co. 281 both held up until December 27, after which date they were unmillable. The acidity of the P.O.J. 36-M was lower than that of the Co. 281, but the purities in both cases were as good as the initial purities on December 3. The severe cold weather from December 18 to 26, followed by rising temperatures on December 27 and 28, was responsible for all varieties of standing cane deteriorating rapidly. All of the canes under test had been split by the cold and showed rapid increase in acidity as soon as the warmer weather came. Previous to this time this standing cane in no case showed acidities high enough to cause trouble in milling.

The results of the 1930-31 season do not show that any of the varieties kept better than the previous year, while some of them did not keep at all. However, this was to be expected. The freeze of November 27, 1930, killed the buds on the cane here at the station, but there were many eyes not killed even on exposed canes and occasional buds were not killed. The condition of this freeze brought the cane to the critical point, but was insufficient to entirely kill the plant. The usual examination made within two days after the freeze might have led one to feel justified in windrowing. At this time the tops, although still green in color, upon being cut open showed dead growing points and would seem to justify the belief that the canes were sufficiently killed. The tops did not entirely lose their green color until acted upon by further freezes later on in the season, and all canes windrowed under these conditions did not keep satisfactorily.

The variety which kept best in the windrow in the 1930-31 season was P.O.J. 213, which almost held its own in purity and acidity until January 28. Co. 281 was second, almost holding its own in both purity and acidity until January 28, although in purity it held almost as well as P.O.J. 213, its acidity being higher throughout. P.O.J. 234 came third, showing a breaking in purity on January 7, after an initial drop in purity of 10 points from the first analysis to the second on December 10. The acidity, however, did not seem to rise very much. P.O.J. 36-M came fourth, showing an almost immediate deterioration in the windrow. The acidity, however, was very low even though the cane had gone to pieces in the windrow. CP. 807 came last, breaking worse than P.O.J. 36-M as soon as windrowed, but the acidity in this cane showed a considerable rise from the normal even at the time of the second analysis on December 10.

The standing canes of these varieties for 1930-31 tell an entirely different story. The most outstanding cane is P.O.J. 36-M, which ranks first in keeping quality as standing cane. This variety did not show any real break in purity until January 21, 1931, its acidity being below 3 cc. until that date, at which time the acidity was 3.6 cc., which would have still been millable cane.

P.O.J. 213 ranks second, holding its purity well until January 7, when it began to drop, and the acidity began to rise considerably, being then 3.8 cc., as against 2.7 cc. for the analysis of the previous week. P.O.J. 234 seems to come third, but with a steady drop in purity from the original analysis. December 31 marks the break in purity of this variety. A week later the purity showed a considerable drop and an increase in acidity from 2.7 cc. on December 31 to 4.6 cc. on January 7. Co. 281 comes fourth. This variety shows a drop of about 5 points between the first and the second analysis, but seems to have then kept its purity fairly well until January 14, when it took a sharp drop in purity and increased a great deal in acidity from 3.4 cc. on January 7 to 5.9 cc. on January 14. CP. 807 is last. It began to show a sharp drop in purity on December 31, with also a decided increase in acidity.

The indications shown by the two sets of analyses seem to lead one to the belief that the variety P.O.J. 36-M as standing cane will consistently stand much colder weather than any of the other varieties, increase in acidity but slowly—both standing and windrowed—and keep better standing than any of the other varieties. Examinations of the stalks of standing canes of all of these varieties at different dates during the 1930-31 season bear out this opinion. The stalks of P.O.J. 36-M standing showed less signs of deterioration than any other varieties.

A very large amount of data was collected from plantations covering the greater part of the cane territory in 1929-30. A study of this data corroborated our findings for that year to the effect that where cane was properly windrowed and comparative records kept, the windrowed cane was good into January.

Cane Freezing Experiments 1930-31

Mr. Whipple presented a two-page mimeographed progress report on cane freezing experiments.

Freedom for the Philippines

(By C. J. BOURG)

Freedom for the Philippines is to receive early attention of next Congress. Although the jam of legislation at the end of the recent session of Congress did not permit the consideration of any subject which would cause as much debate as Philippine independence, there exists an agreement by which the Chairman of the Senate Committee on Territories and Insular Affairs will call up for action the bill to free the Philippines, introduced jointly by Senators Hawes of Missouri and Cutting of New Mexico.

Since the Democrats generally are in favor of releasing the Philippines, and a substantial number of independent Republicans feel the same way, there hardly remains any doubt that the bill will be passed by the Senate. Heretofore, the Republican majority has made it impossible to expect any action from the House, but with the membership evenly divided as to party in the Seventy-second Congress and a growing sentiment among the mid-western farmers against retaining these islands, we may even expect favorable action in the lower house. As long as Mr. Stimpson is Secretary of State we may also anticipate that the President will veto any bill for Philippine independence, hence it will be necessary to educate the public generally on the merits of this legislation so that their views may be reflected in the next Congress, to the extent of at least a two-thirds majority.

In a general way, the Hawes-Cutting Bill (S. 3822) may be said to contain four major purposes, as follows:

(1) To provide for drafting of a constitution for

10 *Minute Handling* of CANE MUDS

... the key to reduced inversion losses brought about by the use of Oliver United Cane Mud Filters.

BUT a few minutes are needed for the hot defecated settlings to be drawn from the tank and pass to the Oliver United filter to be "dewatered", washed and then discharged. For example, in an important Brazilian Central the time interval for this complete step is less than ten minutes.

Thus, by taking out the impurities so quickly, inversion losses are minimized.

Accompanying this reduction in inversion losses, is the negligible mechanical loss of sucrose in the cake. Thorough washing reduces this to $1/4$ the loss with presses. And finally, spillage losses, always present in a filter press station, are eliminated.

Oliver United Cane Mud Filters offer sugar producers a sure way of reducing not only total costs of handling, but unit costs of sugar.

a free and independent government of the Philippine Islands:

(2) To provide for a ratification by the Philippine people of the constitution so formulated, and the election of governmental officials under the new constitution:

(3) To provide a 5-year period of test for the gradual change in the economic and political relationship between the islands and the United States, thus giving the Philippine people an actual experience of such relationship, and an opportunity, following such experience, to decide at a plebiscite whether they approve or disapprove of separation from the United States:

(4) To provide, in the event of an affirmative vote in the plebiscite, for the final withdrawal of American sovereignty over the islands, with such agreements by treaty or otherwise as may be necessary for the protection of American rights and properties in the Philippines, the liquidation of the public debt of the Philippines, and the retention by the United States of sites for coaling or naval bases as the United States may deem advisable.

During the "test" period and under the constitution to be adopted by the Philippine people for this period, the United States, in pursuance of the terms of the bill reported, remains in complete supervision and control of every step taken by the Philippine people toward Philippine independence, and is not to relinquish the islands finally until the provisions of the bill shall have been satisfactorily complied with and until the Congress of the United States shall have approved both the constitution to be framed by the Filipinos and every other step in their progress toward competence as a self-governing people.

The new government having been thus formed and installed, trade relations between the United States and the Philippines shall be, during the 5-year period, upon the following basis:

(a) During the first year, trade relations shall be as at present.

(b) During the second year, 25 per cent of existing duties shall be levied upon all articles imported into the United States from the Philippines, and on all articles imported into the islands from the United States;

(c) During the third year, 50 per cent of such duties shall levied:

(d) During the fourth year, 75 per cent of such duties shall be levied;

(e) During the fifth year, full duty shall be levied upon imports to both countries in the same manner as on all foreign imports.

The proposals for the gradual application of tariff duties during the period of transition from the present status to complete independence were adopted from the provisions of a bill introduced by Senator Vandenberg.

Should the Philippine people fail to ratify the proposal for independence in the plebiscite, the bill provides that tariff relations between the islands and the United States shall be restored to the present basis.

Circulation of this Issue 1900 Copies

THE La. State University, Baton Rouge, La.

SUGAR
BULLETIN

Entered as second-class matter April 13, 1925, at the postoffice at
New Orleans, La., under Act of March 6, 1879.

We stand for the encouragement of Home Industries as against Foreign Competition.

| Vol. 9 | NEW ORLEANS, LA., APRIL 1, 1931 | No. 13 |

Planning Borer Control for 1931

By W. E. Hinds, Entomologist, Louisiana Experiment Station

At the meeting of the Contact Committee with the Experiment Station staff on March 13, the matter of securing the most effective possible borer control through the coming season was discussed. The Entomologist hopes to be of some service to the sugarcane planters by discussing through the columns of THE SUGAR BULLETIN in future issues, in brief, timely articles, some of the phases of the problem on which we feel that we have available at this time information which may be helpful to the planters in studying their own situations and in applying the most effective methods of borer control which may now be available and appropriate.

At the very bottom of the problem lies the determination of the general condition of borer infestation, especially early in the season, or from the latter part of May to the middle of July. The prospects for the scarcity or abundance of moths from the over-wintering larvæ in any season depends upon at least two principal factors. First, the abundance of borers in the cane at planting and harvest times and, second, the favorable or unfavorable conditions of rainfall and minimum temperatures, earliness or lateness of spring, etc., which may affect the percentage of borers entering hibernation which may survive and produce moths to deposit the first generation eggs.

During the fall of 1930 it was the general report that borer infestation in cane was unusually light. Seed cane, as a rule, was exceptionally clean and free from infestation. This fact should mean generally better stands, and much less initial borer infestation in the fields of plant cane this season. In the fields of cane standing late in the fall there was some increased infestation in the tops from the late-developing larvæ. However, there were very few fields seen by the writer or reported to him where the tops of 213 showed a degree of borer infestation which would

be considered even as heavy as "light" in an average season. The early freezing of much of the cane meant low topping and this gave a very large amount of trash on the ground and unusually large basal sections in these tops. Both of these factors were rather favorable for the borers therein. Subsequent burning was generally unusually incomplete. This factor favored the escape of an unusually large proportion of the borer larvæ present at the time of burning. The climatic conditions of the winter have also been rather favorable generally to borer survival. The sum of these considerations leads us to the conclusion at this time that we must anticipate a decidedly "spotted" condition of borer infestation at the beginning of this breeding season. Borer infestation generally appears likely to be "light". However, it seems quite certain that there will be fields occasionally where the borer population was "fairly heavy", where topping was low, burning was poor and soil drainage good, where the survival will be quite heavy and a later heavy infestation will be in prospect. Planters should watch their fields for such a situation.

The borer population in top trash at this time may be found fairly accurately by splitting open the thicker parts of tops and noting the ratio of the number of tops examined per 1 living stage of borer found. If this ratio is less than 50 to 1, we would consider it fairly high and threatening. If the ratio is more than 100 to 1, we would consider the surviving borer population to be "light" and the situation not threatening at this time.

The occurrence of "dead hearts" among the cane sprouts during April and May is worthy of some investigation. Dead hearts may result from cultural injuries, from the attack of the sugarcane beetle, and even from unfavorable growth conditions, aside from those that result from borer infestation. An examination of

THE
SUGAR
BULLETIN

407 Carondelet St., New Orleans

Issued on the 1st and 15th of each month. Official Organ of the American Sugar Cane League of the U. S. A., in which are consolidated
The Louisiana Sugar Planters' Assn.
The American Cane Growers' Assn.
The Producers & Mfgrs. Protective Assn.
Subscription Price, 50 Cents Per Year.

Reginald Dykers, General Manager & Editor of the Bulletin
301 Nola Bldg., New Orleans
Frank L. Barker, Secretary and Treasurer
Lockport, La.
C. J. Bourg, Manager Washington Office
810 Union Trust Building

CHAIRMEN OF COMMITTEES:
C. D. Kemper, Franklin, La.
President of the League and Ex-Officio Chairman of Executive Committee
Andrew H. Gay, Plaquemine, La.
Chairman Agricultural Committee
David W. Pipes, Jr., Houma, La.
Chairman Industrial Committee
Frank L. Barker, Lockport, La.
Chairman Finance Committee.
Edward J. Gay, Plaquemine, La.
Chairman Tariff Committee
H. Langdon Laws, Cinclare, La.
Chairman Legislative Committee
J. C. LeBourgeois, New Orleans, La.
Chairman Freight Rate Committee
R. H. Chadwick, Bayou Goula, La.
Chairman Membership Committee
A. H. Rosenfeld, New Orleans, La.
Chairman Publicity Committee

Members of the League desiring action on, or information on, any subject are invited to communicate with
the League or with the Chairman of the Committee
to which it seems to appertain.

---

a considerable number of dead hearts to determine
the cause of injury will help in revealing the condition
of borer infestation.

In addition to the foregoing, the planter and his
managers especially should watch closely the earliest
developing corn on the plantation, or near thereto;
for the "leaf perforation" and other signs of cane
borer infestation. These signs are well known to
most cane growers. They may reveal the centers of
concentration of borer infestation in the first generation and accordingly, may indicate the areas where
special borer control measures should be applied.
These measures will be discussed more fully in later
articles. In the meantime by giving attention to the
signs of borer infestation which we have indicated, the
planter may be securing exceedingly important information which will enable him to decide whether he
may wish to undertake borer control in any areas by
colonization of the egg parasite, *Trichogramma minu-
tum*, in an effort to increase natural control by this
enemy of the borer, or whether the borer population
of the first generation may be reduced in numbers
before the moths emerge by feeding out heavily-in-
fested corn before the moths emerge therefrom.

We shall expect to discuss later the conditions under which the egg parasite may be held in storage
awaiting favorable climatic conditions for their release in the field, and how they may be distributed
so as to secure the maximum benefit from this effort
at borer control.

The Liquid Sugar Case
By C. J. Bourg

The protest of the Savannah Sugar Refining Corporation upon the tariff rate charged by the United
States Government, on an importation of a mixture
of sugar and water, came up for hearing at Savannah, Georgia, Friday March 27th, before the U. S.
Customs Court, Judge W. J. Tilson, presiding. This
is the well-known and much-discussed "liquid sugar"
case.

The Assistant Attorney General of the United
States, Hon. Charles Lawrence, represented the Treasury Department, assisted by counsel specially employed by the Domestic Sugar Producers' Association, the Hawaiian Planters' Association and your
representative.

The importer has designated the material as a
"sugar syrup", but the papers of importation show
that this material was brought in for the purpose of
producing a refined sugar. The importer tendered
payment of $1.68 for duty at the rate of one-fourth
of one cent per gallon, under paragraph 502 of the
Tariff Act. The Collector of Customs required a payment of $116.07, which the corporation paid under
protest.

Only three witnesses were called by the protesting
importer and these merely testified to the facts sur-
rounding the importation, all of which are shown by
the papers in the case, and the analyses of the material imported. There was nothing to indicate what
the legal position or plan of action of either side
would be, from the testimony adduced. The Attorney General did question the corporation's chemist
regarding the use of formaldehyde in the mixture
imported, as a preservative to prevent fermentation.

The Government analysis of the imported material
is as follows:

$$
\begin{array}{rl}
\text{Brix} & 47.6 \\
\text{Polarization} & 45.5 \\
\text{Sp. Gravity} & 1.21863 \\
\text{Sucrose} & 45.54 \\
\text{Invert} & .42 \\
\text{Total Sugars} & 45.96
\end{array}
$$

The Savannah Sugar Refining Corporation submitted an analysis of:

51.5% water
45.71 sucrose
.44 reducing sugars
46.15 total sugars
2.35 ash, etc.
net weight 8499 pounds.

The Savannah Station of the Food & Drug Administration, Department of Agriculture, submitted an
analysis which shows that .04% of formaldehyde was
found in the mixture.

The containers were eight black iron drums, which
were supposed to have been sealed in Cuba, but they
arrived without evidence of sealing and the weight
at Cuba was 309 pounds less than the weight a
point of debarkation.

As there was no argument or discussion of the
legal features of the case, outside of the introduction
of testimony, no comment can be made upon tha
most interesting side.

The matter has now been transferred to the Third
Division of the United States Customs Court, which
is composed of three judges and will sit at New

The Advertisers in the Sugar Bulletin are contributing towards the support of the American Sugar Cane League and should enjoy your special consideration; help them to help the Domestic Sugar Industry by doing business with them whenever possible.

York on Monday, April 27, 1930, to complete the hearing.

It is obvious that no discussion of the legal battle which will come in New York, would be proper in view of the unwillingness of either party to "show its hand" by the introduction of testimony, other than that referred to above. We can anticipate that there will be lexical combat among the chemists, experts and tradespeople to determine when sugar is sugar, and whether it has to be called a syrup when it is all wet. At least, we may be sure that the Court will have to determine upon several definitions of sweetness in various forms, in addition to recognizing the very patent fact that the imported mixture, call it what you will (and the attorney for the importer called it "sugar dissolved in water" when examining a witness), is being brought in as a liquid for one purpose only and that is to avoid paying the rate of tariff duty that Congress intended should be paid. The question is whether it will be construed as a legal subterfuge.

Cane Condition

(A special Sugar Cane Appropriation Report, Department of Plant Pathology, Louisiana Experiment Station, on March 13, 1931.)

Studies on the condition of the cane were made at weekly intervals from the time the cane was cut in the fall up until the present time.

The weather conditions have been quite different from that of the preceding fall and winter. With a cool, dry fall, there was very little development of either plant or stubble cane in the fall, and with January and February being rather warm, spring development began earlier than usual.

Plant Cane: Most plant cane had only begun development when cold weather stopped growth. M36, Co. 281, and C.P. 807 made but little growth, while the other varieties, especially C.P. 177* and P.O.J. 234, in favorable locations had shoots to the surface of the ground. There were but few roots on the seed pieces. During the winter, these roots remained comparatively healthy, though by February, many of the roots of D-74, P.O.J. 213, and P.O.J. 234 had entirely or partially rotted. In the spring development of the shoots, P.O.J. 234, P.O.J. 213, D-74, C.P. 177* and Co. 290* are the most advanced. New roots on seed pieces are up to 3 inches in length. However, even at the present a comparatively small number have developed shoots. C.P. 177* and P.O.J. 234 have shoots above the ground, while P.O.J. 36, P.O.J. 36M and Co. 281 have barely begun growth.

Stubble: Even early cut cane showed little development during the fall. P.O.J. 213, P.O.J. 234, Purple, D-74, and C.P. 177* showed the most development and had shoots above the ground. C.P.

807 and Co. 281 showed less, while P.O.J. 36 and M 36 showed practically none. The shoots that developed for the most part started before the cane was cut. These had a few roots of their own. Late cut cane showed practically no development except for the naturally developing shoots. These had roots.

During the winter and up until the present, there has been comparatively little decay. However, early cut P.O.J. 213, P.O.J. 234, and D-74 for the most part show rotted eyes and shoots, while P.O.J. 213 and P.O.J. 234 still retain from 1 to 4 good eyes.

At present, all varieties have started growth, ranging from M 36 with eyes swelling to C.P. 177* and P.O.J. 234 with shoots 6 to 8 inches above ground. The first shoots out, excepting those that started in the fall, have largely developed from the upper eyes. Late cut cane of all varieties except possibly D-74 shows practically all eyes good.

In the main, the condition of the cane at the present time is much better than that of a year ago. This seems to be due to a less amount of root rot. The better root system at the present time should permit the plants to develop more rapidly.

Red Rot Investigations

A. Effect of red rot organism on sugar cane roots: It was thought to be of some interest to determine whether the red rot fungus is capable of rotting the roots of sugar cane. Preliminary tests in the laboratory had shown that under the most favorable conditions *Colletotrichum falcatum* is capable of causing slight rotting of cane roots. In order to test this out in the greenhouse, pots of sterilized sugar cane soil were inoculated with pure cultures of the red rot fungus, and seed pieces of Purple cane planted in the pots. They were kept in the greenhouse at a temperature of from 70° to 90° F. until the plants had reached a height of about two feet. The soil was then washed away from the roots and they were carefully examined. Most of the roots from the inoculated plants were as healthy as those from the controls, but a few roots had reddish lesions on them caused by the red rot. This test indicates that red rot is not to be considered as an important factor in the rotting of cane roots.

B. Varietal Inoculations: On September 30, 1930, fifty stalks each of C.P. 177*, C.P. 807, P.O.J. 213, P.O.J. 36-M, Co. 281, P.O.J. 234 and 10 stalks of Co. 290* were inoculated with a strain of red rot known to be parasitic on cane. The cane was bedded down behind the greenhouse where good drainage could be provided. On the three dates given in the table, some of the cane was taken up and examined. The total length of the rot in the stalk, the number of joints infected, and the comparative severity of the rot were recorded. The figures given in the table represent the averages of the total number of stalks examined at each date. The number of plus

signs indicates the relative severity of the rot, one plus indicating very slight rot, while five plus signs indicate very severe rot.

Table 1. Results of variety inoculations with red rot, cane inoculated and bedded down September 30, 1930. Cane taken up and examined at 3 different dates in 1931. The plus signs indicate relative severity of rot, one plus shows slight rot, and five plus signs indicate severe infection.

	Examined—Jan. 15			Examined—Feb. 19			Examined—March 9		
Variety	Number Joints infected	Length of rotted area (inches)	Comparative severity of rot	Number Joints infected	Length of rotted area (inches)	Comparative severity of rot	Number Joints infected	Length of rotted area (inches)	Comparative severity of rot
*C.P. 177	4.7	34	++++	5.6	35	+++++	5.0	33	++++
C.P. 807	4.9	30	++++	5.0	32	+++++	4.7	28	+++++
POJ 213	4.0	27	+++	3.5	26	+++	3.1	22	+++
*Co. 290	4.0	35	+++	6.0	39	+++			
POJ 36M	3.3	20	+++	5.2	25	+++	4.0	25	+++
Co. 281	3.8	26	++	3.2	20	++	2.8	21	++
POJ 234	2.5	18	+	3.0	20	++	3.3	20	+++
	15 stalks of all except Co. 290—5 stalks Co. 290			5 of Co. 290, 15 of others			15 stalks of each. No Co. 290 was examined		

An examination of the table shows that C.P. 177* and C.P. 807 are quite susceptible to the disease under the conditions of this test. P.O.J. 213 and Co. 290* are slightly less susceptible, P.O.J. 36-M is moderately susceptible, while Co. 281 and P.O.J. 234 are quite resistant.

There was a considerable development of red rot between the January 15 and the March 9 examinations. On the last date, secondary organisms had begun to develop and complete the rot started by the red rot organism. Many stalks of C.P. 177* and C.P. 807 were completely rotted when examined March 9.

* Not released.

National Co-operative Dehydrated Hay Association

A very interesting conference was held at Reserve, La., on February 25, 1931, under the auspices of Mr. Walter Godchaux, and under the chairmanship of Mr. Howard T. Greene, of Wisconsin, for the purpose of discussing our stock feed producing possibilities in Louisiana and taking steps to develop and expand this industry.

Mr. Greene addressed the meeting and stated the general topics to be considered were the growing of suitable forage crops, the harvesting and the drying of the crops. It was suggested that the drying of the crops be discussed first.

Mr. Carl Nadler stated that he felt it should be decided whether or not there was any objection to cutting hay into short lengths as this was a necessary step in the use of the Arnold, Koon and Louisiana type driers. It was agreed that there was no objection to cutting other than the fact that it made baling more difficult. Mr. Godchaux's experience with baling cane tops and hay in a Celotex type baler was cited as a proof that even when cut into very short lengths hay could be successfully baled.

Mr. Greene stated that dairy cows prefer the hay in meal form and will eat off grade hay when ground to meal which they would refuse before being ground. He said that at Brook Hill Farm they were grinding all hays to meal including the sun cured hays. Dr. J. C. Robert of the South Mississippi Experiment Station said grinding to meal would make the hay more digestible. Mr. Greene said they had once experienced some trouble from impaction from very fine ground meal, but that they had had no other trouble on this account. Molasses eliminates the dust trouble *but molasses costs $60.00 a ton in barrels in Wisconsin.*

Mr. Greene stated that Louisiana shippers should ship meal with molasses content. It was stated that soy bean hay ground to meal absorbs ½ gallon per ration.

Mr. J. J. Munson stated that the South Coast Company was feeding 1½ gallons of molasses per day per mule, using some cotton seed meal to furnish protein. Mr. W. G. Taggart of the Louisiana Experiment Station gave results of molasses feeding tests at L. S. U.

Mr. Greene said that alfalfa meal sells for $5.50 per ton more than #1 baled hay in Wisconsin, the freight rate is $2.00 less per ton. Mr. H. N. Hefferman said the cold process of rubbing molasses into the meal is better than the hot process and recommended the use of thicker molasses than is usually sold on the market. The suggestion was made of drying to 5% moisture and mixing with heavy molasses. It was agreed that hay driers are a success commercially. It was stated that ensilage cutters of the flywheel type instead of the lawn mower type will cut to ¼″ and if back geared to ⅛″ cut. Mr. Nadler stated that due to irregularity of feed, much of the hay is improperly cut with any ensilage cutter. Mr. Whipple told of improved cutting with 16″ McCormick Deering Ensilage cutter after removing half the fan blades to reduce the power load and running faster than rated speed. It was agreed that finer breaking up of fibre is desirable and that this phase of the process needs development.

Mr. Greene spoke about the report soon to be released by Burlingane, King and Duke, whose business is management of farms and country estates, giving costs of drying hay in the different types of hay driers; also a report of Professor Duffee, University of Wisconsin, giving results of a survey made by him. The cost per ton included depreciation and interest on investment with fuel oil 5 cents per gallon, coal $5.00 per ton, labor 40 cents per hour and varied from $23.70 per ton to $6.32 per ton. The lowest cost per ton was in the rotary drum type and the highest quality of the product was in the Koon type drier. The Jeffers product had a distinct burnt taste, the Arnold product a slightly burnt taste and the Koon product very little burnt taste. Mr. Greene promised to send copies of the reports to members as soon as they were off the press. Mr. Greene reported a test showing protein and calcium content of alfalfa hay dried in the laboratory, in the field under ideal conditions which could not be approached on a large scale, and in his Koon and Arnold driers in Wisconsin.

Lab. Sample	Field Dry Ideal	Koon	Arnold
Protein 19.6	18.3	17.65	16.25
CaO 2.2	1.98	1.90	1.73

The calcium content and protein in the leaves are more than twice the percentage in the stems, so that the figures for the driers indicate leaf loss. Flue gas analyses show: For the Koon drier, about 6.2% CO_2 and 11 to 13% oxygen; for the Arnold drier, 3.4% CO_2 and 17% oxygen. Mr. Greene stated that he was absolutely committed to the Rotary drier, that its fuel efficiency was very high and that he favored caacities of 6000 pounds of moisture per hour or igher.

The subject of standard data sheets for recording rying operations was discussed and Mr. William Vhipple of the Louisiana State University was reuested to draw up such a form. It was decided that he difference between the weight of green hay and ry hay could be considered the moisture removed.

Mr. Greene described the method of harvesting sed by him, using a Farmall tractor with mower atachment and side delivery rake. The hay is loaded nto International Dump 1-ton truck, with a hay oader attached, which dump at a cement platform nto a pit where it takes five or six men to feed one utter and one hay drier. The use of a cutter in he field and suction fan with one man at the spout vould cut down the labor cost at this dryer point. Iarvesting machines can be used to cut and elevate ut will not chop up. A set of crushing rubber rollrs are being used on the Pacific Coast for drying lfalfa in the field.

A resolution was unanimously passed requesting L. . U. Experiment Station to investigate methods of reparing forage crops for hay driers by a finer breakig up of fibre.

The Mason type harvester was described by Mr. Godchaux and Mr. Muntz gave his experiences in cuting corn and soybeans in the field with a Ronning orn harvester and feeding the drier with a suction an..

The growing of crops for hay driers was then disussed. Mr. Greene stated that grain is probably ot necessary for cows if hays with the proper mixure of proteins are produced, since cows naturally at grasses only.

Alfalfa proteins seem to make other proteins availble and digestible. Heavy nitrogen fertilization inreases the protein in grasses in a marked degree. he number of days to make hay crops is not yet etermined if cutting is to be done at period to roduce highest protein per acre. It is necessary to lan crops to keep hay drier busy without swamping y too much at one period, such as cutting from irge acreage of alfalfa.

Mr. A. Montz of LaPlace, La., stated that he sold is corn and soybean meal for about $20.00 per ton rithout molasses and about $25.00 per ton with molsses, he was able to put more weight in a sack with lolasses.

Dr. Graves' method of "rehydrating" hay to reemble pasture grass by moistening with steam was iscussed. Wide leafed oats and other leafy crops rere discussed. Dried thistles contain 16% protein. Dried Melilotus Indica does not taint the milk and Ir. Greene said a carload bought from Mr. Montz ave very good results in Wisconsin. Dr. Robert said eef cattle in Mississippi thrive on Mellilotus Alba nd get very fat. Lespedeza does very well in acid ind in Mississippi. Alsike should grow in the delta s it is similar to White Clover. Mr. Godchaux said lsike does well in poorly drained land on Red River. ed Clover will cut four tons on first cutting. The ifficulty of curing is probably the reason for not rowing it, as it grows waist high. Sudan grass grows verywhere and cows like it, but people are afraid to row it because the seed resembles Johnson grass. rotalaria has been grown by Dodson and Robert in

Louisiana and Mississippi with extremely heavy yields. White Clover crops have possibilities in selling the seed and saving the hay.

Mr. Greene stressed the fact that quality of feed is most important in marketing and it is necessary to harvest at an earlier stage than the South is accustomed to. The marketing of legumes is no problem; Northern mills are now asking for 2,000 tons. The freight rate on all the Eastern Coast will not be prohibitive. In the West we must compete with western meals. State boards will recommend good feeds.

Alfalfa if cut in next few weeks before flowering state will make leaf meal worth $45.00 f.o.b. Minneapolis and will run 20% protein. It is necessary to

adjust freight rates and railroads will be glad to d so if approached.

Mr. Jeffers is interested in feeding the Walke Gordon herds only artificially dried hay which con tains seven times the vitamin A content of naturall cured hay and thus produces superior milk. He wi buy a large amount of suitable dehydrated hays.

It was decided to organize an association with com mittees to study the different problems, to be calle National Cooperative Dehydrated Hay Associatior

The above report was furnished to THE SUGA BULLETIN by Prof. Wm. Whipple who acted as Sec retary of the meeting.

Moth Borer Damage to Different Varieties of Sugar Cane

Editor Sugar Bulletin:

In an interesting little article under this title i the "Journal of Economic Entomology" some tim ago, Messrs. Holloway and Haley gave as an explana ation of the fact that, after the P.O.J. canes replace the striped and purple in the Argentine Republic damage by the moth borer ceased to be a problem the following:

"The new varieties have given a number o stubble crops in Argentina as against one or tw stubble crops of the old varieties. This means tha less and less cane is planted, and more and mor springs up each year from the stubble. Now it ha been found that a dangerous source of borer infesta tion is in the planted stalks, the borer larvæ develop ing in the stalks into issuing adults making their wa through the slight covering of soil ready to ovapos on plants of the grass family. Thus, the less can there was planted, the fewer borers were planted i the stalks, and as more and more of the long stu bling varieties were planted, the hibernating larv were progressively reduced."

This theory, while an ingenious one, and supe ficially sound, must be abandoned as it is based on a absolutely erroneous hypothesis that the old canes i the Argentine produced only one or two stubble crop As a matter of fact, in the old days in the Argentin with the old striped and purple varieties, eight an ten stubble crops were not particularly uncommo and the average up to the time of their replaceme by the P.O.J. varieties was between four and fiv stubble crops. While it is true that the P.O.J. can seem to produce several more stubble crops than tl old native cane, inasmuch as sixth, seventh and eigh year stubble has been largely handled in recent crop just the opposite conditions to those assumed by H loway and Haley prevailed during the period th reduced borer damage was particularly noticeable the Argentine. That is to say that, during the yea 1917 to 1920, the entire cane area of the Province Tucuman was being laid down to the new varietie and in these years, which coincided with a subsiden of moth borer injury, larger proportions of plant ca were probably harvested than in any similar peric before or since in the history of Tucuman cane cu ture.

Furthermore, we have to face the fact that, dt to the world's surplus of sugar during the past fe years, there has been little cane planted in Tucuma

nce about 1924. Nevertheless, despite the fact that
ıe last four crops have been very largely of stubble
ıne, borer damage has again been on the increase
uring these years.

Arthur H. Rosenfeld.

Tew Orleans, Jan. 12, 1931.

CONFERENCE ROOM
The American Sugar Cane League takes
plasure in offering a comfortable

PRIVATE CONFERENCE ROOM

to any of its members who may have occasion to use it. Business conferences in
New Orleans may thus be held in a
secluded and entirely neutral atmosphere,
which is sometimes preferable to using the
office of one of the conferring parties.
No advance notice necessary. Just use the
room at your convenience.

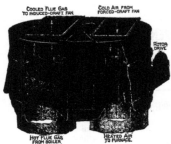
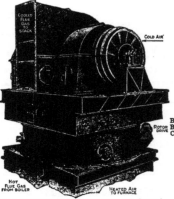

Circulation of this Issue 1900 Copies

Dr. Chas. E. Coates,
Baton Rouge, La.

May 14   May 14

THE
SUGAR
BULLETIN

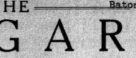

Entered as second-class matter April 13, 1925, at the postoffice at
New Orleans, La., under Act of March 6, 1879.

*We stand for the encouragement of Home
Industries as against foreign competition.*

Vol. 9	NEW ORLEANS, LA., APRIL 15, 1931	No. 14

Watching for Centers of Borer Concentration

By W. E. Hinds, Entomologist, Louisiana Experiment Station

In studying this matter we must consider the two principal host plants of the sugar cane borer which are corn and sugar cane. The comparative degree of infestation in these two crops may depend upon a number of factors, but seems to vary especially with the stage of development of each crop at the time that the moths from the over-wintered generation are most active in laying their eggs. Thus if corn is larger and growing thriftily at this period, the moths will tend to concentrate their egg laying upon this crop; while otherwise their eggs will be scattered through the cane.

Innumerable observations have shown conclusively that corn is a more favorable host plant for the borer than is cane. The borer population per stalk of early garden corn may run up to more than 50 borers, while it is rare that more than a single larva develops in a stalk of cane in the early part of the season. We have always found it far easier to locate borer stages in corn than it is in cane during the first two generations particularly. This condition of concentration should be looked for especially in the earliest maturing corn whether it be planted in gardens for roasting ears or in the fields for forage.

Undoubtedly thriftiness of growth, relative height of stalks and density of tops, as well as the stage of maturity of the host crop, are factors in this attractiveness to borer moths for their egg deposition. It has been found by tests under comparable conditions where several rows of several varieties of corn and sorghum have been planted on the same date and with the same conditions of soil fertility, cultivation, borer infestation, etc., that sweet corn is more attractive to the borers and develops a higher borer population to maturity than does field corn, sorghum, etc. We know that the elimination of corn on any plan-

tation will not exterminate the borers or prevent some degree of infestation, but it is certainly logical to believe that any borer control measures which can be economically applied and which will serve to reduce materially the borer population maturing especially during the first and second generation, will certainly result in a reduction in the borer population developing later in the season and reduce the damage inflicted by these borers on the crop of cane. Examinations made on a number of plantations on which corn was planted and used as an early forage crop for the work stock showed in 1927 at harvest time an average of 12% of the joints bored as compared with over 17% on a group of plantations where corn was planted also but allowed to mature. The transfer of borer moths from maturing crops of corn to fields of cane during July and August when most of the corn matures is a well-known fact and the damage inflicted on cane increases very rapidly, as a rule, after this time.

The signs of borer attack on either corn or cane may be seen most plainly during the first and second generations by watching the leaves for the occurrence of the typical feeding work of the young borers which is done in the leaf roll. As soon as the borer larvæ hatch from the eggs, they travel as directly as possible to the leaf roll of the stalk and there find shelter and extremely tender food and begin their feeding by burrowing into, or through the very tender central rolled leaves. When these leaves unfold later, this feeding appears as pin holes, often arranged in a straight line with three to five holes extending at almost uniform intervals across the blade of the leaf. This work is done by the first and second larval stages and cannot be confused with the work of the corn ear worm in the bud of the stalk, which is much coarser, larger holes and with more ragged edges.

THE
SUGAR
BULLETIN

407 Carondelet St., New Orleans

Issued on the 1st and 15th of each month. Official Organ of the American
Sugar Cane League of the U. S. A., in which are consolidated
The Louisiana Sugar Planters' Assn.
The American Cane Growers' Assn.
The Producers & Mfgrs. Protective Assn.
Subscription Price, 50 Cents Per Year.

Reginald Dykers, General Manager & Editor of the Bulletin
301 Nola Bldg., New Orleans
Frank L. Barker, Secretary and Treasurer
Lockport, La.
C. J. Bourg, Manager Washington Office
810 Union Trust Building

CHAIRMEN OF COMMITTEES:
C. D. Kemper, Franklin, La.
President of the League and Ex-Officio Chairman of Executive Committee
Andrew H. Gay, Plaquemine, La.
Chairman Agricultural Committee
David W. Pipes, Jr., Houma, La.
Chairman Industrial Committee
Frank L. Barker, Lockport, La.
Chairman Finance Committee.
Edward J. Gay, Plaquemine, La.
Chairman Tariff Committee
H. Langdon Laws, Cinclare, La.
Chairman Legislative Committee
J. C. LeBourgeois, New Orleans, La.
Chairman Freight Rate Committee
R. H. Chadwick, Bayou Goula, La.
Chairman Membership Committee
A. H. Rosenfeld, New Orleans, La.
Chairman Publicity Committee

Members of the League desiring action on, or information on, any subject are invited to communicate with
the League or with the Chairman of the Committee
to which it seems to appertain.

Real Progress in the Louisiana Sugar Industry

*By Arthur H. Rosenfeld, Consulting Technologist of
the American Sugar Cane League.*

So much has been published of late regarding the
debacle of the world's sugar industry, especially since
prices, caused by overproduction in the Tropics,
dropped last year to figures far below cost of production in the lowest-cost countries—a condition which
must manifestly correct itself—that a brief statement
regarding the present outlook for the "white gold"
industry of the Pelican State will probably be in
order.

According to the estimate of Mr. Lionel L. Janes
of the United States Bureau of Agricultural Economics, there were about 114,000 acres of cane in Louisiana in 1927, which represented, however, only some
22,000 acres of *P.O.J.* varieties which have since put
the Louisiana industry, producing only 47,166 tons
of sugar in 1926, back on the map, the 1929 crop
totalling 199,609 tons. The 1927 *P.O.J.* cane furnished us with enough seed that fall to lay down
another 114,00 acres in these vigorous and heavily
producing varieties, and last year's cane acreage,
almost entirely in *P.O.J.* cane, reached 171,000 acres,
after a 200,000-ton sugar crop had been made. I
want to say categorically and emphatically that *I am
convinced that the Louisiana cane crop has staged a*

comeback, and a very dramatic one at that. Whi
this past year has been a very difficult one, due
the cold, rainy winter and spring followed by one
the longest droughts known and all-time low pric
for both sugar and molasses, we have made a fai
satisfactory crop under conditions that would ha
caused a complete crop failure with our old can
and there had been a tremendous demonstration
the hardiness of the new canes and a splendid ince
tive to their planting which, with a return to anythi
like normal sugar prices, is inevitably going to res
in far larger acreages than in the "good old days" a
total crops still larger in proportion, inasmuch as t
per-acre yield of the new varieties sponsored by t
American Sugar Cane League, in cooperation wi
the Federal Office of Sugar Plants and the State E
periment Station, is materially larger than that of t
old canes at their best.

Although somewhat ancient history, it should
stated that in 1926, despite the fact that the larg
amount of our *P.O.J.* cane supply was located
Southdown Plantation near Houma, in the very hea
of the district most ravished by one of the earlie
severe hurricanes recorded in Louisiana, that of t
25th of August, the *P.O.J.* canes produced 150% be
ter crops than the average for the entire State, ar
in every mill test which we were able to make, wi
the limited amount of the new cane which we fe
willing to divert from planting that year, the *P.O.*
canes showed up superior in analysis to the old can
under the same conditions—this difference worki
out at 15 to 20 pounds of sugar additional per ton
cane ground. In recent crops, with much larg
yields per acre all around, the superiority of t
P.O.J. canes has again and again been demonstrat
in similar proportion.

We feel that the adaptability of the *P.O.J.* can
to Louisiana conditions and their ability to put tl
Louisiana sugar industry once more on its feet ha
been absolutely demonstrated by the results obtain
in the State during the past three very difficult yea
so that we can look forward with confidence to tl
industry in a very short time assuming a more pron
nent position amongst the State's major industri
than ever before in her history.

Plant Pathology Work at Baton Rouge

*Report on the work of the Department of Pla
Pathology of the Louisiana Experiment Stati
during 1930 by C. W. Edgerton, E. C. Tims,
J. Mills, T. C. Ryker.*

During 1930, investigations were continued on t
following subjects: (1) Studies on root developme
of sugar cane; (2) root rot; (3) red rot; (4) Pokk
bong disease; (5) mosaic; (6) disease resistance
new seedlings.

1. *Root Development:* The principle cane var
ties, 36-M, P.O.J. 36, P.O.J. 213, P.O.J. 234, Co. 2
C.P. 177 and C.P. 807, act very much alike in rega
to root development, the chief differences being
rate and extent of development. The development
roots on the seed pieces is necessary for normal sh
growth. These roots furnish water for the you
plant. If these rot during the early part of the w

The Advertisers in the Sugar Bulletin are contributing towards the support of the American Sugar Cane League and should enjoy your special consideration; help them to help the Domestic Sugar Industry by doing business with them whenever possible.

r, shoot development will be slow. Such a condition occurred in 1929-30. The complete destruction these roots means the loss of nearly a month's owth in the spring. The development and growth the winter and spring of both plant and stubble ine is governed by moisture, temperature and soil inditions. If there is considerable root and shoot owth in the fall, and a wet, severe winter follows, ere may be serious deterioration of the shoots and es. This condition is more apt to occur with P.O.J. 4, P.O.J. 213, and the native canes than with Co. 1, 36-M, and P.O.J. 36. The latter varieties delop more slowly and are not as severely injured by cay organisms during the winter.

There is a correlation between shoot and root owth though it is modified by moisture conditions the soil. During the spring of 1930 the young ots and shoots were about the same length, while 1929, the roots were nearly twice as long. In a dry ason, the roots tend to go downward in the soil and t as many are found in the surface layers. In avy soils, there is a greater concentration of roots the upper layers than in light and sandy soils. The plication of fertilizer to one side of the row did not em to cause a greater production of roots on that le. In stools suffering from root rot, the weights both tops and roots were decreased. The ratio, wever, between the weights of the tops and roots is about the same as with healthy plants.

2. *Root Rot*: A number of soil treatments, made heavy and light soil, failed to increase the elds over the controls in P.O.J. 213 plant and stube cane. This confirms the results of previous years, ich have shown that various chemicals applied to e soil have not reduced the amount of root rot to y appreciable extent.

Studies were made on the effect of corn and grass Pythium development in the field. There were appreciable differences in the root systems or in e numbers of parasitic Pythiums on the roots of veral cane varieties which were grown in fields folwing corn and in fields kept free from corn and asses for two years. The possible effect of Pythium ot rot of mosaic-infected cane as compared to moic-free cane has been a question of some interest.

a test in the greenhouse, selected and unselected 74 and mosaic-free and diseased P.O.J. 36-M were oculated with Pythium. The Pythium injured the althy cane as badly as it did the diseased plants both varieties. The D-74, however, was much re severely attacked by the Pythium than the O.J. 36-M.

3. *Red Rot*: A large number of varietal inoculans have been made with cultures of red rot to demine varietal susceptibility. These tests have wn that P.O.J. 234 and Co. 281 are most resist of the varieties generally grown. P.O.J. 36-M slightly less resistant, P.O.J. 213 and Co. 290 are

moderately susceptible, while C.P. 177, C.P. 807, and Purple are very susceptible. The results of these inoculation tests only show relative susceptibility to artificial inoculations, and may not show the reactions of the varieties under field conditions. While C.P. 807 is quite susceptible to artificial inoculation, it is apparently not injured in the field. This may be due to the unusual hardness of the rind and the comparatively small amount of borer injury. A number of strains of the red rot organism have been found which vary in their ability to rot the different cane varieties. There seem to be physiological strains of this fungus occurring in the cane fields. This may account for some of the severe outbreaks of red rot which sometimes occur in Louisiana. This line of investigation is being continued.

4. *Pokkah-bong*: Large numbers of inoculations were made during the summer of 1930 on several susceptible cane varieties with several strains of Fusarium. Most of these inoculations did not produce typical symptoms of the disease, but caused top killing and other forms of injury to the leaves. In one series of inoculations, however, made with a strain of Fusarium isolated from an infected cane leaf, many typical pokkah-bong infections were obtained. This was during a rainy, warm period when the cane was growing rapidly. Such a combination of factors seems to be necessary for the development of typical pokkah-bong symptoms. Further studies are being made on the organisms causing the disease and the conditions under which it develops best.

5. *Mosaic*: Yield tests were continued to determine the effect of mosaic under field conditions. The following varieties were used: selected and unselected D-74 and mosaic and mosaic-free Striped, P.O.J. 36-M, P.O.J. 36, and P.O.J. 234. The results were similar to those previously reported in that the selected D-74 gave consistently larger yields than the unselected, while the differences in yields between the plots planted with mosaic cane and with mosaic-free cane of the other varieties were not significant.

The disappearing of mosaic in some of the P.O.J. varieties has been reported previously. Studies were continued in 1930 on this phase of the mosaic problem on a larger scale. It was demonstrated again that mosaic disappears in many plants of the P.O.J. varieties 213 and 228, and with much less frequency in the susceptible varieties, P.O.J. 36 and 234. Studies made on the development of mosaic in different parts of the stalk showed that many stalks of the

P.O.J. varieties which show mosaic symptoms ma
have buds that are free of the disease. This ma
account for the fact that even in the fields of th
very susceptible varieties, such as P.O.J. 36 and 23·
there are always many stalks which show no mosai

Experiments conducted in the greenhouse on th
effect of mosaic on root growth have not been entirel
consistent. They indicate that in the very suscept
ble varieties such as D-74 and Striped, mosaic ma
cause some reduction in root growth. Under the co
ditions of the experiments, little or no injury was ol
served on the root systems of P.O.J. 36, 213 and 23

6. *Disease resistance in the seedling canes*: Con
plete disease records were kept on all the varieti·
grown on the six test fields over the cane belt, ;
well as on the large number of seedling canes grow
on the Sugar Station at Baton Rouge.

How Sugar Stands Comparison

In order to demonstrate how cheap a food sug
is, intrinsically, at present prices Mr. Harry Austi
Secretary of the United States Beet Sugar Associ
tion, has prepared a chart showing the present pri
of sugar and the present price of various other food
and, at the same time, showing the price at whic
the other commodities would sell, compared wil
sugar, if prices were based on the food calories co
tained in one pound of each. We endeavor to sho
this in the table below, though of course less grapl
ically than it is shown on Mr. Austin's chart.

	Actual Price	What price would be based on comparati food value, taki sugar as a standa
Sugar	5.9¢	5.9¢
Butter	37.7¢	10.95¢
Bacon	40.2¢	8.45¢
Cheese	32.1¢	6.49¢
Macaroni	18.2¢	5.29¢
Ham	50.6¢	5.27¢
Rice	8.9¢	5.17¢
Beans	9.2¢	5.09¢
Lamb	31.4¢	3.95¢
Bread	8.2¢	3.85¢
Roast Beef	31.5¢	3.27¢
Beef Sirloin	42.5¢	3.11¢
Eggs (doz.)	36.1¢	2.89¢
Fowls	32.7¢	2.44¢
Milk (quart)	13.3¢	2.04¢
Corn (can)	14.7¢	1.45¢
Potatoes	2.9¢	1¢
Peas	15.5¢	8/10¢
Cabbage	4.3¢	4/10¢
Canned Tomatoes	11.2¢	3/10¢

Some of the discrepancies between food value a
price are very glaring. We pay 42.5¢ for a porti
of beef sirloin, for instance, which contains only
many calories as we could buy for 3.11¢ if we bou
them in the form of sugar; we pay 50.6¢ for a p
tion of ham containing only as many calories as
could buy for 5.27¢ if we bought them in the fc
of sugar; we pay 37.7¢ for a portion of butter c
taining only as many calories as we could buy
10.95¢ if we bought them in the form of sugar;
pay 36.1¢ for a portion of eggs containing only
many calories as we could buy for 2.89¢ if we bou

them in the form of sugar; and so on throughout the list.

The mystery is: Why is there always so much said about the price of sugar, which has the lowest price factor of any article of daily food? The hue and cry must be deliberately manufactured. It cannot emanate spontaneously from the consumer at all. It is incredible that it would do so.

Mr. Austin's chart is very instructive and a copy ought to be mailed to every High school in the United States.

Sugar for Canning

The National Canners' Association, 1739 H. Street, N. W., Washington, D. C., has issued a statement to the press in which they point out that there is a growing desire on the part of canners to buy sugar which has been especially tested to determine its suitability for canning purposes. The canners, according to the information now given out by their association, would like to see sugar manufacturers produce sugar under some process of bacteriological control which will be more suitable for canning non-acid commodities than sugar possessing sources of thermophilic infection. The Director of the Research Laboratory of the National Canners' Association, Dr. W. D. Bigelow, has prepared and distributed a description of the procedure to be followed in determining whether or not sugar meets the desired requirements. The description of this procedure is highly technical and we refer to the matter merely because of the general interest it must necessarily possess to those who are largely engaged in producing sugar for use in canning establishments.

A Mechanical Cane Knife

Cane cutting by hand is at best a slow operation. It is inefficient also, as the richest part of the stalk, close to the ground, is usually left in the field as part of the stubble. Sugar planters, of course, look with interest on the development of the cane harvester, but this, when it comes, may be an elaborate and costly machine, beyond the reach of the ordinary planter.

Mr. T. E. Holloway, of the United States Bureau of Entomology, has given some attention to cane cutting on account of its relation to the cane borer problem, some of the borers spending the winter in tall stubble left by laborers using the hand knife, and he now proposes a simple implement which would not do away with the human cane cutter, but would, he thinks, make him more efficient by placing mechanical power at his disposal.

In brief, the device, as suggested by Mr. Holloway, would consist of, first, a convenient wooden handle, some three feet long, in the hands of the laborer. At the end of this handle there would be two revolving circular saws or knives, and a touch of these whirling blades to the base of a cane stalk would sever it at once. It would be just as easy to cut close to the ground as farther up. Topping the stalk could be done as easily. The revolving blades would be operated by flexible shafting (which is on the order of a speedometer cable) connecting with a cog wheel, and the cog wheel would be connected with and turned by a tractor engine. One tractor could operate sev-

eral lines of flexible shafting, each connected with set of knives in the hands of a laborer.

Mr. Holloway visualizes in the future a group (cane cutters advancing across a field as we see toda but each man would hold a mechanical knife or sa which would speed up his work and make it mo efficient. Slowly following the gang would be a tra tor to supply power, by means of the flexible shaftin to the "mechanical knives."

The Editor of the SUGAR BULLETIN recalls distinc ly that a device of the sort suggested by Mr. Ho loway was invented in Australia some twenty-fiv years ago, and a photograph of it was sent to Louis ana, the picture showing the inventor holding in h hand what looked like a stick about three feet lon at the end of which was a small circular saw abou six or eight inches in diameter. There were wir leading from it and it was driven by electricity. was claimed that the little saw applied to a clump (canes at the ground line, cut through the whole clum in a few seconds. Since that long ago day we hav heard nothing of it. Possibly so many toes and fir gers added their juice to the cane juice that crysta lization was interfered with.

Sugar Institute Denies Charges

After the filing in the United States District Cour in New York City by the Department of Justice, on March 30 of a petition asking the dissolution of th Sugar Institute, Inc., of New York City, for allege violations of the anti-trust laws, Wilbur L. Cumming counsel for the institution, issued a statement in whic he asserted that he believes that no such restrair of trade, as alleged, exists. The statement of counse for the institute follows. in full text:

"The organization of the Sugar Institute in 192 was encouraged by the Department of Commerc which then was urging the formation of trade associa tions in the Nation's important industries. The De partment of Justice approved the code of ethics unde which the sugar industry was to operate as an associa tion of manufacturers. The Department reserved th right to change its mind if operations under the cod appeared to bring about an unlawful restraint o trade.

"The Department now feels that such a restrair has been brought about, and that the restraint i unlawful notwithstanding operations have followe the code. I believe that no such restraint exists and tha all actions of the institute have been entirely lawfu However, if the Department doubts this, the institut will welcome a determination by the courts. Since its organization, the institute has given the Department and the Federal Trade Commission full information as to all its activities.

"The cardinal principle of the code was elimination of old trade abuses and unethical trade practices which resulted in unfair discrimination between customers. To accomplish this it has been necessary to require brokers, jobbers, transportation agencies, warehousemen and others engaged in sale and distribution of sugar to deal ethically and respect the principles of the code. Some of these have complained.

"If some of the old and questionable forms of competition have disappeared the institute contends that only those have gone which were essentially unfair and thus unlawful and that the institute was right in abolishing them. The question as it appears to the institute is whether a great industry can police itself to elevate the conduct of its business to a high moral plane, if in so doing some old but unethical forms of competition are eliminated.

"The questions to be decided in this case are far-reaching, because they concern many other great industries which have adopted the code of the sugar industry for the formation of trade associations. These associations have all brought about better conditions in their industry by adherence to the principles of the institute's code."

Washington News

By C. J. Bourg

The 71st Congress has come to an end without much applause excepting from those people who, like the President, feel that the country is better off when Congress is adjourned. There was more applause for the adjournment than for the accomplishments. However, the sugar industry of Louisiana, and in fact all industries in Louisiana that compete with foreign products, have every reason to be pleased over the progress made towards a greater appreciation of the value of tariff protection for our domestic industries, insofar as the Congressional Delegation from Louisiana is concerned.

It will be remembered that when the Underwood Bill was before the House, including its provision for free sugar, on a motion to recommit the Bill we find the Congressman from the Third District, "Couzin" Bob Broussard, the lone Louisianian voting to recommit while the seven other Louisiana Congressmen voted with the Democratic majority against this motion. The same vote appears that day on an appeal from the ruling of Speaker Clark regarding the parliamentary status of the Bill. However, on the passage of the Bill we do find Congressmen Broussard, Dupre, Lazaro and Morgan voting against it. No one is so young in the sugar business as not to remember the terrific battle in the United States Senate on sugar, which was then Schedule E. Louisiana Senators have always fought for the sugar industry.

On the so-called Emergency Tariff Bill of 1921 we find the Louisiana Delegation divided equally, with Dupre, Martin, Lazaro and Favrot in favor of the Bill, while Aswell, Wilson, O'Connor and Sandlin opposed. The following year on September 13, 1922, when the Fordney Tariff Bill was under consideration, the division of votes was the same as in 1921.

On none of these bills did the House have a chance

to vote separately on sugar because of the rules which forced the members to either vote for or against the whole bill. But in 1930 when the Conference on the Hawley-Smoot Tariff Bill was unable to reach an agreement, an opportunity was given to the. House to express itself on several of the more controversial items, including sugar. We again record with appreciation the fact that the entire Louisiana Delegation voted for the higher rate of 2.40 on sugar, which, if they had prevailed, would have meant a tariff of 2.20, the normal compromise figure for the Conference. The final vote on the Bill was as follows: Aswell, Derouen, Kemp, Montet, O'Connor, Spearing and Wilson voting for the Bill, with Sandlin against. Thus from 1913 to 1930 the vote of the Louisiana Delegation changed from a minority of one to seven to a majority of seven to one, and this one voting in our favor on the sugar schedule.

Your representative is pleased to express again our gratitude and appreciation to both of our Senators, Broussard and Ransdell, and to all of our Congressmen named above for their loyal support of an industry which we know to be of vital importance to the progress and prosperity of Louisiana.

We have reason to look back upon the 71st Congress as sympathetic to our interests in the matter of appropriations. These columns have already recognized the active cooperation furnished by Congressman John N. Sandlin, who is the Louisiana member on the House Appropriations Committee and. to Senator Edwin S. Broussard who is the Louisiana member on the Senate Appropriations Committee, towards maintaining the appropriations for the Department of Agriculture to continue its research and the solving of problems facing the sugar cane grower. For the fiscal year 1931 increases were given as follows: Office of Sugar Plants, $10,000 for the development of new cane varieties; Office of Cereal and Forage Insects, $10,000 to bring cane borer parasites from South America; Office of Agricultural Engineering, $2,500 for drainage tests in Louisiana. For the fiscal year 1932 the following increases were granted: Office of Sugar Plants, $5,000 for varietal work; Bureau of Chemistry and Soils, $75,000 for investigation of the utilization of farm waste including bagasse; Bureau of Agricultural Engineering, $10,000 for developing a cane harvester. These increases are over and above the yearly appropriation which have been maintained in both Appropriation Bills. A definite idea of what the continuance of yearly appropriations means will be gained from a reference to the annual allotment for the Office of Sugar Plants alone, which for 1932 is $413,700.

Certain very definite improvements are being advocated by members of Congress so as to make more readily available to the farmer the benefits intended for him by Congress. One bill seeks to combine the Federal Farm Board with the Farm Loan Bureau, which would mean that the agricultural credits and marketing loans would be handled by the same organization. This has possibilities of working out to the advantage of the sugar cane grower.

A recent editorial· in *The Times-Picayune*, while accepting the facts as we reported them in these columns regarding the bills providing Philippine Independence, cautions against our forecast that there will be action 'on at least one of these bills in Congress during the next session. We now amplify our previous report to the extent of saying that the im-

portance of solving the question of Philippine Independence is being accepted nationally as an issue, which if not settled in the First Session of the 72nd Congress, will determine the political fortunes of aspiring statesmen, particularly in the Middle West. The farm organizations are alive to the Philippine question and with all due respect to the beauties of an altruistic point of view regarding the Little Brown Brother, the economic forces are more efficient in determining the course of statesmanship. It will rest with the members of Congress as to whether it is better to project this additional issue into the 1932 national campaign or to dispose of it in advance.

STATEMENT OF THE OWNERSHIP, MANAGEMENT, CIRCULATION, ETC., REQUIRED BY THE ACT OF CONGRESS OF AUGUST 24, 1912.

Of The Sugar Bulletin, published semi-monthly at New Orleans, La., for April 1, 1931. State of Louisiana, Parish of Orleans.

Before me, a Notary Public in and for the State and parish aforesaid, personally appeared Andrew W. Dykers, who, having been duly sworn according to law, deposes and says that he is the Business Manager of the Sugar Bulletin and that the following is, to the best of his knowledge and belief, a true statement of the ownership, management, etc., of the aforesaid publication for the date shown in the above caption, required by the Act of August 24, 1912, embodied in section 411, Postal Laws and Regulations, printed on the reverse of this form, to-wit:

1. That the names and addresses of the publisher, editor, managing editor, and business managers are: Publisher, The American Sugar Cane League of the U. S. A., Inc., New Orleans, La.; Editor, Reginald Dykers, New Orleans, La.; Managing Editor, none; Business Manager, Andrew W. Dykers, New Orleans, La.

2. That the owner is The American Sugar Cane League of the U. S. A., Inc., New Orleans, La.; C. D. Kemper, Franklin, La., President; Percy A. Lemann, Donaldsonville, La., Vice-President; Frank L. Barker, Lockport, La., Secretary-Treasurer.

3. That the known bondholders, mortgagees, and other security holders owning or holding 1 per cent or more of total amount of bonds, mortgages, or other securities are none.

A. W. DYKERS, Business Manager.

Sworn to and subscribed before me this 30th day of March, 1931.

A. A. DE LA HOUSSAYE, Notary Public. (My commission expires at death.)

May 1—   *Circulation of this Issue 1900 Copies*   May 14

THE
SUGAR
BULLETIN

r. Chas. E. ...
Ba... Rou... La.

Entered as second-class matter April 13, 1925, at the postoffice at
New Orleans, La., under Act of March 6, 1879.

We stand for the encouragement of Home Industries as against Foreign competition.

| Vol. 9 | NEW ORLEANS, LA., MAY 1, 1931 | No. 15 |

The Liquid Sugar Case

By C. J. Bourg

The case of the Savannah Sugar Refining Corporation versus the United States was heard before the Customs Court at New York City on April 27th, 28th and 29th. The judges were the third division composed of Judges Young, Evans and Cline, the latter being the woman member of the Court.

At the very outset, the importer admitted frankly that his purpose in bringing his raw sugar into the United States in liquid form, was to pay a lower rate of duty. To the layman this immediately demonstrates that this whole matter is based upon the subterfuge of avoiding the tariff duty which Congress intended when the Tariff Act of 1930 was passed. As written before in these columns, the peculiar jurisprudence of the Customs Court recognizes that in some cases there can be a "legal subterfuge" but we are not at all convinced that the importer can hide behind that liberal interpretation of the law. It should not be necessary to prove criminal fraud in order to keep importers from evasion of customs laws.

From the testimony introduced, it is evident that the importer hopes to be able to have the Court give the most extremely comprehensive definition possible to the term "sugar syrup" contained in paragraph 502 of the Tariff Act. An argument used by counsel for the importer indicated that he contends that any mixture of sugar and water ought to be accepted as a sugar syrup within the meaning of the act. The Court of Customs and Patent Appeals has already ruled in what is known as the Cresca Cases that syrup is a saturated solution, and as the Act of 1930 was passed by Congress since these decisions, without in any way changing the language of the tariff laws, this congressional action has the effect of confirming and adopting the definition and interpretation of the Customs Court. Counsel for the importer would waive aside the *stare decisis* and Congress, because a new way has been found of "getting around the law."

The testimony of the witnesses for the importer was intended to prove almost exclusively, that the term sugar syrup is used for any and all kinds of liquors and liquids. The Customs Courts have repeatedly held that the commercial designation of the article known to the trade and used by it, will determine what is meant. Not one witness on either side testified that he had dealt in a commodity composed of 48% sugar and 52% water. Most of them stated emphatically that not only had this mixture never been used before, in the above proportions, but that it would not be accepted in the trade. Several witnesses stated that this mixture could not be used for the purposes that sugar syrup usually serves. It was shown by a great preponderance of evidence that the transportation of the mixture would make it impracticable on account of the cost. Secondly, that the proportions were such that fermentation would set in so quickly that preservatives would have to be used, more or less successfully. The question of the requirements of the Pure Food and Drugs Act also would enter into whether this mixture could be used in the trade. The use of formaldehyde by the Savannah corporation in the mixture imported, has brought an interesting development to the case. No tradesman using syrups for direct human consumption, was willing to state that he would handle a syrup containing this well-known disinfectant and germicide.

Among the witnesses for the United States were three Louisianians, namely, Mr. Richard M. Murphy of J. C. Murphy & Son, Mr. Walter Sullivan of Gay-Sullivan Co., Inc., and Mr. H. F. Saufley of the New Orleans Coffee Co., all experienced buyers and sellers of syrups. They were excellent witnesses both as to their knowledge of the trade and the manner in which they handled themselves on the witness stand.

The case has been taken under advisement by the Court, time being allowed for the submission of briefs. Incidentally the case of the South Porto Rico Sugar Company versus the United States will be considered

=========THE=========
SUGAR
BULLETIN

407 Carondelet St., New Orleans

Issued on the 1st and 15th of each month. Official Organ of the American
Sugar Cane League and Ex-Officio of the U. S. A., in which are consolidated
The Louisiana Sugar Planters' Assn.
The American Cane Growers' Assn.
The Producers & Mfgrs. Protective Assn.
Subscription Price, 50 Cents Per Year.

Reginald Dykers, General Manager & Editor of the Bulletin
301 Nola Bldg., New Orleans
Frank L. Barker, Secretary and Treasurer
Lockport, La.
C. J. Bourg, Manager Washington Office
810 Union Trust Building

CHAIRMEN OF COMMITTEES:
C. D. Kemper, Franklin, La.
President of the League and Ex-Officio Chairman of Executive Committee
Andrew H. Gay, Plaquemine, La,
Chairman Agricultural Committee
David W. Pipes, Jr., Houma, La.
Chairman Industrial Committee
Frank L. Barker, Lockport, La.
Chairman Finance Committee.
Edward J. Gay, Plaquemine, La.
Chairman Tariff Committee
H. Langdon Laws, Cinclare, La.
Chairman Legislative Committee
J. C. LeBourgeois, New Orleans, La.
Chairman Freight Rate Committee
R. H. Chadwick, Bayou Goula, La.
Chairman Membership Committee
A. H. Rosenfeld, New Orleans, La.
Chairman Publicity Committee

Members of the League desiring action on, or information on, any subject are invited to communicate with
the League or with the Chairman of the Committee
to which it seems to appertain.

upon the same evidence as submitted in the Savannah
case.

It is the opinion of all who sat through the entire
proceeding, that the Government has met every point
offered by the importer. Under the procedure of the
Customs Court, it becomes the burden of the protesting importer to show two things: First, that the ruling of the Collector of Customs was wrong in collecting the higher duty, and second, that the lower rate
of duty should be applied upon the basis that the importer offers. In short, the importer might prove the
Collector used the wrong basis, and still not be able
to show that the basis for which the importer contends is the proper one. In the present case, the ruling of the Collector is that the rate of duty must be
based upon the article of chief value in the mixture
imported; which is sugar and not syrup.

While we await the decision of the Court, we contemplate the reasons for bringing this question before
the Courts of the United States. From all branches
of the sugar industry we hear the hope expressed that
liquid sugar and its attendant developments will not
become prevalent in the trade. Even the present importer knows that should he win this case, Congress
will immediately correct the language of the Tariff
Act and forbid diluted sugar to be used as a subterfuge. But there you have what is generally believed
to be the real motive.

The refiners want a differential in their favor on refined sugar importations. They also prefer to see a

lower rate on raw sugar. By winning the case in
Court, they throw open the Sugar Schedule in Congress.

When they first protested, to the Court, there was
a belief and hope that Congress would in the past session correct this liquid sugar business, and the importer figured it would give the refiners a chance to
insist upon a refiner's differential. Congress took no
action and the case has had to continue. If the Government wins this case, as we believe it will, then the
chances for re-opening the sugar schedule will depend
upon the party-in-power's willingness to have tariff
legislation again before Congress. The experience of
the parties with tariff acts does not argue well for any
decision to start the fight over again.

The protest filed by the Savannah Sugar Refining
Corporation reads as follows:

Now comes Savannah Sugar Refining Corporation, a
corporation under the laws of the State of New York,
and within sixty days after, but not before the decision
and liquidation herein complained of and the payment
made on November 17, 1930, of all duties, charges and
exactions appearing by such decision and liquidation to
be due, respectfully enters this protest and objection,
as provided for in Section 514 of the Tariff Act of 1930,
to the decision made respecting the classification of, and
the rate of duty applicable to, said entry, and to the
liquidation thereof at said rate, said decision and liquidation having been made on November 17, 1930, in the
matter of the entry through the Savannah Custom
House of 8 drums of sugar sirup aggregating 834,679
gallons, net weight 8472 lbs., brought from Sagua La
Grande, Cuba, on the American Steamship "Menardan,"
which arrived at Savannah November 1, 1930, bearing
marks S. S. R. Co., having consular invoice No. 091,
given consumption entry No. 85, date of entry November 1, 1930, testing by the polariscope 45.50 sugar degrees, testing 45.96 total sugars, variously designated by
the Customs authorities as "sugar solution" and "sugar
diluted with water," and finally liquidated November
17, 1930, at the rate of 1.7125 cents per lb. less 20%
C. R., "as sugar testing by the polariscope less than
75 degrees," on the authority of T. D. 44275.

The address of the protestant is Savannah Sugar Refining Corporation, Savannah Bank & Trust Company
Building, Savannah, Georgia. The address of its attorney is Robert M. Hitch, Esq., Savannah Fire Insurance
Company Building, Savannah, Georgia.

The reasons for the objection to the decision and
liquidation above mentioned, and to the classification
given said merchandise, and to the rate of duty imposed
thereon and which the protestant was required to pay
are as follows:

(1) There is no such classification as that given
this merchandise, to-wit, "Sugar solution," or "sugar
diluted with water," to be found in paragraph 501 of
the Tariff Act of 1930, under which a duty of 1.712
cents per lbs., less 20% C R., was imposed.

(2) Said merchandise was not "Sugars," nor "sirup
of cane juice," within the meaning of said paragraph
501, nor was it mixtures containing sugar and water
"within contemplation of said paragraph 501 which is
restricted to such mixtures testing by the polariscope
above 50 sugar degrees," whereas the said merchandise
tested by the polariscope is only 45.50 sugar degrees.

(3) Said merchandise was not lawfully dutiable at
the rates prescribed in said paragraph 501 as "mixture
containing sugar and water" by virtue of the "similitude" portion of paragraph 1559. Said statute prescribes
expressly the condition in which a mixture containing
sugar and water must be found before the rates prescribed therein can lawfully be made to apply, i. e., the
mixture must test by the polariscope "above 50 sugar
degrees." Said paragraph 501 must therefore be taken
to preclude the application of the "similitude" portion
of paragraph 1559 to a mixture containing sugar and
water which has a lower polariscope test than the
prescribed.

(4) Said merchandise was not in essence a sugar

The Advertisers in the Sugar Bulletin are contributing towards the support of the American Sugar Cane League and should enjoy your special consideration; help them to help the Domestic Sugar Industry by doing business with them whenever possible.

and therefore dutiable as sugar under said paragraph 501, since the classification and rate are to be determined by the condition of the merchandise at the time of its importation, rather than by the condition to which it may afterwards be brought by some process of manufacture or otherwise.

(5) Said merchandise was not lawfully dutiable at the rates prescribed in said paragraph 501 by virtue of the provisions contained in the latter portion of paragraph 1559 as a non-enumerated article manufactured of two or more materials, since it is within the enumerated classes, being either a sugar sirup within the meaning of paragraph 502 or a mixture containing sugar and water within the meaning of paragraph 501, although not taking the duty prescribed by paragraph 501 for mixtures containing sugar and water because not coming up to the polariscopic test provided for such mixtures in said paragraph 501. The fact that it may not be specially provided for does not take it out of the enumerated classes.

(6) Said merchandise did not come within any classification covered by said paragraph 501, nor could the rates of duty authorized by said paragraph 501 be lawfully imposed upon said merchandise by virtue of any provision contained in paragraph 1559 of said Tariff Act of 1930.

(7) Said merchandise should have been held dutiable at the rate of ¼ of 1 cent per gallon as "sugar sirups, not specially provided for," within the meaning of paragraph 502 of said Tariff Act of 1930, or at the rate of 20% ad valorem as "articles manufactured in whole or in part, not specially provided for," within the meaning of the latter portion of paragraph 1558 of said Tariff Act.

WHEREFORE Protestant respectfully prays that the Collector review and modify his decision, as provided for in Section 515 of the said Tariff Act of 1930, and thereafter refund the duties found to have been assessed and collected in excess, or, in case of affirmance of said decision, that he thereupon transmit the entry and the accompanying papers, and all the exhibits connected therewith, to the United States Customs Court for due assignment and determination, as provided by law, to the end that the errors herein complained of may be considered and corrected.

Dated at Savannah, Georgia, December 2, 1930.

　　　　SAVANNAH SUGAR REFINING CORPORATION
　　　　　　By (Sgd.) B. O. Sprague,
　　　　　　　　　　　B. O. Sprague,
(Sgd.)　Robert M. Hitch,　　　　　President.
　　　　Robert M. Hitch,
　　　　Counsel.

The Cane Saw

Dr. T. E. Holloway's suggestion relative to a rotary cane cutter, comprising a small circular saw driven by a flexible shaft from a tractor and operated by hand seems to have occasioned serious thought in a number of practical minds. As we jocularly pointed out, the contrivance might cut off fingers and toes as well as cane stalks, but this was meant as a tribute to its cutting efficiency and not as a serious criticism. Certainly a man equipped with such a device ought to be able to march down a cane row and lay the cane low at a gait of perhaps a mile an hour. The flexible shaft and the movable power represented by the tractor change the complexion of the situation as compared with that existing years ago when such an idea was first conceived in Queensland.

The Contact Committee

Meeting of American Sugar Cane League Contact Committee with Louisiana Experiment Station Workers Held at Baton Rouge, La., March 13, 1931

The meeting was called to order by Mr. Wallace, Chairman. · Present:

Contact Committee: Mr. A. W. Wallace, Mr. Percy Lemann, Mr. Stephen Munson, Mr. Elliot Jones. **Station Staff:** Dr. C. T. Dowell, Mr. W. G. Taggart, Dr. C. W. Edgerton, Dr. E. C. Tims, Mr. Truman Ryker, Mr. Percy Mills, Dr. W. E. Hinds, Mr. B. A. Osterberger, Mr. G. H. Reuss, Mr. Wm. Whipple, Mr. C. B. Gouaux. **Visitors:** Dr. A. H. Rosenfeld.

The reading of the minutes of the last meeting was dispensed with.

Department of Entomology Report

A four-page mimeographed progress report was presented by Dr. Hinds. *Trichogramma Breeding Work:* We have completed the installation in the second moth breeding room. Yellow Creole corn was found to be the best variety for our work and we have stocked the room with moths from Room No. 3 which has been running since last spring. Before we stock the room with moths the corn is fumigated very thoroughly with carbon disulphide and left long enough to make sure we have killed all insect life in the corn. The corn is then put in the trays and sometimes fumigated again. The idea is to kill out all forms of insects that might infest it and then stock with what we would call "pure cultures" of the eggs of Angoumois grain moths. Following up the results of previous laboratory tests upon the effect of moisture and drinking water supply upon the duration of life of adult moths and their egg deposition, we have completed the moisture-proofing of walls, floors and doors and have installed humidifying apparatus which has been built by Mr. Stracener. The form of humidifier which may work very satisfactorily during the winter when heat also is required may, apparently, be quite simple and yet secure fairly satisfactory uniform conditions with only manual control. The installation of automatic control of temperature and relative humidity through the introduction of thermostats and hydrostats in each room may add somewhat to the uniformity of results but we have yet to determine whether this improvement is sufficient to justify the added investment in control equipment. This equipment made by commercial companies costs hundreds or thousands of dollars, so if we succeed in regulating humidity and temperature within 5 degrees at a cost of under $50.00, we think we will be doing fairly well. This is what we expect to do. During the summer season when the problem is to reduce rather than to increase the temperature in the room, a different form of humidifier must be used and this is now being devised.

We have recently sent Trichogramma parasitized eggs to Dr. A. W. Morrill in California to enable him to rear our Louisiana strain of Trichogramma for commercial distribution, and we have also sent a small shipment of parasitized eggs to a research worker in Wisconsin to enable him to go on with his work.

The proposition of Dr. A. W. Morrill, Los Angeles, California, to supply Louisiana growers with Trichogramma from his commercial production plant was discussed quite fully. It appears that this will be the only available source of commercial supply for Louisiana growers this season. Some of those present expressed the conviction that arrangements should be made in the future whereby such service for Louisiana planters may be provided here in Louisiana. The sentiment was expressed that the Station should issue some publication that would give to the planters full information in regard to the egg parasite and methods by which they may be able to determine for themselves whether their conditions would call for Trichogramma colonization and if so, how to determine approximately the number of parasites that they can use economically and how to handle these so that they may secure the largest possible value from their colonization. Dr. Hinds stated that such information will be prepared and also that from time to time brief articles may be placed in THE SUGAR BULLETIN that will help in preparing the planters for this work.

Borer Population in Hibernation: We have made several examinations to get some idea of the borer population in hibernation. In regard to hibernation in corn stalks, in field examinations made at Plaquemine and Baton Rouge, we found in a total of 317 stalks, 72 pupal skins, 8 alive and 15 dead larvæ, ratio of 40 stalks to 1 living stage. In sugar cane tops, not burned, 1200 stalks were examined and revealed 1 pupal skin, 11 alive and 2 dead larvæ, or a ratio of 110 to 1, which is light. In 213 plant cane at Island Plantation, Plaquemine, we found the ratio to be 10 to 1, or eleven times as heavy borer infestation in this particular area as we found here on the average at the station. At the station examinations made on February 12 of 225 stalks showed no borer stages in two cuts of P.O.J. 213 plant, while in 333 stalks of D-74 and Purple, the ratio was 56 to 1. These latter stalks lay on the ground just as left by the cutters, had been burned over and still showed 6 living and 6 dead borer larvæ in the 333 stalks.

In March, 1929, at Cinclare on trash disposal plats, the average ratio of tops to living larvæ was 58 to 1. At the Sugar Station the ratio in cane, unburned, was 46 to 1 and where burned thoroughly 1200 to 1. At Baton Rouge in March, 1929, among corn stalks, the ratio was 80 to 1.

White Grub Control Tests: In order to secure as early as possible in the season further information regarding insecticidal control materials which might be applied in the field tests for the control of the sugar cane beetle at Franklin later in the season, Mr. Osterberger collected behind the plows at the Sugar Experiment Station a large number of white grubs, not specimens of the sugar cane beetle but other species that come in the group of white grubs, so as to carry on some laboratory work. For this work, upland soil, which was much drier than bottom soil, was thoroughly sifted to eliminate additional specimens. This soil was placed in open, 1-gallon sirup pails, to a depth of 5 to 6 inches. In each pail were placed 12 grubs which were mixed with the soil at various depths. All insecticidal materials were placed on the surface of the soil and not in direct contact with any grubs, and the soil was moistened by sprinkling it with water every other day. The amount of insecticidal material applied was determined on the general basis of what was considered a reasonable application per acre.

The mortality records from these series of tests showed a total of 132 grubs started, 17 died during tests—or a total mortality of 13%; while the checks showed 36 grubs started and a total mortality of 22.2%. The results of these preliminary laboratory tests failed to show any increase in grub mortality on account of the various materials used. However, we know that the sugar cane beetle grubs, which do not feed upon living roots, are more delicate to handle in the laboratory than most species of white grubs which do, as a rule, feed on living roots. Therefore, in our field work at Franklin for this season we have included plans for applying a number of possible control materials in field applications. The prolonged cool weather occurring during the past three weeks has delayed the opening of the field work at Franklin. We do not wish to have Mr. Osterberger in the field until the spring flight of beetles begins. Most of the equipment for this field work has already been transferred to Franklin, and we expect that Mr. Osterberger will be located there for a few weeks to get this work well under way and that it may be started very soon now.

Soil Animal Work: The stocking of the 56 new drums planted on the upland Station this past fall has been continued and is approaching completion.

The main difficulty in completing this work earlier has been the fact that the species of greatest importance probably, *Lepidocyrtus violentus*, which is usually most abundant, has been exceptionally hard to find this winter. Drainage conditions in the present location appear to be ideal and the cane is beginning to germinate in these drums.

Department of Plant Pathology Report

A six-page mimeographed progress report was presented by Dr. Edgerton. This was published in THE SUGAR BULLETIN of April 1, 1931.

A resume of the work done in the department during 1930 was given, on the following subjects: Root development of sugar cane, root rot, red rot, Pokkahbong disease, mosaic and disease resistance of new seedlings. This was published in THE SUGAR BULLETIN of April 15, 1931.

Report of Test Field Work

A three-page mimeographed progress report was presented by Mr. Gouaux.

Early Season Field Work: During the months of January and February there was considerable activity and progress with sugar cane field work in the various sections of the Cane Belt. In most cases, planters took advantage of prevailing spells of favorable weather in performing necessary field operations such as middle wrapping, off-barring, stubble shaving, cane scraping, planting spring cane, preparing lands for corn and legumes, and in some cases, planting corn and legumes. The extremely mild weather conditions of the fall and winter months have been quite favorable for the new cane crop. Examinations of first and second stubble indicate an unusually sound condition of eyes, from the surface to the bottom. The fall plant cane in general is showing excellent germination; while seed cane for spring planting kept well in the windrow. The shaving of stubble, which is very light and mostly to cut off dried cane stalk remnants from last year's crop and clean off the row, is on a more extensive scale than in 1930. The revolving disc-type shavers which are more popular, are doing better work.

Plans for Fertilizing Cane and Corn: Throughout the Belt preparations are either completed or under consideration for fertilizing cane and corn crops. On the Mississippi alluvial first bottom soils, in most cases, only nitrogenous materials will be used; while in the areas west of the Atchafalaya some of the planters will use phosphoric acid with nitrogen. The rates of application of both plant foods for stubble cane will be practically in accordance with Experiment Station recommendations. Sulphate of ammonia and cyanamid, the two lowest priced nitrogenous materials, will be used exclusively.

Five-Acre Stubble Cane Fertilizer Demonstrations: The Chilean Nitrate of Soda organization is cooperating this season in a series of ten stubble cane fertilizer demonstrations. This Extension project, as usual, is under the supervision of county agents. Arrangements with cooperating planters in the following parishes have already been completed: Assumption, Lafourche, West Baton Rouge, Pointe Coupee, St. James, Rapides, Lafayette, Vermilion, Iberia and St. Mary.

Sugar Cane Potash Tests: A series of twenty-one sugar cane potash tests are being undertaken this season throughout the Cane Belt with cooperative

planters by the N. V. Potash My. It is an experimental project to determine if any real benefits can be derived from heavy potash cane fertilization, using sulphate of potash. The project includes the securing of field and chemical data from large-scale mill tests, and is somewhat on the same basis as similar work conducted in Hawaii and Porto Rico. Arrangements for this work have already been completed.

Experiment Station Test Fields: During the 1931 season, the sugar cane variety work in the Cane Belt will consist of a series of six plant cane fields and six first stubble test fields at the following established test fields: Cinclare, Glenwood, Reserve, Meeker, Sterling and Youngsville; and four second stubble fields at Cinclare, Meeker, Sterling and Youngsville.

Second Stubble: Cinclare: Middles wrapped, off-barred and shaved. No shoots of any variety out.

Meeker: Middles wrapped and off-barred. C.P. 807 and P.O.J. 234 most advanced.

Sterling: Middles wrapped, off-barred and shaved. C.P. 807 out most. P.O.J. 36, 36-M, 213 and Co. 281 few shoots out.

Youngsville: Middles wrapped. C.P. 807 and Co. 281 most advanced.

First Stubble: Cinclare: Middles wrapped, off-barred and shaved. No shoots of any variety out.

Glenwood: Middles wrapped. C.P. 807 and P.O.J. 234 most advanced.

Reserve: Middles wrapped and shaved. C.P. 807 most advanced; only few shoots of P.O.J. 234 out.

Meeker: Middles wrapped and off-barred. C.P. 807 and P.O.J. 234 most advanced.

Sterling and Youngsville: Middles wrapped. C.P. 807 most advanced. P.O.J. 234, 213 and Co. 281 only few shoots out.

At Youngsville the plant cane varieties were the most backward, with only few shoots showing up in plots of C.P. 807 and Co. 290.

Sterling showed the most advanced germinations. The germination counts were made during the period of February 26 to March 5 (this was before the recent frosts killed back sprouts) and compare favorably with last year's counts of March 25 to 31. At all of the plant cane variety fields, C.P. 807 is the leading variety in early germination, followed by P. O.J. 234 and Co. 290.

Discussions

Dr. Hinds told of the fellowship secured from The Grasselli Chemical Company and that "Dutox" will be tested out in experimental tests, and this information will help us in our sugar cane insecticidal tests. We have secured a very capable graduate student in agriculture to carry out these field tests.

Meeting adjourned.

Vauable Information from Dr. Hinds

In this issue of THE SUGAR BULLETIN, and in the two previous issues, Dr. W. E. Hinds, Entomologist of the Louisiana Experiment Station, has published some very valuable information in connection with the sugar cane borer and the sugar cane beetle. This information is for the benefit and guidance of the members of the American Sugar Cane League who grow sugar cane, as about 95% of them do. It should be carefully read and digested.

The Sugarcane Beetle and Some Suggestions for its Control

By W. E. Hinds, Entomologist, and B. A. Osterberger, Assistant Entomologist, Louisiana Experiment Station

At this time we wish to discuss briefly the second most important sugar cane insect in Louisiana. The sugar cane beetle is known also as the "corn stalk beetle" and bears the scientific name *Euetheola* (Ligyrus) *rugiceps*. This beetle occurs throughout Louisiana but appears to be most abundant in St. Mary Parish, where it has been recorded as a serious pest on cane for more than 50 years past.

The beetle is a very hard-shelled, black beetle with broad, oval body. They are about one-half inch long by slightly more than one-quarter inch broad and have very strong spiny legs which enable them to dig into and work their way through the soil. The dirt is pushed backward, filling the burrow behind the beetles. They avoid daylight and few, if any, may be seen without digging even in a heavily infested field. The damage is done by the adult beetles only and they may attack the succulent sprouts of young corn, cane or rice particularly. In extreme cases the entire stand of corn or cane may be destroyed. In one case reported to us at Anna Plantation, in a tract of 75 acres of 1929 fall plant P.O.J. 213 cane, where the soil is of a very light sandy type, the total crop harvested in the fall of 1930 was but 65 tons.

We believe that some recent observations made on this species may have considerable interest for planters whose fields are infested. This condition is indicated most plainly by the large number of dying sprouts which show upon examination that they have been gnawed into below the surface of the ground and the tissues left in a very rough shredded condition.

The females began egg laying this year at about the middle of April but only a small proportion at that time showed that they were ready to deposit eggs. The eggs are small, white egg-shaped bodies about one-sixteenth of an inch long and are laid singly in the loose soil near where the beetle may be feeding. From the eggs hatch grubs, which grow to look much like the common "white grubs" found in the soil, but they are very different therefrom especially in their food habits. White grubs feed upon living root tissue, while the sugar cane beetle grubs do not feed at all on living roots and seem to be of no economic importance whatever during the grub stage. The damage results from the feeding done by the adult beetles. There seems to be but one generation a year. They pass the winter in the adult stage and the adults become injurious soon after the soil temperatures rise above an average mean temperature of 55 degrees F.

In the half century since Dr. L. O. Howard first studied these beetles on the property which is now Sterling Plantation, little has been found in the way of practicable control measures. It has been known for a long time that these beetles fly to lights in large numbers and some use has been made of trap lights for these and other injurious insects on sugar planta-

tions. At the present time we are testing the efficiency and value of two types of lights as a method for decreasing the population of sugar cane beetles. Beside these beetles, trap lights collect large numbers of several other injurious species or groups of species of insects. These include the so-called May or June beetles, which are the parents of white grubs, many sugar cane borer moths and also large numbers of small click beetles which are the parents of wireworms which also feed on plant roots. We find that large numbers of these insects are flying actively and come to such trap lights before 9:00 p. m.

In certain types of very light sandy soil, where corn had been planted and following a rain which had packed the soil and smoothed the surface along the drill, we found that it was quite easily possible to locate very definitely the spots where sugar cane beetles had emerged and also where they had re-entered the soil. Emergence holes are just the size of the beetle bodies and are left open until the soil is disturbed or the next rain occurs. Entrance holes are not open but are indicated by the slight elevation of loose soil which is left on the surface where it is simply pushed back by the burrowing beetles. These entrance places are located generally very close to a corn plant. It is quite evident that many of the beetles come to the surface during the night and crawl or fly around and re-enter the ground close to some attractive food supply.

Following such "beetle signs" it was found possible to dig down beside the plant, preferably with a narrow trowel, and locate the beetle, or beetles, and remove them before they had destroyed or injured the corn. In this way in a heavily infested area beetles could be dug out and destroyed at an average rate of about one per minute. At even one-third of this rate it would seem that such hand collection, repeated twice a week as long as beetles remain abundant, may constitute the cheapest and most efficient method for reducing the sugar cane beetle population for such favorable locations. If applied immediately, it will forestall the deposition of most of the eggs of this species in this particular season and may save a stand of corn or cane. It is possible that this hand collection method may be applied in many fields of plant cane, but it will surely be more difficult where the surface soil is very rough or lumpy and in fields of stubble cane.

The beetles collected may be crushed immediately, or if it is desired to keep them for counting, they may be placed in a tin can containing a little dirt into which they will burrow immediately and not attempt to escape. They show little tendency to fly in the daytime. One planter is known who is paying one-half cent each for beetles thus collected, and the laborer is making good wages.

There are reasons for believing also that it is worthwhile to keep the soil stirred frequently and as close to the plants as possible, but there is no repellent or insecticidal chemical treatment that we can recommend at this time for application to the infested soil. It is quite possible that fertilization may pay and with later planted corn we would now advise using an abundance of seed and thinning only after the corn has gotten a good start.

How to Tell Them Apart

Dr. Ernst Artschwager, of the Bureau of Plant Industry, United States Department of Agriculture, is the author of an article entitled "A Comparative Study of the Stem Epidermis of Certain Sugar Cane Varieties," and a reprint of this article, which appeared in the Journal of Agricultural Research, has been sent to the Editor of the SUGAR BULLETIN.

It seems that Dr. Artschwager has found that the different varieties of cane show different characteristics in the epidermis of the stem, and in the cases where there is uncertainty as to the classification of a cane this uncertainty can be removed by a microscopic study of the epidermis. We understand the epidermis to be the thin outer layer of the stalk, what the unlearned might call the skin, but Dr. Artschwager assumes that everybody knows just what the epidermis of the cane is and does not tell us. The article is highly technical and was evidently written for scientific consumption only.

One beautiful colored plate, which is marred by the misspelling of the word "Sugar Cane" at the top of it, and several photographs accompany the article showing just how the cells in the epidermis are arranged in the different varieties of cane. The arrangement of these cells in the case of the variety D-74, for instance, is very different from their arrangement in P.O.J. 213, and so it is with all the other varieties. The difference in the arrangement of the cells in the epidermis is obvious at a glance.

In his article Dr. Artschwager relates at length just how he proceeds in his examination and comparison of the cells and the conclusion he arrives at is that the method he describes will be useful in identifying varieties, with which all will doubtless agree. So far as general plantation practice is concerned any experienced man can generally tell one variety from another by looking at it and it is not likely that Dr. Artschwager and his microscope, nitric acid, potassium chlorate and chloroiodide of zinc will be much needed in the rude vortex of a farm. As a new facet on the bedecked and brilliant walls of the chemical cloister, however, it scintillates with becoming radiance, and that this method will be applied frequently in research work among new cane varieties by the scientists engaged in their classification is very probable.

Etomologie D'Haiti

By George N. Wolcott
(Published by "Service Technique" of the Department of Agriculture Port-au-Prince, Haiti, 1927.)

Editor Sugar Bulletin:

So much of our sugar planters speak and read French with greater than or equal facility as English, that the appearance of a book on the insects of several of their principal crops written in the language of the forefathers of a great many Southern Louisiana agriculturists, should be of decided interest in the Pelican sugar bowl.

With the publication of his *"Insectae Portoricensis"* and his *"Entomologia Economica Puertoriquena"* Dr. Wolcott had several years ago entitled himself to the gratitude of all those interested in the entomology of the West Indies, and the insects of the sugar cane. With the appearance of the volume un-

der review, an exceedingly important addition has been made to these subjects. It is particularly satisfactory to have such a comprehensive work covering the entomology of a country like Haiti, which heretofore 'has been almost unknown entomologically. Dr. Wolcott prepared the work in connection with his teaching in the Agricultural School of *Service Technique* and for a text book of entomology in tropical America it appears to the writer that this volume may serve as a model.

The book is divided into four parts: Part one discusses the general economic relations, anatomy, physiology, and development of insects and consists of five chapters. Part two, consisting of seven chapters, is an exceedingly complete, though necessarily popular, discussion of their ecology. Part three consists of eighteen chapters, the first being devoted to nomenclature and classification and the remaining seventeen each to one order of insects. Part four consists of twelve chapters, the first of which is devoted to the general introduction on the relation of insects to the farmer and the remaining eleven are devoted to the particular insects which attack distinct crops or animals. These are divided as follows: Sugar cane, coffee, cotton, tobacco, fruits, grain and legumes, stored products, domestic articles, fowl, live stock and men.

The book is very well illustrated, a great many of the drawings being original. It consists of 440 pages, is well indexed and substantially bound in cloth. Dr. Wolcott is to be congratulated on the completion of this very excellent treatise.

Arthur H. Rosenfeld.

January 27, 1931.

THE
S U G A R
La State University
Baton Rouge,
BULLETIN

Entered as second-class matter April 13, 1925, at the postoffice at
New Orleans, La., under Act of March 6, 1879.

*We stand for the encouragement of Home
Industries as against foreign competition.* May 20

| Vol. 9 | NEW ORLEANS, LA., MAY 15, 1931 | No. 16 |

The Chadbourne Plan

The Chadbourne Plan was formally signed on May 9, 1931, by the countries supposed to be signatory thereto and is now *un fait accompli*. Whatever justifiable skepticism may have existed as to whether the plan would ever be adopted can no longer have any basis, and such doubts as may be entertained regarding it must be transferred to the question of how it will work.

Mr. Chadbourne has never at any time contended that the mere holding off of the market of the stock of surplus sugar that has accumulated would be sufficient to help prices; nor does his plan include any agreement to reduce production. It does provide, however, that the countries adhering to it, among which are all the large exporting countries, shall limit their exports to certain totals that have been expertly arrived at, and this is calculated to prevent the flooding of the world's markets. Inferentially the limiting of exports will lead the countries thus limited to curtail their production, as there will be no point in the accumulation within their borders of quantities of sugar which they are notified beforehand that they cannot sell. Cuba, for instance, the chief market for whose sugar is the United States, has agreed not to export to the United States this year more than 2,577,000 tons, and it is already apparent that the Cuban sugar producers have decided to cut their output far below what it might have been, and it seems reasonable enough to suppose that the knowledge that they could not export unlimited quantities was a material factor in this reduction, because Cuba has hitherto been inclined to disregard economic conditions, that is to say, the price factor, in her sugar operations, and has apparently been able to, and disposed to, produce more and more sugar every year regardless of what it would bring. We believe, therefore, that whatever the reduction may be this year in the output of the Cuban factories will not be occasioned by the fact that they could not find some way to produce sugar at current prices but will be because they realize that they cannot sell sugar at all, beyond the Chadbourne Plan quota. The same indirect influence will operate to curtail actual production in all the other exporting countries that have joined in the pact, and thus we find a limitation of production which has never been successfully accomplished in the case of any staple commodity by direct agreement, in a fair way to be accomplished in the case of sugar by the indirect action devised by Mr. Chadbourne.

From now on we are relieved of the necessity of wondering whether or not the machinery of the Chadbourne Plan could be set up, which there was abundant reason to doubt, but which has been done, and we are free to observe the actual operation of one of the most noteworthy economic experiments ever set in motion. It is certain to be of absorbing interest from day to day as the underlying theory of it is subjected to the strain of practical tests. The Einsteins and Michelsons of economics, and a host of lesser minds, not capable of analyzing all the principles involved but realizing keenly that their bread and butter is at stake, will follow the Plan's progress as eagerly as any gallery ever followed Bobby Jones.

=====THE=====

SUGAR BULLETIN

407 Carondelet St., New Orleans

Issued on the 1st and 15th of each month. Official Organ of the American
Sugar Cane League of the U. S. A., in which are consolidated
The Louisiana Sugar Planters' Assn.
The American Cane Growers' Assn.
The Producers & Mfgrs. Protective Assn.
Subscription Price, 50 Cents Per Year.

Reginald Dykers, General Manager & Editor of the Bulletin
301 Nola Bldg., New Orleans
Frank L. Barker, Secretary and Treasurer
Lockport, La.
C. J. Bourg, Manager Washington Office
810 Union Trust Building

CHAIRMEN OF COMMITTEES:
C. D. Kemper, Franklin, La.
President of the League and Ex-Officio Chairman of Executive Committee
Percy A. Lemann, Donaldsonville, La.
Chairman Agricultural Committee
David W. Pipes, Jr., Houma, La.
Chairman Industrial Committee
Frank L. Barker, Lockport, La.
Chairman Finance Committee.
Edward J. Gay, Plaquemine, La.
Chairman Tariff Committee
H. Langdon Laws, Cinclare, La.
Chairman Legislative Committee
J. C. LeBourgeois, New Orleans, La.
Chairman Freight Rate Committee
R. H. Chadwick, Bayou Goula, La.
Chairman Membership Committee
A. H. Rosenfeld, New Orleans, La.
Chairman Publicity Committee

Members of the League desiring action on, or information on, any subject are invited to communicate with
the League or with the Chairman of the Committee
to which it seems to appertain.

Circular No. 162

The United States Department of Agriculture has
issued Circular No. 162, which is entitled "Variety
Tests of Sugar Canes in Louisiana During the Crop
Year 1928-29". The date of publication is April,
1931, and the manuscript was completed in July,
1930, but if anyone be disposed to gnash his teeth
over the time that has elapsed since the date at
which the tests were conducted and the date at which
the results have been officially promulgated it will
be advisable for him to pause and reflect that the only
result will be to wear out his teeth. The Government, like God, moves in a slow, mysterious way
its wonders to perform. The redeeming feature, in
both cases, is that wonders are indeed performed
and it is our part to regard them with appropriate
awe and respect. In the case of Circular No. 162
there is a mitigating circumstance, to-wit, that we
were very kindly allowed to publish the "Summary
and Conclusions" thereof in the SUGAR BULLETIN of
September 15th, 1930, through the courtesy of Dr.
Sidney F. Sherwood of the Bureau of Plant Industry. It will therefore not be necessary to republish
them now.

Circular No. 162 was compiled and written by
Mr. George Arceneaux, Agent, and Mr. R. T. Gib-
bens, Assistant Agronomist, of the Office of Sugar
Plants, United States Bureau of Plant Industry.

Both of these gentlemen are stationed at Houma,
La., and the data they have assembled is based on
tests made by them some two or three years ago on
the canes known as P.O.J. 36, P.O.J. 36M, P.O.J.
213, P.O.J. 234, C.P. 807, Co. 281, P.O.J. 2725,
C.P. 177, P.O.J. 2354, P.O.J. 2878, C.P. 71B, C.P.
130, C.P. 766, P.O.J. 228, P.O.J. 979, P.O.J. 826,
P.O.J. 2727, U.S. 1444, and C.P. 123. Complete information concerning results obtained with these
different varieties is given and there is no doubt
that no stone was left unturned by Messrs. Arceneaux and Gibbens in their efforts to find out all
about them and determine their suitability, or the
lack of it, for our Louisiana conditions.

Circular No. 162 should be read by all the members of the American Sugar Cane League and those
who have not seen it should write to the Washington office of the League, 810 Union Trust Building,
and request that a copy be sent them.

L. S. P. A.—the Initials of a Friend

On May 6th, 1931, thirteen surviving members of
The Louisiana Sugar Planters' Association, in meeting assembled as required by law, voted to dissolve
that corporation, and three liquidators—Messrs. Ernest A. Burguieres, Emile A. Rainold and Reginald
Dykers—were appointed to wind up its affairs.
These three morticians are proceeding with their
task.

The Louisiana Sugar Planters' Association was
formed in 1877 and was chartered in 1888. Its
Presidents, in the order named, were Duncan F.
Kenner, John Dymond, Judge Emile Rost, Henry
McCall, Charles V. Moore, James D. Hill, Edward
J. Gay, L. M. Soniat and Andrew H. Gay. With
the exception of Senator Edward J. Gay, every one
of them is dead.

From the date of the formation of The Louisiana
Sugar Planters' Association in 1877 to its final dissolution in 1931 was over half a century. During that
time it exercised an imperishable influence on the
sugar industry of this State and it was during a
considerable part of that time that Louisiana led
the whole sugar world in agriculture and in sugar
manufacturing technique. The era embraces all of
the brilliant careers among us of Doctor W. C.
Stubbs and of the erudite John Dymond, the skillful
and successful Daniel Thompson, Lewis S. Clarke,
Leon Godchaux, John N. Pharr and J. M. Burguieres,
the patrician William Porcher Miles, the able D. D.
Colcock and the courtly Benjamin Oxnard. Scores
of others, too numerous to mention, left their beneficial imprint on the times. The Association met
monthly, at night, to discuss pertinent field and
factory problems. For many years the meetings
were held at the old armory of the Continental
Guards on Camp Street, opposite Lafayette Square.
Later the meetings were held in various places, including the St. Charles Hotel, and the minute books
of the organization are a record of the halcyon days
of sugar production in this State. Those days are,
alas, no more, but we hope for their return.

Corporations have no souls. This accusation has
been flung into their teeth a million times, and is
accepted generally as a fact. So far as The Louisiana
Sugar Planters' Association is concerned, however,

we like to believe that it has a soul, and that its spirit lives still in some strange limbo of the law. We like to imagine the ghosts of all its departed Presidents assembled on the other side of some statutory Styx, a phantom *corps d'elite*, obtaining the legal wraith from Charon by a spectral writ of habeas corpus and gathering in the Shades to discuss the subject of when and how and whether they shall shave the Celestial stubble. We like to believe that the discussion will run true to form and that they will be careful to arrive at no agreement because that would prevent discussing the whole thing over again a little later on.

We do not care to placidly admit that L. S. P. A. stands for nothing now. It stands, as it has always stood, for the desire to find the truth that is buried so deeply, sometimes, at the bottom of the economic well. This quest for the truth which shall make us free from all industrial ills is being conducted now by the American Sugar Cane League, with which The Louisiana Sugar Planters' Association was merged in 1922. Like The Louisiana Sugar Planters' Association, the League is carrying high the torch. May its life be as long, as full, as useful and as resplendent as that of its predecessor.

International Conferences

(By C. J. Bourg)

It would seem to one who has listened in on some of the international conferences and followed the sessions of them all in the press, that each time the United States is an active participant, we either give something away, assume an additional obligation or listen to lectures from foreigners as to how to run our country. Even from those international groups where we have no official representation, the United States receives suggestions as to how we can contribute, or should, or something.

The latest has been the meeting of the International Chamber of Commerce in Washington where we were told what kind of tariff would be best for our own good, among other things. Quite naturally the politicians immediately vulture up and in more or less definite language, blame the world depression upon the Hawley-Smoot Act of 1930. Statistics, the friendly expert of the college professor and demagogue, which can be used to prove either side of any proposition, have been compiled on world trade with the United States to show how the recent tariff act has just ruined everything. The papers are full of statements from the merchants and bankers of Europe, the American capitalist who invests his money in foreign countries and the politician who finds an opportunity to help his party's chances in the next national election; hence what they say need not be discussed here. But we do pause to wonder whether the farmers of the country are going to be deceived. Everybody who has followed events in Washington for the past several years knows that the recent tariff revision was brought about at the insistence of agriculture and its champions. Certainly none can deny that agriculture received the largest measure of benefits and added protection from the Tariff Act of 1930. Having allowed foreigners to oppose the tariff while it was in the making, through questionable diplomatic mediums, it really seems that the citizens of the United States are being asked to show favorable reaction, instead of resentment at this meddling in our domestic affairs. Let the farmer, in whatever part of the country he may live and whatever he may produce, remember that the greatest criticism and most active opposition from foreign sources to our present tariff laws, are directed against rates upon agricultural products.

The laboring man of America had been thoroughly convinced that it is just as bad for America to compete with foreign laborers who are permitted to immigrate, as to have the foreign-made products of cheap labor brought into the United States, without protection to him against the competition with the American product and robbing him of his home market. This is no longer a partisan matter, although some of the few living free traders are trying to make it appear so. The Republican Party has always advocated protection. The Democratic Party beginning with a majority of free traders, changed first to "tariff for revenue only," then later to "tariff with incidental protection." In 1928 the party declared itself in favor of a competitive tariff for the protection of domestic industry and labor. In short, and in fact, the Democrats are as much in favor of protection now as the Republicans, although they are inclined to slightly lower rates. In most cases, let it be said in fairness and in truth, this difference in the amount of the rates levied, depends upon whether it applies to the "home state product" of the particular statesman.

Eager to center attention upon sugar, one of the Americans who has joined in the recent European attacks on our tariff is Senator Walsh of Montana. He points out that there was 4.2 per cent less cane sugar imported into the United States in 1930 than in 1929. He offers this as an indication of what he calls "the deplorable slump in our foreign trade." However, he is unwilling to go any further than to state that this is caused by the Tariff Act of 1930, adding merely that "the reader will be able to judge for himself." Of course, the Senator would never admit that the below-cost price of sugar being paid in the United States markets, and the unemployment depression which started at least a year before the tariff act was passed, have had anything to do with this "gigantic slump" of 4.2 per cent. This is cited as an indication of the whole situation.

Consistently with what has been said above we can

refer now to the signing of the Chadbourne Plan at Brussels last Saturday. We want to record with emphasis that this international sugar conference did not include any official representative of the United States Government or of the domestic sugar industry of the United States. Therefore, we anticipate that our domestic industry has more than an even chance of benefiting from the Chadbourne Plan. As the newspaper reports on the Chadbourne Plan have played up the price feature of the agreement, because of its probable news value, it is believed that a more or less elementary statement of the whole proposition will not only be interesting but informative, based upon facts taken from trade journals and sugar publications.

The Chadbourne Plan is an agreement signed by the Governments of Cuba, Java, Germany, Belgium, Poland, Czecho-Slovakia and Hungary. France has not signed the agreement but has taken action towards restriction of sugar production in keeping with the Chadbourne Plan. Further efforts will be made to secure the official cooperation of Peru, San Domingo and Russia in these restriction plans.

The world sugar situation which caused Mr. Thomas Chadbourne to originate his plan has been given in the following figures of the past crop year:

World's production of sugar 27,690,000 long tons.

World's consumption of sugar 26,374,000 long tons.

Amount of sugar consumed in countries which import sugar, 20,084,000 tons.

Net amount of sugar these countries imported over and above the amount of sugar they produced, 11,072,000 tons.

Amount of sugar produced by the sugar exporting countries of the world, 19,120,000 tons.

Net amount of sugar exported by these countries, 10,894,000 tons.

Amount of sugar consumed by these countries, 6,290,000 tons.

Surplus of sugar produced by these countries above amount of sugar exported and consumed, 1,936,000 tons.

The total visible stock of sugar existing in the world at the end of the past crop year, 10,566,000 tons.

Total visible stock of sugar existing at the end of 1927-28 8,160,000 tons.

A very reliable report from New York states that the sugar trade generally believes that the existing invisible supply of sugar in the hands of distributors and consumers throughout the world, is at a very low point. The discouraging sugar market condition has caused the trade to work to carry the smallest possible stock, leaving to the producers the excess supply. It is estimated that the invisible supply of sugar varies from 3,000,000 tons in times of distress to as high as 10,000,000 tons in a period of confidence and advancing prices. Under average market conditions in sugar it is reasonable to assume 6,500,000 tons of invisible stock, which means there is room for an unusually heavy movement of sugar into the hands of the distributing and consuming trade, as soon as there is confidence of an upturn in values.

The Chadbourne Plan calls for the liquidation of 2,500,000 tons excess sugar over the five-year period. By gradual liquidation and a curb on production it is hoped that sugar prices will be restored to a profitable basis. The Chadbourne Plan is intended to stabilize the industry through the restoration of equilibrium between world production and consumption. It is not only an accord between sugar producers but the governments of the countries joining the plan, will protect the integrity of the export and crop restrictions agreed upon.

Already Cuba has restricted her crop to 3,122,000 tons, which is a reduction of 1,549,000 tons from the last crop. The beet acreage in Europe has been reduced more than 15 per cent, outside of Russia.

Contrary to the efforts of certain newspapers to create the impression that the Chadbourne Plan is a price fixing proposition, the agreement makes no geographical restriction of markets nor does it fix any price. Each of the signatory countries has agreed to segregate a certain number of tons of sugar to be sold over a five-year period. There is a provision that in the event of sugar prices reaching 2 cents per pound f.o.b. Cuba and the price maintained for thirty days, the export quotas will be automatically increased 5 per cent. Should sugar prices advance to $2\frac{1}{4}$ cents per pound f.o.b. Cuba and remain there for a period of thirty days, the International Sugar Commission has been given the power to release an additional $2\frac{1}{2}$ per cent of the export quotas. Another provision stipulates that should prices advance to $2\frac{1}{2}$ cents per pound f.o.b. Cuba for a thirty-day period, then 5 per cent of the export quotas must be released, including the $2\frac{1}{2}$ per cent optional increase above authorized.

The plan provides that the agreement shall be carried out under the direction of a committee which will very likely be headed by Senator Beauduin of

Belgium, but the active executive will be Mr. Francis Powell, an American who has had considerable experience in the sugar markets of Europe. The function of this committee will be to supervise the crop restrictions and the exportations of sugar, and as can be seen from the preceding paragraph, it will also serve to insure against any undue or unreasonable rise in the price of sugar, unwarranted by the supplies of sugar throughout the world. The sugar under the control of the committee will thus help to provide a price which is above the cost of production but it will also keep that price within reasonable bounds.

Contact Committee

Minutes of
Meeting of American Sugar Cane League Contact
Committee with Louisiana Experiment
Station Workers
Baton Rouge, La., April 10, 1931

The meeting was called to order by Mr. Wallace, Chairman. Present:

Contact Committee—Mr. A. W. Wallace, Mr. Percy Lemann, Mr. Stephen Munson, Mr. Elliot Jones. *Station Staff*—Dr. C. T. Dowell, Mr. W. G. Taggart, Mr. E. C. Simon, Dr. C. W. Edgerton, Dr. E. C. Tims, Mr. Truman Ryker, Dr. W. E. Hinds, Mr. G. N. Reuss, Mr. Wm. Whipple, Mr. C. B. Gouaux, Mr. S. J. Breaux. *Visitors*—Dr. A. H. Rosenfeld, Mr. A. M. O'Neal.

Department of Entomology Report

A three-page mimeographed progress report was presented by Dr. Hinds, as follows:

Trichogramma Work: During the past month we have made considerable progress in the development of humidifying apparatus such as will be adaptable for summer conditions. The one we are using now is simple but one without heat and which will give us high humidity in the summer time and yet hold temperature down is another proposition entirely, and we are working on this at the present time. We can get fairly good control of both temperature and relative humidity as long as we can use heat to vaporize water. Breeding Room No. 1, which was stocked after December, is now producing 5,000 to 6,000 moths per day. We will have a supply available for field colonization on first brood eggs, which will be during the latter part of April or first of May if centers of fairly heavy infestation can be found to maintain them.

The planting of trap corn for the concentration of the eggs of Diatraea and Heliothis has been completed at Island Plantation, Plaquemine on March 24th, and here at the Sugar Station on March 25th. We waited until we thought the soil conditions favorable for the growth of corn, but little progress has been made in the growth of this corn on account

of the cold weather which has since prevailed. In accordance with the discussion at the last meeting of the Committee, an article entitled "Planning Borer Control for 1931" was prepared and was published in the Sugar Bulletin on April 1st. We are planning on other articles to follow.

We have been trying to determine further the place and manner of hibernation of Trichogramma. Last winter at the Cleveland meetings the matter was discussed with a Northern entomologist and he stated that Trichogramma parasitism has been found occasionally in the eggs of the bagworm during the winter there, and so we have been trying to locate bagworm eggs here. The bagworm is a species of caterpillar that feeds especially on evergreens; the worms construct a silken cocoon, weaving into that little particles of twigs and leaves so that it looks like trash, and this is their protection. During the early part of their life this cocoon is entirely movable and is carried with them. Later on they attach it to a twig and inside of this the female develops. The female never leaves the cocoon and lays her eggs on the inside. There is a fair chance that there may be survival of Trichogramma here in a location like that. We have searched extensively around Baton Rouge for eggs of the evergreen bagworm, but have failed to find any in this section. We are trying to secure some from a center of infestation which has been reported to us from Mississippi. We have examined cabbage fields late in March for eggs of the cabbage looper and cabbage butterfly, but no parasitism by Trichogramma was found.

Borer Development: A number of moths have emerged in the laboratory since March 21st. The first of these moths come from sections of cane that we have carried in the laboratory since last December. There has been no moisture whatever and still they have gone ahead and completed development and moths have emerged in spite of this very dry condition.

Examinations of top trash material brought from Island Plantation, Plaquemine, and including material taken from several different cuts in the series of trash disposal tests, showed on March 20th, among 400 tops examined, 37 stages alive and 15 dead. This gives a ratio of approximately one living stage per 11 tops examined. Among the living stages were found the following: 1 second stage larva, 2 third stage, 11 fourth stage, 15 fifth stage, 3 living pupae and 5 empty pupal skins. It is very surprising that second stage larvae should have survived up to this time.

Soil Animal Work: During the past month Mr. Stracener and student assistants have completed the collection of small soil animals and have completed the stocking of the drums in this experimental work.

Due to the scarcity of funds and the necessity for conserving them to the utmost, it was deemed advisable to delay the beginning of the Ligyrus work at Franklin until temperature conditions become more favorable for the flight of these beetles. Mr. Osterberger left Baton Rouge on April 6th and is now at Franklin. A few statements from him are included in this report.

Tests have been started to determine the effect of applications of superphosphate, cyanamid, "P. D. B.," calcium cyanide and lime, in varying dosages, upon the activity, development and injuriousness of the sugar cane beetle. The corn is 3 to 4 inches high and is still yellow from the recent cold. The beetles are active in the ground feeding on cane and corn, and mating in the ground, but no eggs or young grubs could be found in the soil. So we are actually ahead of the breeding season this year, which is considerably later than the season of 1930. There is apparently little if any flying of beetles as yet. Trap lights are also being used in this work.

Climatic Conditions: Climatic conditions, of course, affect borer development the same as they affect cane development, and it is important for us to keep close watch of the prevailing conditions of temperature and rainfall especially. In comparing these records, particularly for last year and this year, it is very evident that 1931 is an unusually cold, late season. You will recall that January, 1930, experienced a number of severe freezes and the month was considered as being unusually cold. During that month the average mean temperature was 50° and the minimum went to 32° or lower on 10 dates. The temperature stood at 40° or lower, with prospects of frosts or freezes on 15 days. In comparison with these figures, we find in 1931 an average mean temperature of 49.4° with a minimum of 32° or lower on only 5 days, but with a temperature of 40° or below on 18 days. February, during both seasons, was fairly warm and, in fact, considerably warmer than March of each year. In 1930 the February average mean was 58.5°, while in 1931 it was only 55.4°. The lower average of 1931 is due especially to the lower average maximum temperature experienced. In March, 1930, the average mean temperature of the air was 55.4°, while that of 1931 was 53.5°. Mean temperatures of below 55° are not often favorable to plant growth. In March, 1930, the temperature was at or below 40° with frost on 8 dates and freeze on 1, while in 1931 the temperature of 40° or below with frosts was experienced in 12 days. These frosts continued at Baton Rouge as late as April 6th with a heavy frost at 37° on April 6th and a very light frost in spots on April 7th. These temperature conditions will explain fairly clearly the very slow development of cane and corn this year.

Department of Plant Pathology

A two-page mimeographed progress report was presented by Dr. Edgerton.

Cane Conditions: A month ago we brought out the statement that cane was in much better condition fundamentally than it was a year ago The roots are still on the seed pieces and a good growth should follow when weather conditions are favorable. Cane development, however, has been materially held back due to the unfavorable weather. Nevertheless, the cane at the present time is better than it was a year ago. Plant cane of the varieties P.O.J. 213, 36, 36M and Co. 281 has grown very slowly. P.O.J. 234, C.P.

Statistics Award the Prize to the OLIVER UNITED CANE MUD FILTER

ABOUT three years ago the first Oliver United Cane Mud Filter went into service, and has made three campaigns. Its user has obtained a substantial profit by its operation.

Since then eight other companies (widely separated) have bought this machine for the profit it provides.

The rapid acceptance of this machine by the industry shows how its users realize the immediate benefit by lower handling costs and by a greater recovery of sugar from the cane milled.

The prize for the development most profitable to the cane sugar industry goes to the Oliver United Cane Mud Filter.

Benefits Obtained by Using
THE OLIVER UNITED CANE MUD FILTER

Cleaner and quicker handling of cane muds
More sugar in the bag
Minimum water for washing cake
Long life of filter medium
Reduction in labor

177 and Co. 290 are almost up to a stand. A few buds and shoots of P.O.J. 213 and 234 have rotted recently, but these are exceptions. There has been a somewhat greater deterioration in first year stubble, especially the early cut cane of P.O.J. 234 and 213. The upper eyes are the most developed. P.O.J. 36M is the only variety showing primary root development. In second stubble of P.O.J. 213 and 36M, a considerable percentage of the eyes and shoots have rotted. Unless there is further decay, there are sufficient eyes left to produce a good stand. A trip over the State on March 17th, 18th and 19th showed the cane the most advanced at Meeker; good at Reserve and Houma; and somewhat backward at Youngsville. Similarly to last year, there has been practically no decay of the roots or shoots at Meeker. Cultures made from roots from different localities showed very little Pythium development except at Donaldsonville.

Germination Counts: These germination counts were made by planting the stalks and counting the eyes. The cane was planted on October 22nd and 23rd and on April 6th counts were made of the shoots showing above ground. Last year on April 10th there was much more cane on the ground than at the present time. The percentage of germination is not much over half of what it was a year ago with most of the varieties.

Resistance to Mosaic: At previous meetings of this Committee it has been brought out that certain of the P.O.J. varieties have the ability to throw off mosaic or to produce healthy shoots from eyes on stalks that were known to be mosaic-infected. At present it would seem that the usual freedom from mosaic of varieties like P.O.J. 213 is due to this. Mosaic in any variety that constantly throws off a large percentage of healthy shoots from diseased seed pieces apparently becomes a problem of no important.

A test carried on recently in the greenhouse has given some interesting results. Twelve stalks each of P.O.J. 36, 213, 234 and 228, which were known to be infested with mosaic, were planted. Shoots from these stalks were examined. P.O.J. 234 produced the least number of healthy shoots, while P.O.J. 213 and 228 produced a high percentage of healthy shoots.

Report of Test Field Work

A four-page mimeographed progress report was presented by Mr. Gouaux.

Field Work in March: The cane crop did not make very much progress during the month of March on account of the unfavorable weather conditions which existed. The shoots of cane, both plant and stubble, that were out were badly hit by frost and thin ice. With favorable growing weather, the cane will grow out very quickly and regain its green color. The fall plant crop is now scraped and off-barred and in a good many cases hoed and is showing excellent germination. P.O.J. 234, as usual, is much more advanced than is P.O.J. 213, 36 and 36M. There are some complaints about red rot damage, mostly with the P.O.J. 213 variety, and usually in lands where drainage is poor. This condition occurs frequently in fields where the seed cane is planted too deep, covered with too much dirt and where the dirt was scraped off late. C.P. 807 is the most advanced variety; P.O.J. 234 comes next in order from comparative standpoint in the field, not including the test fields. Co. 290 in the test fields is making very good showing; Co. 281 in all cases is slower in germination and is not to be compared with C.P. 807 or P.O.J. 234. The stubble crop has received all preliminary cultivation work with a great deal of shaving going on throughout the cane belt. The first stubble is more advanced than second stubble, although there is some very good second stubble out in the State. P.O.J. 234 first stubble is more advanced than P.O.J. 213, 36 and 36M, and in some cases has already been fertilized. P.O.J. 213, 36 and 36M second stubble is in a more sound condition than P.O.J. 234 second stubble. During the latter part of March some of the more advanced stubble fields were being fertilized. During the month of March the planting of feed crops has been one of the main field activities throughout the section. The planters are interested in obtaining higher yields of corn to fully meet their mule feeding requirements. More attention is being given to planting better seed corn, and in many cases the planters have bought fresh seed corn. Most of the planters are planning to use some fertilizer during the early growing period and will use practically the same material as they use for stubble cane. The Biloxi soybean continues to be the standard summer legume in all sections of the cane belt, with smaller plantings of the Otootan variety.

Cane Fertilization and Cultivation: Cane cultivation is being discussed more freely by sugar planters this year than ever before, and the method of cultivation as practiced at the Louisiana Experiment Station has met the favorable approval of many planters in the various sections of the cane belt. The method takes into consideration the following important points:

1—Deep work with plows and middle-burster, early in the season before the cane roots are out.
2—Subsequent cultivations with Moline type cultivator, spring-tooth and shovel attachments.
3—Early lay-by of crop with Moline type cultivator and disc cultivator.
4—Minimizing the cutting of cane roots as much as possible at all times.

Experiment Station Test Fields: The plant cane varieties are more advanced than first and second stubble varieties. Sterling shows the most advanced condition, while Cinclare and Glenwood are ahead of Reserve, and Youngsville is slowest in germination. The variety C.P. 807 is showing the highest germination counts at all of the test fields. Co. 290 is second ranking variety at Cinclare, Glenwood, Meeker and Youngsville, while P.O.J. 234, also high ranking early germination variety, is second at Meeker, Reserve and Sterling. P.O.J. 36M is slower than both P.O.J. 213 and Co. 281, while Co. 281 has a slight advantage on P.O.J. 213. Plant cane varieties at the same time in 1930 were more advanced.

First Stubble: The condition of first stubble varieties for the period of March 25-31 was more advanced in 1930. In three alluvial section test fields Reserve is most advanced, followed by Glenwood. Meeker is more advanced than Reserve and Sterling. Germination is slowest at Youngsville. C.P. 807 is leading in highest shoots counts at all the test fields except Glenwood and Meeker, where Co. 281 and P.O.J. 234 are just as high. In the majority of cases Co. 281 outranked P.O.J. 213 and P.O.J. 36M is

slower than P.O.J. 213, while P.O.J. 234 was higher than Co. 281 four out of six times.

Second Stubble: At the four second stubble test fields C.P. 807 is the leading variety in having more shoots out. P.O.J. 234 is second ranking variety at Cinclare and Meeker. Co. 281 is second at Sterling and P.O.J. 36M and P.O.J. 213 are second at Youngsville.

On March 17th, Mr. E. J. Badeaux, Field Manager, Sterling Sugars, Inc., made germination counts of the Sterling test field plant cane varieties and observations on root development and general appearance. He reports as follows: "The best root development was found on P.O.J. 36 and 807 next. The poorest was found on P.O.J. 213 and 234. The longest roots were found on C.P. 177. There are three varieties that do not show any signs of having been affected by the cold, Co. 290, Co. 281 and C. P. 807. C. P. 177 shows the best growth."

Department of Agricultural Economics

A brief mimeographed report of Cane Yields on 135 Small Farms for 1930 was presented by Mr. Reuss. The extremely low yields on these small farms were discussed at length. The low yields secured are no doubt due to the fertilization practices and the predominance of spring planting.

Circulation of this Issue 1750 Copies

Jun 12

Jun 12

THE
SUGAR
BULLETIN

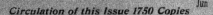

Entered as second-class matter April 13, 1925, at the postoffice at
New Orleans, La., under Act of March 6, 1879.

*We stand for the encouragement of Home
Industries as against Foreign competition.*

| Vol. 9 | NEW ORLEANS, LA., JUNE 1, 1931 | No. 17 |

Planning Trichogramma Colonization

By W. E. Hinds, Entomologist, Louisiana Experiment Station

Sugarcane borer moths from overwintered larvæ have been emerging since about the middle of April, at which time males and females were taken at trap lights at Franklin. It is certain, therefore, that eggs have been deposited in some numbers since that time, but we have not yet (May 11, 1931) found either borer eggs or the feeding work of first generation borer larvæ in either corn or cane at Baton Rouge. No trace of parasitism by Trichogramma has been found in the fields this season on the eggs of any possible host species, although several examinations have been made.

In THE SUGAR BULLETIN of April 15, 1931, appears an article entitled "Watching for Centers of Borer Concentration." The suggestions given in that article should be followed closely in making field examinations to determine where favorable locations for Trichogramma colonization may exist, and what areas, or acreage, of corn or cane should be included in such an experimental effort at borer control.

It appears generally that corn is relatively more advanced in growth this season than is cane. We believe therefore, that there will be a much larger proportion of the first generation of borers produced in corn this season than has occurred for several years. Accordingly we shall expect to find the principal centers for colonization of Trichogramma in the field to be in corn that is quite closely adjacent to cane fields. In the corn at this time may be found a rather large proportion of stalks showing the feeding work of the larvæ of *Heliothis obsoleta*. These larvæ are known as corn budworms or corn earworms since the same species feeds in the leaf roll early in the growth of the stalk and later upon the ears as they develop. Eggs of this species are present continuously from early in the season, and these eggs are subject to a high degree of parasitization by Trichogramma. They may maintain Trichogram-

ma in the field at times when Diatraea eggs are scarce. In our experimental work for this season we are just now beginning the release of Trichogramma in corn fields even though infestation by Diatraea is not yet apparent.

For the sugar planter as a rule, however, we would not think it advisable for him to attempt any field colonization of Trichogramma before the latter part of June this season. By that time the egg laying by the earliest of the first generation cane borer moths should be under way and a continuous supply of the eggs of these two species should then be present in corn to provide a favorable situation for Trichogramma colonization with good prospects of successful maintenance.

The practical question which many growers may have in mind at this time is: How shall I determine how large a supply of Trichogramma I shall need to meet the requirements for successful colonization under my conditions? In an attempt to help answer this question we would make the following suggestions: First, watch the early-maturing corn especially for evidences of infestation by both the corn earworm and the sugarcane borer. If areas of even moderately heavy infestation are found, and the location is such that the spread of cane borer moths and of parasites may readily occur from this area to cane fields, then we would estimate the acreage included in this area and plan to colonize Trichogramma therein. The benefit of colonization may be experienced by the corn crop as well as by the nearby areas of cane. It is our opinion at the present time that it is better policy to release a small number of Trichogramma at a time and repeat the releases at intervals of a week or ten days, rather than to release the entire number at any one time. In accordance with this policy, we would expect to arrange with some commercial Trichogramma production organization to supply the material desired and

THE

SUGAR
BULLETIN

407 Carondelet St., New Orleans

Issued on the 1st and 15th of each month. Official Organ of the American
Sugar Cane League of the U. S. A., in which are consolidated
The Louisiana Sugar Planters' Assn.
The American Cane Growers' Assn.
The Producers & Mfgrs. Protective Assn.
Subscription Price, 50 Cents Per Year.

Reginald Dykers, General Manager & Editor of the Bulletin
301 Nola Bldg., New Orleans
Frank L. Barker, Secretary and Treasurer
Lockport, La.
C. J. Bourg, Manager Washington Office
810 Union Trust Building

CHAIRMEN OF COMMITTEES:
C. D. Kemper, Franklin, La.
President of the League and Ex-Officio Chairman of Executive Committee
Percy A. Lemann, Donaldsonville, La.
Chairman Agricultural Committee
David W. Pipes, Jr., Houma, La.
Chairman Industrial Committee
Frank L. Barker, Lockport, La.
Chairman Finance Committee.
Edward J. Gay, Plaquemine, La.
Chairman Tariff Committee
H. Langdon Laws, Cinclare, La.
Chairman Legislative Committee
J. C. LeBourgeois, New Orleans, La.
Chairman Freight Rate Committee
R. H. Chadwick, Bayou Goula, La.
Chairman Membership Committee
A. H. Rosenfeld, New Orleans, La.
Chairman Publicity Committee

Members of the League desiring action on, or information on, any subject are invited to communicate with the League or with the Chairman of the Committee to which it seems to appertain.

to deliver it in accordance with the time scheduled for making the various releases. We believe that a fairly safe basis for estimating the stock of Trichogramma required would be at the rate of approximately 2,000 parasites per acre at each of 3 release periods. This would mean a total stock of not less than 5,000 parasites per acre for the area to be colonized. The actual number would likely range between 5,000 and 7,000 per acre. In placing an order for material, it should be specified that the "Louisiana strain of Trichogramma" is desired. This stock has been bred from parasites coming originally from cane borer eggs taken at Franklin, Louisiana, in March, 1927, and we have good evidence that it is superior to the strains produced in some other sections in the readiness with which it attacks the eggs of Diatraea.

In a future article we shall expect to discuss the conditions under which Trichogramma stock may be held in storage to delay the emergence of parasites or to prolong the life of adults while awaiting favorable climatic conditions for making the actual release in the field and describing the conditions which we consider as most favorable to successful field colonization work.

Baton Rouge, Louisiana, May 12, 1931.

The Chadbourne Plan

The International Sugar Journal (London) devotes several pages of its editorial space in its May, 1931, issue to a discussion of the Chadbourne Plan, in the ultimate efficacy of which the editor seems to firmly believe. So far as the immediate situation is concerned, however, he says:

"But for the time being the bears have dug themselves in, and New York, their headquarters, has been encouraged in its resistance by the fact that the Philippines have made it a present of the whole of its current crop at today's prices. So there is no material improvement in the market for the time being, and indications point to the possibility that several more months will elapse before certain inexorable factors have full play on market prices. These include: (1) The fact that nearly three million tons of surplus sugar out of an annual production of 28 millions is being taken off the market; (2) that the Cuban crop is now coming to an end so that storage congestion in Cuba will tend to easen and there will be no need to throw Cuban sugars on the American market at cut prices; (3) that the European beet crop (bar Russia) to be marketed next Autumn and Winter promises to be appreciably less, not only on account of reduced sowings but from the fact that last year's favorable weather and much more than average yield cannot be counted on to repeat themselves."

The following is an extract from a communication from one of the personnel of the Lamborn & Company organization which was published in their market letter this week:

"I shall not attempt to criticize or defend the Chadbourne plan, which can be twisted and turned in exactly the way that your mind is working or your position on the market makes you feel like doing. I do believe, however, that inasmuch as the pact has been officially signed and a treaty agreed upon, we can deal more with facts, and it will be rather amusing to take a look around. Ever since the Chadbourne plan originated, those who opposed this idea have always had the advantage of having a loophole where this scheme would come to naught, and break up all negotiations, which would result in throwing millions of tons of sugar on the market. This is now settled—the treaty cannot be broken, and consequently, it is a fact that these sugars which are segregated cannot at a minute's notice be thrown on the market.

"The big factor recently has been the continued propaganda that the consumption in the United States is decreasing by leaps and bounds, principally based on the decreased deliveries and meltings of the United States refineries to date.

"Would it not be well to remember that during the first five months of 1930 there were large quantities of refined sugars stored away, with the idea of taking advantage of the new tariff, which would be effective later on?

"Are we forgetting entirely that during the months of June, July, August and September we had a continued bear market in 1930, where deliveries fell off rapidly?

"Would it, therefore, not be fair to take the exact deliveries of all white sugars given out privately by the Sugar Institute during the year 1930? These figures must be correct, because the Institute receives them from the refiners, beet people and importers of all white sugars.

"I understand that in the United States during 1930 there was delivery of white sugars in the amount of 5,765,000 long tons. Now, if we go further and reduce the raw sugar into the equivalent of refined, all the beet, Louisiana, Porto Rican, Mexican, Philippine, Hawaiians and allotted Cubas to the United States into white sugars, we will find that we will have approximately (taking every pound into consideration) 5,800,000 long tons of white sugars, or an excess of 35,000 long tons.

"We are today on the basis of 12 points below the

The Advertisers in the Sugar Bulletin are contributing 'owards the support of the American Sugar Cane League and should enjoy your special consideration; help them 'o help the Domestic Sugar Industry by doing business with them whenever possible.

vorld's parity, which can only be accounted for by the oncentrated efforts of the free duty sellers to give heir sugars away as fast as the market will take them.

"At today's spot market of 1.14 c. and f. New York, I ionestly believe that every sugar producer is selling his iroduct at a loss.

"I have tried to reason why this should happen, and vhy these holders would let go of their product at this idiculous price, and the only answer I can give is to iuote from the Bible: 'Please forgive them, as they :now not what they are doing.'

"The trade has no sugar—the refiners have a fair itock, but not excessive, and not the amount which will ie required as we very shortly enter the heavy con- iuming season.

"I consider raw sugar at 1.14 c. and f. a bargain and feel sure that soon better prices will be witnessed."

Later advices are that Russia is reported to have iurchased 10,000 to 20,000 tons of German crystals ind is inquiring for more. It is also reported that Russia endeavored to re-buy sugars sold to Holland ind other continental countries. London cables in- licate that the Russian crop is apparently falling :onsiderably below expectations.

Domino Vobiscum

One of the outstanding entertainment features n connection with the convention of the American Wholesale Grocers at New Orleans, May 12th-14th, vas a trip to the Chalmette Refinery of the American Sugar Refining Company on Tuesday afternoon, May 12th.

In company with public officials of the State of Louisiana and the City of New Orleans, together with prominent business men of the city, members of the Association and their wives, a total party of ver 800, boarded the steamer "New Orleans," spe- :ially chartered by the refining company and, leaving he foot of Canal Street, New Orleans, at 1:30 p. m., iailed to Chalmette.

Historic interest attaches to the site upon which he Chalmette Refinery is located for it was here that Andrew Jackson's military genius repulsed the British luring the war of 1812.

On arrival at Chalmette, a luncheon was served in he form of an old fashioned Southern barbecue. following luncheon the guests were conducted in iroups on a tour of the refinery, where much interest vas shown in the many intricate processes employed n the production of the popular Domino Package Sugars.

After inspection of the refinery the guests re-em- iarked on the steamer for the return trip to New Orleans in time for dinner.

The admirable way in which the affair was con- lucted was in keeping with the reputation for effi- iency that the host enjoys. Mr. Ralph S. Stubbs, /ice-President of the American Sugar Refining Com- iany, came down from the New York headquarters for he occasion, and Mr. W. J. Crane, the General Vlanager of the company at New Orleans, and Mr.

J. Clifford Pierson, head of the local raw sugar pur- chasing department, and all the other New Orleans men connected with the company outdid themselves in courtesy and hospitality, with the result that many blushes were brought to their sophisticated cheeks by the compliments heaped upon them.

The Coincidence of a Century

By C. J. Bourg

The literary theory that history repeats itself cer- tainly finds a dramatic substantiation in the present litigation before the United States Customs Court. It was just one hundred years ago that an attempt was made to dodge the sugar duty by introducing sugar in a liquid form. For some years thereafter the practice continued, bringing about governmental action and investigations which it was hoped might curb and prevent these frauds.

Some writers have given credit for originality to the Savannah Refining Corporation in respect to im- porting sugar dissolved in water, so as to evade the payment of the higher duty on sugar and to have applied the lower rate on molasses. The same stunt, was tried unsuccessfully a century ago and while it seems to have troubled the Government for some twenty years thereafter, the practice was finally given up in the face of Treasury regulations and legislative improvements.

While delving in the mysteries of one of Wash- ington's many bookstores, your correspondent came upon certain Senate documents referring to sugar and with the aid of a gray-haired librarian collected six of such documents dated from 1832 to 1851, in- clusive. These documents contained correspondence and reports of the problems which confronted the Treasury Department and which were eventually passed on to the Congress of the United States, with regard to the importation of sugar under vari- ous disguises in an attempt to avoid paying the full duty.

A letter which forms part of Senate Document No. 139, 22nd Congress of the United States, could have been written in 1931 instead of 1831, by the Gover- nor of Louisiana without changing any of the state- ments therein made and still be a correct recital of the present situation.

The letter from his Excellency A. B. Roman, Gov- ernor of Louisiana, to the Secretary of the Treasury, relative to the importation of sugar in the form of syrup, is somewhat long and only the most important excerpts are reproduced hereinbelow.

"New Orleans, September 28, 1831.

"Hon. Louis M'Lane,

"Secretary of the Treasury.

"Sir:

"Having been informed of a fraud on the revenue laws of the United States, attempted in this city, which, if not suppressed, would tend not only to diminish materially the revenue of the National Government, but would also have the effect of inflicting a most fatal blow to the prosperity of Louisiana, I consider it as a duty to add my observations to those which, as I understand, have been addressed to you on the subject. * * *

"Some individuals concerned in sugar refineries, have purchased sugar in the island of Cuba, and after having had it there dissolved in some warm water in order to render it liquid, have shipped it to New Orleans as molasses or syrup. This operation of boiling the sugar with water, is an indispensable preparation to the refining of it, and the importers have only had done in Cuba what they would have been obliged to do in their own refining houses in this city, if the sugar had been in its natural state. The simple statement of those facts, * * * would seem sufficient to show that the importation could have no other object but the evasion of the legal duty; * * *

"It cannot be contended that, if the substance is not to be considered as molasses or syrup, it can no more be called sugar; and that if the importer were to state plainly at the custom-house how the liquid was composed, it would have to be classed amongst the non-enumerated articles, and be entered on paying a duty of fifteen per cent. ad valorem. Such a doctrine, if it were admitted, would only tend to legalize fraud, provided it was openly and boldly committed. * * * But can it be supposed that, when the law has enumerated an article, and classed it with those which the interest of the nation requires to be submitted to a heavy duty, it should only be necessary to disguise that article, to mask its appearance without changing its nature, to alter its name, or to pretend that it has no name at all, in order to class it legally among those which that same law has considered as too insignificant to be named? I cannot believe it: I cannot admit that the laws of the country are so easily trampled under foot. If sugar refiners find an advantage in preparing their sugars with water before they import it, they should certainly be permitted to do so, but they should pay the usual duty on the sugar which the water contains. If that were not the case, the planters of Louisiana would be less favored by the laws of the Union than those of Cuba, and the protecting duty on sugar could be considered as totally repealed.

"* * * Our fellow citizens deprived of their just rights, would be condemned to an unavoidable ruin for the benefit of foreigners, and a few sugar refiners in the United States, who would accumulate immense wealth by defrauding the national revenue.

"I have every reason to expect, however, that you will be of opinion that such a course cannot be permitted, and that the necessary means will be immediately taken to prevent in future this fraudulent traffic, not only here, but also in the northern cities, where it has, no doubt, been likewise attempted.

"Very respectfully,
"Your obedient servant,
"A. B. Roman."

On September 20, 1831, Martin Gordon, Collector of New Orleans, reported to the Secretary of the Treasury that several small importations from Cuba of an article invoiced and entered as "sirop de batterie" were entered at New Orleans. He states that the article is in fact "sugar dissolved by the intro-

duction of steam or boiling water and holding in solution the largest possible quantity of sugar." He reports that an extensive establishment has been erected at Matanzas where sugar is thrown into kettles, mixed with water and after undergoing a slight boiling is called sirup de batterie and shipped to the United States. He comments, "under those circumstances, you will readily perceive that the importation of this article operates as a serious and positive fraud on the Government, as well as being, in the highest degree injurious to the interest and well-being of this State." On October 5, 1831, Mr. Gordon reported the arrival of another cargo which was entered as "sirup made from sugar and water," which he reports contains nine parts sugar and one part water.

Mr. Gordon sends correspondence to the Treasury Department to show that he has requested a certain number of sugar planters to examine the imported article stating that because of their experience in the culture of cane and manufacture of sugar they would be able to ascertain the precise character of the article. These gentlemen in turn signed a statement declaring the "casks to contain sugar which has been dissolved in water and apparently holding in solution a very large portion of sugar."

It should be interesting to read the familiar names of some of the planters called in to make the examination, viz.:

W. W. Montgomery, M. S. Cucullu, G. Villere, David Urquhart, L. Millaudon, J. H. Shepherd, C. Zermiguel, F. Dorville, G. B. Milligan, F. Bienvenu, Z. Cavelier, P. Baron Boisfontaine, F. Fazende, W. Lavergne, M. Andry, F. L. N. Labarre.

While the details of these investigations and reports give a most interesting historical background to the whole thread of sugar tariff legislation, the writer is somewhat hesitant to extend his enthusiasm to these columns for the recitation of what to him are romantic facts. We read of how it was decided at one time "that the duty on molasses should be charged per pound and not per gallon; because the more saccharine in molasses or syrup, the more the weight; and the quantity and not capacity should thereby be taxed." By referring to the Tariff Act of 1842, we find an interesting provision which states in part: "In order to prevent frauds and to prevent the introduction of sugar, syrup of sugar, syrup of cane, or batterie syrup under the title of molasses, or in any other improper manner," inspection shall be made by the Secretary of the Treasury. In Tariff Act of 1861 this enactment was made stronger by the following provision: "That all syrup of sugar, or of sugar cane, concentrated molasses, or melada, entered under the name of molasses or any other name than syrup of sugar or of sugar cane, concentrated molasses or concentrated melada shall be liable to forfeiture to the United States." A similar forfeiture provision appears in all Tariff Acts, until the Tariff Act of 1883, when the tariff law was first divided into separate schedules, and sugar was specially treated under Schedule E.

One would think that with all of these precedents and with the information so long before Congress and the Treasury Department, that legislation could be drawn which would prevent of a rather striking repetition of history. It is amusing, although disappointing, that one of the reports submitted to the

ited States Senate by the Secretary of the Treas-
' suggests that as a result of the researches being
de and the reports incident thereto, "the Govern-
nt may be in possession of all the facts necessary
enlightening and illustrating its policy with refer-
:e to this subject; frauds, being rendered of ready
ection will be prevented, and the attempt finally
indoned." The Secretary was right in so far as
immediate contemporaneous attempts of import-
, but he little reckoned that despite the enlighten-
nt of one hundred years, his successor in office
)uld in 1931 have to face the same problems.
It might be historically important to record the
e of the clever importer of 1831; "in connection
'h the importation of syrup in 1831 at New Or-
ns, Mr. Goodale, then and now a refiner of that
y, caused to be built at Matanzas, as I have been
d by himself and by persons residing near Matan-
i, a house furnished with a train of pans for dis-
ving sugar in water. The sirup thus formed was
: article he imported, and which was seized by the
llector of New Orleans. Mr. Goodale had thus
)ended several thousand dollars, believing that he
ild, under the then existing laws, introduce sirup
th profit and without liability to seizure. But the
s he sustained, in consequence of the seizures of
i sirup, the costs of suits in which he became in-
lved with the government, and the sacrifice of
)perty he was obliged to make, effectually put an
d to his operations."
The reading of these historical documents, so im-
rtant and yet so ineffective in the wealth of in-
rmation which they give, in so far as concerns the·
1guage of our present tariff laws, leads to the belief
at it might be well worth the while for some stunt sincerely interested in the welfare of the domes-
sugar industry of the United States, to delve
eply into the history of tariffs and to bring his
search to the attention and notice of those who
1ke tariffs as well as those who apply them. An
1bitious student, filled with the zeal of a just cause
d believing in the industrial expansion of the
1ited States, despite depressions, theorists, ·or poli-
ians who inherit their principles of statesmanship,
ght well ask that the scientists and practical execu-
·es of all branches of the industry, join in a con-
·ence with the scientists and customs officials of
e United States Government, with a view to deter-
ning upon simple language which shall ·compre-
1sively and finally state the actual and purposeful
:ent of the Congress of the United States.

Doles

In these days of strange eventualities, when the
richest nation in the world hears within its borders
an occasional discussion of the dole as a palliative
for the evils of unemployment, it may not be amiss
to call attention to a recent statement of Herr Her-
man Dietrich, Finance Minister of Germany, who has
suggested that instead of governments paying money
directly to the unemployed in the shape of a dole
they should pay the same amount as a subsidy to
some domestic industry producing an article that is
under-produced in the country that makes the payment, the money thus paid to the industry to be used
entirely to pay wages to extra help to make more of
the under-produced commodity.

That has a sane sound to it. In the United States,
for example, we lack some 3,000,000 tons of sugar
every year and have to buy it abroad. If, instead
of giving our unemployed a dole (which we hope will
never be necessary) our government would pay the
money to the owners of cane and beet sugar farms
and factories and see that they use every cent of it
to pay wages to additional men and women to grow
more cane and beets and manufacture more sugar,
until we produce all we need at home, hundreds of
thousands of our American people would get work
and hundreds of thousands of dollars now sent abroad
for sugar would stay in the United States. Of course,
a government wise enough to do that would be wise
enough to see that the cane and beet sugar producers were not put out of business, and their labor put
out of jobs, by cheap sugar from abroad, which is
what is happening to them now.

The Contract Committee

Minutes of

Meeting of American Sugar Cane League Contact Committee with Louisiana Experiment Station Workers Baton Rouge, La., May 8, 1931.

The meeting was called to order by Mr. Munson, acting Chairman, in the absence of Mr. Wallace. There were present, of the Contact Committee, Mr. Percy Lemann, Mr. Stephen Munson, Mr. Elliot Jones, and of the Station Staff, Dr. C. T. Dowell, Mr. W. G. Taggar Mr. E. C. Simon, Dr. C. W. Edgerton, Dr. E. C. Tims, Mr. P. J. Mills, Mr. Truman Ryker, Mr. B. A. Osterberger Mr. C. L. Stracener, Mr. G. H. Reuss, Mr. Wm. Whipple Mr. Harold T. Barr, Mr. C. B. Gouaux. Visitors, Dr. A. H. Rosenfeld, Mr. W. B. Mercier.

A five-page mimeographed progress report was presented by Dr. Edgerton. Germination Counts: The results of the condition of cane at the present time compared to a year ago from counted buds in the fall at approximately the same date. The germination this year is consistently behind what it was a year ago.

Cane Conditions: The information is comparable t last year, the condition of the length of plant cane shoot and stubble shoots and roots being under as nearly identical conditions as we could get them. The plant can is shorter as is also the stubble in most cases. While the roots do not show as great a length as last year they are more numerous this year, and we would consider the cane in better condition with favorable weather.

Deterioration of Cane, especially Stubble: Studies during the past month on stubble cane were in the field here at the Station. One hundred stubble pieces from each of these plots were dug up without selecting, just as they came, in order to get a fair idea of the condition of the cane. This gives the information on th varieties, first and second year stubble, date the can was cut and date examined this spring. Bearing in mind that these stubbles should have anywhere from to 10 eyes to the piece, it is possible to figure what these ought to have by the number of good eyes remaining on the stubble pieces. C.P. 807 and P.O.J. 21 showed the greatest number of stubble pieces dead. The last column shows the number of stubble pieces discolored or rotten at the base.

Variety	Year Stubble	Date Cut	Date Examined	Number of Good Eyes Per 100 Pieces	Number Stubble Pieces Dead	Number Stubble Pieces Discolored or Rotten at Base
P.O.J. 234	First	11–26–30	4–13–31	321	4	3
P.O.J. 234	First	12–10–30	4–13–31	234	8	10
C.P. 807	First	10– 1–30	4–13–31	119	23	23
C.P. 807	First	10–20–30	4–11–31	97	19	16
C.P. 807	First	11–25–30	4–11–31	234	10	10
P.O.J. 36-M	First	10–15–30	4–13–31	220	5	8
P.O.J. 36-M	First	12–10–30	4–13–31	253	6	9
P.O.J. 213	First	11–26–30	4–13–31	365	6	6
P.O.J. 213	Second	October–30	4–20–31	67	32	18
P.O.J. 213	Second	October–30	4–13–31	97	71	26
Co. 281	Second	October–30	4–20–31	391	2	3
Co. 281	Second	October–30	4–20–31	263	5	5
Co. 281	Third	Dec.–30	4–20–31	51	22	12
C.P. 177	First	10–28–30	4–20–31	257	8.	4
Purple	First	10–26–30	4–20–31	27	36	27

The vitality of the cane is cut down when decay infection occurs at the basal portion.

These same stubble pieces were split and held at high humidity, each piece being separated to permit th organisms to grow out of them. While it is impossib to obtain all the organisms present, the high percentag of red rot obtained is noteworthy. The relatively hig percentage of red rot occurring in certain varietie particularly P.O.J. 213, one lot of C.P. 807 and one l of P.O.J. 36-M, should be noted. It is probable that th actual percentage of red rot was a great deal high than this.

Variety	Year Stubble	Date Cut	Number with Red Rot	Fussa-rium sp.	Maras-mius sp.	Tricho-derma	Miscel-laneous Fungi
P.O.J. 234_	First	11–26–30	0	10	4	4	8
P.O.J. 234_	First	12–10–30	1	15	5	6	9
C.P. 807___	First	10– 1–30	15	23	9	6	27
C.P. 807___	First	10–20–30	3	26	---	4	2
P.O.J. 36-M	First	12–10–30	29	7	7	8	26
P.O.J. 36-M	First	10–15–30	9	12	0	9	5
P.O.J. 213_	Second	Oct.–30	24	17	4	8	5
P.O.J. 213_	Second	Oct.–30	8	17	---	9	8
Co. 281___	First	Oct.–30	26	18	5	7	--
Co. 281___	Second	Oct.–30	7	22	12	15	--
Co. 281___	Third	Dec.–30	6	20	12	22	--
C.P. 177___	First	10–28–30	13	30	2	17	--
Purple____	First	10–26–30	47	24	11	18	--

It is believed that the red rot is very largely the reason for the stubble deterioration from an organism standpoint. There is no reason to believe that the red rot infection is any worse than the average this year. C.P. 807 is particularly susceptible and in bad years may be seriously injured.

A discussion followed on the deterioration of cane, and very much interest was expressed in this report. It was brought out in the discussion that no cane is immune to red rot but some show a resistance, Co. 281 being a variety of this type. The depth of planting and quickness in getting the dirt off in the spring has quite an influence on the germination. Experiments are being conducted at Houma on the depth of covering of several varieties.

A three-page mimeographed progress report was presented by Mr. Osterberger.

Trichogramma Work: Room 3, which has been our carry over supply of moths for our winter rearing of Trichogramma and the supply for stocking the fresh corn in Rooms 1 and 2, has been cleaned out, fumigated and is now ready to be prepared for a new supply of corn. Room 2 is just beginning to produce and in about three weeks the production will be well under way. Very few collections have been made in this room and, as a consequence, the adults emerging have deposited eggs in the room and re-stocked the new corn. The production in Room 1 for April was 112,084 moths from which 1,917,156 eggs were obtained, or an average of 34.28 eggs per female. This is rather high and we think the humidity has helped quite a bit. Mass production of parasites has been started, and we now have on hand more than 350,000 parasites which will be liberated as soon as we find host eggs in quantities that will justify liberations. Up to this time we have been unable to find parasites in the field, either in cabbage loopers, cabbage butterfly eggs or any other host eggs. Our searches have not been as extensive as in previous years, but we have made systematic searches on a reduced scale. These reports are confirmed by reports from workers in neighboring states for this month.

Borer Development: At Franklin in our trap light work we have collected a few adult borers. Up to this time we have found no eggs in the field, but this doesn't mean that the borers have not been depositing eggs. In the sections of cane which have been kept in the laboratory since December 1, 1930, we are still finding fifth stages, pupae and pupal skins, which indicates that the drying of cane does not prevent the development of borers, if the cane is protected, as in the steam heated laboratory.

Examinations of tops are being continued in our trash disposal tests at Island. Plantation, Plaquemine, and we found the following ratios and averages:

1.2 pieces of top per 1 row. ft.

1.24 ft. of top per 1 row ft.

48 top pieces per 1 living stage (unemerged).

Population rate 200 living larvae per acre.

1 living larva per 40 row ft.

1 living larva per 50 lin. ft. tops.

Soil Animal Work: The Ligyrus work has been started at Franklin, Sterling Sugars. The observations on this work have been published in THE SUGAR BULLE-

TIN of May 1 under the title of "The Sugarcane Beetle and Some Suggestions for Its Control."

We collected 75 adult beetles in a short time and these were examined for sex and eggs. Of the 75 beetles collected, 33 were males and 42 were females. The average per female was 3.64 and the number of eggs per female was 0 to 12. These findings, with the finding of many mating pairs in the soil, indicated that the egg-laying period is just beginning and searching for eggs has been almost negative up to April 21.

A heavy infestation of Ligyrus at Cut Off in D-95 has been reported.

We are in the process of trying some trap baits for the control of these beetles, but the work is not as advanced enough for any definite plan or procedure. We are collecting beetles now for a small-scale test of various materials to determine food preference or attractant materials, which may be a plant, plant products or chemicals.

The drums have all been inoculated with the soil animals and Pythium. Germination is fair in all drums except the ones very heavily inoculated with Pythium.

A discussion on the progress of the work at Franklin followed. The failure of lime to repel the beetles as heretofore was attributed to the unusual cool weather, which rendered the beetles inactive. Dr. Rosenfeld brought out the fact that the soil differentiation is not nearly so marked as in previous years.

A three-page mimeographed progress report was presented by Mr. Gouaux.

Cane Crop Conditions: In spite of the unfavorably cool weather, there has been a marked improvement in cane stands over the period of a month ago. The weather was excellent for field work, permitting excellent progress to be made in helpful field operations, such as hoeing, rotary-hoe and stubble digger work, all of which tended to promote better conditions for the germination of the crop. The fertilization of stubble cane was another important field activity. The bulk of the stubble acreage was fertilized during the interval of April 13 to 30. In the northern and western sections, this work will not be completed until some time in early May. In the season of 1930, the stubble cane was fertilized during this same period.

Field Varieties: In all sections of the Cane Belt P.O.J. 234 as plant and first stubble has germinated earlier and, in general, has given very uniform stands. Second stubble of this variety is also good, where the previous crop was harvested late in the season. This variety is extremely popular with sugar planters in every section of the Belt. Its popularity is increasing in sections that are subject to early cold weather and lower temperatures. P.O.J. 213 is more popular in Terrebonne, Lafourche, St. Mary and portions of Assumption, St. James and St. John Parishes. This variety has been losing ground mostly in the upper Mississippi and Atchafalaya and Red River sections. In general, P.O.J. 213 plant cane is at its best, where the plantings were made in the early fall, late September and early October; while the late fall and spring plantings show slower germination and gappy stand conditions.

P.O.J. 36 is outstanding as a ratooning variety, surpassing in germination both P.O.J. 213 and 234 as second stubble, and being excellent as first stubble. The plant cane is slightly slower than P.O.J. 213, but stands are generally better.

The P.O.J. 36-M variety, which has all of the good qualities of the P.O.J. 36 with additional early maturity, is showing up well in all sections of the Cane Belt, as plant cane, first and second stubble.

Experiment Station Test Fields: The six sugarcane variety test fields were visited during the interval of April 24 to 29. The variety plots were inspected and the regular stalk or shoot counts were made in each of the fall plant, first stubble and second stubble test fields.

In the plant cane test fields, in most cases, all varieties show substantial increases in number of shoots per acre over the condition of a month ago. In the majority of cases the counts for last year run higher than for the present season.

C.P. 807 continues to be the leading variety in highest

number of shoots per acre at all of the test fields. Co. 290 is second ranking variety at Cinclare, Glenwood, Youngsville, and was second with P.O.J. 234 at Sterling. At Reserve and Meeker, P.O.J. 234 is second ranking variety. P.O.J. 36-M gave higher counts at Reserve, Sterling and Youngsville than P.O.J. 213; while at the other three places P.O.J. 213 was higher. Co. 281 gave higher counts than P.O.J. 213 at Cinclare, Reserve, Meeker, Sterling and Youngsville.

The first stubble varieties showed greater improvement during the past month than the plant cane. With the exception of some of the varieties at Sterling and Youngsville, the first stubble is now ahead of the plant cane in number of shoots per acre.

The Meeker first stubble test field shows the most advanced condition, with the others in about the following order: Glenwood, Reserve, Cinclare, Sterling and Youngsville.

At all test fields C.P. 807 shows the highest number of stalk counts, P.O.J. 234 is second ranking at Cinclare, Reserve and Meeker. At Glenwood and Youngsville, P.O.J. 36-M is second highest in number of shoots per acre; while at Sterling, P.O.J. 213 is second.

The condition of first stubble varieties for the period of April 24 to 29 was more advanced in 1930.

The condition of second stubble varieties for the end of April period was more advanced last year than the present season. C.P. 807 is the leading variety in the highest number of stalks per acre. At Cinclare and Sterling P.O.J. 36-M ranks second; at Youngsville Co. 281 is second; and at Meeker P.O.J. 234 is second.

It was suggested and agreed that the next meeting be held at the Houma Station with the Federal authorities. Dr. Dowell suggested that the Experiment Station workers dispense with their reports at this meeting and learn more about the work and results of these workers.

Louisiana Exceeds Quota

As will be recalled we published some time ago an announcement by Dr. W. L. Owen of Baton Rouge, Vice-Chairman for Louisiana, to the effect that he had been entrusted with the work of securing memberships in Louisiana for the International Society of Sugar Cane Technologists. It was indicated that the quota for Louisiana was 25. We are now advised by Dr. Arthur H. Rosenfeld, Secretary of the Society, that this number has been exceeded, the following membership from Louisiana having been enrolled.

Arceneaux, George......U. S. Sugar Plant Field Station, Houma, La.
Abbott, E. V...............Bureau of Plant Industry, Houma, La.
Burguieres, C. P.........J. M. Burguieres Co., Ltd., 827 Union St., New Orleans, La.
Burguieres, Ernest......J. M. Burguieres Co., Ltd., 827 Union St., New Orleans, La.
Barker, Frank L.........Valentine Sugars, Inc., Lockport, La.
Coe, Dana G..............Am. Cyanamid Co., 736 N. Blvd., Baton Rouge, La.
Dahlberg, C. F............South Coast Co., 1248 Canal Bank Bldg., New Orleans, La.
Dykers, Reginald ....Am. Sugar Cane League, 407 Carondelet St., New Orleans, La.
Gouner, L. E..............2514 Lowerline St., New Orleans, La.
Gilmore, A. B............P. O. Box 771, New Orleans, La.
Grayson, Wilmer........Am. Biochemical Products Co., P. O. Box 80, Baton Rouge, La.
Godchaux, Walter......Godchaux Sugars, Inc., Masonic Temple Bldg., New Orleans, La.
Godchaux, Jules.........Godchaux Sugars, Inc., Masonic Temple Bldg., New Orleans, La.
Greven, J. P..............Reserve Refinery, Godchaux Sugars, Inc., Reserve, La.
Holloway, T. E..........Entomologist, Bureau of Entomology, 8203 Oak St., New Orleans, La.

Hegenbarth, F.................Fulton Iron Works, 505 N. O. Bank
            Bldg., New Orleans, La.
Hinds, W. E.................Entomologist, La. Exp. Station,
            Baton Rouge, La.
Kemper, C. D.................Sterling Sugars, Inc., Franklin, La.
LeBourgeois, J. C.......LeBourgeois Brokerage Co., 405 N. O.
            Bank Bldg., New Orleans, La.
Laws, H. Langdon........604 American Bank Bldg.,
            New Orleans, La.
Meade, George.................Colonial Sugars Co.,
            Gramercy Refinery, Gramercy, La.
Munson, Stephen C....Assumption Sugars, Inc.,
            Napoleonville, La.
Nadler, Carl.................Southdown Sugars Co., Houma, La.
Nelson, Horace, Mgr..Raceland Refinery, Godchaux
            Sugars, Inc., Raceland, La.
Owen, W. L.................P. O. Box 1345, Baton Rouge, La.
Pipes, David W.........Estate H. C. Minor, Houma, La.
Rosenfeld, A. H.........Gen. Secretary Int. Society of Sugar
            Cane Tech., 1005 N. O. Bank Bldg.,
            New Orleans. La.
Whipple, William.......La. State University,
            Baton Rouge, La.
Webre, Jos. M.................830 North St., Baton Rouge, La.
Wale, James H.........South Coast Sugars Co.,
            Montegut, La.
Webre, Louis A.........830 North St., Baton Rouge, La.

Tiles from Bagasse

Mr. Robert L. Mayer, of Jacksonville, Florida, called at the office of the American Sugar Cane League recently and exhibited for inspection some tiles and slabs composed, as he says, largely of bagasse. The purpose of Mr. Mayer is to obtain some money with which to manufacture this material on an industrial scale. He says $10,000 will be enough.

In appearance and weight the tiles and slabs resemble cement, but the bagasse fibre is easily discernible and probably acts as a binder. The tiles are highly polished and the process by which they are made is not patented, but neither is it divulged by Mr. Mayer.

The Committee in Washington, headed by Dr. E. W. Brandes, one section of which is trying so assiduously to find ways and means of utilizing the by-products of our sugar industry, especially bagasse, may see fit to get in touch with Mr. Mayer and investigate his claims. Dr. Henry G. Knight, Chief of the Bureau of Chemistry and Soils, is, we believe, in particular charge of bagasse utilization problems.

Borer Active

Baton Rouge, May 25, 1931.

Editor Sugar Bulletin:

Possibly some of your readers may be interested in the following information regarding borer development and abundance in vicinity of Baton Rouge.

The first work of borer larvæ of 1931, first generation, was found in corn at Baton Rouge on May 13. This represented second stage larvæ and all of the work found was in one row of corn within a distance of about 25 row ft. and undoubtedly represented the egg laying of 1 female in this plat of garden corn.

On May 15 no borer work could be found in some 1200 row ft. of 213 stubble corn, or in 2,000 row ft. of the most advanced field corn on the Sugar Station grounds at Baton Rouge.

On May 18 on a plantation at Plaquemine, we located what appears to be an extremely heavy first generation infestation in 213 stubble, where we found an average of a leaf perforation; stalk per every 4 or

5 row ft. These stalks showed the presence of first and second stage larvæ. A batch of eggs in process of hatching was found on this date and no evidence of the presence of Trichogramma. On this plantation and near to this cane, which was heavily infested with borers in the fall of 1930, we found numerous stalks of corn showing borer infestation with first, second, third stage larvæ common and one fourth stage larva taken.

On May 22 in the above location in an examination of 40 rows of the oldest corn (rows averaging about 300 ft. long) we located 17 first stage larvæ, 37 second stage, 34 third stage, and 2 fourth stage larvæ.

The foregoing observations indicate that we may expect the maturity of many first generation moths and the beginning of egg laying for the second generation after about June 10 to 15.

W. E. Hinds, Entomologist.

THE SUGAR BULLETIN

La. State Universi
Ba[...] Rouge

Entered as second-class matter April 13, 1925, at the postoffice at
New Orleans, La., under Act of March 6, 1879.

*We stand for the encouragement of Home
Industries as against foreign competition.*

| Vol. 9 | NEW ORLEANS, LA., JUNE 15, 1931 | No. 18 |

Effective Trichogramma Colonization

By W. E. Hinds, Entomologist, Louisiana Experiment Station

The most effective time for colonizing Trichogramma on the sugar cane borer is undoubtedly during the ten or fifteen days after moths of the first generation emerge in considerable numbers so that eggs for the second generation may be available commonly for parasitization by the wasps. The determination of this time has been made by the entomologists for several years past by extensive splitting up of the stalks of infested corn and sugar cane to find the stage of development of the majority of the borer population therein. These records begin with examinations of the earliest maturing corn which can be found in gardens and fields. Invariably, the first pupae and the first empty pupal skins, which show the emergence of moths of the first generation, are to be found in this earliest maturing corn.

The maturity of the first generation varies from year to year according to the season and also according to the stage of development of the host plant. It is much later this season than it has been during some other seasons. Recent examinations made in South Louisiana show that a large proportion of the first generation of borers in early corn has now reached the stage of full-grown larvae. Large numbers of pupae may also be found, but up to June 6th there were very few empty pupal skins, and these were found only in very small corn plants which had been so heavily infested as to stunt their growth and cause the premature death of the stalks before the first of June.

The simplest possible basis for the average planter to determine the time when first generation moths begin to emerge is to be found in the beginning of tasselling and ear formation in the corn. When the earliest maturing corn reaches this stage, the planter should examine for evidences of borer infestation as shown most conspicuously by the leaf perforation signs and also, as the larvae become full-grown, by the burrows and larval excrement appearing in the axils of lower leaves and usually within two feet of the ground. If many pupae are then found, it indicates that the emergence of moths may be expected within a few days, and if empty skins are found, the emergence has already begun. At this stage of borer development, the decision regarding the disposition of the corn should be made. Under many conditions it may be advisable to cut out the entire crop of corn and feed it out green or make it into silage in order to prevent the emergence of moths therefrom. Usually, if more than 20 per cent of the corn stalks are infested by borers, the destruction of the entire crop is advisable instead of attempting to cut out only the borer-infested stalks and allow the balance to mature.

During the recent examinations in St. Mary and Iberia Parishes, especially, a number of areas of corn were found in which the percentage of stalks infested by borers ranged from an average of 30 to as high as 70 per cent. The areas involved ranged from home gardens with a few rows of corn to about 20 acres in one location. It happened in the latter case that no sugar cane is grown within a mile of this corn area and the hibernation of the cane borers occurred very certainly in the stubble of Johnson grass principally.

Favorable climatic conditions should be chosen for releasing Trichogramma in the field. We believe that such conditions include a fair day with temperature above 70 degrees F. and without heavy winds. Under such conditions the wasps may be expected to have a period of activity which is favorable for their finding host eggs and ovipositing therein. If weather conditions are distinctly unfavorable, we would not attempt the release of parasites but would prefer to hold the stock in refrigerators awaiting more favor-

======THE======
S U G A R
BULLETIN
407 Carondelet St., New Orleans

Issued on the 1st and 15th of each month. Official Organ of the American
Sugar Cane League of the U. S. A., in which are consolidated
The Louisiana Sugar Planters' Assn.
The American Cane Growers' Assn.
The Producers & Mfgrs. Protective Assn.
Subscription Price, 50 Cents Per Year.

Reginald Dykers, General Manager & Editor of the Bulletin
301 Nola Bldg., New Orleans
Frank L. Barker, Secretary and Treasurer
Lockport, La.
C. J. Bourg, Manager Washington Office
810 Union Trust Building

CHAIRMEN OF COMMITTEES:
C. D. Kemper, Franklin, La.
President of the League and Ex-Officio Chairman of Executive Committee
Percy A. Lemann, Donaldsonville, La.
Chairman Agricultural Committee
David W. Pipes, Jr., Houma, La.
Chairman Industrial Committee
Frank L. Barker, Lockport, La.
Chairman Finance Committee.
Edward J. Gay, Plaquemine, La.
Chairman Tariff Committee
H. Langdon Laws, Cinclare, La.
Chairman Legislative Committee
J. C. LeBourgeois, New Orleans, La.
Chairman Freight Rate Committee
R. H. Chadwick, Bayou Goula, La.
Chairman Membership Committee
A. H. Rosenfeld, New Orleans, La.
Chairman Publicity Committee

Members of the League desiring action on, or information on, any subject are invited to communicate with
the League or with the Chairman of the Committee
to which it seems to appertain.

able conditions in the field. The purchaser of commercial stock of Trichogramma should be informed
with each shipment as to the probable day of emergence of the wasps. Shipments should be made so
that the material will reach its destination at least
two days before emergence is expected. This will allow for slight delays enroute and the occurrence of
high temperatures which favor more rapid development of the parasites. Therefore, there should be
some opportunity for the planter to select a favorable time for release. Parasitized grain moth eggs
may be kept in refrigerators at temperatures ranging
from about 38 to 55 degrees F., which will retard
the development and delay the emergence of the
wasps. If wasps have already emerged, their activity
is checked and their life prolonged under such low
temperature conditions.

If the foregoing general suggestions are followed,
it should not be difficult to secure an effective colonization of Trichogramma in areas of heavy borer infestation by releasing a few thousand wasps at a time
and repeating the releases at least once in about eight
or ten days, or preferably repeating releases in about
weekly intervals until three releases are made during
the fifteen days after the second generation egg laying begins in some abundance.

The Co-operative Fertilizer Experi-
ments on Sugar Cane

The 1930 Results and Summaries for Past
Three Years

By Arthur H. Rosenfeld,
Consulting Technologist, American Sugar Cane
League

In 1928 the writer published (1) the records of
five series of tests of the application of varying
quantities of nitrogenous and phosphoric acid fertilizers on P.O.J. plant cane in large scale trials on six
distinct Louisiana sugar plantations during the year
1927, as well as the results of a series of tests made
at the Baton Rouge Experiment Station. In all cases
without exception the results shown on plant cane
were *commercially* negative, i. e., although in a few
cases a very small tonnage gain could be shown from
the application of fertilizer, in no case was this gain
sufficiently large to show a definite profit after payment for the fertilizer and its application. As far
as nitrogen was concerned, it was felt that a logical
explanation of the failure of plant cane to respond
to fertilization was the fact that without exception
all of these experimental plantings were made on
land on which the standard Louisiana practice of
turning under a good crop of soy beans in the fall
had been followed and that, therefore, the soil had
been rather liberally supplied with this most expensive and essential element. All the experimental evidence having shown definitely that the fertilizing of
plant cane after turning under soy beans cannot be
justified as an investment, the fertilizing of plant
cane in Louisiana has been practically discontinued
during recent years.

Beginning with the 1928 season, all of our co-
operative fertilizer demonstrations have been made on
stubble cane exclusively. In the stubble cane experiments in 1928 (2) and 1929 (3), contrary to the
results obtained from experiments made on plant
cane, there was, in the case of first and second stubble of all of the P.O.J. varieties, a most decided and
uniform response to all nitrogenous fertilizers, with
the most profitable amount of nitrogen seeming to
lie between 30 and 40 pounds per acre. In the nitrate tests the most profitable limit seemed to lie between 30 and 35 pounds of nitrogen, or say between
200 and 250 pounds of nitrate of soda or nitrate of
lime per acre; whereas, with cyanamid and sulphate
of ammonia, which have larger contents of nitrogen
and are considerably cheaper per unit, the point of
most advantageous commercial return seemed to be
at about 40 pounds of nitrogen per acre, corresponding roughly to 200 pounds per acre of either substance. The results of 1928 and 1929 showed that
larger amounts of nitrogen than the above in many
cases gave *some* additional tonnage of cane, but it
was doubtful, taking into consideration the depressing effect on the sucrose content of the juices due to
higher nitrogen applications, if there was any material final gain from applying more than 40 pounds

(1) Results of Some Co-operative Fertilizer Tests. The Sugar
Bulletin, V-1-28.
(2) The 1928 Co-operative Fertilizer Experiments. The Sugar
Bulletin, II-1-29.
(3) The 1929 Co-operative Fertilizer Experiments. The Sugar
Bulletin, V-15-30.

of nitrogen per acre under the conditions of Louisiana's extremely short growing season.

As to phosphoric acid, the majority of the experimental trials with stubble cane, as in the previous plant cane demonstrations, showed no profit derived from such application. In the few potash applications no response whatsoever was shown, although Mr. Claude Gouaux, sugar cane specialist of the L. S. U. Experiment Station, obtained some results last year from potassic applications, indicating the need of further trials along this line.

The 1930 Tests of Nitrate of Soda and Calcium Super-Phosphate

These tests were made on plats or cuts running from one and one-half to four acres each, the large size of these permitting of all operations, both of cultivation and harvesting, being carried out on the regular field scale and the harvesting and milling data obtained without any interruption of the normal course of plantation practice, due to the plats being large enough to permit regular plowing, hoeing and harvesting gangs to carry out their work in the same manner as in other fields. The fertilizers in all cases were applied as early as was practicable after off-barring in the off-bar furrow and as near to the cane as was possible. The results of the harvesting of this second series of stubble demonstrations are shown in detail in Table I, together with soil type, variety of cane employed and the harvesting date of each demonstration.

Table I

Tests with Nitrate of Soda and Superphosphate on First Stubble*

Pounds Fertilizer Per Acre**	Tons Cane Per Acre		Chemical Analyses of Juices			Pounds Available Sugar per Acre***
	Yield	Gain over average of Check Plats	Brix	Sucrose	Purity	
Levert, St. John, Inc., Levert						
Sandy Silt Loam					Harv. XI-26-30	
P.O.J. 213						
200 N. S.	15.48	5.24	16.19	13.91	85.92	3144
Check, No Fert.	11.40		16.06	13.97	87.00	1973(a)
200 N.S. & 200 P.	14.84	4.60	14.92	11.74	78.42	2422
Check, No Fert.	9.08		16.38	12.92	78.90	....
300 N.S. & 200 P.	17.90	7.66	15.88	12.61	79.41	3161
Oaklawn Plantation, Franklin, The South Coast Co.						
Teche Silt Loam					XI-1-30	
P.O.J. 213*						
200 N.S.	11.49	4.17	15.99	11.87	74.23	1835
Check, No Fert.	6.77		15.18	11.97	78.83	1109(a)
200 N.S. & 200 P.	13.05	5.73	15.72	12.28	78.12	2224
Check, No Fert.	7.86		15.17	10.56	69.59	....
300 N. S. & 200 P.	14.23	6.91	16.09	12.61	78.37	2495
Presqu'ile Plantation, Terrebonne Parish,						
The South Coast Co. Sandy Mixed Loam					XI-9-30	
P.O.J. 213						
200 N.S.	23.15	7.32	15.63	12.42	79.46	4028
Check, No Fert.	14.18		16.07	13.28	82.62	2918(a)
200 N.S. & 200 P.	22.87	7.04	15.68	12.17	77.61	3847
Check, No Fert.	17.50		16.23	12.83	78.98	....
300 N.S. & 200 P.	27.51	11.68	15.58	11.58	74.33	4292
Tally-Ho Plantation, Bayou Goula, Geo. M. Murrell Plg. Co.						
Mixed Black Miss. Alluvium						
P.O.J. 36						
200 N.S.	20.54	5.21	14.63	10.89	74.44	3015
Check, No Fert.	16.21		14.72	11.23	76.29	2367(a)
200 N.S. & 200 P.	20.80	5.47	14.65	10.86	74.13	3037
Check, No Fert.	14.45		14.85	11.34	76.86	....
300 N.S. & 200 P.	21.40	6.07	14.32	10.40	72.63	2953
H. K. Bubenzer, Bunkie						
Miller Fine Sandy Silt Loam					XII-2-30	
P.O.J. 213						
200 N.S.	25.37	3.26	13.66	9.80	71.74	3273
Check, No Fert.	21.56		14.42	11.15	75.35	3312(a)
200 N.S. & 200 P.	24.23	2.12	14.51	11.13	76.71	3702
Check, No Fert.	22.66		14.59	10.83	74.19	....
300 N.S. & 200 P.	26.38	4.27	14.01	10.19	72.73	3569
Averages of Above Five Demonstrations						
200 N.S.	19.21	5.04	15.22	11.78	77.40	3059
Check, No Fert.	14.02		15.29	12.32	80.58	2336(a)
200 N.S. & 200 P.	19.16	4.99	15.11	11.64	77.04	3046
Check, No Fert.	14.31		15.44	11.70	75.78	....
300 N.S. & 200 P.	21.48	7.31	15.18	11.48	75.62	3294
General Averages for 1928, 1929 and 1930—Thirteen Demonstrations						
200 N.S.	20.84	6.47	16.03	13.11	81.78	3915
Check, No Fert.	14.53		16.10	13.44	83.48	2729(a)
200 N.S. & 200 P.	19.96	5.59	16.16	13.24	81.93	3733
Check, No Fert.	14.20		15.50	13.03	84.06	....
300 N.S. & 200 P.	21.70	7.33	16.11	13.04	80.94	4011

*The Oaklawn demonstration was on second stubble.
**N. S.—Nitrate of Soda. P—Calcium Superphosphate.
***Calculated by employing "Java Formula" (Winter-Carp), assuming 75% extraction and 100% boil. house efficiency.
(a)—Average of check plats.

A study of these results shows that they are on the whole again quite uniform—indeed exceptionally so for what are, after all, large scale demonstrational tests rather than carefully controlled replication ex-

This is The American Sugar Cane League's Buy and Sell Column

If you are interested in any item below write to the League about it, at 407 Carondelet St., New Orleans, mentioning the item BY NUMBER and full information will be supplied.

WANTED TO PURCHASE

(B-200) Filter Press Plates and Frames for 36" x 36" Shriver Presses Side Feed, 1½" thick.

FOR SALE

(A-200) 1 Reducing Tee 6 x 8—not drilled

(A-201) 1 Reducing Tee 8 x 12—not drilled

(A-202) 2 12" Globe Valves—drilled

(A-203) 1 12" Reducing Valve—high and low pressure

(A-204) 3 8" Elbows—drilled

(A-205) 1 6" Elbow—not drilled

(A-206) 11 8" Flanges—not drilled

(A-207) 1 6" Flange—not drilled

(A-208) 1 12" Tee—not drilled

(A-209) 1 12" Elbow—not drilled

(All of the above material is extra heavy Crane Brand, in first class condition)

(A-210) 1 Bancroft Plate and Frame Filter Press 34" x 34"

(A-211) 1 Number four Shaper, manufactured by S. W. Putman & Sons, year 1886

(A-212) 1 Large iron Pulley and Shaft size Pulley Face 4' 2" Dia. 6' Shaft 8" Dia. 12' long

(A-213) 1 8' Pan complete with connections and pump

(A-214) 1 Anderson Crude Oil Engine, 3 cylinders, upright, 135 I.H.P.

periments—if we bear in mind that the two tests showing somewhat erratic analyses (those at Oaklawn and Bunkie) were both located in districts most affected by the prolonged drought of the summer of 1930. In both cases the cane had to withstand more than three continuous months of rainless weather at the most critical period of their growth (the so-called "boom stage" of Hawaii) and it is but natural that under such conditions response to fertilization should be abnormal. Furthermore, in both the Teche and Red River sections we have had some indication of a slight response to phosphoric acid applications, in contradistinction to the lack of reaction of the Mississippi alluvial soils to this fertilizing element. On the whole, however, just as in the former stubble demonstrations, three things seem to stand out clearly from a careful study of this table:

Firstly, about 30 pounds of nitrogen per acre, as represented by 200 pounds of nitrate of soda containing roughly 15 per cent of nitrogen, seems about the commercial maximum to apply to stubble cane under the conditions of these experiments;

Secondly, in general there is no apparent benefit obtained on tonnage or sucrose content by adding phosphoric acid to our fertilizer application, this being in accord with three previous years of experimentation with phosphoric acid applications. The evidence is now undoubtedly sufficiently strong to justify our advising quite definitely against the former almost general practice in Louisiana of applying about 200 pounds of super-phosphate per acre to both plant and stubble, except only on certain outlying soil types such as the rolling lands in the extreme western edge of the belt and the Red River clay soils at the extreme northern edge, as the application of phosphoric acid shows no apparently definitely beneficial results in tonnage or sucrose of cane, with the possible exception of the Oaklawn test, which in 1929 as first stubble showed negative results from applications of super-phosphate. In no case has there been obtained any evidence that the application of phosphoric acid has had any of its theoretical effect of hastening maturity and, hence, increasing the sugar content of the juices. In fact, in these experiments and in previous ones, for some reason which the author is at a loss to explain, not only has the addition of phosphoric acid to the nitrogen application shown no increase in cane tonnage in general—certainly no commercial increase—but in a great many cases the sucrose and purity of the juice from the plats receiving at the rate of 200 pounds of nitrate of soda plus 200 pounds of super-phosphate have been lower than those of the juice from cane receiving 200 pounds of nitrate of soda alone. This is evident in three out of the above five tests, while one exception, the Bubenzer experiment, shows an appreciable increase in sucrose content which, however, accompanies actual loss of tonnage for the nitrogen and phosphoric acid plats. This point is clearly brought out in the figures showing the averages from the five 1930 demonstrations, wherein we see that the best purity and sucrose content of the fertilized plats correspond to the cane plots receiving 200 pounds of nitrate of soda alone, and the "nitrate only" plats actually produced an average of 13 pounds of sugar per acre more than the nitrate and super-phosphate combined!

Thirdly, the addition of 100 pounds of nitrate of soda to what we might call the *standard ration* of

200 pounds has shown no *commercial* advantage. The average figures for the three years of stubble demonstrations show plot No. 5 with a slightly increased tonnage over the "nitrate only" plats, amounting to less than a ton of cane per acre per year, which would not even pay for the additional fertilizer at present sugar prices. Examining the general averages, again, we find that the gain in sugar for this extra 100 pounds of nitrate of soda, or 15 pounds of nitrogen, is less than 100 pounds per acre, while the average gain of the 200 pounds of nitrate per acre over the check is almost 1200 pounds of sugar per acre—a splendid return on the fertilizer investment.

The Cyanamid Tests in 1930

These carefully replicated experiments were conducted in three series, one to test out the effects of the addition of 200 pounds of super-phosphate to the 250 pounds of cyanamid tried on second stubble (four demonstrations), one of a similar nature with 200 pounds of cyanamid on first stubble (six demonstrations), and the other to study the effect of varying quantities of cyanamid which were applied at the rate of 100 pounds, 200 pounds and 300 pounds per acre respectively, corresponding roughly to 20, 40 and 60 pounds of nitrogen (two demonstrations). In 1930 these tests were conducted by the Louisiana State University under a fellowship financed by the American Cyanamid Company. They were under the general direction of Dean C. T. Dowell and Assistant Director W. G. Taggart, while the actual field operations were supervised by Mr. A. K. Smith, graduate student on the fellowship. The data have been calculated from a mimeograph progress report issued on 30th January last by Dr. Dana G. Coe, agriculturist for the American Cyanamid Company, Baton Rouge. Dr. Coe calls attention to the necessity of bearing in mind the effects of the late spring and summer drought when comparing these figures with data from the 1929 experiments, particularly to the lower sugar contents and purities, even the check plats showing decreases of one or two points in sucrose and four or more points in purity as compared with the 1929 figures.

In Table II will be found the data for the second stubble replicated trials, with indications as to soil type, variety, number of replications and dates of fertilization and harvest in each case.

The object of reducing the size of the check plats in the first three experiments and applying cyanamid in an extra plat where no fertilizer was applied was to investigate the possible cumulative effect of previous nitrogenous applications. There was quite a generalized idea among the planters last season that, due to the cold spring and succeeding drought, the cane had not been able to assimilate nitrogen applied during the normal growing season—had not been able to "use it up" in the usual parlance—with the consequence that the late growth was characteristic only of the fertilized fields and that a decided reduction in ripe cane tonnage, sucrose content and purity of the juice must have resulted. If there were any surplus nitrogen from plats fertilized the previous year, therefore, it would be expected to reduce tonnage and sugar recoveries more in such plats fertilized two years in succession than in the plats receiving no nitrogen in 1929.

Table II
Cyanamid Second Year Stubble Tests*

Pounds Fertilizer Per Acre	Cane Tons Per Acre	Gain Over Check	Normal Juice Analysis			96 degree Sugar Pounds per Acre
			Brix	Sucrose	Purity	
Godchaux Sugars, Inc., Mary, Sandy Loam						
P.O.J. 213—3 replications, Fertilized April 1 and 2						
Harvested October 22, 23 and 24, 1930						
Check, No Fert. (Ck. 1929)	10.05	------	14.63	11.44	78.20	1596
250 Cyan. (Ck. 1929)	16.72	6.67	14.13	10.61	75.35	2410
250 Cyan. (200 Cyan. 1929)	13.10	3.05	14.41	11.06	76.69	1989
250 Cyan. & 200 Superphos.	14.22	4.17	14.35	10.95	76.27	2131
300 Cyan. (same 1929)	15.52	5.47	14.29	10.92	76.28	2319
Estate Harry L. Laws, Cinclare, Sandy Loam						
P.O.J. 213—3 replications, Fertilized April 21 and 22						
Harvested October 24 and 25, 1930						
Check, No Fert. (Ck. 1929)	11.83	------	13.52	9.72	71.92	1516
250 Cyan. (Ck. 1929)	18.98	7.15	13.17	8.88	67.45	2126
250 Cyan.(100 Cyan. 1929)	19.92	8.09	12.82	8.49	66.26	2105
250 Cyan. & 200 Superphos.	20.77	8.94	12.75	8.19	64.28	2068
300 Cyan. (same 1929)	19.33	7.50	12.87	8.57	66.58	2089
Glenwood Sugars, Inc. Napoleonville, Sandy Loam						
P.O.J. 213—2 replications, no check retained, Fertilized						
April 10 and 11						
Harvested October 27 and 28, 1930						
250 Cyan. (Ck. 1929)	17.52	------	14.65	11.37	77.63	2753
250 Cyan. (200 Cyan. 1929)	17.41	------	14.60	11.39	78.07	2751
250 Cyan. & 200 Superphos.	17.84	------	14.64	11.09	75.72	2694
300 Cyan. (same 1929)	20.82	------	14.12	10.24	72.50	2826
South Coast Co., Ashland, Silt Loam						
P.O.J. 36—2 replications, Fertilized March 31						
Harvested November 27 and 28, 1930						
Check, No Fert. (Ck. 1929)	14.81	------	16.61	13.56	79.50	2814
250 Cyan. (200 Cyan. 1929)	20.42	5.61	15.85	12.34	77.86	3491
250 Cyan. & 200 Superphos.	20.94	6.13	16.37	12.90	78.81	3767
300 Cyan. (same 1929)	22.00	7.19	15.65	11.73	74.95	3495
Averages of Three Demonstrations Above Having Checks						
Check, No Fert. (Ck. 1929)	12.23	------	14.92	11.57	77.55	1975
250 Cyan.	17.83	5.60	14.08	10.28	73.01	2424
250 Cyan. & 200 Superphos.	18.64	6.41	14.49	10.68	73.71	2655
300 Cyan.	18.95	6.72	14.27	10.41	72.95	2628

*Continued from 1929 with same plats.

A study of the two series of comparative plats at Mary, Cinclare and Glenwood, however, fails to show any trend whatsoever. In the first case the previous check plats receiving nitrogen in 1930 showed a tonnage gain over the checks twice that of the plats fertilized two years in succession, while the sucrose content and purity of the old check plats was materially lower. At Cinclare just the reverse is the case, the "twice-fertilized" plats producing a ton more cane than the old check plats fertilized in 1930 and having slightly lower sucrose and purity in the juice. At Glenwood tonnage, sucrose content and purity were almost identical in the two series of plats, the resultant theoretical recovery working out with a difference of only two pounds of sugar per acre between the two. The writer is inclined to believe, however, that fifty pounds of nitrogen per acre is too much to apply even to second-year stubble, with the short growing season which we must contend with in Louisiana, and feels that just as good or even better results would have been obtained had 200 pounds of cyanamid, or roughly forty pounds of nitrogen, been employed instead of 250. This is indicated by the generally lower sucrose content and purities of all fertilized plats as compared with the checks in each demonstration, while the average increase in cane produced by the plats receiving 300 pounds of cyana-

mid works out at just about a ton more per acre than that harvested from the plats fertilized with 250 pounds. Undoubtedly the most profitable investment in the second stubble series has been the application of nitrogen alone at the lower rate.

Let us now consider the cyanamid and superphosphate applications to first stubble. Table III gives the complete detailed results secured from the eight experiments, together with notations of variety, number of replications and fertilization and harvesting dates.

Table III
Tests with Cyanamid and Superphosphate on First Stubble

Pounds Fertilizer Per Acre*	Tons Cane Per Acre		Chemical Analyses of Juices			Pounds Available Sugar per Acre**
	Yield	Gain over Check	Brix	Sucrose	Purity	
Ashland Plantation, Terrebonne Parish, The South Coast Co. Fert. III-31-30						
P.O.J. 213—2 replications Harv. XI-27&28-30						
Check, No Fert.	19.43	--------	17.15	14.66	85.51	4149
200 Cy.	26.73	7.30	16.17	13.25	81.94	5045
200 Cy. & 200 P.	26.40	6.97	15.86	12.80	80.67	4775
300 Cy.	29.18	9.75	15.22	11.94	78.43	4844
Midway, Bayou Sale, The J. M. Burguieres Co., Ltd. Fert. IV-9-30						
P.O.J. 213—2 replications Harv. XII-5&6-30						
Check, No Fert.	10.36	--------	16.70	13.68	81.90	2019
200 Cy.	17.54	7.18	16.40	13.10	79.90	3229
200 Cy. & 200 P.	17.31	6.95	16.80	13.22	79.30	3202
300 Cy.	19.86	9.50	16.50	13.05	79.10	3622
Enterprise, Patoutville Fert. IV-15-30						
P.O.J. 234—2 replications Harv. X-31-30 & XI-1-30						
Check, No Fert.	14.91	--------	16.25	13.01	80.40	2735
200 Cy.	17.04	2.13	15.60	12.39	79.10	2950
200 Cy. & 200 P.	18.63	3.72	14.90	11.85	79.50	3094
300 Cy.	17.79	2.88	15.00	11.73	78.20	2897
Enola, Napoleonville, W. N. Bergeron Fert. IV-11-30						
P.O.J. 213—2 replications Harv. XI-19 & 20-30						
Check, No Fert.	13.88	--------	15.14	12.07	79.73	2351
200 Cy.	18.66	4.78	15.09	12.08	80.03	3170
200 Cy. & 200 P.	20.58	6.70	15.35	12.18	79.36	3510
Kinsale, Bayou Goula, J. Supple's Sons, Ltd. Fert. IV-12-30						
P.O.J. 213 Harv. XII-10-30						
Check, No Fert.	15.53	--------	15.30	11.39	74.30	2381
200 Cy.	24.72	9.19	14.60	10.50	71.90	3422
200 Cy. & 200 P.	25.62	10.09	14.80	10.35	70.00	3433
Valence, Labadieville, E. G. Robichaux Co., Ltd. Fert. IV-8-30						
P.O.J. 234—2 replications Harv. XII-27-30						
Check, No Fert.	16.95	--------	16.90	14.03	82.80	3407
200 Cy.	24.73	7.78	16.10	13.30	82.30	4697
200 Cy. & 200 P.	25.03	8.08	16.00	12.91	80.70	4749
Averages of Above Six Demonstrations						
Check, No Fert.	15.18	--------	16.24	13.14	80.91	2840
200 Cy.	21.57	6.39	15.66	12.44	79.44	3752
200 Cy. & 200 P.	22.43	7.25	15.62	12.22	78.23	3794
General Averages for 1928, 1929 and 1930—Fourteen Demonstrations*						
Check, No Fert.	16.76	--------	16.35	13.34	81.59	3160
200 Cy.	23.86	7.10	16.03	13.03	81.29	4356
200 Cy. & 200 P.	24.33	7.57	16.12	12.99	80.58	4425

*Cy—Cyanamid. P—Calcium Superphosphate.

**Calculated by employing "Java Formula" (Winter-Carp), assuming 75% extraction and 100% boiling-house efficiency.

Levert, St. John, Inc., Levert   Fert. IV-9-30
P.O.J. 213—3 replications   Harv. XI-24 & 25-30

Check, No Fert.	22.37	--------	16.07	13.58	84.60	4401
100 Cy.	26.49	4.12	15.80	12.87	81.50	4843
200 Cy.	29.33	6.96	15.54	12.60	81.10	5236
300 Cy.	31.13	8.76	15.09	11.84	78.50	5128

Angola, La., State Penitentiary   Fert. IV-23-30
P.O.J. 36—2 replications   Harv. XII-1 & 2-30

Check, No Fert.	15.05	--------	13.10	7.96	60.83	1389
100 Cy.	22.25	7.20	13.02	7.65	58.82	1915
200 Cy.	21.94	6.89	12.57	7.33	58.34	1795
300 Cy.	22.48	7.43	12.47	7.13	57.16	1753

Averages of Above Two Demonstrations

Check, No Fert.	18.71	--------	14.59	10.77	73.82	2895
100 Cy.	24.37	5.66	14.41	10.26	71.20	3379
200 Cy.	25.64	6.93	14.06	9.97	70.91	3516
300 Cy.	26.81	8.10	13.78	9.49	68.87	3441

General Averages for 1928, 1929 and 1930—Seven Demonstrations****

Check, No Fert.	16.97	--------	16.00	12.63	78.94	1990
100 Cy.	22.50	5.53	16.00	12.57	78.56	3930
200 Cy.	24.82	7.85	15.82	12.45	78.69	4264
300 Cy.	26.50	9.53	15.53	11.98	77.14	4351

***Southdown, Greenwood and Mary in 1928 and Crescent Farm, Camperdown, Mary, Glenwood and Ashland in 1929.

****Hollywood in 1928, and Hollywood, Waterford, Cinclare and Belle Terre in 1929.

Examining first the effect of the addition of 200 pounds of super-phosphate to the 200-pound cyanamid application, we find that the results are very much in accord with those already shown in the nitrate and second stubble cyanamid tests. At Bayou Sale and Ashland the tonnage produced where 200 pounds of super-phosphate were added to the 200 pounds of cyanamid was slightly inferior to the tonnage obtained from 200 pounds of cyanamid alone, and at the four others of this series the increase shown from the addition of the phosphoric acid was only around one ton per acre. The average for the six tests receiving the 200 pounds of phosphoric acid plus the 200 pounds of cyanamid shows a gain of less than one ton of cane and only 42 pounds of sugar per acre over the "nitrogen only" plats. Again, as regards the effect of phosphoric acid on the juice, there are actual decreases in sucrose and purity in the phosphoric acid plots at Ashland, Kinsale and Valence, decreases in purity at Midway and Enola and a decrease in sucrose at Enterprise, not a single demonstration showing an increase in both sucrose and purity where the phosphoric acid was added to the nitrogen application as against the 200 pounds cyanamid applied alone. Examining the averages again, both for 1930 and for the three years, we find that 200 pounds of cyanamid alone shows a slightly better sucrose content and purity than where phosphoric acid has been added.

Now as regards the addition of some 20 pounds of nitrogen to what we have taken as our standard here of about 40 pounds, we find a quite uniform commercial response up to 200 pounds of cyanamid per acre and a still uniform, but decidedly smaller proportionate increase of tonnage from the 300-pound application as compared with the 200 pounds. Studying our averages again, we find that 100 pounds of cyanamid have given an increase of about five and one-half tons over the check plots and that 200 pounds of cyanamid show an increase of less than half that amount over the yield from the 100 pounds. The gain from still an additional 100 pounds of cy-

HANDLING
of CANE MUD
. . . where production costs can be *definitely* and *appreciably* lowered

IN MILL AFTER MILL, a great improvement in the handling of cane mud is being brought about. In Brazil, Hawaii, Porto Rico, Argentina, Mexico, The Philippines . . . sugar producers are installing Oliver United Cane Mud Filters to reduce their operating costs.

Operating costs are lower:

One man operates the filter station.

The filter medium lasts several crops.

Sugar losses are greatly reduced.

The filter station is small and clean.

Maintenance is low.

Yes, with this method handling costs are considerably less than by any other method. Inversion losses are practically eliminated.

Progressive sugar mills should install Oliver United Cane Mud Filters.

anamid, however, is just a little over a ton of cane per acre, showing an average juice containing about half a point less sucrose and a point and a half lower purity than that from the 200-pound application, signifying a higher cost of manufacture due to the necessity of handling more cane to produce one ton of sugar. While during the three years, 200 pounds of cyanamid alone have produced well over a ton of sugar per year more than the check plots, our return from an additional 100 pounds of cyanamid is only at the average rate of less than 100 pounds of sugar per acre. Here again our previous conclusions seem amply confirmed, the question suggesting itself, however, in view of the much larger proportionate gain from 20 pounds of nitrogen as compared with that from 40, of the advisability of reducing the 200-pound applications so commonly employed with cyanamid and sulphate of ammonia to about 175 pounds, corresponding to the 35 pounds of nitrogen which the nitrate demonstrations indicated as about the commercially most profitable amount per acre.

Summary and Conclusions

Summing up the results of three years of these co-operative demonstrations with fertilizers on P.O.J. stubble cane, we find that almost without exception applications of nitrogen alone at the rate of 30 to 40 pounds per acre have resulted in a net gain over the unfertilized checks of from six to eight tons of cane per acre, while equally consistently and with only a few notable exceptions on certain isolated soil types, such as in the Teche and Red River sections, the addition of 200 pounds of super-phosphate to our 30 to 40 pounds of nitrogen has resulted again in a commercial loss. That is to say, with the exception of these outlying soil types, the addition of 200 pounds of acid phosphate has not produced a sufficient additional number of pounds of sugar per acre over the application of nitrogen alone to pay for the cost of the super-phosphate—to say nothing of the mixing and application cost.

While undoubtedly further investigational work should be done by our experiment stations with super-phosphate, particularly on the few types of soil where phosphoric acid seems to give any commercial returns and although assuredly the last word has not as yet been spoken as to future eventual use of phosphoric acid in our cane fertilizing program, in view of the generally depressed economic conditions we should, in making our fertilizer recommendations, consider the case from the angle of this current situation and the absolute necessity of economizing at every possible point along the line where such economy will not actually mean a smaller return in tonnage of cane and sugar during immediately coming crops.

We have proven pretty definitely for the past three years in large scale practical demonstrations scattered all over the State that an investment of $3 to $4.50 per acre in applying 30 to 40 pounds of nitrogen to stubble cane will result in a sure profit of 150 to 300 per cent on the investment, and the writer knows of no other single phase in the cultivation of sugar cane, from the time the ground is broken until the crop is at the conductor, where an investment of any amount can secure such a large and almost certain percentage return. Pass 40 pounds of nitrogen per acre—and possibly 35—and there seems to be a depressing effect on the sucrose in the juice to the extent that, were we to make considerably more sugar per acre, the cost of handling a larger number of tons of cane in order to manufacture a ton of sugar makes the profit per additional pound of sugar very much less and the percentage return on our additional investment, therefore, considerably less than when the 30 to 35 pounds of nitrogen are applied. Hence the writer is of the opinion that, *with the exception of a few outlying soil types*, our planters will receive the best return on their fertilizer investments by omitting phosphoric acid entirely from the fertilizer program and applying their nitrogenous fertilizers to stubble cane at the rate of 30 to 35 pounds of nitrogen per acre, putting this fertilizer as close as possible to the cane just as early in the spring as it is practicable to distribute it.

Acknowledgments

For the 1930 nitrate experiments both the nitrate of soda and super-phosphate were furnished by the Chilean Nitrate of Soda Educational Bureau through their district manager, Mr. F. R. Curtis, of Alexandria, whose hearty co-operation in the laying out and control of these demonstrations is gratefully acknowledged. The writer also desires to express appreciation of the co-operation of Mr. Claude B. Gouaux, Extension Cane Technologist of the L. S. U. Experiment Station, in carrying out these tests, as well as of that of the managers and agriculturists of the various plantations on which all of these co-operative demonstrations were conducted and of the following county agents: Mr. Joe G. Richard, of Terrebonne Parish; Mr. J. C. Nargassans, of St. Martin; Mr. P. J. de Gravelles, of St. Mary, and Mr. F. A. Swann, of Avoyelles.

Application for Increased Sugar Duty

Just as this issue of the SUGAR BULLETIN goes to press we are advised by the Washington office of the American Sugar Cane League that several beet growers' organizations in the Western States, as well as several individual beet farmers in that territory, have filed an application with the United States Tariff Commission for an increase in the duty on raw and refined sugar, edible molasses, cane syrup and blackstrap molasses. The action of Congress in placing the duty on Cuban 96° raw sugar at 2¢ instead of the 2.40¢ asked for by the domestic sugar producers as the minimum that would enable them to survive, has played havoc with the beet growers, just as it has with the cane growers.

No details are yet at hand concerning the text of the petition and until we have further information we withhold comment, except to say that the importance of the move made by the beet farmers can hardly be overemphasized.

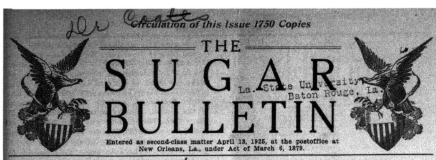

Circulation of this Issue 1750 Copies

THE
SUGAR
BULLETIN

La. State University
Baton Rouge, La.

Entered as second-class matter April 13, 1925, at the postoffice at
New Orleans, La., under Act of March 6, 1879.

We stand for the encouragement of Home Industries as against foreign competition.

| Vol. 9 | NEW ORLEANS, LA., JULY 1, 1931 | No. 19 |

This Sugar Business of Ours

We think it is timely to make a little survey of the Louisiana sugar industry and cast up, as well as we may, the balances against it and those in its favor. It is now some three years since the new varieties of canes, from which so much was expected, began to be cultivated on an industrial scale and since then they generally replaced on our plantations the D.74, D.95 and purple and striped canes of invalid and pathetic memory. A sufficient time has elapsed for some practical insight to be had into the question of whether these new canes have fulfilled the task assigned to them, which was, in brief, to save the Louisiana sugar industry from destruction.

The industry having been virtually extinguished just before the new canes were introduced, the production going down to 47,000 tons, and having now recovered to some 200,000 tons, an extent equal to about 2/3 of its normal volume, there can be only one answer to such an inquiry. That the new canes restored the Louisiana sugar industry is beyond dispute. It is a fact, however, that some pessimism exists based on the absence of a succession of similar miracles arriving, one after another, to exorcise low prices, make it rain at the right time and keep it from freezing at the wrong time. These afflictions have been visited upon us without much restraint and that our sugar business has suffered from them is indisputable, yet there is no doubt at all that the Louisiana sugar industry can, and does, rise superior to all of them with the exception of the low prices. These are brought about by the practice of sugar producers elsewhere selling their sugars on our markets at less than their own production cost, and when we take into consideration the fact that the producers of sugar all over the world and the producers of virtually every other staple commodity in the United States, are operating at a loss at the present time because of low prices no pessimism concerning the Louisiana sugar industry is justifiable on this especial ground. We have only to look around us to see a score of other businesses worse off, from this cause, than sugar.

Intrinsically the Louisiana sugar industry is as sound as the new canes were supposed to make it. In recent months there has been a tendency to decry one of the new cane varieties, P.O.J. 213, because of its susceptibility to red rot, and as this particular variety was thought by some to be the best of those introduced here, the discovery that it suffered from red rot in certain localities has given rise to an amount of pessimism that is entirely unjustified by the facts. Nobody has to keep on planting P.O.J. 213 if they do not want to; the day has gone when we all had to plant one sort of cane or none at all. That fact is the very crux of the varietal situation. No longer need we go down to an annual production of 47,000 tons of sugar, or less, because some certain variety of cane gets something the matter with it. That was the tragedy of our situation before the United States Department of Agriculture came to our rescue with the new canes, for at that time our cane, our only cane, got mosaic disease, and we had nothing to replace it. Now,

===THE===

SUGAR BULLETIN

407 Carondelet St., New Orleans

Issued on the 1st and 15th of each month. Official Organ of the American Sugar Cane League of the U. S. A., in which are consolidated
The Louisiana Sugar Planters' Assn.
The American Cane Growers' Assn.
The Producers & Mfgrs. Protective Assn.
Subscription Price, 50 Cents Per Year.

Reginald Dykers, General Manager & Editor of the Bulletin
301 Nola Bldg., New Orleans
Frank L. Barker, Secretary and Treasurer
Lockport, La.
C. J. Bourg, Manager Washington Office
810 Union Trust Building

CHAIRMEN OF COMMITTEES:

C. D. Kemper, Franklin, La.
President of the League and Ex-Officio Chairman of Executive Committee

Percy A. Lemann, Donaldsonville, La.
Chairman Agricultural Committee

David W. Pipes, Jr., Houma, La.
Chairman Industrial Committee

Frank L. Barker, Lockport, La.
Chairman Finance Committee.

Edward J. Gay, Plaquemine, La.
Chairman Tariff Committee

H. Langdon Laws, Cinclare, La.
Chairman Legislative Committee

J. C. LeBourgeois, New Orleans, La.
Chairman Freight Rate Committee

R. H. Chadwick, Bayou Goula, La.
Chairman Membership Committee

A. H. Rosenfeld, New Orleans, La.
Chairman Publicity Committee

Members of the League desiring action on, or information on, any subject are invited to communicate with the League or with the Chairman of the Committee to which it seems to appertain.

if any particular variety gets diseased we have only to discard it and use another. Six varieties are already released, of which two besides P.O.J. 213 are in such plentiful supply that they can be switched to in one season, and additional varieties are scheduled for release from time to time, so the situation in this regard is utterly different and incomparably safer than it used to be. Cane disease need no longer be a bugbear to the Louisiana sugar district, any more than yellow fever is a bugbear to New Orleans; both belong to the limbo of the obsolete. Let us remember this.

As a matter of fact most of the trouble with P.O.J. 213 is due to one or the other of three things; it was either planted on black land, for which it has not proved suitable, or it was planted too deep, or in poorly drained localities. P.O.J. 213 is a cane that should be planted early in the fall, never in the spring, and in the spring the dirt should be taken off of it as soon as possible, and, where properly planted, it is said to give the most sugar per acre and, furthermore, the first year stubble of P.O.J.

213 is generally excellent wherever there was a good crop of plant cane the previous year. In the years 1928-1929 and 1930 the yield from P.O.J. 213 in Louisiana averaged 2440 lbs. of sugar per acre, in spite of the yields on some places that were inordinately low due to improper treatment, and by contrast the yield of the old varieties of cane throughout the 15 years from 1909 to 1924 was only 2000 lbs. of sugar per acre. We are not attempting to persuade those who do not think well of P.O.J. 213 to plant it, because every man should do as he pleases about that. We do think, however, that the amount of criticism of P.O.J. 213 has gone beyond conservative bounds and that this criticism is being transposed in some quarters into a peculiar and wholly unjustified attitude of pessimism towards all the new canes, which is sheer folly. Those who do not like P.O.J. 213 should plant another variety as soon as feasible and rejoice over the fact that they can do so.

Now let us consider last year and this year, up to date, from a weather standpoint. Does anyone believe that, given the cold spring of last year, with hardly a moderately warm day before the middle of June, followed by a drought prevailing nearly all summer, the old varieties of cane would have made half a crop? The new canes made nearly a normal crop. Does anyone believe that with the present cold and dry spring (the months of March, April and May this year were cooler than these months have ever been before in the history of the Weather Bureau), the old canes would present the stand and appearance that the new canes present today or that they would speed up like race-horses in the home stretch in August and September as the new canes so invariably do as if to make up for lost time? Juggling different varieties of canes around is now a remunerative pastime in all the sugar countries of the world, and those very successful sugar countries Java and Hawaii are the leaders in all this. They stay with no one variety very long, but continuously transfer their fields to others that they like better and from which they believe they will get better returns. We, too, must get to the point where changing from one variety to another, for any cause at all, is commonplace with us.

So far as the physical condition of the Louisiana sugar district is concerned we are incomparably better off than we were three years ago. Nearly every sugar factory that is required for the milling of the crop has been put in fair shape, and some of them in splendid shape. The soil is in good tilth, many ways have been

The Advertisers in the Sugar Bulletin are contributing towards the support of the American Sugar Cane League and should enjoy your special consideration; help them to help the Domestic Sugar Industry by doing business with them whenever possible.

found for doing things more cheaply and efficiency methods have been adopted all down the line. Last, but not least, the United States Department of Agriculture has established a clinic at Houma, housed there in three splendid buildings built by the American Sugar Cane League, and the Louisiana Experiment Station has another clinic at Baton Rouge that is functioning actively, through the aid of the annual $40,000 secured for it from the Louisiana Legislature by the League. The economic benefit derived by our sugar industry from these two sources is almost incalculable.

After a survey of the whole situation the conclusion is inevitable that there is nothing whatever wrong with this sugar business of ours except the price of sugar. That factor has wrecked nearly the whole sugar world today, and in the universality of this trouble lies the hope of our salvation from it, because while the Louisiana sugar producers, owing to their small output, can do nothing to help prices, the sugar world at large can, and has already taken intelligent action to that end through the adoption of the Chadbourne plan, the effects of which are already being felt.

Let us take heart, therefore. Let us look at our sugar business in the true perspective. If we do that we shall see it for what it is—the safest, surest, most enduring and most permanent agricultural undertaking in the State of Louisiana today. It is easy to find fault, in general terms, with anything. In the case of sugar let us insist that critics either become specific and categorical or keep silent, and, above all, let us not be unreasonably critical ourselves.

NEW ORLEANS, LA., JUNE 15, 1931

Notice

Through an error in our printing office the date line on the SUGAR BULLETIN of June 15, 1931, was printed June 1, 1931. Attached to this page will be found a small gummed sticker of the proper size to place over the erroneous date. Those of our readers who preserve files of the SUGAR BULLETIN will be glad to take advantage of this opportunity to correct the date line.

Cane Crops in Spite of Cold Springs

By Arthur H. Rosenfeld, Consulting Technologist, American Sugar Cane League.

Once again the Louisiana cane regions have had to withstand a long, cold spring—in fact the coldest since the United States Weather Bureau records were started here, the average daily mean temperature for March, April and May having been just $4\frac{1}{2}°$ below the normal for those months—and once again our cane, though showing an excellent stand in general, is very short for this season of the year.

To the sugar man accustomed only to the Tropics, visiting Louisiana early this summer, it seems totally impossible that sugar cane which is practically just starting to grow can produce excellent crops of fair sugar content only four or five months hence. He thinks of what seven or eight months old cane in the Tropics would be like, and, were it not for the fact that he knows that all cane is winter killed each year in Louisiana, he would be inclined to seriously doubt the veracity of his Louisiana cicerone.

It is a fact, however, that in both Louisiana and Tucuman, the sister sub-tropical cane-producing regions north and south of the equator, growth is much more rapid and luxuriant during the maximum seven or eight months' growing season than in almost any part of the Tropics, and, of course, the incidence of cool weather causes the cane to start ripening at a much earlier age than is the case where such a climatic stimulus is lacking. The writer is inclined to believe that nowhere in the Tropics does sugar cane grow so rapidly in a similar period as during the three or four months of high temperatures, humidity and rainfall characteristic of the summer and early fall of both Louisiana and Northern Argentina. Particularly favorable to rapid and continuous growth are the excessively hot and humid nights so typical of both sub-tropical countries and which the writer has never experienced over similar periods in the true Tropics, as well as the large number of daylight hours during the principal growing season, the length of day reaching $12\frac{1}{2}$ hours the latter part of March, rising to 14 hours in June and not falling below 13 hours again until September.*

Even in these sub-tropical countries after a late spring, such as Louisiana experienced this year, the planters themselves are inclined to forget previous experience and wonder if there will be time to make a crop. For a number of years the writer has kept photographic records of the status of fields of different varieties in various sections of the State and he has found of late that the showing of some of these series, of what might be called visual records of growth in other years, to some of our alarmed planters has served, to a large extent, to dissipate their pessimism. The most recent comparison with the present late spring in Louisiana was the crop year 1930, when practically the entire development

*McDonald, W. F.—A Study of Weather Influences on Sugar Cane Production in Louisiana. The Pltr. & Sug. Mfr., 1926.

of that reasonably good cane crop occurred after the 1st of July as demonstrated by numerous photographs taken at stated intervals. Those made in 1928 on Belle Terre Plantation near Donaldsonville, Louisiana, by Mr. Percy Lemann (**) are also most convincing in this regard. Without the backing of such series of photographs, it would be difficult to credit such remarkable development to but four months of growth, yet Mr. Lemann's photographed fields of P.O.J. plant cane produced from 25 to 32 tons of cane per acre at harvest time and showed excellent sugar content.

An idea of the rapidity of growth during a normal Louisiana summer may be obtained from the two tables following, the first being a series of measurements from the top of the cane ridge to the bud of the cane, made by Dr. M. V. Marmande (***) on his plantation at Theriot in the Parish of Terrebonne with marked stools of the three commercially propagated P.O.J. canes. As will be observed from this table, during a period of almost six weeks these varieties made an average growth of about 85/100 of an inch per day.

The second table is a record of the growth of these P.O.J. canes and the Louisiana Purple on the five test fields conducted by the American Sugar Cane League and the Louisiana Experiment Station under the supervision of Mr. Claude B. Gouaux (****). These figures show that, for the month of July, the growth of the P.O.J. canes in the test fields averaged over an inch per day.

TABLE I.

		Height VII-23 Inches	Height VIII-31 Inches	Gain in 39 days Inches
Variety	Age			
P. O. J. 36	Plant	54	89	35
P. O. J. 36	Stubble	54	84	30
P. O. J. 213	Plant	48	81	33
P. O. J. 213	Stubble	49	81	32
P. O. J. 234	Plant	55	85	30
P. O. J. 234	Stubble	47	78	31

GROWTH OF CANE IN TERREBONNE PARISH—1928

TABLE II.

AVERAGE DAILY GROWTH RATES OF TEST FIELD VARIETIES

(Expressed in Inches)

Variety	Cinclare	Glenwood	Reserve	Sterling	Youngsville
	7-6 to 8-2	7-5 to 7-31	7-6 to 8-3	7-3 to 8-4	7-2 to 30
(Plant Cane)					
P. O. J. 36	1.08	1.03	.97	1.15	1.07
P. O. J. 36M	1.04	1.15	1.14	.97	1.00
P. O. J. 213	1.11	1.23	.78	.97	1.11
P. O. J. 234	1.00	1.23	1.04	.97	1.11
Purple	.92	.80	.89	.97	1.21
(First Year Stubble)					
P. O. J. 36	.78	.80	.89	1.09	.75
P. O. J. 213	.85	.88	.96	1.00	1.00
P. O. J. 234	.96	.92	1.32	.94	1.35
Purple	.44	.42	.75	.60	.71

It may be of interest, also, in this connection that the writer, in measuring growth during three or four day periods of excessively warm rainy weather and oppressive nights in Louisiana and Tucuman, has found average daily growth to run from two to two and one-half inches!

In connection with the above table showing the slower development of the Louisiana Purple cane as compared with that of the P.O.J.'s, some reference to the acre stalk population of the P.O.J. canes as compared with the Purple, determinations of which were made in July, 1928, is illuminating, par-

**Rosenfeld, Arthur H. The Growth of Cane in Louisiana. Int. Sug. Jour., XXXII, 1930.
***The Rate of Growth of the P.O.J. Canes. Sug. Bull. VI, 24, 1928.
****Reports to Contact Committee.

ticularly as illustrating the difference in potential and realized yields of cane and sugar per acre. A large number of counts were made that month in various sections of the State of the average number of what were considered then probably millable stalks per lineal feet, each count being made on several 100-foot sections of rows. The number of stalks per 100 feet was then calculated to the 7200 lineal feet per acre existing where cane is planted in six-foot rows. With the old Louisiana Purple and Striped canes, only the best of these in the western section of the belt around Youngsville, where the virulence of mosaic disease had not at that time attained its maximum, were counted, whereas the P.O.J. canes of all conditions and of all varieties were included in the estimates.

The average for these counts—and well over 100 of them were made—show that they were at that time some 12,000 stalks per acre in the case of the Louisiana "native" canes as against an average of nearly 40,000 stalks for the three P.O.J. varieties. The crop figures amply bore out the promise of these stalk counts, as the P.O.J. canes on the fields under consideration produced an average of around 20 tons of cane per acre against just under seven tons for the Purple and Striped!

Last year at this time the cane section was in the throes of an exceptionally severe drought following upon a late spring, though not so late as this year. At the present time the growth of the cane is probably ten days behind that of last year in general, or about three weeks behind the normal growth condition. However, the whole sugar district has had more or less scattered showers of late and satisfactory precipitations in a few limited sections, while temperature conditions are now ideal for rapid growth where there is anything like ample moisture in the soil. The writer feels that, with normal July rainfall, we have more than a good chance of catching up with last year's condition and even of making a yield per acre intermediate between that of 1930 and what might be called normal, thus giving to the hoped-for July rain-clouds not the proverbial silver, but a "white-gold" lining.

Embargo on Soviet Products

Statement of Hon. Numa F. Montet, a Representative in Congress from the State of Louisiana, at Hearing Before Committee on Ways and Means, Washington, February 20, 1931.

The CHAIRMAN. Give your name, address and business connections to the committee and the stenographer.

MR. MONTET. Numa F. Montet, Representative in Congress from the third Louisiana district.

Mr. Chairman, I do not propose to utilize more than 10 minutes which, by order of this committee, is supposed to be allotted to each witness. I do not propose to engage in a general discussion of the Russian situation, because I have every reason to assume that, generally speaking, this committee has more information in hand than I am able to supply. However, as I have my own conclusions in the matter, I want to say that they are these: I personally view the Russian situation as a menace to the economic and political system of this country; and not only do I view this problem from the immediate present, but were it not that I view it in anticipation of the future, the facts that I desire to submit to this committee would probably be held irrelevant.

My district is practically 100 per cent an agricultural district. Our main product is sugar made from sugar cane. You gentlemen all know that the sugar industry of the world, at least most of it, has been trying to stabilize the production and the marketing of sugar for some months, just as we are trying, through Government agencies in this country, to stabilize the market for wheat, cotton, and so forth. Russia last year had 1,050,000 hectares in sugar beets. It produced some 2,000,000 tons of sugar. This year it has 1,300,000 hectares of land in cultivation in sugar beets. Its production this year is anticipated to be 2,500,000 tons of sugar—not enough to take care of the needs of its 150,000,000 of population.

We consume in this country, with 120,000,000 people, over 5,000,000 tons of sugar annually. So it is obvious that Russia's increased production of this year is not sufficient to supply its local needs.

The reason that sugar comes into this picture, as I say, is because I look upon the Russian situation in anticipation of the future. According to a report issued by Willett & Gray, of New York, sugar brokers and sugar statisticians, since the 1st of January of this year the Russian Government has shipped to India over 40,000 tons of sugar and sold it there at a price 10 points below the price that the Javanese are able to deliver sugar in India. The effect that has on the sugar business is this: When those shipments entered into India, Java threatened to withdraw from the world agreement to stabilize sugar unless Russia entered into the agreement. Right at this time, there is no certainty that Russia will enter into the agreement and, if Russia does not enter into the agreement it may disrupt the whole stabilization program for sugar.

Now, we might say, how does the United States come in contact with that situation? As I say, I look into the future. If Russia can ship sugar into New York at a price 10 points below that which the Javanese can meet, we have every reason to assume that Russia can and will, in the future some time, ship sugar into the United States in competition with the very substantial sugar industry we have in this country. As you gentlemen know, the sugar industry in this country of beet and sugar cane is quite a substantial industry. It represents hundreds of millions of dollars of investment and, as I say, I look at the matter in the future. I can readily see that if Russia continues to success with her so-called 5-year program—and I am not ready to say she will not succeed—that sugar will be dumped into this country at a price (in spite of the existing tariff) not only that America will not be able to meet, but even that Cuba will not be able to meet.

We can talk about exports from this country into Russia. That is true at this time. I feel if we look at the situation simply from a consideration of the immediate present, it is advantageous for us to trade with Russia; but, in my opinion, there is no difference whatever between the economic and political system of Russia; the economic system is the political system and the political system is the economic system.

Our own Government has refused to recognize the political system and when we do that, in my opinion, the Government is officially condemning the Russian economic system.

As I said a few months ago, Russia is importing, as is the evidence I have heard here before this committee, probably $150,000,000 of our products; but the day will soon be here when Russia will be self-sufficient, when she will be supplying her own needs—and what is going to become of us then? Her economic program, then her political program, will be a success. We might suffer right at this time if an embargo is levied against Russia, maybe for two or three or maybe for four or five years; but, for myself, I look at the question from a viewpoint of the future and not exactly the immediate present. Sugar is not affected at this time in this country, but without question, in my opinion, it will be affected; because Russia is continuing to increase her production, and her intention of destroying the economic systems of the balance of the world is well indicated in her shipping of sugar out of Russia where they need it so badly. Russia wants cash; those in charge of the Government do not seem to be interested in supplying the local demand right in their own country. If that were true, this 40,000 tons of sugar would have been retained there. And I submit, Mr. Chairman and gentlemen of the committee, in my opinion it is time this country practiced a little enlightened selfishness.

I thank you.

MR. CRISP. I think my friend, of course, made his position very clear as to this embargo legislation on Russia and he gave reasons for the belief that was in him. We have other embargo bills pending before us, one, notably the Burtness bill, dealing with an embargo on a great many agricultural products, on the ground that agriculture is in a distressed state, which we all concede and deplore. But if there is to be an embargo on agricultural products to aid the farmers in obtaining a better price, do you not think those farmers engaged in the production of sugar are entitled to the same benefits and the embargo should also apply to sugar, as well as to certain other enumerated agricultural products?

MR. MONTET. I certainly do think so; because certainly no one will maintain at any time, anywhere, that sugar is not a substantial industry of this country. I believe if we are going to have an embargo to protect one class of farmers, let us protect them all.

MR. CRISP. I agree with that, but some of the proponents of that bill are opposed to an embargo on sugar.

MR. MONTET. I am just as much for protection to the wheat farmer—while there is not a grain of wheat grown in my district—as I am for the protection of the sugar cane farmers.

MR. CRISP. I am frank to say I am not in favor of an embargo on world agricultural products; I am in favor of giving an adequate tariff. But I do say, if our Government is going to change its historic policy and start into the embargo business, I think all ·industries of the United States and all agricultural interests are entitled in equity, to the same benefits as a few enumerated products.

MR. MONTET. If I may say to the gentleman from Georgia, I view the Russian situation as an extraordinary situation, as an extraordinary problem, and such problems always justify extraordinary remedies. Now, if this Government, in my opinion, did not view the Russian situation as a menace, we would recognize the Russian Government. I believe this country should do one of two things—we should either recognize the Government in Russia and deal with it as we do with all other countries, or we should continue our present policy and sever all relations of any and every kind whatsoever, including trade. Because, in my opinion, the reason why we do not recognize Russia is because her principles run counter to the principles of government of the balance of the countries in the world. Then, if we do that, we necessarily have in mind the ultimate destruction of that form of government and, in my opinion, the governmental system of that country and the economic system are one and the same; when you speak of the economic system, it is the government; when you speak of the government, it is the economic system.

MR. CRISP. I think my friend made his position very clear as to an embargo on Russia and in most cases I am not altogether out of sympathy with him on that proposition; because I think there is the fundamental principle involved in an embargo against Russia. But I wanted to draw his attention to the other bill that was not an embargo against Russia alone, but was an embargo against the world on certain named agricultural products, and I know his vital interest in agriculture.

MR. MONTET. Yes.

MR. CRISP. And I wanted to get your views if you did not think sugar should also be included in that program.

MR. MONTET. I am dealing in my remarks solely with the extraordinary problem of the Russian situation.

MR. COLLIER. Supplementing what Judge Crisp said regarding the Burtness bill, on which we have been holding hearings for practically all of the week until yesterday afternoon, that bill provides for an embargo on a great number of agricultural products against all the world, but the proponents of that bill are antagonistic to sugar, because they claim they want the embargo only to be laid against those agricultural products of which we produce a surplus. So

that in no sense could sugar fall within the provisions of that bill.

MR. MONTET. My position has to do solely with the Russian situation and I feel any substantial industry in this country, whether it supplies our demands and needs in this country in their entirety, or not, is entitled to the same treatment that we would give to the industry that supplies all of our demands.

Pertinent to the above are the resolutions below adopted at the regular monthly meeting of the Executive Committee of the American Sugar Cane League held June 24th, 1931:

WHEREAS—It is a matter of public knowledge that raw materials, as well as manufactured products, of all kinds, are being produced in Soviet Russia under labor conditions that are not only far beneath the standard prevalent in the United States, but which are abhorrent to our ideas, practices, customs and principles, and

WHEREAS—The products of such labor, which is compelled to its tasks by both direct and indirect methods, by the Russian Government, will inevitably undersell the products of American labor, which rightfully expects and receives wages commensurate with the American standard of living, and thus undermine and destroy our industries and lead to an increase of distress and unemployment, therefore be it

RESOLVED—That the American Sugar Cane League of the U. S. A., Inc., opposes the entry into the United States of the products of Soviet Russia and believes adequate steps should be taken by the Government of the United States to prevent such products coming into competition with the products of the labor and industry of the United States where our whole economic system is of a better and higher order and this better and higher order and the ideals and principles on which it has been constructed we must use every effort to defend and maintain, and be it further

RESOLVED—That it is our opinion that there is no difference whatever in the harmful effect on our domestic industries whether articles and commodities imported into this country, to compete with similar articles and commodities made here, are produced by Russian labor working through governmental compulsion under conditions that are different from and far below the economic standards sought and attained after nearly a century of effort by American labor, or whether they are produced in any other foreign country by labor working under similar conditions without governmental compulsion. The ruin that such importations inflict on our home industries is just as harmful in one case as the other. We believe that in considering the importations from Soviet Russia attention should be directed to the obvious fact that other importations from other countries, produced by poorly paid workmen living under low economic conditions, are likewise threatening the existence of many of our domestic industries because of the lack of an adequate protective tariff against them.

The Chadbourne Plan in Operation

There is reproduced below cablegram sent by Mr. Thomas L. Chadbourne for presentation at the first session of the International Sugar Council, which assembled in London June 22d:

"Please present my greetings to the International Sugar Council on this occasion of its first meeting. From my point of view it is a most significant occasion. The agreement which brings the council into being represents the most comprehensive accomplishment to bring into equilibrium on a world-wide scale the production and consumption of a universally used commodity.

"Taking 1930 consumption as a basis, the plan provides for a production throughout the world, which will result in a normal price being established sufficient to compensate for all normal costs. The elasticity of the plan provides for ample response to any increase in consumption requirements, without permitting unusual speculative profits.

"It should be a function of the council to so guide the operation of the plan that these results may be achieved normally and intelligently. Assuming our statistical knowledge of sugar conditions is correct, the plan, which you are to administer, is certain to succeed.

"I believe export countries like Peru, with which you are negotiating, and Santo Domingo with which I resume negotiations next week, will realize the advantages and join the international agreement. I believe that Russia's internal requirements will absorb practically the whole of her expected sugar production during the next few years and, as a matter of fact, that she will be a buyer on balances for some time to. come.

"I am satisfied that the co-operation the respective governments and sugar producers of the exporting countries have given to the plan, and the obvious interest of all these countries in seeing to it that the plan is carried out, will assure the fulfillment of the provisions of the agreement to the letter. The surplus sugar segregated by the agreement in the exporting countries will be held off the market and only liberated in the orderly fashion established by the contract.

"As to world consumption, it is agreed by experts that 1930 was an abnormally low year in actual consumption. · Figures now in hand show clearly that during the eight months from September 1, 1930, to April 30, 1931, the sugar consumption of Europe actually increased 4.3 per cent, notwithstanding an economic depression fully as serious as we are undergoing in America. A careful study of conditions justifies the opinion that consumption requirements in the United States are not diminishing. It is fair to assume, therefore, that the use of sugar is increasing throughout the world. ·

"With reference. to production, it is clearly established that this year will see a greatly reduced output of sugar throughout the world. Figures already in hand indicate a reduction in Europe of at least 1,865,000 tons, or more than 18 per cent. Cuban production is already less than last year by 1,550,000 tons.

"It is probably fair to say that world production will be 4,000,000 tons less this year than last year, when it is realized that under the plan 2,614,000 tons of sugar, the surplus over normal stocks, are segregated in the exporting countries, with only one-fifth of it available to the export market this year.

"It is thus not inaccurate to say that there will be available to the world market upward of 6,000,000 tons of sugar less this year than was the case in 1930, against probable actual consumption this year in excess of that of 1930.

"Such are the results already achieved by looking the facts squarely in the face and having the sugar industrialists of the important countries agree upon a common co-operative plan of meeting those facts. It will be the function of your council to continue this co-operative undertaking for the next five years.

"I am sure the results of your efforts will be greatly to the advantage of the sugar industry

throughout the world and at the same time will make the industry readily responsive to all developments in the market requirements for sugar. I pray for your success and wish I were with you at this, your first, conference."

The New York Journal of Commerce of June 22 says:

"With the details of the Chadbourne plan now to hand a feature has become known which heretofore was not generally understood," Farr & Company say in a recent report. "In so far as Cuba is concerned the size of the crop during the next five years is regulated by the sum total of the local Cuban quota plus the foreign quota, plus United States actual exports during the previous year. In other words, next year's Cuban crop must be reduced by whatever quantity is carried over in Cuba from the current production. The object, of course, is to build up no further surpluses anywhere but to carry out the plan for diminishing those already existing at the agreed upon rate of 260,000 tons a year so far as Cuba is concerned. The above provisions make quite a difference in the mental attitude of those who prefer to carry sugar until later in the year or even into next year in the knowledge that they will not be holding the umbrella and, furthermore, they should be well repaid in the price ruling next year as a result of the decrease in the size of the 1932 crop in the likely event of a fair sized carryover this year. As we see it, unless the price improves substantially above the present, the carryover in Cuba will amount to about 500,000 tons, which would make production for 1932 only about 2,750,000 tons."

Washington News

By C. J. Bourg

The report that the Cuban Chamber of Commerce had forwarded a petition to the President of the United States asking that the tariff rate on raw sugar be reduced for the benefit of the Cuban sugar industry, preceded by only a few days the filing of an application by a large group of beet growers in the western part of the United States, stating that under present conditions an increase in the rate of duty on raw sugar was necessary to make beet growing profitable for them. The Tariff Commission has not yet ordered an investigation as a result of this application of the beet growers, which application asks for investigations looking to increases of duty on raw and refined sugar, edible molasses, cane syrup and blackstrap molasses.

Considerable publicity has been given recently to reports regarding certain processes through which sugar is to be utilized for other purposes besides human consumption. The process which has received greatest notice required nine years of experimental and research work and has developed the use of sugar in the manufacture of transparent rubber, artificial leather, paints, varnishes and non-inflammable celluloid. The discoverer of the process has stated that the plastic material can be manufactured into fountain pens, lamp shades, table and deck tops of any color. There is also under way several experiments looking to the use of sugar as cattle feed, and especially in the ration of the dairy cow. Preliminary information gives rise to the hope that this latter consumption may reach sufficient proportions to count. None of these discoveries have yet reached the development which would justify too much enthusiasm, but they all go to demonstrate that the sugar industry is moving forward and will be in much better condition as soon as the formal control of the surplus of world production has been put into effect.

Sugar Freight Reduction Before I. C. C.

A very interesting report has been submitted by an examiner of the Interstate Commerce Commission upon the application by transcontinental rail lines for reduction of rates on refined sugar between the Western Coast and Mississippi Valley points. The application is grounded principally on recently developed actual competition with route operating through the Panama Canal, through New Orleans and up the Mississippi River, or through New York City and by Canal and the Great Lakes. The examiner recommends that the application be denied on the principal ground that this sugar traffic has been developed by Panama Canal lines and does not particularly represent traffic that has been drawn away from the rail lines.

Liquid Sugar Brief Filed

The Savannah Sugar Refining Corporation has filed in the United States Customs Court the brief upon which is based its case in the matter of liquid sugar importations. A summary of its contentions is as follows:

(1) There is no such classification as that given this merchandise, to-wit, "sugar solution," or "sugar diluted with water," to be found in paragraph 501 of the Tariff Act of 1930, under which a duty of 1.7125 cents per pound, less 20% C. R. was imposed.

(2) Said merchandise was not "sugars," nor "sirups of cane juice," within the meaning of said paragraph 501, nor was it "mixtures containing sugar and water," within the contemplation of said paragraph 501, which is restricted to such mixtures testing by the polariscope above 50 sugar degrees, whereas the said merchandise tested by the polariscope only 45.50 sugar degrees.

(3) Said merchandise was not lawfully dutiable at the rates prescribed in said paragraph 501, as "mixtures containing sugar and water" by virtue of the "similitude" portion of paragraph 1559. Said statute provides expressly the condition in which a mixture containing sugar and water must be found before the rates prescribed therein can lawfully be made to apply, i. e., the mixture must test by the polariscope "above 50 sugar degrees." Said paragraph 501 must, therefore, be taken to preclude the application of the similitude portion of paragraph 1559 to a mixture containing sugar and water which has a lower polariscopic test than that prescribed.

(4) Said merchandise was not in essence a sugar, and, therefore, dutiable as sugar under paragraph 501, since the classification and rate are to be determined by the condition of the merchandise at the time of its importation, rather than by the condition to which it may afterwards be brought by some process of manufacture or otherwise.

(5) Said merchandise was not lawfully dutiable at the rates prescribed in said paragraph 501 by virtue of the provisions contained in the latter portion of paragraph 1559 as a non-enumerated article manufactured of two or more materials, since it is within the enumerated classes, being either a sugar sirup within the meaning of paragraph 502 or a mixture containing sugar and water within the meaning of paragraph 501, although not taking the duty prescribed by paragraph 501, for mixtures containing sugar and water because not coming up to the polariscopic test provided for such mixtures in said paragraph 501. The fact that it may not be specially provided for does not take it out of the enumerated classes.

(6) Said merchandise did not come within any classification covered by said paragraph 501, nor could the rates of duty authorized by said paragraph 501 be lawfully imposed upon said merchandise by virtue of any provision contained in paragraph 1559 of said Tariff Act of 1930.

(7) Said merchandise should have been held dutiable at the rate of ¼ of 1 cent per gallon as "sugar sirups, not specially provided for," within the meaning of paragraph 502 of said Tariff Act, or at the rate of 20% ad valorem as "articles manufactured in whole or in part, not specially provided for," within the meaning of the latter portion of paragraph 1558 of said Tariff Act.

Plaintiff also contends that even if the commodity imported by it should be deemed not strictly a "sugar sirup" within the meaning of paragraph 502, it is nevertheless dutiable as a sugar sirup by virtue of the "similitude" provisions of paragraph 1559.

Briefs of the United States through the Assistant Attorney General, and of the Domestic Producers who have intervened as *amici curiae* will be filed within the next thirty days.

Jul 31

Circulation of this Issue 1750 Copies

Dr. Chas. E. Coates,
Baton Rouge, La.

THE
SUGAR
BULLETIN

Entered as second-class matter April 13, 1925, at the postoffice at
New Orleans, La., under Act of March 6, 1879.

*We stand for the encouragement of Home
Industries as against Foreign competition.*

| Vol. 9 | NEW ORLEANS, LA., JULY 15, 1931 | No. 20 |

What Have We To Look Forward To?

We frequently hear it said that the Louisiana sugar industry isn't what it used to be, and never will be what it used to be. The statement is usually accompanied by a dismal shaking of the head. Tempora Mutantur; the Times are Changed. We sail on, like agricultural Columbuses, but Spain with its flesh pots lies astern and we shall never see it more!

There is no disputing the fact that times have changed, all along the line. Every industry in every progressive country in the world is carried on differently now from the way it was carried on 25 or 30 years ago. This is true not only because of new inventions and new ways of doing things but because of the universal levelling process that goes on throughout all human affairs as the years pass by. We admit that the Louisiana sugar industry is not what it used to be. The differences, substantially, are these:

Twenty-five or thirty years ago the Louisiana sugar industry presented the spectacle of a gorgeous *robe de chambre* wrapped around a body of considerable flabbiness. Notwithstanding the fact that we shall, and should, forever cherish the memory of the thirty years from 1880 to 1910 as an era of brilliant accomplishments, achieved in an atmosphere that was fragrant with Victorian dignity and impregnated with the charming doctrine of noblesse oblige, it witnessed the existence in the Louisiana sugar district of a social body so constructed that it could not stand the gaff. There is proof positive of this, for when the gaff did strike the whole thing collapsed.

During the 31 years from 1880 to 1910, inclusive, the average price of sugar, duty paid, or bounty paid, was 5.049 cents per pound. The canes were healthy, labor was plentiful and cheap and many buyers eagerly competed for our plantation grades of sugar. It was not reasonable, however, to expect that favorable conditions would continue always, nor did they. The tragedy of it all was that the body inside the showy dressing gown lacked stamina. It was soft and flabby and, although it had abundant courage it did not know how to fight. It could not live on short rations nor make forced marches, because all that sort of thing had been left out of the curriculum of the school in which it was brought up.

In contrast to that we find ourselves today moulded by hardship and adversity into a regiment of Micky McGuires. We are graduates of the school of hard knocks, and it is a school that has carried us into the highest branches of the science of survival. If there were any economic advantages of the 1880 to 1910 situation that are forever lost to us—and there are some—we have certain other advantages to offset them. As against the higher average prices of that era we can set our vastly more efficient operating methods; as against the lower labor costs we can set our hardier canes, earlier lay-by, our mechanical cultivation, our mechanical cane loading, and our mechanical carrier feeding. In addition we have today a thorough, scientific system for breeding and developing new canes which was unheard of prior to 1910. We have reduced our selling

=======THE=======

SUGAR BULLETIN

407 Carondelet St., New Orleans

Issued on the 1st and 15th of each month. Official Organ of the American Sugar Cane League of the U. S. A., in which are consolidated
The Louisiana Sugar Planters' Assn.
The American Cane Growers' Assn.
The Producers & Mfgrs. Protective Assn.
Subscription Price, 50 Cents Per Year.

Reginald Dykers, General Manager & Editor of the Bulletin
301 Nola Bldg., New Orleans
Frank L. Barker, Secretary and Treasurer
Lockport, La.
C. J. Bourg, Manager Washington Office
810 Union Trust Building

expenses, we have found new uses for our bagasse, we have hard surfaced roads instead of
muddy dirt roads on which to move the bulk
of our cane that does not move by rail and we
have motor trucks to move it with. We have
found out how to make a crop and how to grind
a crop with far less men and mules than were
considered necessary prior to 1910. We have
learned how to get nitrogen from cheaper
sources; we have learned economical stock feeding methods and we are inaugurating cheaper
transportation systems for our sugar and our
supplies. We have set our house in order
through the insistence of necessity, which is
the mother of invention. We can toss aside our
robe de chambre now and show legs and arms
and chest developed to the nth degree, and if it
happens that the stomach is a little flat, so
much the better.

. The only obstacle that really lies in the way
of the Louisiana sugar industry becoming as
prosperous as it was in what are called "the
good old days" is the low price of sugar. This
re-acts on the cane supply, for less cane is
raised by cane growers when the price is unsatisfactory, and that, in turn, prevents the factories from getting a full grinding, which is
economically harmful. So far as the prevalent
price is concerned it is as detrimental to the
sugar industries of other countries as it is to
ours. It is not as if other countries are all
doing well at these prices, while we are not. A
price that is below the production cost of virtually all the sugar countries of the world
must assuredly rise before long, and when it
does the Louisiana sugar industry will reap the
full benefit of its new and hardy canes, its economic house-cleaning and its aroused, energized
and forward-looking people.

Everything in this world passes away and we
like to contemplate and visualize the effect on
the Louisiana sugar district of the passing of
this epoch of abnormally low prices. Thousands of abandoned acres will blossom into
cane overnight; factories will have full grind-
ings and will benefit therefrom doubly in an
economic sense; all the thousand and one
things needed to make more cane and mill it
will be bought from a delighted army of dealers and manufacturers; transportation systems of all kinds will be taxed to capacity; employment will be plentiful; banks will show
color in their cheeks, and Dr. Brandes and his
varietal disciples will prance exultantly among
us because the proof of the pudding is in the
eating and we will be eating it at last.

There is nothing wrong with that picture.
The logic of the situation points to its coming
true.

Peruvian Insects Flown to Louisiana

(Reprinted from The Grace Log)

The wasp Ipobracon rimac, native of Peru, and, it
is sincerely hoped by the Department of Agriculture,
sworn enemy to the sugar cane moth borer, Diatraea
saccharalis, which ravages not only cane but corn in
the United States, Mexico, West Indies, and Central
and South America, is the latest patron of the Pan
American-Grace Airways.

Ipobracon rimac, experimented with and carefully
observed by United States Department of Agriculture entomologist . H. A. Jaynes, on Peruvian sugar
plantations such as W. R. Grace's Cartavio property,
was formerly shipped north by vessel, but travel
times by sea between its native republic and the
United States did not favor it. Only 1½ per cent
of the wasps were wont to reach New Orleans, headquarters of the army against the cane borer, alive.
Now, with Panagra planes as transports, 30 per cent
arrive in fighting condition, six days after shipment.
Twenty-two days were required by vessel.

Mr. Jaynes, an expert in his line, houses Ipobracon
rimac in large ventilated tin cans containing rations
of water and lump sugar and sends them on their
way to Miami, where they are taken in charge by
Inspector of the Plant Quarantine and Control Administration J. V. Gist, and forwarded to T. E. Holloway, the Department of Agriculture's senior entomologist in New Orleans. Mr. Holloway, assisted by
W. E. Haley and E. R. Bynum of Houma, Louisiana,
then sends them against Diatraea saccharalis, brigad-

ed with another Peruvian army corps composed of
the fly Paratheresia claripalpis, dispatched by Mr.
Jaynes via the Grace Line, packed in cold storage.
The flies arrive in the cocoon stage, 90,000 at a
time, and emerge in insectaries provided by the Department. Ipobraçon rimac, however, leaves Peru
when adult.

The Borer's Tactics

The borer's method of attack is invariable. Diatraea saccharalis, whose damage to sugar cane in
Louisiana alone amounts to five millions yearly, lays
its eggs on the leaves of the cane in flattened, circular clusters, and after a week or so the young are
hatched. These then feed on the cane plant's ten-
derest leaves and then bore into the stem, killing the
innermost part of this and causing the disease known
as "dead heart." The borer is a busy breeder, and in
a year's time four or five broods afflict Louisiana. It
has not even the decency to leave the attacked plant
when its larva is full grown, but transforms itself
into the pupa or cocoon state in the cane stem, into
which it has gnawed its way, leaving a sort of trap
door behind it. Because of this system of dugout
warfare airplane dusting with sodium fluosilicate is
almost useless, and the only system of attack or
defense against it is constituted by the loosing of
enemy parasites upon it.

The Wasp's Counter-Attack

Ipobracon rimac will, it is hoped, help to rub out
the borer by some such system as this. It will insert
its egg into the borer's egg and when the wasp is hatched
it will gnaw its way out of the borer's egg and go
right on to the next borer's egg. Ipobracon rimac
has not, however, yet been employed on this job.
The fly Paratheresia claripalpis, somewhat larger
than the house fly, more hairy and carrying its wings
at a wider angle, deposits its larvae on or near the
borer, and the larvae eat themselves into it, saving
its vital organs for the last. Finally they get seriously
to work and the borer dies, after which the larvae
pass into the pupal stage, appearing as brown cocoons
three-eighths of an inch long.

Assembled in Vacuum Cleaner

Paratheresia claripalpis, once it has emerged from
its pupa in the insectaries in New Orleans, leads a
complicated life. It is placed in an emergence box
where it is kept close, lest secondary parasites which
have attacked its pupa escape to attack it further in
the fields, and when ready for release, is collected
in the celluloid nozzle of a Hoover vacuum duster.
The nozzle is then inserted into a release cage, and
the thousands of flies collected go their ways. The
cage is then taken to the field of action, opened and
emptied.

This work of introducing parasites is not new. The
Japanese beetle, the European corn borer, and the
gypsy and brown-tail moths have all been attacked
by introduced parasites, but of these Ipobracon rimac
alone flies 4000 odd miles from base to battle front
in planes which serve two continents.

A Cane Yardstick

Considerable discussion has occurred lately in Louisiana concerning the proper method to determine
the comparative merit of different varieties of cane
and the practice of using tonnage of sugar per acre
as the basic factor in such determinations has met
with more or less criticism, inasmuch as this method
does not necessarily indicate the most desirable cane
from a purely dollars and cents standpoint. A committee of the American Sugar Cane League composed
of Mr. David W. Pipes, Jr., Mr. Percy A. Lemann
and Mr. A. W. Wallace was appointed to investigate
this matter and under date of June 22nd they made
a preliminary report, in the preparation of which
they were assisted by Mr. W. S. Daubert, superintendent of the Cinclare factory in West Baton Rouge
Parish. This report handles the subject from an agricultural point of view only, and is to be followed
later by one which will carry the idea on through the
manufacturing aspect of the case.

Messrs. Pipes, Lemann and Wallace say in their
report:

"As suggested by you, we have drawn up a method
for the purpose of valuating canes from a standpoint
of return in dollars and cents to the agricultural
division.

Due to the purchase of cane on a sucrose basis,
the manufacturing end of the industry has a definite
spread between the cost of the raw material—cane—
and the finished products. This spread is calculated
that all qualities of cane will yield a definite amount
of return over and above the cost of cane. For this
reason the valuating of the cane as set forth below
is from an agricultural point of view only and is an
attempt to rate the different varieties not only from
a tonnage basis but from a point of relative net returns after harvesting.

In making any comparison it is necessary to set up
some basis to which everything may be compared.
In all cane contracts a definite base has been set up
and a standard price paid for cane of a definite sucrose content. This base in practically all instances
is a cane the normal juice from which has a sucrose
content of 11 to 12 per cent. Cane with a normal
juice of this quality commands the standard base
price per cent, and variations from this quality of
juice are paid in accordance with a definite scale up
and down from the base.

Having such a standard now definitely established
and thoroughly understood by all sellers of cane, it
seems logical that canes of various qualities can be
referred to this base in order to properly evaluate
them.

In estimating the ratio of any quality cane to this
base, the net return to the field is the factor that is
considered. Appended to this report is a chart, de-
noted as Chart No. 1, giving the gross values per

ton of cane with sugar at 3.50 cents per pound and using the standard scale of payment:

14% — $1.20 per cent	10% — $0.90 per cent
13% — 1.10 " "	9% — 0.70 " "
11-12% — 1.00 " "	8% — 0.40 " "

These gross returns show the actual value of the cane as delivered to the cars. From an agricultural point of view the value of the cane as delivered must be decreased by the cost of harvesting to give the actual net return or the value of the cane per ton as standing in the field ready for cutting. A cost of $1.00 is estimated for cutting and hauling and the lower curve on the Chart No. 1 gives the actual net value of one ton of standing cane to the agricultural department.

As may be seen, the net return for standard cane is between 11 and 12 per cent sucrose. This is assumed as the basis on which the other qualities are based.

By dividing the net return of one ton of standard cane by the net return of one ton of cane of any different quality gives the number of tons of cane which will give an equivalent net return as one ton of standard cane. The reciprocals of these numbers expressed as decimals give a quality factor to reduce all grades of cane to a standard quality.

On Chart No. 2 are plotted the equivalent tons of cane to equal the net return of one ton standard cane as well as the quality factor at the various per cent sucrose. With sugar at 3.50 cents and $1.00 per cent as a base, the calculated points on the two charts are:

	Gross Return	Net Return	Tons Equiv. to 1 ton Std.	Quality Factor
8.00	1.40	.40	6.25	.16
9.00	2.45	1.45	1.72	.58
10.00	3.15	2.15	1.16	.86
11.00	3.50	2.50	1.00	1.00
12.00	3.50	2.50	1.00	1.00
13.00	3.85	2.85	.88	1.14
14.00	4.20	3.20	.78	1.28

In order to compare different varieties of cane whose tonnage per acre and sucrose per cent normal juice is known, it is only necessary to multiply the tons per acre by the quality factor corresponding to the analysis to reduce the cane to tons of standard cane per acre.

In this way all types and qualities of cane can be referred to a basis of economic return, instead of being referred to a fictitious pounds of sugar per acre. Assuming as an example that a cane yielding 35 tons per acre having a sucrose content of 9.50 and a purity of 72.0 is to be compared to a cane yielding 22 tons per acre having a sucrose of 13 per cent and a purity of 79. In actual practice in the average Louisiana sugar house the expected yield per ton would be 119.07 pounds in the first case and 172.46 pounds in the second case.

Sugar per acre would be

$$35 \times 119.07 = 4167.45 \text{ for the first; and}$$
$$22 \times 172.46 = 3794.12 \text{ for the second and showing}$$

a decided advantage for the low sucrose, high tonnage cane.

From Chart No. 2 the quality factor for 9.5 per cent cane is .72 and for the 13.00 per cent cane is 1.14, then—

$35 \times .72 = 25.2$ tons standard cane
$22 \times 1.14 = 25.08$ tons standard cane

Difference
           .14 ton

which at a net return of $2.50 per ton of standard cane shows only an advantage of 35 cents per acre in favor of the 13 tons more per acre than the low yielding, high sucrose cane."

We are not able to reproduce the charts referred to in the Report. The tenor of it can be readily understood, however, without them.

Louisiana's Coming Sugar Crop

(By Dr. Arthur H. Rosenfeld).

On account of the record-breaking late spring and unusually dry June in general—up to the rain on the morning of June 13th, the precipitation had been the lowest of any June since the United States Bureau records were established here—and the consequent backwardness of our cane crop, the writer has received numerous rather nervous requests for an estimate of acreage and probable production for Louisiana this year. While it is yet extremely early to attempt to estimate probable production, with our normally best growing months ahead of us, I am glad at this time to give my idea of the approximate acreage planted in P.O.J. cane this fall and a long range estimate of the probable sugar to be produced therefrom, although these figures are very largely hypothetical and it will be sometime yet before we can have definite calculations of the sugar to be produced this winter.

Judging from observations I have made in going around over the sugar belt, I should say that there has been about 8 per cent less acreage laid down to plant cane this past fall and spring than in the previous year, but the large amount of second stubble carried over ought to bring our total acreage to about 178,000, or a couple of thousand acres more than last year. Based on results of the past year, this ought to give us at least 2,800,000 tons of cane for milling next crop, and, on a most conservative basis of recovery, around 185,000 tons of sugar, both of which are well above Louisiana's ten-year averages and which indicate that the industry will be back on its feet as soon as prices normalize. Most of the skeptics have been convinced by the good results given by the new canes in the past climatically bad crop year. If prices improve now, the outlook is indeed very bright for the Louisiana sugar industry—firmer I think than at any time in the past hundred years, inasmuch as we now have canes which we are sure will produce crops; poorer ones under more unfavorable conditions and better ones naturally, under good conditions, but at any rate without much likelihood of any more such crop failures as we have experienced in past years. The existing mills will this year have no difficulty in taking care of the crop in prospect, but when sugar prices get back to anything like normal, our industry will expand very considerably.

Mixed Feed

During the hearings before the Committee on Ways and Means of the United States House of Representatives held in the winter of 1929, the President of one of the large mixed feed mills in St. Louis, Mo., gave some interesting testimony concerning the price and composition of so-called "mixed feeds" for live stock in which blackstrap molasses is an ingredient. According to this witness, who ought to know, this industry produces over ten million tons of mixed feed annually, worth, or perhaps we should say sold for, some $400,000,000, which is an average of $40 a ton. Of the total of 10,000,000 tons of mixed feed manufactured annually about 6,000,000 contain, said the witness, blackstrap molasses as the essential ingredient, the amount ranging from 20 to 50 per cent of the total according to the purpose for which the feed is to be used. The witness objected to an increase of 2 cents a gallon in the duty on blackstrap molasses because, on a ton of his feed selling for $40 the increased duty would make him pay $1.71 more for the blackstrap he put in it.

We believe these mixed feeds are now selling for $30 to $35 per ton and blackstrap, which was 10½ cents a gallon when this testimony was given, is now selling for approximately one-third of this price, so the expense of the blackstrap ingredient is negligible. To what extent such mixed feeds are being bought by the Louisiana sugar producers we do not know, but for years the amount bought was considerable and the sugar district has been overrun with mixed feed salesmen who seem to be doing a good business. With corn purchasable at 70 to 75 cents a bushel and the molasses right here on our plantations a ton of mixed feed composed wholly of corn and molasses can apparently be made at home for less than the price of a ton of mixed feed made somewhere else and the maker knows what is in it. Only an inexpensive mill and mixing device is needed for the mechanical part of the work. We may be able to live at home with profit so far as mixed feed is concerned. The mixed feed manufacturers, to our discomfiture, fought us rather bitterly in the matter of an increased duty on blackstrap, which would have helped our industry and not hurt theirs. We can perhaps get along without them and save money in doing it.

Some Comments from Washington

(By C. J. Bourg)

There is something of historical significance in the signatures to the application which has been filed with the United States Tariff Commission, asking for an investigation of the tariff differential between the duty on raw and refined sugar. All branches of the sugar industry in the United States have joined in this petition. The signers represent all of the sugar refining industry, more than 99 per cent of the beet sugar production and almost as large a percentage of the cane sugar production of continental United States.

We know of no other occasion where there has been such unanimity of purpose and action in the domestic sugar industry and the significance should lie in the realization and acceptance that in most matters which concern both our government and our industry, there is greater general benefit to be attained by collaboration than by suspicious aloofness or working at cross-purposes.

The basic rate of 2 cents on raw sugar from Cuba is not sought to be changed by the application and will not be involved in the investigation, if one is ordered by the Commission. The application merely asks that the producers of white sugars in the United States be afforded some protection against foreign imports. Under the Tariff Act of 1930 the duty on Cuban sugar is 1.37 at 75 degrees polariscopic test, and with an increment per degree of .03 cent, it becomes 2 cents at 96 degrees and 2.12 cents at 100 degrees. It is accepted that 107 pounds of raw sugar is required to produce 100 pounds of refined sugar. The duty on 107 pounds of raw sugar is $2.14. The duty on 100 pounds of refined sugar is $2.12. Hence our own laws in effect actually grant a tariff preferential to the Cuban refined sugar exporter of 2 cents per hundred pounds in addition to the 20 per cent granted on all Cuban exports entering the United States.

Now, under the Tariff Act of 1922 the United States refiner had protection which amounted to 2.47 cents per hundred pounds, yet we quote the figures of the Department of Commerce that in 1925 the imports of refined sugar from Cuba were 2,647,149 pounds, and in 1929 they had mounted to 511,931,377 pounds.

Impressive as these increases may be, the aim of the application is not so much to keep the imports out, but to remove the incentive for Cuba sending all of her sugar into the United States in the refined instead of the raw state. This is an excellent example of the true worth of the protective tariff policy, as it safeguards domestic industry with its thousands of employees in every important port of the land without directly or necessarily increasing price. That the Cubans are not unmindful of the possibilities of the situation, let us read from the Havana paper, El Commercial, issue of April 20, 1929, the following:

"If the Cuban producer could obtain an absolute and irrevocable guarantee that at no time would the duties on sugar refined in Cuba, be raised within the next ten years, there would not be left standing a single cane sugar refinery on the Atlantic Coast or on the Gulf of Mexico.

"Only the fear of an increase in duty hinders the Cuban planters from investing their money in adapting their centrals to refining and this affords one proof more that the interests of the refiner and producer are in direct conflict."

The July issue of the Review of Reviews publishes an interview with Mr. Thomas L. Chadbourne, which gives with such clarity the reasons for, the workings

of and expectations from the Chadbourne Plan, that we consider several excerpts worthy of reproduction in these columns.

He begins by stating that while "the results of our agreements thus far are largely negative" * * * "in the last few days there has been a disposition on the part of the brokers to believe that perhaps the plan will work after all."

Mr. Chadbourne then makes the all important statement: "I am firmly convinced that before the end of this year the price of sugar will have risen to two cents."

The article discusses overproduction, blaming the World War for the increased production in Cuba and Java.

It has been written often that the Chadbourne Plan does not provide a restriction in production, but it is interesting to read that at the first meeting between Mr. Chadbourne and the Java sugar producers, when asked to explain his plan, he is quoted, "Gentlemen, the plan can be put into two sentences. It is this: Java produced last year 3,017,000 tons of sugar; this year she must produce only 2,500,000 tons. Cuba produced last year 4,670,000 tons of sugar; this year she must produce only 3,122,000 tons."

The interview states: "Though the Chadbourne plan entails complicated agreements between groups of producers, legislation by interested governments, tariffs, and a vast array of technical and statistical matters, it rests on two principles. They have been lucidly and simply stated, on behalf of Mr. Chadbourne, by Ivy Lee:

" '1. Each exporting country shall segregate its entire unsold surplus stocks of sugar and finance that surplus for five years, with the understanding that at least one-fifth of the segregated amounts shall be sold each year. The period of five years is selected because the industry has been sick for that long a period, and because it is felt that at least that much time must be allowed for the thorough convalescence of the world situation.

" '2. Reduce production and export the next five years by the extent to which there has been overproduction this year, it being understood' that one-fifth the segregated carry-overs shall be regarded as new production for each of the next five years until the stocks carried over are exhausted.'

"This means that the entire unconsumed surplus is considered as part of the production of the next five years. Actual production is automatically limited each year to home consumption and the export quota, allowing for liquidation of one-fifth the segregated sugar. Here are the figures:

	Segregated Surplus (tons)	Last Uncontrolled Crop (tons)	Average Chadbourne Plan Crop*	%Crop Reduction
Cuba	1,300,000	4,670,000	3,420,000	27
Java	850,000	3,027,000	2,750,000	9
Germany	243,000	2,500,000	1,881,000	25
Czecho	95,000	1,175,000	889,000	24
Poland	75,000	770,000	657,000	15
Hungary	20,000	225,000	181,000	20
Belgium	31,000	275,000	241,000	12
	2,614,000	12,642,000	10,019,000	20

"*Home consumption plus average export quota, less annual proportion of segregated surplus."

Mr. Chadbourne recognizes and admits the true situation: "Cuba restricts her production more than the others because, in the words of Mr. Chadbourne (who is himself heavily interested in Cuban sugar), 'she was the worst offender'."

When confronted with the opinion of critics that his plan will meet the same fate as experiments in the control of rubber and coffee, Mr. Chadbourne answers:

"The differences between the plan for sugar stabilization and the previous ones are two. These are the related factors of government control of exports and the automatic restriction of production.

"We are concerned only with export, since that is the upsetting factor in world sugar prices. It is true that the plan includes countries accounting for only 45 per cent of the world's sugar production, but it comprises those accounting for 80 per cent of the export. The plan is to have the governments of these exporting nations regulate, through legislation providing export licenses, the amounts of sugar shipped abroad, in accordance with the figures we have determined.

"So far as new production is concerned, individual growers are assigned their share of the new growth provided in the plan. The shares are determined on the basis of their production during the two previous years. And here is what is new, the teeth in this plan which comparatively few persons seem as yet to appreciate: the grower has no incentive, as he has had under all previous commodity-stabilization plans, to produce more than his share. If he does, he himself has to finance it. He cannot export it, because the government will not let him. There is nothing he can do with his excess sugar but stand the loss its production entails under the plan."

Mr. Chadbourne sums up the problem, in the opinion of his interviewer, in the words which he used to the Germans who were the last to be convinced regarding the Chadbourne Plan.

"There is today an unmarketable surplus of sugar in the world which has caused disaster to the world sugar market. It is this condition which we are attempting to remedy. If there existed a situation where there was an actual market for all the sugar produced, we would have little difficulty in arranging the respective proportions of the exporting countries so as to provide for their full share of production, but the difficulty is that there is no market for a substantial portion of the sugar which is now pouring upon the world."

So far, so good! But now that Mr. Chadbourne has become an international figure, and we have every reason to be pleased with what he has accomplished internationally, he gets invitations to make speeches and his remarks have made "copy." An Arthur Brisbane, or surely a Will Rogers, might columnize "Stick to your knitting, Tom!" Mr. Chadbourne went far afield in his discussion of the sugar tariff as it affects Cuba and was not too careful in the facts and figures which he used, if he is quoted correctly in every important newspaper in the East. He did not get away with his statement that the sugar tariff is the cause of the economic distress in Cuba. The New York Journal of Commerce lost no time in reminding him editorially, "Mr. Chadbourne's own insistence upon the need for world-wide restriction of sugar exports indicates his personal belief that the cause of Cuba's difficulties and the source of the economic distress of sugar producers in all parts of the world lie in the excessive increases in productive

output that have outstripped demand. Reduction or elimination of tariffs on Cuban sugar would allow for greater sales perhaps at the expense of present tax free imports, but so long as total world supplies of raw sugar are excessive in relation to consumptive demand there is little reason to believe that the benefits of tariff remission could be retained by sellers of raw sugar. The more likely result would be that buyers and refiners in the United States would gain by insisting upon paying less for duty free imports from Cuba."

The International Society of Sugar Cane Technologists

Dr. F. W. Zerban, general chairman of the International Society of Sugar Cane Technologists, 80 South Street, New York City, has issued the following notice to the members of the society:

"The Fourth Conference of this Society will be held at San Juan, Puerto Rico, in March, 1932. The meeting itself will last about one week, and will be followed by another week of excursions to plantations and other points of interest.

"The Third Congress, held in Soerabaja, Java, was attended by delegates from fourteen different countries, and it is expected that the next one will be even more truly international in scope. Official invitations will be sent out during the summer.

"There will be one or two meetings at which problems of general interest will be taken up, and then the Congress will divide into several sections, each one under a separate chairman, to discuss the various special branches of sugar technology, such as,

"Protective Sugar Cane Quarantine, Insect Pests of Sugar Cane, Diseases of Sugar Cane, Varieties, including Propagation and Selection, Cultivation and Field Operations, Description and Identification of the Original Cane Varieties, Soils, Irrigation and Drainage, Technique of Field Experiments, Factory Operation and Chemical Control, Uniformity in Reporting Factory Data, Forestry.

"The technical committees having charge of these various subjects are to present at the meeting reports on progress made in their particular fields since the last Congress. These reports will be supplemented by brief individual papers relevant to the topics under discussion.

"In order to make proper arrangements for the Congress, we should like to know whether you expect to attend. If you are planning to do so, please notify at your earliest convenience the Local Secretary, Mr. Manuel A. del Valle, Central Constancia, Toa Baja, Puerto Rico.

"If you wish to present a paper, please state the *title* of it in your letter to Mr. del Valle, and add a brief *summary* of it.

"*Manuscript copy* of all papers should later be sent to Mr. del Valle so that it will reach him by October 1st, 1931, or as soon as possible thereafter. This will enable him to have reprints prepared for distribution before or at the opening of the Congress, and will facilitate discussion.

"Detailed information about ship and airplane connections to and from Puerto Rico, local accommodations during the Congress, and similar matters will be sent to all who notify Mr. del Valle of their intention to attend the Congress."

Circulation of this Issue 1750 Copies

THE State University,
Baton Rouge, La.

SUGAR BULLETIN

Entered as second-class matter April 13, 1925, at the postoffice at
New Orleans, La., under Act of March 6, 1879.

We stand for the encouragement of Home Industries as against Foreign competition.

| Vol. 9 | NEW ORLEANS, LA., AUGUST 1, 1931 | No. 21 |

The Use of Motor Trucks in Hauling Cane

By G. H. Reuss, Assistant Economist, Department Farm Economics, Louisiana State University.

As the 1931 harvest season approaches, planters are again confronted with the problem of determining the cheapest methods of hauling their cane. In addition to a low cost method each planter desires a system which will work satisfactorily in favorable and unfavorable weather, for straight and for crooked cane, and one flexible enough that it will operate smoothly through any unforeseen adverse conditions which may arise.

The use of motor trucks in the hauling of cane increased rapidly during the last two harvest seasons, and will, no doubt, be more common than ever before during the 1931 season. Planters who hauled cane by truck in 1930 experimented in size of truck, type of body, type of road, and length of haul in an effort to determine what conditions were necessary to cheap and rapid truck hauling. A representative of the Department of Farm Economics of Louisiana State Agricultural Experiment Station visited a number of these planters to observe the trucking operations and to determine something of the costs incurred on these plantations. A brief resume of the 1930 practices and results will serve as a summary of the progress made to date in adopting the motor truck to cane harvest conditions.

There are definite limits to the type of hauling which trucks can do satisfactorily. As a general rule motor trucks cannot be relied upon to haul over dirt roads. Exceptions to this occur in good weather and on well kept plantation roads, but since this favorable condition may exist throughout only a small part of the harvest season, it is thought unwise to rely on trucks as a means of moving any appreciable part of the crop over dirt roads.

Most plantation managers have deemed it wise to improve short sections of road where necessary in order to facilitate the use of trucks. This is true of the entrance from the highway to the mill derrick and of the approaches to field hoists which are situated near the highway. The construction of a road to extend from the highway through the plantation so as to serve a number of loading points is thought by some managers to be feasible for plantations which are located some distance from the mill and which now ship all their cane by rail. Up to date, however, no extensive graveling of plantation roads has been undertaken as a means of furthering truck use.

On surfaced roads, there are two hauls which are adapted to truck use. The first is the two to five mile or long cart haul and the second the short rail haul varying in length from two to twelve or fifteen miles. Since the truck can replace mules only on that portion of the haul which is on surfaced roads, truck use necessitates an additional handling of the cane in transferring it from the wagon to the truck. The truck does not require this additional handling in its substitution for the railway haul.

In many sections, particularly along the Teche, few plantations own the trucks which they use, but trucks are hired on a per ton basis. The rate paid varies between loading points according to the distance from the mill. Small farmers, village draymen, and in some cases long distance drayage services are hired to haul the cane. In addition to the operation of a fleet of trucks, many of the small farmers operated a hoist on their farm.

The railway's rate for hauling cane at all distances at which the motor truck may be a competitor is 60 cents per ton. If the cane being shipped is produced on plantation owned property, a loading station is maintained and operated by the plantation organization. The cost of operation of such a loading station ranges from 7 to 15 cents per ton. If, however, the cane is being purchased and shipped to the mill, it is commonly the practice for the mill to set up the hoisting equipment and to hire it run by a local man on a tonnage basis. In areas where the

THE
SUGAR
BULLETIN

407 Carondelet St., New Orleans

Issued on the 1st and 15th of each month. Official Organ of the American
Sugar Cane League of the U. S. A., in which are consolidated
The Louisiana Sugar Planters' Assn.
The American Cane Growers' Assn.
The Producers & Mfgrs. Protective Assn.
Subscription Price, 50 Cents Per Year.

Reginald Dykers, General Manager & Editor of the Bulletin
301 Nola Bldg., New Orleans
Frank L. Barker, Secretary and Treasurer
Lockport, La.
C. J. Bourg, Manager Washington Office
810 Union Trust Building

CHAIRMEN OF COMMITTEES:
C. D. Kemper, Franklin, La.
President of the League and Ex-Officio Chairman of Executive Committee
Percy A. Lemann, Donaldsonville, La.
Chairman Agricultural Committee
David W. Pipes, Jr., Houma, La.
Chairman Industrial Committee
Frank L. Barker, Lockport, La.
Chairman Finance Committee.
Edward J. Gay, Plaquemine, La.
Chairman Tariff Committee
H. Langdon Laws, Cinclare, La.
Chairman Legislative Committee
J. C. LeBourgeois, New Orleans, La.
Chairman Freight Rate Committee
R. H. Chadwick, Bayou Goula, La.
Chairman Membership Committee
A. H. Rosenfeld, New Orleans, La.
Chairman Publicity Committee

Members of the League desiring action on, or information on, any subject are invited to communicate with
the League or with the Chairman of the Committee
to which it seems to appertain.

supply of cane is large and where there is little
competition between mills for the cane, the hoistman
has little difficulty in getting a sufficient supply of
cane to keep his hoist busy and in furnishing a good

supply to the mill. In such cases the rate paid for
the operation of the hoist is as low as 15 cents per
ton. However, if competition is strong, the mill may
pay as high as 35 cents a ton to the hoist operator,
who in order to load a large supply of cane must
solicit the farmers of the area to get it and must give
a part of his fee as a bonus for the delivery of cane
to his derrick.

In order to successfully compete with the railways
for the hauling of owned cane, truck rates must be
under 60 cents per ton. Two sources of saving may
be opened in hauling purchased cane by truck; first,
a truck rate of less than 60 cents per ton and, second, a decrease in fee paid hoist operators due to
the fact that the operators of the trucks will in many
instances solicit the cane and in some cases pay a
small bonus to the producers in order to get the business for their trucks.

In Table I at the bottom of this page are shown
some of the custom rates paid in 1930, together with
the length of haul, type of road, loading charges
and cost of competing methods of hauling.

On these plantations the saving from the use of
custom trucks varied from 0 to 30 cents per ton.
The length of haul for cases in which trucks had sup-
planted the railway ranged from 3½ to 12 miles.
Since truck hauling rates vary with the distance, but
rail rates do not (up to 25 miles) the greatest economies are obtained from the shorter hauls. In 1930
truck rates were such that 12 to 15 miles was the
longest distance at which trucks could compete with
the railway. This maximum length of haul will vary
inversely with the general custom rate of hauling.
A further advantage of truck use results from the
shorter period of time which elapses between the cutting of the cane and its arrival at the mill.

Trucks were used to replace mules on hauls of 1
to 4 miles. The cost of transferring the cane from
wagon to truck was estimated by the plantation managers to be approximately 15 cents per ton. Although there was not sufficient cost information
available on these plantations to determine the outlays which would have been necessary to do this road
hauling by mules, each plantation manager believed

Plantation	Custom Rate per Ton	Road	Miles	Av. Size** of Load, Tons	Hoist Operation	Hoist Rate	Competing Method	Hoist Rate Under Former Hauling System	Tons Hauled by 1 Truck per Day, Av.
A	.50	Gravel	6.0	5–7	Custom	15c	Rail 60c	.35	60
	.60	Gravel	8.0	5–7	Custom	15c	Rail 60c	.35	60
B	.50	Gravel	4.0	4–5	Custom	25c	Rail 60c	.25	?
C	.50	Paved	7.0	5–6	Owned	07c	Rail 60c	.07	45
D	.30	Paved	2.0	3–5	Owned	15c	Cart	0	50
E	.40	Gravel	4.0	5–7	Owned	15c	Cart	0	70
	.30	Gravel	2.9	5–7	Owned	15c	Cart	0	90
	.25	Gravel	2.5	5–7	Owned	15c	Cart	0	90
F	.40	Gravel	4.5	4½–5	Owned	06c	Rail 60c	.06	60
G	.30–*	Gravel	7.6	4	Owned	?	Rail 60c	?	40
H	.60	Gravel	12.0	-----	Custom	35c	Rail 60c	.35	?
	.60	Gravel	4.0	-----	Custom	35c	Rail 60c	.35	?
I	.35	Gravel	3.5		Owned	?	Rail 60c	?	?
J	.35	Gravel	4.0	5	Custom	18c***	Rail 60c	.18***	45
K	.325	Gravel	1.0	4	Owned	15c	Cart	0	?
	.40	Gravel	3.5	4	Owned	15c	Cart	0	?
	.40	Gravel	4.0	4	Owned	15c	Rail 60c	.15	?
	.50	Gravel	7.0	4	Custom	20c	Rail 60c	.20	?
L	.40	Gravel	3 to 5.5	6	Owned	15c	Plantation Railway	.15	60

*Trucks hired at $10 per day, operating time, plus $2.25 for drivers, plus gasoline and oil.
**Variations in size of load are due to the relative straightness of the cane.
***Includes weighing.

that truck use resulted in a considerable saving. In addition to any cash saving which may have been made, the release of a large number of mules from road work made them available for bringing the cane out of the field and increased the tonnage which it was possible to handle each day. This is particularly significant since the amount of mule power available is the limiting factor in determining the rate of harvesting on practically all plantations.

A few plantations operated their own trucks during the 1930 season. A statement of the expenditures incurred in truck operation on two such plantations is presented in Table II.

TABLE II. COST OF HAULING CANE BY OWNED TRUCKS ON TWO PLANTATIONS, 1930

Plantation	A		B	
Expenses	Per Day Dollars	Per Ton Cents	Per Day Dollars	Per Ton Cents
Gasoline and Oil	$3.08	5.7	$1.54	3.7
Repairs and Tires	2.00	3.7	.94	2.2
Driver's Wage	2.37	4.4	2.00	4.8
Total Cash Expense	7.45	13.8	4.48	10.7
Depreciation	3.33	6.2	3.00	7.1
Interest	.73	1.3	.60	1.4
Total Overhead Exp.	4.06	7.5	3.60	8.5
Total Expense	$11.51	21.3	$8.08	19.2
New Cost of Truck with Trailer and Body			$1,100	$1,200
Size of Load:				
Bundles			3	2
Tons			4.9	4.0
Length of Haul, One Way			7.3 Mi.	4.5 Mi.
Average Trips per Day			11—	11+
Average Tons per Day			54	42

Only major cost items are included. Detailed costs were not available on these plantations.

A majority of these trucks were purchased in 1930. Consequently repairs, expenditures for tires, and gasoline and oil outlays were somewhat lower than is to be expected, as an average of the entire useful life of the truck. Table II presents the major cost items, but does not includes charges for chore labor or for minor repairs done by plantation employees other than the driver. These figures, however, do indicate that a considerable margin exists between the actual cost of truck operation and custom rates charged in the area. Planters owning a small number of trucks find use for them in the general plantation work throughout the year. Should the number of owned trucks be markedly increased, however, all overhead charges will necessarily be borne by the cane harvest.

A variety of questions of a technical nature have risen concerning the use of trucks in the hauling of cane. The development of a truck which will work satisfactorily on dirt roads or in the field has been attempted, but as yet has not reached a practical

degree of perfection. The problems which most commonly arise concern the size of the truck and the capacity and design of the body. Most of the trucks used are rated at 1½ tons. The length of the cane bundle is such that it cannot be loaded cross ways of the body and yet remain within the legal width for vehicles on public highways. A large part of the weight carried high in the load introduces the risk of turning the truck over due to a shifting of the load or to a slanting road. Finally a poorly dimensioned body may allow the bundles to wedge so tightly that they are broken or that the truck body is lifted from the chassis in unloading. These difficulties have been overcome to a large extent by the use of a body long enough to hold two bundles of cane and so narrow as to prevent a bundle, laid on top of these, from shifting to one side. The chains on the upper bundles are loosened to permit it to spread evenly over the top of the load.

It is desirable to haul as large a load as possible at each trip. Since 1½ ton trucks are usually limited to three bundles of cane per load, (several trucks observed carrying only two, but a few hauled four) the desired increase in tonnage is usually achieved through a heavier loading of the wagons in the field. Rather wide differences in size of load occur due to variations in the straightness of the canes. These cannot be eliminated but the average load on most plantations may be increased by the use of lighter wagons, the improvement of plantation roads, decreased length of wagon haul, etc. Truck hauling facilitates many of these changes which tend to the heavier loading of wagons and this in turn increases the efficiency of the truck.

The use of trucks larger than those of the 1½ ton rating is not common. A few dray services haul cane in trucks which have a capacity of 8 to 10 tons per load. To date, no trucks of this size have been purchased by plantations for the hauling of cane.

Summary

For planters who are not using trucks at the present time, the adoption of this method offers a possibility of considerable saving on hauls of from two to twelve miles in length of surfaced roads. The saving is marked as compared with existing rail rates and it is generally accepted among plantation owners and managers that long cart hauls are more expensive than truck hauls for corresponding distances plus the cost of transferring from wagon to truck. The surfacing of the approaches to loading and unloading points to facilitate the use of the motor truck has proven economical. There is the possibility of achieving economies by surfacing plantation roads to loading derricks situated some distance from an improved highway. The time required to move cane from the field to the mill by truck is comparatively

short. Consequently the deterioration which takes place in transit is less than by rail hauling methods.

Due to the large proportion of new trucks in use in 1930 a definite comparison cannot be made between the relative economy of hiring custom trucking and of owning and operating a plantation fleet of trucks. The available information, however, seems to indicate that custom rates are comparatively high. These will tend to adjust themselves somewhat as the number of both custom and owned trucks increases.

Truck users are now primarily concerned with the adoption of the truck to cane harvest conditions so as to make possible the hauling of larger loads over all types of roads, with a minimum of delay and expense from the turning over of trucks, breakage, wedging of bundles, and shifting of the load. Of these factors the size of load and the adoption to road conditions are the most significant.

HARRY AUSTIN

By C. J. Bourg

The death of Harry A. Austin on July 17th was a serious loss to the sugar industry of the United States. Mr. Austin had been connected with the U. S. Beet Sugar Association since 1911 and had been its Secretary-Treasurer since 1921. Although a comparatively young man, being 56 years of age, he had been ill for some time and failed to recover from a recent operation.

Mr. Austin's work brought him in intimate contact with the officials and policies of the American Sugar Cane League. He was ever a very courteous and cooperative type and was personally held in high regard by men in all branches of the industry. He possessed a disposition of the finest quality, impressing everyone with his excellent character and consideration.

Mr. Austin enjoyed an unusual spread of experience in national affairs. A native of Washington, he lived for a time in Nebraska but returned to the Nation's Capital as secretary to Senator Willia Allen of Nebraska. He maintained his contacts wit the affairs of the middle west as Washington cor respondent for the Omaha World Herald. He late became a civilian employee at the Army War Colleg as secretary to General Tasker Bliss, with whom h traveled extensively, spending more than a year i Cuba on a military mission. In later years his con tacts in Nebraska and Cuba proved very valuabl to give him a better understanding of his work i the sugar industry.

Mr. Austin's permanent contributions to the suga industry are his work as statistician and editor c *Concerning Sugar*, the world's best known encyclc pedia of sugar, and as author of the History an Development of the Beet Sugar Industry. But h wrote many articles dealing with sugar and other na tional problems for trade journals and importan magazines.

The sugar industry has known him best in hi work with the United States Congress. He was rec ognized as a most reliable source of information an his testimony before the Committees of Congress ha belped immeasurably to secure favorable legislation for the domestic sugar industry.

He has gone to join those other beloved dead who contributed so largely towards the advancement of the interests of sugar cane and beet growers, Truman Palmer, John Rogers, Bob Broussard, and Whit Martin, and we give expression to our gratefulness for their beneficent contributions. We recognize his work and appreciate his accomplishments, yet for ourselves we shall remember Harry Austin best because above all things he was a gentleman, always considerate of the feelings of everyone.

Contact Committee

Minutes of Meeting of American Sugar Cane League Contact Committee with Louisiana Experiment Station Workers, Baton Rouge, La., July 10, 1931.

The meeting was called to order by Mr. A. W. Wallace, Chairman. There were present of the Contact Committee: Messrs. A. W. Wallace, Elliot Jones, Percy Lemann; of the Station Staff: Messrs. C. T. Dowell, W. G. Taggart, E. C. Simon, C. W. Edgerton, E. C. Tims, Truman Ryker, W E. Hinds, B. A. Osterberger, G. H. Reuss, Wm. Whipple, Harold T. Barr, C. B. Gouaux. Visitors: Messrs. C. D. Kemper, President, American Sugar Cane League, A. H. Rosenfeld, E. J. Badeaux, W. B. Mercier, Floyd Spencer and Guillot.

DEPARTMENT OF ENTOMOLOGY REPORT

A five-page mimeographed progress report covering the past two months' work was presented by Dr. Hinds, of which the following is a summary:

Cane Borer Seasonal History: Leaf perforation signs in cane and in early corn showed that first generation borer eggs had hatched and young larvae were developing in considerable numbers during the latter part of April and early part of May. On May 13 in some cane carried over in the laboratory at Baton Rouge we observed an infertile female in the act of oviposition. During a period of 6 hours this female deposited 160 eggs. This observation gave us considerable new information regarding oviposition and was decidedly interesting.

The development of borer stages in the fields was watched as closely as possible at Baton Rouge and at Plaquemine. The heaviest infestation this year is at Island Plantation, Plaquemine, and in one hour's examination of P.O.J. 213 stubble on May 18, 176 stalks showing lead perforations in 800 row ft., 1 batch of eggs just hatching and numerous first and second stage larvae were found. At the same time in adjoining early planted corn, a heavier and more advanced condition of infestation with larvae ranging from first to fourth stage, but mostly third stage in size was found. The first 2nd stage larvae occurred here on May 13, and the first 5th stage larvae were found in corn on June 2, showing considerable more advancement in corn than in cane.

Observations from Franklin, Centerville, Jeanerette, New Iberia, to Baton Rouge revealed that the main development of first generation adults occurred this season about June 10 to 20, and the beginning of the second generation followed immediately.

Trash Disposal Tests: These tests were started at Island Plantation, Plaquemine, last November and we planned to carry on different tests, but on account of a misunderstanding on the part of the plantation workmen it was not possible to carry out all the tests as originally planned. Seven plats of 1 acre each were involved. On plat 1, cut November 20, the trash was partially buried on November 25, while still green. On the other plats a very poor burn was given by the laborers about February 1, 1931. We applied 200 lbs. ammonium sulphate per acre to test the effect of an application of nitrogen in hastening the decomposition of partially buried trash to plat 6 on February 5 and immediately followed this with a uniform partial burial of the un-

burned trash on this plat and also that on plat 5, which had no nitrate, for comparison.

Final examinations were made May 28 to determine a comparison of the amount and condition of decomposition, and the borer population also as they occurred in the various plats. The material was raked out very thoroughly, collected, brought to the laboratory and examined. One hibernating 5th stage larva was found in the material from plat 1 on May 28, whereas 6 4th stage larvae were found on May 8. In the March examinations 1 2nd stage larva was found, and we were quite struck with the fact that a 2nd stage larva was hibernating successfully.

Trash Disposal Tests—Final Examinations, May 28, 1931
Island Plantation, Plaquemine
Material from 100 row feet for each plat

Plat No.	Treatment	No. Firm Pieces Found	Total Length Feet	Borer Stages Larvae 5th St.	Pupae	Skins
1	Trash part buried green, 11/25/30..	270	240	1	0	8
2	Poor burn, 2/1/31.	170	148	0	0	10
3	Poor burn, 2/1/31.	190	132	0	0	5
4	Poor burn, 2/1/31.	100	195	0	0	1
5	Part buried also, 2/5/31..........	170	158	0	0	0
6	200 lbs. Am. Sul. per A. part buried, 2/5/31..........	123	99	--	0	0
7	Plantation Practice part burned 2/1/31	170	237	1	1	1

The plat No. 6, treated with nitrate, shows decidedly less solid top butt material than from any other plat and no living borer stage was found in it.

We do not find it advisable to try burying trash immediately after it is cut early in the fall. The volume of undecomposed material was very great in the spring when cultivation started. Had applications of nitrate been made, the results might have been different.

Sitotroga Moth Production: It was after December 15, 1930, before we could buy our corn and start the breeding of moths. We stocked Room 1 as soon as possible with yellow corn, as previously reported, and the introduction of moth eggs followed during the next four to six weeks. This room reached its peak of production about the last of April. Daily records are kept on the number of moths collected from each room. Up to the end of June we have collected more than 500,000 moths. Practically one-half of these are females, and we have secured an average production of 35 eggs per female, or about 9,000,000 eggs from this one room as stock for Trichogramma parasitization.

The second room was stocked with corn and moth eggs in February and has added much more to our available egg material.

Trichogramma Production: Only a very small maintenance stock of wasps (which has been breeding continuously since March, 1927, when Mr. Osterberger found the first in the fields at Franklin) was carried along during the winter. The strain which we have been breeding successfully is the brown strain. In the fields this spring and in previous years we have found as natural occurrence a yellow strain. Whether these are two distinct strains or whether they are interbreeding, we do not know. It may possibly be a difference in coloration at different seasons of the year.

No heavy centers of borer infestation could be found in the immediate vicinity of Baton Rouge. The nearest fairly heavy infestation found was at Island Plantation, Plaquemine, in early planted corn and in 213 stubble cane. Field colonization of Trichogramma was started for this season on May 19 with the hope that the parasites might find sufficient eggs of the cane borer or of the corn earworm on the corn to maintain themselves and to be ready for the parasitization of second generation borer eggs as soon as they were deposited. From May 19 to July 4 we had colonized in Louisiana cane and corn fields approximately 3,000,000 Trichogrammas.

The summary of observations made in the southern cane sections June 26 and 27, where colonizations were made June 13, shows an average of 54% parasitized among 4,704 eggs collected from 12 fields. In 7 uncolonized areas only one location shows any considerable parasitism, and this was at Jeanerette which shows a parasitism of 36.8%. This field of uncolonized corn is located near and between two large colonized areas and may have received some Trichogramma therefrom. The average parasitism in 7 uncolonized areas was 25% among 1401 eggs.

A comparison of the percentage of eggs parasitized as shown in colonized and uncolonized areas indicates that the destruction of borer eggs has been more than doubled within two weeks by the Trichogramma colonization.

The first natural field occurrence of Trichogramma this season was found at Baton Rouge in cabbage looper eggs on May 29. These wasps were of the "yellow" strain, while our bred material is "brown." At Midway Plantation on Bayou Sale on June 13, we found quite a

percentage of Heliothis eggs on tomato and parasitized naturally by the "yellow" strain.

Trichogramma Production Cooperation: At the March meeting of the Committee the matter of commercial production of Trichogramma for the supply of Louisiana cane planters, as proposed by Dr. A. W. Morrill of Los Angeles, California, was discussed and approved in general. We anticipated supplying Dr. Morrill with sufficient breeding stock of our Louisiana brown strain of Trichogramma to enable him to supply any calls that might come from our cane growers, in case they should find centers of heavy borer infestation developing during the first generation and should desire to undertake on their own account this experimental method of borer control.

It happened that Dr. Morrill encountered some unexpected difficulties in his moth production work and Trichogramma parasitization early in the season. Accordingly he inquired of us whether we could supply him with para-sitized grain moth eggs, up to the number of 500,000 Trichogramma at a price of 25c per thousand, which he would pay us for such stock. As our own borer infestation was rather light and we had the material on hand, this seemed advisable and so with the approval of the Director and the Chairman of the Contact Committee, we have prepared and shipped to Dr. Morrill a total of 625,000 Trichogramma for which he has made us a cash payment. These funds enabled us to carry some of our students for field work and thus enabled us to carry out further important field work which would rapidly facilitate our own investigations and which could not have been done otherwise.

Publications: A series of five short timely articles dealing principally with the basis for, and practice of, Trichogramma colonization for the benefit of those planters who might be interested in testing this out on their own account has been prepared and published in THE SUGAR BULLETIN.

The work on Ligyrus was practically closed about June 1 this year. The results have not been completed yet, but these will be completed and discussed at a later date.

DEPARTMENT OF PLANT PATHOLOGY REPORT

A three-page mimeographed progress report was presented by Dr. Edgerton of which the following is a summary:

Mosaic on Test Fields: During June, counts were made of mosaic on newer varieties at the different test fields. C.P. 807 showed no mosaic on any of the test fields. It appeared very suddenly in Co. 281 last year and the year before, and considerable variation in the amount of mosaic is noticeable. The high percentage of mosaic at Reserve should be noticed. P.O.J. 213 at Reserve showed up especially high last year and is showing up the same this year, as did Co. 281. Co. 290 showed more mosaic at Reserve than any place—in fact, it was practically the only place that showed an appreciable amount of the disease.

Recovery from Mosaic: It was brought out from time to time here that certain varieties infected with mosaic, when planted for several generations, would continually throw off a very high percentage of healthy stalks. Last year we not only conducted these experiments with cane from the Station here, but we brought came from the heavily infested region around Reserve and planted it at Baton Rouge. Neither Co. 281 nor P.O.J. 213 from Reserve threw off mosaic disease, while ordinarily mosaic at Baton Rouge continued as it had been doing in the past.

Growth of Roots and Shoots During Three Years: The years 1929, 1930 and 1931 were very unlike, 1929 being one of the most advanced seasons on record, while the last two years have been the reverse. Measurements have been made of roots and shoots in the early spring, during the period that the roots are growing out into the middles. In each case, the figures are based on 10 stalks. The stalk height represents the distance between the seed piece in the soil and the highest visible leaf sheath ring. The root length is the distance the roots

extend out into the middles in the upper 6 to 8 inches of soil.

In 1929 the root length was practically twice that of the stalk height. On May 14, when the stalks were 8 to 11 inches high, the roots were 17 to 19 inches in length, long enough to be injured by deep cultivation and by May 30 the roots were meeting in the middles.

In 1930 and 1931 the roots were less than twice as long as the shoots, and cane 12 to 13 inches high did not have roots long enough to be seriously injured by cultivation. In 1930, the middle of the row was not reached by any great number of roots until after June 6. In 1931, the growth was even slower than in 1930.

From the three years' results, it would seem that deep cultivation should be discontinued some time between May 14 and June 6, depending upon the advancement of the season.

Bulletin on Root Development: During the last week we have written up and handed in for publication a bulletin on root development, various phases of root correlation and growth. This covers the results of two years' work.

Dr Hinds inquired as to the method of getting the root length, and Dr. Edgerton replied that it was the longest root—not the length of the roots at all but the extension into the middles.

Director Dowell asked "how deep" does "deep cultivation" mean, and it was explained that by "deep cultivation" was meant the turn plow method.

REPORT OF TEST FIELD WORK

A five-page mimeographed progress report was presented by Mr. Gouaux of which the following is a summary:

Cane Cultivation: With the dry weather conditions that have prevailed during the months of May and June, the number of field cultivations performed for the period ending in early July averaged five, and in some instances was as high as seven and eight times.

The old system of cultivation, which involves the use of plows and heavy implements, by which the rows are ridged high and the drill closed in with too much dirt, is very much in evidence throughout the Cane Belt. However, there are some planters who are using the moderate row and shallow method of cultivation with very good results, while others have made progress in reducing the height of the rows and minimizing to some extent the cutting of cane roots.

The present season closely resembles the 1930 crop year, with a slightly more adverse late cold spring and somewhat similar drouth conditions. During the early May period the cane crop was less advanced in stands and size than in 1930. At the end of June, the crop showed considerable improvement, to such an extent that the two seasons now compare closely.

Field Extension: In cooperation with some of the County Agents of the sugarcane parishes, plantation field trips were made and advice given on cane cultivation and varieties. During the month of June an inspection trip was made with Mr. A. C. Morris, representative of N. V. Potash My., to inspect the series of twenty-one cooperative sugarcane potash tests, which are being conducted in the Cane Belt parishes. The series of ten Chilean Nitrate of Soda cane fertilizer demonstrations were also inspected.

A field trip was made with Dr. Hinds for the purpose of locating centers of cane borer infestation in the parishes of St. Mary and Iberia. Trichogramma releases were made in heavily infested corn fields in the following localities: Bayou Sale, Centerville, Franklin, Jeanerette and New Iberia.

The Station Test Fields: Since the last report given at the meeting of May 8, the six Experiment Station test fields have been visited and inspected during the intervals of May 29 to June 5, and the latter part of June and early July. On these two trips, the regular stalk counts and measurements of the varieties, as plant cane, first and second stubble, were made.

Plant Cane: The stalk counts indicate that in most cases all varieties, except C.P. 807, showed better germination and suckering in the May and June counts last year than the present season. The counts of a month later showed that the varieties were close together for the two seasons.

All the varieties at Meeker show very low counts in comparison with the other fields. This is caused by covering the drill with too much dirt early in the season and choking out or checking the development of suckers.

P.O.J. 36-M runs slightly higher in counts than P.O.J. 36; while P.O.J. 213 compares favorably with P.O.J. 36-M. However, both P.O.J. 36 and 36-M have a decidedly better germination of original mother stalks. P.O.J. 213 is such a vigorous suckering cane that even with a gappy stand it will show a higher number of shoots than varieties like P.O.J. 36 and 36-M with full stands.

Co. 290, promising new seedling, gave the highest counts at Glenwood, Meeker and Sterling; C.P. 807 was highest at Cinclare; Co. 281, highest at Youngsville and P.O.J. 234, highest at Reserve. At all test fields these four varieties gave higher counts than P.O.J. 36, P.O.J.

36-M and P.O.J. 213. Co. 281 showed the greatest number of late suckers; while P.O.J. 234, Co. 290 and C.P. 807 show a more advanced stage of suckering

The plant cane measurements indicate that the varieties were more advanced in 1930 than the present season. From height comparisons the test fields are in the following order: Cinclare, Glenwood, Sterling, Reserve, Meeker and Youngsville.

First Stubble: In the comparisons of June and July counts, the varieties show higher 34 times for 1931 and 36 times for 1930. Both P.O.J. 213 and Co. 281 show consistently lower counts this year than 1930. P.O.J. 36-M has a greater number of shoots than P.O.J. 36 and P.O.J. 213. C.P. 807 has the highest number of shoots at Cinclare, Sterling and Youngsville; while P.O.J. 234 ranks higher at Glenwood, Reserve and Meeker. At all of the test fields C.P. 807 is the tallest variety, followed by Co. 290.

In the first stubble variety height comparisons, Cinclare is the most advanced field; while Glenwood, Reserve, Meeker and Sterling are about on an equal basis, and Youngsville is smallest in size.

At all of the test fields, P.O.J. 36-M first stubble shows a greater number of shoots and suckers per acre than P.O.J. 36.

Second Stubble: In the stalk counts P.O.J. 36-M has a slight advantage over P.O.J. 36. P.O.J. 213 shows up comparatively very poor at all test fields except Meeker. Although at this place the stand is somewhat thin, and the high counts are attributable to extra heavy stooling.

P.O.J. 234 showed stand failures at Sterling and Youngsville; while it is at its best at Cinclare and Meeker.

Co. 281 shows up well at Cinclare, Meeker and Youngsville; while at Sterling the stand is comparatively poor.

C.P. 807 has its heaviest stand at Meeker, while Cinclare, Sterling and Youngsville compare closely with good stands.

The test fields rank as follows from height comparisons:

Meeker, Cinclare, Sterling and Youngsville.

DEPARTMENT OF AGRICULTURAL ECONOMICS REPORT

Mr. Reuss presented an interesting survey of 129 small farms in the Cane Belt of which the following is a summary:

The net cash income of these farms averaged $4.38 per acre, or $426.00 per farm. Only 30% made more than enough to pay depreciation, family labor and capital charges. On the average, all farms lacked $4.50 per acre of meeting these charges. Quite marked variations occurred in the earnings of individual farmers. Cotton included in the farm organization in any considerable proportion was associated with a decrease in both net cash income and labor income. Farms growing large proportions of truck made relatively large net cash returns per acre, but due to their small size and to the large amounts of family labor employed did not return a satisfactory income when considered on per farm basis. Farms having less than 30% of the crop area in cane made relatively low incomes. On the average, 50% of the crop area in cane was the optimum organization. This figure, however, varies somewhat, depending on cane yields, feed crop yields, labor expenses, etc.

Labor expense was found to be an important factor in determining income. The most significant factor affecting the income of these farms was the yield of cane. This yield was 14.68 tons per acre on the average.

DISCUSSIONS

It was felt that the low yields received on these small farms resulted from failure to adopt an improved system of fertilization, cultivation and the growing of legumes. County Agents could do much towards teaching these small farmers modern and improved practices.

It was thought that Mr. Gouaux would be able to work with these County Agents and point out the benefits to be derived from the planting of cane and the use of modern methods in working their cane. Mr. Spencer of the Extension Service stated that the extension work is to be built upon scientific information coupled with facts of successful men in the territory.

Much interest was expressed in the report given by

Mr. Reuss, and this information is being published as an Experiment Station bulletin and will be available within the next few weeks.

DEPARTMENT OF AGRICULTURAL ENGINEERING REPORT

Mr. Barr presented in an interesting way the work being carried on in cane cultivation and the use of more power and tractors. The problem is to find an economical and practical method of getting the cane out of the fields.

The new project "Draft of Cane Wagons" was discussed by Mr. Barr. The purpose of this project is to determine the influence upon the draft of a wagon as offered by:

(1) Determine supporting ability of soil in pounds per square inch under different moisture conditions and then design wheel to support the load.

(2) Rolling resistance (height of wheel, width of tire, nature of road, type of wheel).

(3) Axle friction (load of wheel, radius of wheel, radius of skein, efficiency of lubrication, materials used in skein and wheel boxing).

(4) Grade resistance.

(5) Rate of travel.

(6) Angle of hitch.

(7) Placement of load.

(8) Dynamometer test of present available wagons.

In order to render some relief for this season dynamometer test will be made on several different types of wagons during July and August. We hope to obtain a wagon with a range of wheel heights and tire widths, in which the type of bearing can also be changed. With the above equipment we will make a series of tests with different loads on muddy and firm field conditions, firm dirt, grassy and gravel headlands.

A discussion followed and it was decided to try to get commercial concerns to make loans of different types of wagons for such experimental work. Mr. Lemann stated that some concerns would not make changes in their equipment unless one paid for same.

The meeting was adjourned.

Excitement About the Philippines

The visit of Senator Harry Hawes of Missouri to the Philippine Islands this summer has developed from what was intended as an instructive vacation into an affair of primary national importance. Whether the Senator expected it or not he has been welcomed and received everywhere on the Islands as a national saviour. Impartial reports from the Philippines tell us that the parade given in his honor was the most enthusiastic national demonstration ever held. At any rate the recent reports supposed to emanate from the Philippines and published in the press of the United States, that the sentiment in favor of independence among the Filipinos was diminishing, have certainly been effectively denied. In fact, the suggestion of Governor-General Davis in his report to the Philippine legislators that they should consider economics instead of politics, has been interpreted by the native leaders to mean dollars instead of liberty.

It is somewhat significant that the same national newspapers which favor dollar diplomacy and are always clamoring for the protection of foreign or insular investments of American capitalists, are now seeking to point a finger of scorn at the farmers whose low-priced or unsold cotton seed, dairy products and beets might lead them to favor the elimination of preferred competition through the granting or independence to the Filipinos. Questioning the motives of the same members of Congress who actually provided or planned Filipino independence by legislation in 1916 will hardly impress anybody excepting those who feel that they know better than the "little brown brother" what is good for him, and whose feelings can be traced in many cases to an investment.

The proposed visit of Secretary of War Hurley, to the Philippines late this summer has been interpreted as an administration move to develop a compromise of some kind, or to get the facts upon which the justification for a veto might be built. Considering recent events, the Secretary of War is not likely to get the enthusiastic response that has been accorded his neighbor from Missouri.

Embargoes

A recent ruling of the Attorney General of the United States on the power of the President to declare an embargo against importations which depress our domestic markets, is of considerable importance to all persons engaged in the manufacture of products which feel the effect of competition with imported goods which sell below cost. The opinion was issued upon the appeal of independent oil producers, but the Attorney General carefully broadened his message to take care of all appellants who might be looking embargo-wise for help.

While the ruling offers no consoling hope for any of our great industries, it does very clearly interpret the Tariff Act of 1930 with reference to "unfair methods of competition" and "unfair acts" by importers. This opinion of the Attorney General indicates rather conclusively that the Administration does not believe that relief by embargo should be exercised for the benefit of any domestic industry, except in the specific cases of importers guilty of those practices which legally constitute unfair competition.

This will be considered as strict construction by those who are suffering, but it can be accepted not only as the official legal position of the Administration but also as a part of its foreign policy towards the establishment or maintenance of international good will.

Circulation of this Issue 1750 Copies

THE
SUGAR
BULLETIN

Entered as second-class matter April 13, 1925, at the postoffice at
New Orleans, La., under Act of March 6, 1879.

*We stand for the encouragement of Home
Industries as against foreign competition.*

Vol. 9　　　　　　NEW ORLEANS, LA., AUGUST 15, 1931　　　　　　No. 22

Sugar Cane Harvesting Methods and Cost, 1931

By G. H. Reuss, Assistant Economist, Department Farm Economics, Louisiana State University.

The cutting, loading, and hauling at harvest makes up a major item in the cost of producing cane. The various phases of these operations are inter-related in their effect on costs, on volume of cane hauled by any particular unit, and on the quality of the cane when it reaches the mill. These inter-relationships form a complicated problem, the solution of which must necessarily be made to fit local plantation conditions. A somewhat detailed study of the effects on harvest efficiency of variations in straightness of the cane, length of haul, type of equipment, road conditions, and varieties grown is planned for 1931. During 1930 a general preliminary survey of cane harvesting methods was made. In discussing the methods which were in use during 1930, examples from specific plantations are used and the comparative advantages or disadvantages which are presented are those found by plantation managers. Whenever possible the data are presented in physical as well as monetary units. This facilitates its application to the 1931 harvest season which will no doubt be marked by a lower general wage rate than that which prevailed in 1930. The conditions existing on the individual plantation must be given due weight in projecting the effect of a new system on the costs of any operation. Hauling in this discussion will be limited to the mule haul from the field to the mill or to a point at which the cane is loaded on railway cars, barges, or motor trucks.

The cutting of cane by the ton is commonly practiced in the Lower River, Lafourche, and Teche sections. The Northern River area and several local communities scattered throughout the cane growing section have maintained the labor method of cutting principally due to the reluctance of the labor to change. There has been some difficulty in getting the labor to understand the new system particularly when the cane is cut by the ton, but not hauled and weighed immediately. On the first pay day a part of the cane cut by each man has not been hauled and so the cutting charge is not paid at that time. However, this difficulty is, at its worst, short lived and the individual cutter learns to prefer the ton rate method. Almost without exception, more cane is cut per day by each man and the wage earned is increased over that of the day labor rate. A variety of methods were found in the actual use of custom or per ton system of cutting cane. A common practice is to organize the work as follows: Small crews of from two to four members each are formed. Many of the crews are composed of the members of one family. Each crew is given a number and each works in the cutting of one heaprow. The overseer places the number of the crew which cut each row at the head of that heaprow. As each load is hauled the driver carries a note of the number of the crew which cut the cane. At the scales the weight is credited to the crew and each day entries are made on the pay roll records as to the amount of cane hauled and crew which did the cutting. Daily statements of the weight hauled and wage earning on the preceding day are returned to the cutters and payments are made at weekly or bi-weekly intervals. The members of the crew share equally in the total wage of that crew.

In working under this system the loaders must keep the cane from each heaprow separated. The loading crew judges the number of loads in each row and loads so as not to have fractional loads remaining in any row. Some planters require that the personnel of the crew remain intact throughout the cutting of each heaprow. Others divide the row and give the crew a new number if a member of the crew stops work or a substitution is made. This practice adds to the amount of bookkeeping which is necessary and may result in light loads from uneven lengths of row.

A common variation of the above method is for

THE
SUGAR
BULLETIN

407 Carondelet St., New Orleans

Issued on the 1st and 15th of each month. Official Organ of the American
Sugar Cane League of the U. S. A., in which are consolidated
The Louisiana Sugar Planters' Assn.
The American Cane Growers' Assn.
The Producers & Mfgrs. Protective Assn.
Subscription Price, 50 Cents Per Year.

Reginald Dykers, General Manager & Editor of the Bulletin
301 Nola Bldg., New Orleans
Frank L. Barker, Secretary and Treasurer
Lockport, La.
C. J. Bourg, Manager Washington Office
810 Union Trust Building

CHAIRMEN OF COMMITTEES:

C. D. Kemper, Franklin, La.
President of the League and Ex-Officio Chairman of Executive Committee
Percy A. Lemann, Donaldsonville, La.
Chairman Agricultural Committee
David W. Pipes, Jr., Houma, La.
Chairman Industrial Committee
Frank L. Barker, Lockport, La.
Chairman Finance Committee.
Edward J. Gay, Plaquemine, La.
Chairman Tariff Committee
H. Langdon Laws, Cinclare, La.
Chairman Legislative Committee
J. C. LeBourgeois, New Orleans, La.
Chairman Freight Rate Committee
R. H. Chadwick, Bayou Goula, La.
Chairman Membership Committee
A. H. Rosenfeld, New Orleans, La.
Chairman Publicity Committee

Members of the League desiring action on, or information on, any subject are invited to communicate with the League or with the Chairman of the Committee to which it seems to appertain.

the overseer to estimate the yield of each cut and to set the rate of pay at so much per row or per set length of row based on the rate per ton and the estimated yield. The letting of a contract to cut certain blocks of cane is a less commonly used method. The man who takes the contract receives the full pay for the cutting. He hires cutters either by the day or by the ton. The responsibility of getting the cane cut at a set rate per day is his as is the function of supervising the cutting crew. The same rate is paid per ton regardless of the method used in the field administration of this system.

All of these custom systems have certain marked advantages over the day labor method. Almost without exception the use of a custom cutting system results in more tons cut per day by each man and so fewer cutters are required. This reduction in the number of cutters has been estimated by plantation managers to be from 20 to 40 per cent. Labor transportation and housing charges are proportionately reduced. Many women who would not ordinarily be in the field will work for a few hours each day helping members of their family. Particularly is this true when the wage scale is based on the length of row cut. High stubble is practically eliminated by this method of cutting and the amount of supervision is decreased.

However, this system has some disadvantages.

There is danger of high topping. The cutters usually overestimate the amount of cane cut each day and they tend to fall behind due to working short hours unless statements are given them each day or unless the overseer estimates the amount cut. Some planters observed a tendency to stop work in rainy or disagreeable weather and to disagree over the cutting of low yielding rows or cuts. These disadvantages were not serious on plantations which maintained a fair degree of supervision over the cutters.

The following are some comparative labor expenditures* between day labor and custom cutting methods both for clean cutting and for cutting top and bottom and laying the canes across the row preparatory to burning:

*Does not include labor, transportation or supervision.

Plantation	Custom Rates		Day Wage Rate	Cost Under Day Wage System	
	Cut and Strip Per Ton	Cut for Burning Per Ton		Cut Clean Per Ton	Cut for Burning Per Ton
A	60c	--------	Men $1.30 Women 1.00	69c	--------
B	70c		------		
C	70c	--------	------	--------	49c
D	65c		------		
E	60c	--------	Men 1.25 Women 1.00	80c poor yield 65c good yield	--------
F	75c*		------		
G	65c good yield 75c poor yield	50c	------	------	
H	------	--------	Men 1.25 Women 1.00	60c	--------
I	------	--------	Men 1.55 Women 1.30	94c	--------
J	70c	35c	------	--------	
K	60c		------		
L	60c		------		
M	70c		------		
N	70c Stubble 60c Plant		------		
O	70c P.O.J. 234 65c P.O.J. 213 60c P.O.J. 36	60c 55c 50c	------	--------	
P	------	--------	------	--------	49c**

*Includes Loading.
**Average of six plantation units ranging from 45 to 50 cents.

The labor expense of cutting and stripping cane by the ton basis varied from 60 to 70 cents per ton on cane yielding 14 tons or more. Most plantations use the day labor basis of pay when cutting poor yielding cane. Plantation G increases the rate by ten cents on cane which yields under twelve tons per acre. Plantation O varies the rate with the variety being cut and plantation N pays ten cents more for cutting stubble than for plant cane. Most of these variations are efforts to equalize the rate of pay to meet variations in the cane which affect rate of cutting. Very crooked cane is usually cut on the day labor basis. The expense of cutting and stripping by the day labor basis was practically the same as by the ton basis. A small advantage exists in favor of the ton basis. One exception to this was found on a plantation paying more than the prevailing rate for harvest labor. The advantages of the per ton basis of cutting lie in the saving in supervision charges, in a reduced number of cutters and a consequent reduction in transportation and housing charges.

The expense of cutting top and bottom and laying across the row ranged from 45 to 50 cents by the day labor method and from 35 to 60 cents by the per ton system. The advantage was in favor of the day basis when considered on the basis of cash labor expense only, but the above mentioned advantages of the ton rate method no doubt equalize the cost of the two systems when total costs are considered.

Field loading on plantations large enough to use a mechanical loader ranged from 9 to 13.5 cents per ton. Hand loading on small plantations cost approximately 20 cents per ton when done by day labor. The prevailing custom rate for hand loading was 20 cents per ton. On a number of plantations using the per ton method of cutting and hand loading, it was the practice for the cutters to load their own cane. This method worked quite satisfactorily when cutting crews were large enough to load at a maximum rate for the loss of time which occurs when a loading crew must wait for wagons was eliminated. However, if one or two men only composed the loading crew the time required to load each wagon was increased and the efficiency of the loading organization was decreased.

The cost of hauling cane is influenced by many factors. The straightness of the canes, which often reflects varietal differences, has a marked effect on costs. The distance from the hoist, the type of equipment, weather and road conditions are all important factors. The effect of these factors on hauling costs is to be studied in detail in 1931.

General or average hauling costs were determined on a number of plantations for 1930. The following were the costs incurred when calculated at labor rates paid, with a charge of $1.33 per day for mule use, and a 29-cent wagon charge.

Planta-tion	Length of Haul	No. of Wagons	Tons Per Day Ave.	Cost Per Ton
A	¼ to 1½	4	60	43.7¢
B	1 to 1½	9*	190	39.9¢
C	¼ to ½	12	200	42.0¢
C	1 to 2	10	140	50.7¢
D	¼ to 1	4	100	28.4¢
E	1	3	65	33.7¢
E	¼	3	85	26.4¢

Costs ranged from 26.4 cents to 50.7 cents. They seemd to vary quite consistently with the distance hauled although other factors no doubt also caused variations.

The common method of plantation bookkeeping does not report hauling costs but determines loading and hauling labor expenses. These include all cash expenses for machine loading and the wage of the wagon drivers, but do not contain wagon, mule, or supervision charges. The following are cash costs per ton (mostly labor) incurred in the loading and hauling of cane on nine plantaions in 1930.

Plantation	Cash Expense of Loading and Hauling
1	18¢
2	21¢
3	16¢
4	20¢
5	16¢
6	22¢
7	15¢
8	16¢
9	12¢

Nearly a 100 per cent variation occurs between plantations on this one item. The actual cost differences were no doubt extremely large on these plantations when considered on the total cost basis for mule and wagon charges will be expected to follow labor expenses closely in their variations between plantations.

*Tractors used to pull three wagons.

Washington News

By C. J. Bourg

While Congress is in vacation, one might think that all official business is quiet in Washington, but there are always governmental activities affecting the domestic sugar industry.

The United States Tariff Commission still has for consideration the applications of the refiners and of the beet growers, and has not decided whether it will order investigations into the differences in costs of production for either or both raw sugar and refined. Mr. Fletcher's announcement that he will resign as Chairman of the Commission, was quickly followed by the statement that he will remain until November 15th so that all matters now before the Commission may be disposed of before he leaves. That should mean some action this Fall.

The briefs for the United States and for the domestic producers of sugar in re the protest of the Savannah Sugar Refining Corporation, have been filed in the United States Customs Court. Assistant Attorney General Charles D. Lawrence presented one on behalf of the United States, and there were two presented as *Amici Curiae*, one by DeVries Crawford & McCook, attorneys for the Domestic Sugar Producers' Association, and one by James L. Gerry, attorney for the Hawaiian Sugar Planters' Association. The brief on behalf of plaintiff was submitted some time ago by its attorneys, Hitch Denmark & Lovett in Savannah.

These briefs are now a part of the Court Record and since they are being considered by the Court in reaching its decision, a discussion here is not apropos. However, for the information of the readers of THE SUGAR BULLETIN there is submitted hereinbelow a summary prepared by each of the above-named attorneys in his brief.

Mr. Lawrence summarizes:

"The record plainly discloses that the importation is not a sugar syrup commercially, commonly, or in any statutory sense. It is not, therefore, dutiable directly under paragraph 502 of the tariff act of 1930.

"The similitude clause in paragraph 1559 of the tariff act of 1930 cannot be properly invoked to bring the article within the terms of paragraph 502 of said act.

"The merchandise was properly assessed for duty at the rate applicable to sugar under paragraph 501 of the tariff act of 1930, by virtue of the "mixed materials" clause in paragraph 1559 of said act.

"There is grave doubt as to the legality of the methods employed in manufacturing, transporting, invoicing and entering the merchandise into the United States.

"There was absolute failure on the part of plaintiff to establish that the merchandise is commercially known as sugar syrup under well known rules for proof of that fact. A solution of the kind under consideration is not, and never was known as an article of trade. Moreover, it is not so constituted as to properly identify it with any well known commercial product.

"There was likewise a failure of proof to establish that the commodity is commonly known as sugar syrup. The common meaning of the term "sugar syrup" was defined by the courts several years ago in the Cresca cases, *supra*. That meaning has received legislative approval and adoption by its reenactment into the tariff act of 1930. That question is therefore *stare decisis.* Moreover, the commodity is new, unique and experimental. It is not commonly known to manufacturers, dealers, administrative departments of the Government, or the generality of the public. It is not, therefore, known as sugar syrup in any proper sense.

"It is not dutiable as a sugar syrup by similitude of material, quality, texture or use because substantial similarity in any of those particulars does not exist.

"If, as alternatively claimed by plaintiff, the commodity is an unenumerated article, paragraph 1559 declares how it shall be assessed for duty. It is there provided that "on articles not enumerated manufactured of two or more materials, the duty shall be assessed at the highest rate at which the same would be chargeable if composed wholly of the component material thereof of chief value." Sugar being the component material thereof of chief value it is properly dutiable at the rate of 1.7125 cents per pound, as provided in paragraph 501. It follows, therefore, that the rate adopted by the collector of customs was the correct one, whether the importation be regarded as sugar in fact or as mixed material unenumerated in which sugar is the component material of chief value.

"Judgment should be entered herein dismissing the protest, or in the alternative affirming the decision of the collector."

Mr. DeVries summarizes:

"Intent of Congress is paramount rule of statutory construction and is shown in Sugar Schedule as rating all ascertainable sugar in whatever form and however imported at the standard rate provided in Paragraph 501.

"Words and Phrases in Paragraphs 501 and 502

including the phrase "Sugar Syrups," are not used by Congress in a trade or commercial sense but according to their common, popular understanding.

"Both lexical and judicial authorities confine the meaning of the term "Sugar Syrups" in Paragraph 502 to the category of molasses and like substances, as a by-product in the process of refining sugar, being a saturated solution.

"Plaintiff had the burden of showing but failed to show a commercial usage including the imported solution within the term "Sugar Syrups," if that term was used by Congress in a commercial sense, the records showing the term "Sugar Syrups" as employed in the trade, to comprehend a different commodity from the importation.

"Importation consists only of raw sugar in an inner container of water, with a preservative added, which was bought and used solely for the sugar content, as raw sugar in the making of refined sugar.

"Plaintiff's obligation to pay just and legal duties on an imported product intended to be and actually used as raw sugar, was not discharged by previous advices to customs authorities for the purpose of avoiding penalties.

"The imported product is dutiable as sugar under Paragraph 501 either directly, or by similitude thereto, or by virtue of the mixed material clause in Paragraph 1559; and is not dutiable as "Sugar Syrup" under any provision of the law.

"In conclusion, the imported product is dutiable directly under Paragraph 501 as being in fact an importation of raw sugar testing less than 75 sugar degrees by the polariscope."

Mr. Gerry summarizes:

"A simple solution of raw sugar and water and .04% formaldehyde is not dutiable directly as a mixture containing sugar and water, under paragraph 501. Neither is it dutiable as a mixture indirectly, being expressly excluded therefrom and, consequently cannot be included.

"The imported merchandise is not dutiable under paragraph 502, because it is not a commercial sugar syrup, bought, sold or traded in the comerce of the country.

"The merchandise in suit is not dutiable by similitude under paragraph 502, there being no likeness or similarity in material, quality, texture or use, to a commercial sugar syrup.

"Similitude under paragraph 502 cannot be established by showing similarity to an article provided for in paragraph 501.

"Neither can similitude under paragraph 502 be established by showing similarity to a mixture of sugar and water which is expressly excluded from paragraph 501.

"Commercial designation differing from the common meaning has not been established and cannot be established by witnesses who admit that they have never bought nor sold the merchandise and to their knowledge such merchandise never has been bought nor sold in the commerce of the country.

"The merchandise is a nonenumerated manufactured article, but the provisions of paragraph 1559 must be invoked and exhausted before the provisions of paragraph 1558 become applicable.

"Alternatively, whereas the merchandise is not dutiable directly or indirectly under paragraph 502, nor directly or by similitude to "mixtures containing sugar and water" in paragraph 501, it is dutiable as sugar

under paragraph 501 on the solid substance of the mixture.

"It is immaterial whether plaintiff's production was known at and before the present tariff act, but if produced thereafter, the fact that it was bought and sold in the commerce has to be established.

"No doubt can be resolved in favor of plaintiff, in the absence of any testimony to raise a doubt.

"The plaintiff has failed utterly to make a *prima facie* case, and the protest should be dismissed."

It is of some importance to make reference to a decision rendered on July 22nd by the United States Customs Court, in the case of Revere Sugar Refinery versus United States.

In this case it seems that bilge water became mixed with a cargo of raw sugar en route between Cuba and Boston, so that the importer pumped and bailed into tanks this mixture of sugar and water and afterwards recovered therefrom 80,077 pounds of sucrose and a quantity of blackstrap. The importer thereupon claimed that the importation was a syrup and asked that the commodity be entered under Paragraph 502. The Court held that in spite of the presence of water, the article which was intended to be and actually was imported, was raw sugar and the rate of duty under Paragraph 501 was applied.

A comparison of this Revere case with the Savannah case leads us to the conclusion that the importation was the same and the chief difference in the facts is that in the Revere case the sugar and water were mixed by accident, while in the Savannah case the mixture was deliberately done under instructions of the importer.

Fundamental Investigations of Sugar Cane Pests

By Arthur H. Rosenfeld, Consulting Technologist American Sugar Cane League.

There is no doubt that there is a great field today for broad scientific research which seeks to better humanity indirectly as well as directly. Through the Rockefeller Foundation, the Carnegie and others wonderful work is being done in studying disease of mankind, improving sanitary conditions, etc., but the major projects of Federal and State Experiment Stations have as their aim the betterment of the food and economic conditions of the people of whole districts through elimination or reduction of the ravages of diseases or insects affecting their staple crops, and hence, their entire economy.

Here in Louisiana's sugar bowl there are two projects—one pathological and one entomological—which should be undertaken in a very broad way and could render untold service to all the inhabitants of our sugar belt. The first one would be a complete study of the *Pythium* fungus, which is largely responsible for the destruction of the roots of cane the world over, and particularly in the moist and cold conditions of Louisiana springs. There is no doubt that if this fungus. could be controlled we could easily increase by fifty per cent the per acre production of cane in this State, and one can figure for himself what an immense blessing that would be, particularly to the small growers who constitute the overwhelming numerical majority of cane. planters.

There are several factors which require broad and uninterrupted study over a series of years in regard to *Pythium* infection in the soil, two of which might be called "climatic" and one strictly "agricultural." We know that *Pythium* does most damage at low temperatures and with relatively high concentrations of soil moisture, hence a project to ultimately determine the minimum moisture content which this fungus can stand and the soil temperatures most inimical to its development would naturally point the way to means of obtaining these desired conditions through better drainage and other practices. The other point which needs determination is the length of life of the fungus in the soil in the absence of its preferred host plants, which are all of the grass family. Could this be determined and established at a reasonable number of years it is possible that by rotations with entirely distinct families of plants, such as legumes for instance, we might be able to prac_

tically stamp out the *Pythium*, while at the same time employing in ideal rotation for sugar cane.

The other project, which is already under way in the United States Bureau of Entomology, is concerned with the importation and establishment of parasites of the sugar cane moth borer, our most general insect pest. Here in Louisiana we have but one native parasite, while in other countries there are dozen or more helping to keep the borer pest in check, with Dame Nature paying the bill instead of the farmer investing annually in insecticides. Efforts to introduce tropical parasites from Cuba, Porto Rico and adjoining countries have practically universally resulted in failure to establish the visitors on account of our severe winters. In the Tucuman sugar district of the Argentine Republic, however, the climatic conditions of which are very similar to our own, there are *six distinct species* of parasites of the cane borer,

and the vast possibilities of benefit which could be obtained for the sugar planters of this country through the establishment of these Argentine or other adaptable parasites here in the United States are almost inconceivable.

The whole matter is too complicated for discussion in a short paper of popular nature, but considerable meditation over the principles involved might be stimulating for our planters as well as our scientists.

Soil Analysis and the "Law of the Minimum"

By Arthur H. Rosenfeld

There is a pronounced tendency on the part of the layman, and even of the soil chemist and agronomist, to rather overestimate the direct value of soil analyses as an index of the exact fertilizer requirements of soils. Of course, complete soil surveys of given areas are of fundamental importance if coordinated with agronomic experiments to elaborate and define the indications of the chemical and physical data, since the deficiencies or excesses of certain plant foods, for instance, as indicated by chemical analyses, do not show how much or how little of these particular nutritive elements should be applied to that particular soil. All that chemical soil analyses can definitely show are glaring deficiencies or comfortable excesses in certain important elements, but they cannot tell exactly just what these deficiencies are in relation to the agronomic environment or the exact degree of availability to the plant roots of the elements shown as present in greater or lesser degree. These facts can be practically determined only by the laborious and painstaking process of field experimentation, using the soil analyses as a useful, but far from omniscient guide. With sugar cane, particularly, this is a slow and complicated, but essential process if cane-growing is to be made a commercially satisfactory industry.

Until fairly recent years, in fact, the composition of a soil, as obtained by chemical analyses alone, was considered the principal factor involved in the determination of its fertility. With added experience, however, has come the recognition of the vital importance of such other factors as physical condition, state of tilth and drainage, micro-organic life and the presence or absence of relatively small amounts of obnoxious substances.

Fourteen chemical elements have been shown as probably being essential in some quantity for the normal development of plant life. Usually, however, it is only one or more of the three elements, nitrogen, phosphoric acid and potash, which are likely to be present in a soil in quantity less than that required for satisfactory plant growth. Nitrogen seems most important for its influence on the growth and rapid development of the plant, phosphoric acid seems to have a direct relation to plant maturity, although with sugar cane no definite results have been obtained showing an increase in sucrose content following heavy artificial applications of phosphoric acid to the soil, and potash appears to function rather particularly in relation to firmness of texture and other physical conditions, such as the keeping characteristics of certain fruits or the burning qualities of leaf tobaccos.

These three important elements may occur in a

given soil in sufficient quantities for maximum growth of the crop thereon, but in forms unavailable to the plant roots, such a condition arising as a result of a variety of causes. It may be that the soil must have improved æration before these elements can assume the proper available form or the trouble may be due to the closely related factor of insufficient drainage, both with their inhibiting effects on the micro-organic life in the soil so vitally affecting the availability of the plant food therein. Furthermore, it very frequently happens that one only of these three important elements is present in insufficient quantity, while the other two exist in sufficient or greater quantities than those needed for maximum plant growth and yet the crop cannot take advantage of these excess supplies even though they exist in what is normally an available form. In such a case, according to Liebig's well-known "law of the minimum," the element present in the smallest quantity is the "limiting element," as each class of plants seems to require these elements in *certain definite proportions* to each other and the amount of the three which can be taken up by the plant roots will be determined by the lowest amount of any of the three present which can combine in the necessary proportions with the other two.

Just as a fleet of warships, although it possess a number of very fast battle cruisers, must adapt its speed to its slowest vessel, so the availability of these highly important plant foods in the soil depends upon the *smallest amount of one of them* which is available for entering into the proportionate combination with the other two, although it must be borne in mind, too, that the other less frequently deficient elements must undoubtedly be assimilated by the plants in certain definite proportions also. A soil, for example, may contain quantities of available phosphoric acid and potash far in excess of the requirements of the plants growing upon it and nevertheless the crop be unable to develop beyond a certain point because the amount of nitrogen in that soil is less than is required by the plants *in the proper proportions* with the excess phosphoric acid and potash, which, to all intents and purposes, might as well be absent from the soil as unable to combine with this "limiting element" in the proportions necessary before the plants can make use of them.* Such a soil would be denominated as "nitrogen-hungry," while those in which the limiting element is potash or phosphoric acid are known as "potash-hungry" or "phosphate-deficient" soils.

The "law of the minimum," then, is probably as important in governing the productivity of a soil as the combined effect of all other factors combined, since, according to that law, the crop yield is largely determined by the *deficiency in one single element* and not by a sufficient or even superabundant supply in others. While Liebig's enunciation of his law had reference mainly to the chemical composition of the soil, it may and should be extended to other such influences as the physical condition and available water supply of the soil, its suitability as the environment for beneficial soil organisms, etc., etc., since, as Mitscherlich has repeatedly demonstrated, it is only

*Rosenfeld, A. H.—"Los Ensayos con Abonos en la Estación Experimental Agrícola de Tucumán, Rev. Ind. y Agra. de Tucumán, V, 1915."

when these conditions are at an optimum that optimum crops may be secured.**

On the other hand, it must be remembered that, even when no condition apparently essential for successful crop production be lacking, the presence of certain undesirable factors such as excessive quantities of chlorides or iron, aluminum or magnesia salts, high acidity or undue alkalinity, may render a soil partially or entirely infertile. Also, as regards the response of Louisiana cane soils to fertilization, it must be borne in mind that there must be a vast difference as regards the nitrogen supply in a field of plant cane, laid down after a heavy soy-bean crop has been turned under, as is almost general practice now in the Pelican sugar bowl, and in fields of stubble, when a good part of the nitrogen supplied by

**For an excellent discussion of Mitscherlich's growth-factor principle the reader is referred to Dr. O. W. Willcox's "Principles of Agrobiology," N. Y. 1930.

the legumes will have been used up in the production of the plant cane crop. It practically never pays to apply nitrogenous fertilizers to plant cane in this state where this cane follows interred soybeans, whereas almost always applications of 30 to 40 pounds of nitrogen per acre to stubble cane produce excellent financial returns on the investment.

Soil Investigations

The Editor of THE SUGAR BULLETIN has received a copy of a bulletin just published by the Louisiana Agricultural Experiment Station entitled "Soil Fertility Investigations in the Sugar Cane District of Louisiana," the authors being Dr. Oswald Schreiner, Chief, Division of Soil Fertility Investigations, Bureau of Chemistry and Soils, U. S. Department of Agriculture, Dr. L. A. Hurst, in charge of U. S. Soil Fertility Investigations in connection with the sugar cane soils of Louisiana, Dr. A. M. O'Neal, likewise of the U. S. Bureau of Chemistry and Soils, and Mr. S. J. Breaux, Jr., of the Louisiana Experiment Station. It seems, therefore, to be predominantly a report on the soil investigation work of the Federal scientists located at the U. S. Sugar Plant Field Station at Houma, but is published by the Louisiana Agricultural Experiment Station at Baton Rouge, probably through some co-operative arrangement.

As Dr. Oswald Schreiner is the pioneer and protagonist of the famous triangle system of fertilizer experimentation which he promulgated at the tenth annual meeting of the American Society of Agronomy at Washington on November 13, 1917, and which has demonstrated its reliability and soundness during the intervening years, it is natural for the report to show numerous experiments conducted on this system at various test fields in the Louisiana sugar district. The different types of soil met with in the sugar parishes of Louisiana are described and their characteristics enumerated and the results of a large number of fertilization experiments on the various kinds of soil are given, the whole yielding a mass of data which is, however, not yet fully digested, chiefly because the experiments show the results of only one season. The authors recognize the inconclusive nature of the results and have omitted to include in the Bulletin the customary summary. To draw a conclusion one must study each experiment, first endeavoring to reconcile the nature of the soil on which it was conducted with his own soil. This is not particularly difficult as a majority of the fields on which the tests were made are composed of the widely prevalent Yazoo very fine sandy loam, the customary "sandy land" of our Louisiana cane belt. We recommend that the Bulletin be applied for and read by the members of the League. Copies of it can doubtless be obtained free of charge from the Louisiana Agricultural Experiment Station at Baton Rouge. The attractiveness of it is somewhat marred by the careless misspelling of the name of Mr. W. G. Taggart, Assistant Director of the Louisiana Agricultural Experiment Station, on the title page.

After reading this Bulletin it will be interesting to read Dr. Arthur H. Rosenfeld's article entitled "Soil Analysis and the Law of the Minimum" published elsewhere in this issue of THE SUGAR BULLETIN. ......

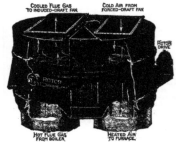
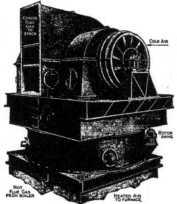

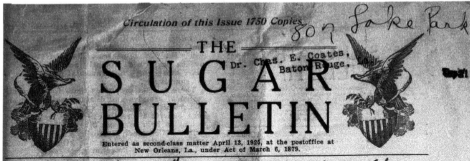

THE
SUGAR
BULLETIN

Dr. Chas. E. Coates,
Baton Rouge,

Entered as second-class matter April 13, 1925, at the postoffice at
New Orleans, La., under Act of March 6, 1879.

We stand for the encouragement of Home Industries as against Foreign Competition.

| Vol. 9 | NEW ORLEANS, LA., SEPTEMBER 1, 1931 | No. 23 |

The Circumlocution Office

The most extraordinary spectacle the people of the United States are witnessing today is the frantic effort of Federal agencies and boards to somehow help the producers of wheat and cotton. It is probable that there has never before, in all the history of the world, been such a mobilization of public money to bring about by some means the restoration of adequate price levels for certain crops, and, as we all know, complete failure to remedy the situation has resulted and the producers of wheat and cotton see prices going from bad to worse instead of getting better. The law of supply and demand wins every round of the fight and the Federal funds are used futilely to buy and store immense quantities of cotton and wheat, hoping to accomplish the purpose for which such action is intended.

The insuperable difficulty in the case of cotton and wheat is that we make more cotton and more wheat than we, in the United States, can consume, or that can be sold abroad, and this fact vitiates every relief program based on the use of Federal money in the shape of loans or for the purpose of purchase and segregation. When we see Federal money used so generously and promptly in behalf of all sorts of plans to help the wheat and cotton growers whose plight is now recognized as virtually hopeless because of the vast overproduction of wheat and vast overproduction of cotton and at the same time see how difficult it is for our cane growers here in Louisiana, who produce something of which there is a shortage in this country, to get prompt and liberal crop loans through the Government agencies established for such purpose, it leads us to wonder as to the source of such ineptitude.

In the case of sugar, or sugar cane, there does not exist the obstacle of vast domestic overproduction which has rendered abortive all the efforts to help the cotton and wheat growers. We produce only about one-half the sugar that we need, and with a tithe of the aid and interest by Federal agencies that is shown in other directions the expansion of the cane growing area could be rapidly increased, much land now idle or growing practically worthless cotton in Louisiana, Texas, Florida, Georgia, Alabama and Mississippi could be planted in cane and a vigorous industry developed, the product of which could be sold without reaching, or even approaching, the needs of the United States for it.

In the case of sugar, a crop that is so circumstanced that it could and would respond immediately to relief measures, we find the attitude of the Federal agencies based apparently on a policy of reluctant parsimony and interminable red tape. The organizations acting as intermediaries between the Federal financial institutions and the cane growers encounter delay, discouragement and indifference where they have every reasonable right to expect alert co-operation. This is not as it should be, and is out of keeping with the widely advertised policy of the Federal Gov-

=====THE=====

S U G A R
BULLETIN

407 Carondelet St., New Orleans

Issued on the 1st and 15th of each month. Official Organ of the American
Sugar Cane League of the U. S. A., in which are consolidated
The Louisiana Sugar Planters' Assn.
The American Cane Growers' Assn.
The Producers & Mfgrs. Protective Assn.
Subscription Price, 50 Cents Per Year.

Reginald Dykers, General Manager & Editor of the Bulletin
301 Nola Bldg., New Orleans
Frank L. Barker, Secretary and Treasurer
Lockport, La.
C. J. Bourg, Manager Washington Office
810 Union Trust Building

CHAIRMEN OF COMMITTEES:
C. D. Kemper, Franklin, La.
President of the League and Ex-Officio Chairman of Executive Committee
Percy A. Lemann, Donaldsonville, La.
Chairman Agricultural Committee
David W. Pipes, Jr., Houma, La.
Chairman Industrial Committee
Frank L. Barker, Lockport, La.
Chairman Finance Committee.
Edward J. Gay, Plaquemine, La.
Chairman Tariff Committee
H. Langdon Laws, Cinclare, La.
Chairman Legislative Committee
J. C. LeBourgeois, New Orleans, La.
Chairman Freight Rate Committee
R. H. Chadwick, Bayou Goula, La.
Chairman Membership Committee
A. H. Rosenfeld, New Orleans, La.
Chairman Publicity Committee

Members of the League desiring action on, or information on, any subject are invited to communicate with the League or with the Chairman of the Committee to which it seems to appertain.

---

ernment towards agriculture in the present crisis.

Throughout the Louisiana sugar district the cane growers should be now breaking their land for next year's cane crop. This operation is known as fall plowing and is a necessary procedure. Participants in Federal aid, however, applying through the recognized channels, are unable, in practically every case, to get the advances to cover the cost of this work at the present time. In order to do fall plowing at all they are obliged to try to get the money to do it with from some other source, with the understanding that the lender will be paid when the Federal loan is finally forthcoming, which may be several months from now. The same situation prevails in regard to nearly every farming operation that has to be conducted under the existing system prevalent in the cane growing section of Louisiana, and as it is imperative that each character of farm work be done at the time that Nature requires, if it is to be done at all, the whole cane growing community, trying to produce one of the few agricultural commodities of which there is not enough in this country to supply the requirements, is hipped and hamstrung, and the security for the money finally obtained from the

Government, to-wit, the crop, has its safety and abundance curtailed and jeopardized because the various phases of its cultivation cannot be performed promptly and properly. A more shortsighted Governmental policy is hardly conceivable.

These are not propitious times for the application of complex and dilatory methods in aid of agriculture, especially a form of agriculture that Federal aid really can help when it is impotent to help so many others. The Circumlocution Office, made famous by Charles Dickens, and the motto of which was "How not to do it" seems to have its counterpart today.

Fall Plant Cane Suggestions

By C. B. Gouaux, Cane Specialist

In the Louisiana sugarcane belt, during the months of August, September and October, the preparation of land, harvesting of corn and legumes and planting of fall cane, are all very important field activities. In making plans for the plant cane of the next crop, the matter of selection of varieties for the different soil types, is one of the most important problems with field men and overseers. With the information on cane varieties that has been obtained from the work of the Louisiana Experiment Station, the Government Field Station, variety test fields and practical field variety work, the planting of varieties best suited for the various sections can be readily determined. Along with this plan of using a definite system for arranging a field variety planting program it is also of the utmost importance to improve fiel practices. The suggestions for improvement in thi line of work, are made for the purpose of improvin the condition of plant cane stands in the sugar bel parishes.

Seed Cane. The cane that is to be used for plant ing purposes should be taken from fields where t cane is sound and healthy, free as possible from dis ease and insect injuries, good stand and growth an good cultivation. Fields of cane with thin stand: stunted growth, badly overrun with grass and weed: heavy borer infestation and poor cultivation, shoul be completely discarded for seed cane purposes.

In harvesting seed cane, every effort should b made to avoid bruising, cutting or damaging eyes i any way. Oftentimes in stripping the cane, the eye are cut or injured. This condition decreases vitalit of the seed cane, besides furnishing ready points c entrance for disease and insect enemies. Closely ad hering green leaf sheaths should be left on; whil the dry leaves can be brushed or shaken off i handling.

In cutting off the top portion, when cutting see cane, the growing bud should be cut off and the knif lowered to the first hard portion of the top. Lon tops that are generally left on, continue to grow an come out of the ground, using stored food from th stalk to the detriment of the eyes that are depende on to give a good germination. The bottom part c the stalk should be cut at surface of ground. Knive for cutting seed cane should be sharp, so as to giv a good clean cut, and avoid any bruising, tearing o splitting of the stalk in any way.

Seed cane should not be cut too long in advanc

The Advertisers in the Sugar Bulletin are contributing towards the support of the American Sugar Cane League and should enjoy your special consideration; help them to help the Domestic Sugar Industry by doing business with them whenever possible.

and should be planted as quickly as possible. Where weather conditions interfere, it is good practice to cover the seed cane with cane trash, as a measure of protection from the sun.

Topping seed cane before planting. The practice of topping cane and allowing it to remain standing for intervals of 4 to 7 days to force germination of the eyes, is an old practice that was used by some of the planters with the old varieties. For the past few seasons the practice has been revived to some extent, and used on slow germinating varieties like P. O.J. 36 and P.O.J. 213. Planters who have tried it out are satisfied that they have obtained better stands. The main disadvantage in connection with topping cane, is the danger of breaking off or injuring the sprouted eyes, in the handling of the seed cane. This system can doubtless best be used by careful small cane growers.

Number of stalks to plant. For all practical purposes the two-running stalks with light lap method should be used in all fall plantings with all varieties. In placing the cane in the planting furrow, tops should be alternated with butts.

Cutting seed cane in the rows. It is a general practice all over the cane belt to cut the seed cane in several pieces, after it has been placed in the planting furrow. This is done mainly to facilitate the covering of the cane. It is a field practice that should have good supervision, as a lot of injury to seed cane can result from improper work. The unnecessary cutting of eyes, hacking the cane in small pieces, and leaving ragged cuts should not be allowed. The work of cutting seed cane in the row is very simple with straight cane, one clean cut with two at the most sufficing; while with crooked cane two to four cuts are generally required. In every case, an effort should be made to cut the cane in the middle of the joint, between the two nodes.

Depth of planting and covering. In all sections of the cane belt the matter of drainage is an important factor. This is especially true when applied to a fall plant cane crop; planted in September and October, and being in a more or less dormant condition until late February and early March. The matter of opening planting furrows so that the lowest point where the cane is placed, will be higher than the level of the middles, is an old recommendation that should be closely followed. The quarter drains should be 4 to 6 inches lower than the middles with good outlets to a clean system of ditches.

The seed cane should be covered with three to four inches of soil, in a broad row with sides gradually sloping to the middles. This sort of a row is ideal for planting winter cover crops of melilotus indica. The peaked or high ridged row and deep covering of seed cane, are considered unfavorable factors for the proper keeping qualities of plantings of P.O.J. canes.

Germination of field varieties. Early germinating canes: P.O.J. 234, C.P. 807.

Late germinating varieties, in following order: P. O.J. 213, Co. 281, P.O.J. 36M and P.O.J. 36.

Suckering of varieties. Early suckering: P.O.J. 234, C.P. 807.

Late suckering: P.O.J. 213, Co. 281, P.O.J. 36M and P.O.J. 36.

Time of planting. September and early October planting: P.O.J. 36, P.O.J. 36M, P.O.J. 213 and Co. 281.

October-November planting: P.O.J. 234 and C.P. 807.

Sandy land varieties: P.O.J. 213, P.O.J. 234, P.O.J. 36M, Co. 281 and C.P. 807.

Black land varieties: P.O.J. 234, Co. 281, P.O.J. 36 and C.P. 807.

Distinguished Guests

About the middle of last month a notable group of scientific men connected with the United States Department of Agriculture made their appearance virtually unheralded at the Southdown Plantation of the Estate of H. C. Minor at Houma, La., where they were the guests for two days of Mr. and Mrs. David Pipes, Jr. The party was composed of Dr. A. F. Woods, Director of Scientific Work, U. S. Department of Agriculture, Dr. S. H. McCrory, Chief of the Bureau of Agricultural Engineering of the U. S., Department of Agriculture, Dr. E. W. Brandes, Principal Pathologist in Charge Sugar Plants, Bureau of Plant Industry, U. S. Department of Agriculture, and Dr. B. Youngblood, Agricultural Economist associated with the Bureau of Experiment Station Administration of the U. S. Department of Agriculture. These gentlemen came to Louisiana to look over the work being done at the Federal Experiment Station at Houma, the intelligent conduct of which is of so much importance to the Louisiana sugar industry, and to familiarize themselves with the varietal cane situation up to date, to see the country and its condition at first hand and to gain such personal knowledge as may be necessary to enable them to plan and carry on the work of the U. S. Department of Agriculture in this field to the best possible advantage. They had, while here, an opportunity to learn the requirements of our industry in the directions of cane-breeding, cane disease prevention, fertilizer work, drainage, irrigation, entomology, mechanical development and other fields of study. All this is very important.

The men who comprised the group are all high in rank in the U. S. Department of Agriculture and their personal interest in our problems and their clear comprehension of our needs and our difficulties means a great deal more to us than can readily be

expressed in ordinary language. They went away,
for instance, fully aware of the fact that something
like half a million people are dependent on the financial success of the Louisiana sugar industry for a living; that the soil and climate of the 17 "sugar Parishes" of Louisiana are such that sugar cane is incomparably the most suitable crop for cultivation
here, and that the production of that crop must be
carried on successfully if all those people are to be
saved from suffering, disaster and want. That they
realized their responsibilities and were eager to meet
them is shown by their having come here, and we are
all to be congratulated on having established direct
contact with men of their high calibre and conscien-
tiousness who have the resources, financial and technical, at their command to help us solve the rather
pressing field and factory problems that are constantly confronting us.

Men like these able and sympathetic visitors loom
large on the economic horizon today. They hold in
their hands the well-being of great communities.
Their intelligent direction of the forces at their command may mean, and does often mean, that count-
less modest homes are happy homes rather than foci
of despair.

Scientific work and research has become a thoroughly practical proposition, to be handled by level
headed men who strive with an eye single towards
the objective of pecuniary benefit to those who earn
their bread from industry. If there still be theorists,
dreamers and dilletantes in the ranks of scientific
investigation they are being rapidly weeded out. The
gentlemen who have just visited us belong to the
new and practical school, and nothing is more certain than that their visit, which their agreeable per-
sonalities made most enjoyable to all who met them,
will tend to lead us toward material welfare, peace
of mind and contentment. They know it is their
job to bring about such eventualities.

A Forward Step in Cultivation

For a great many years the adoption of tractors for
agricultural work in the Louisiana sugar district made
very slow progress, due to the fact that there were
conditions to be met that were peculiar to our work,
and there was no very marked disposition on the part
of tractor builders to construct a tractor especially suited to sugar cane cultivation in Louisiana. A great
deal of money was spent in persuading the Louisiana
sugar planters to buy tractors that only partially
filled their requirements, and a great many were sold,
but if one-tenth the money had been spent in perfect-
ing a tractor for this territory that was spent to sell
here the ordinary models very much better results
would have accrued to all concerned. The proper implements to use with the tractors also offered a considerable field for study that was never fully utilized.

Recently Mr. C. T. Wadsworth and Mr. W. H.
Hauserman have been carrying on some experiments
at Southdown, and also at Cedar Grove and Sterling
for the purpose of combining deep tillage with cultivation work on crops, such as cane, that stand high
enough to require considerable clearance. They used
the Caterpillar Hi-clearance Ten Tractor, which has
a 22-inch clearance, and a set of what are known as
Killefer chisels, which loosened the ground 22 inches

below the surface. As far as we can recall, our experience of more than 30 years, such deep plowing as this has never been done in Louisiana and we believe that, so far as the sugar world in general is concerned, only cable-drawn steam plows, very cumbersome and very expensive, have been used to break the ground to such a depth. Of course ordinary mould-board plows can also be used with the "High Clearance Ten."

The work of Mr. Wadsworth and Mr. Hauserman was watched with a great deal of interest by the members of the staff of the U. S. Sugar Plant Field Station at Houma, and a great many of the sugar planters from different parts of the cane belt also went there to see it. It seems to be generally believed that the Killefer chisels and the Caterpillar Hi-clearance Ten tractor will save a substantial percentage of the crop production costs. A serious attempt is evidently being made to perfect a power-drawn implement that will suit our needs, and every encouragement ought to be given Mr. W. H. George, President of the New Orleans Tractor Company, agent at New Orleans for the Killefer Mfg. Co. and the Caterpillar Tractor Co., in return for his practical, and probably, up to this time, unremunerative work in a direction that is bound to be helpful to our sugar planting community. When you get down 22 inches in the ground you reach what is practically a new farm, and when you get up 22 inches in the air you avoid injury to your growing crop. Mr. George has his outfits rigged up both ways and they will doubtless be in use very generally before long.

Chasing Our Own Tail

Mr. B. B. Jones, the able Agricultural Secretary of the New Orleans Association of Commerce, who supplies an interesting "Market News Letter" to a wide circle of readers every week, says in his letter of August 17th, 1931:

"Agriculture plays an important part in the export business of the country as is shown by the fact that over a five-year period the average annual exports total $4,800,000,000, of which amount agriculture contributes an average of $1,800,000,000. Because of the importance of the export business in agricultural products, world conditions mean much to our industry. Before our recovery can become complete our export business must return to normal, and our markets become free users of agricultural products at profitable prices."

We believe that the method of reaching prosperity suggested by Mr. Jones is too circuitous, and is like

- chasing our own tail. A quicker and more direct way would be to stop bringing in the vast aggregate of agricultural imports that we are now guilty of importing, which compete with the sale here at home of our own agricultural products.

In the years 1926, 1927, 1928, 1929 and 1930 our imports of agricultural products exceeded our exports of agricultural products by the following amounts:

1926	$561,312,000
1927	300,307,000
1928	304,249,000
1929	267,410,000
1930	345,751,000

We brought in, in 1930, because the tariff was inadequate to keep them out, $21,000,000 worth of live stock, $31,000,000 worth of dairy products, $8,-000,000 worth of eggs, $129,000,000 worth of hides and skins, $23,000,000 worth of meats, $42,000,000 worth of cotton lint, $61,000,000 worth of fruits, $167,000,000 of vegetable oils, $200,000,000 of sugar, $49,000,000 worth of vegetables, and a long list of other agricultural products in greater or less volume, which not only replaced, in a majority of cases, a similar amount of agricultural products grown here and made them unsaleable, but lowered the price on those that were sold. Mr. Jones feels that this dead stock of ours, defrauded of its own home market by imports, ought to be exported if we are to become prosperous. Of course it must be, if we keep up this paradoxical policy, but a much simpler way would be not to let our agricultural products be defrauded of their own home market and use them right here.

There is a great deal of bric-a-brac being published about the necessity of export trade. What we really need is less imports so that our own home market will belong to us. Taking just one single item, vegetable oils, what a considerable help it would have been to our producers of cotton seed oil and other vegetable oils if the $167,000,000 paid for foreign vegetable oils in 1930 had been paid to the domestic producers of such commodities!

Sugar Institute Dissolution Suit

By C. J. Bourg

The proceedings instituted by the Department of Justice seeking to abolish the Sugar Institute, have been met by formal answer from the Institute. The Department of Justice charged the Institute with the maintenance of a comprehensive scheme in violation of the Sherman Anti-Trust Act. This action on the part of the U. S. Attorney General was unexpected and caused considerable surprise because of the fact that in 1928 the Code of Ethics and the charter of the Sugar Institute having been submitted to the Department of Justice, had received its formal sanction. Since the organization of the Institute no important changes had been made. In the Code was outlined the purpose and activities of the Institute, all of which have been under the surveillance of the Federal Trade Commission.

A major complaint stipulated by the Department of Justice is that the refiners have entered into "a conspiracy to control the price of sugar" and that "the consuming public had been required to pay large sums in excess of what it would have been re-

quired to pay for sugar in a market free from the artificial restraints." In view of the ridiculously low prices of sugar which have prevailed since the Institute was organized, the cause for which always has been laid to world overproduction, it is intriguing to wonder what evidence can be submitted by the Government to place the responsibility for such price-fixing upon the defendants in this case.

The Attorney General likewise blames the Institute for the differential of 20c per hundred-weight which exists between the price of cane sugar and beet sugar. As this difference is a trade custom established when the beet sugar industry was in its infancy, we shall give an attentive ear to learn what unfair practice has been resorted to by the defendants to maintain the price concession, and whether it is proposed to stop this marketing practice.

Of course, the Government makes many another complaint and gives particulars which it contends would justify a permanent injunction and dissolution of this Sugar Institute.

Now into Court has come the defendant protesting that instead of violating any law or operating in restraint of trade, it has in fact by its organization checked what might have become a monopoly in the hands of favored buyers of sugar, based on unfair and uneconomical discriminations between customers, which tended particularly to favor the larger consumers. The Institute points with pride to its Code of Ethics which has eliminated these discriminations and unethical practices.

Without attempting to prejudge the case or to express an opinion, it is well known that the Code of Ethics of the Institute, in addition to having the approval of the U. S. Department of Justice and the sanction of the Federal Trade Commission, has served as the standard for dozens of similar organizations in other industries, some of which have adopted the Code in its entirety. The Domestic Sugar Bureau is a trade organization composed chiefly of beet sugar manufacturers but includes some Louisiana producers who sell in the upper Mississippi Valley, and this Bureau has adopted the Code of the Sugar Institute.

The Institute in its answer refers specifically to the letter of approval from the office of the Attorney General of the United States which says in part: "Based on our understanding of the purposes to be accomplished by the organization of the Sugar Institute, Inc., and the adoption of the By-Laws and the Code of Ethics, referred to, we believe this organization represents a bona fide combination of persons engaged in the refining and marketing of cane sugar to stabilize the economic conditions affecting their business by means of a trade association whose activities shall be conducted in accordance with the law."

It is well known that the Department of Commerce has for some years been urging the formation of trade associations within all our national industries. It has been reported in certain publications that Secretary of Commerce Herbert Hoover gave his active support to this program and encouraged the organization of the Sugar Institute. There are some who think that the Federal Administration in Washington intends by means of this suit to secure for this trade policy the judicial sanction of our Courts, or to have pointed out in a court decision what abuses must be brought within the law.

Important Events

The annual meeting of the membership of
e American Sugar Cane League will be held
Thursday, September 24th, at 1:30 p. m., at
e rooms of the League, 407 Carondelet Street,
ew Orleans.

The annual Field Day at the Louisiana Ex-
riment Station, Baton Rouge, known as the
'lanters' Field Day," will be held on a date
t to be selected during the latter part of the
ird week in September or the early part of
e fourth week in September, the exact date
be announced later.

Note on Fineness of Division in Liming Materials

By Arthur H. Rosenfeld

Inquiries have been received from time to time at
is office regarding the comparative merits for soil
ning purposes of ground limestone, powdered oyster
ell and other substances, based on their content of
lcium carbonate or oxide. It should be under-
ood in this connection that the prime consideration
any of these materials is, naturally, the calcium
ntent, but, while this is the logical *chemical*
sis of comparison, the *physical condition* of
e materials, *i. e.*, their fineness of division and
oisture content, is even more important as far as the
vailability of the calcium corbonate for the purpose
r which it is to be employed is concerned. If all of
ese materials are sufficiently dry and non-hygroscopic,
that lumps will not be formed to make mechanical
stribution difficult or impossible, and if all are so
nely ground that they are in the *form of a powder
hich will pass thru a 100-mesh screen*, their value
soil amendments would probably be equal per unit
calcium carbonate content; naturally, then, the
termination of the material to purchase would de-
nd on the cost per unit of calcium carbonate or
lcium oxide, after taking into due consideration the
creased freight rate per unit on materials having
wer percentage composition of calcium units. Where
e material is to be shipped over long distances, par-
ularly by water, special attention should be paid
the hygroscopicity, *i. e.*, the water-absorbing ten-
ncies, of the substance, as a product leaving its
anufacturing point in a perfectly dry state, if of
ch a nature that it absorbs moisture readily from
e air, might possibly reach its destination in a
mpy or pasty condition—to such an extent, even,
at economical mechanical distribution would be im-
ssible.

Blackstrap Molasses for Mules

M. G. Snell and W. G. Taggart

In the summer of 1929, the Sugar Station of the Louisiana State University started a series of molasses feeding experiments with mules, the object being:

(1) To find out how much molasses could be included in a work mule's ration;

(2) To determine the feeding value of molasses for mules in comparison with corn.

The first trial attempted to replace corn grain entirely with molasses. A second trial included three pounds of molasses in one ration and six in the other ration, molasses replacing corn grain pound for pound.

The results of these first two trials are shown in Animal Industry Circular No. 2.

Worming and Molasses Feeding

Before explaining the 1931 molasses feeding work, we would like to say that we treat the mules once a year for worms. Likewise, we would like to emphasize that in all of our molasses feeding work the molasses has been poured on the ground feeds at the time of feeding—consequently, every feed is a fresh mixture.

Over a period of more than twelve months of continuous molasses feeding at levels varying from 3 to 9 pounds, the Sugar Station has not had a case of colic nor a mule lose a day's work. Furthermore, the mules are in excellent condition at the present time. The Station is inclined to attribute these excellent results to worming, good care, the method of feeding the molasses, and the molasses as a feed.

1931 Results

Six teams of mules which had been used in the previous molasses feeding trials were divided into two lots of six mules each, one mule from each team going into each lot. Water and salt were available in the feed lot. Each group has similar lot and stall space.

The rations are shown in Table I.

TABLE I

Daily Ration Fed Mules on Work Days February 10 to June 16, 1931—126 days

LOT	I	II
Ration:		
Corn gr. whole (72% grain)	9.1	4.90
Molasses	6.0	9.0
Soybean Hay	9.68	9.68

The mules were weighed three days at the beginning and at the end of the trial. The experiment is to continue 252 days, only the results of the first 126 days are shown in Table II.

TABLE II

Summary of Results of Feeding Molasses to Mules—1931 February 10 to June 16—Table based on one mule

LOT (6 mules per lot)	I Corn gr. whole ear. molasses 6 lbs. soybean hay	II Corn gr. whole ear molasses 9 lbs soybean hay
Period days	126	126
Initial weight, lbs.	1270	1266
Final weight, lbs.	1330	1348
Gain, lbs.	60	82
Daily ration, lbs.:		
Corn gr. whole ear	7.93	3.68
Molasses	4.80	7.21
Soybean hay	9.68	9.68
Feed cost per day:		
Molasses:		
15c per gal.	26.04	25.73
9c per gal.	23.99	22.03
6c per gal.	22.76	20.19
Feed cost per 1000 lbs. live wt.:		
Molasses:		
15c per gal.	20.03	19.76
9c per gal.	18.46	16.86
6c per gal.	17.51	15.45
Days worked	50.67	50.67

Price of Feed:

Corn, 85c per bu.

Grinding corn, 3.71 cents per 100 lbs.

Soybean hay, $25 per ton.

The mules were fed twice a day, one-third of t grain ration at noon and the remainder plus the h was fed at night. On Sundays and days when they were idle, the mules were turned on a grass paddock and only the night feed fed.

At the end of the first 126 days, both lots had gained in weight. Lot I, 60 pounds, and Lot II, 82 pounds.

This shows that molasses is a good conditioner of mules. Some trouble has been noted from over-heating, especially after the mules have been idle for some time. However, as yet we are undecided whether to blame this on the molasses feeding or to the fact that the mules were fat and soft.

Molasses, insofar as these and previous results go, is apparently fully equivalent to corn as a conditioner of farm work mules. Up to the present time, no mule has lost a day's work due to colic, indigestion or any digestive disturbance, or to any other cause that could be laid to molasses. This indicates that molasses has a feeding value for work mules equal to that of corn, when fed up to nine pounds per mule daily.

The price which one could afford to pay for molasses to feed to mules when corn is at varying prices is shown in Table III.

TABLE III
The Value of Molasses as a Mule Feed in Comparison to Corn

Corn, 56 lbs. grain to the bushel.
Molasses, 11.7 lbs. to the gallon.

Corn per bu.	Molasses per gallon	Corn per bu.	Molasses per gallon
$.20	4.18c	$1.00	20.88c
.25	5.22c	1.05	21.93c
.30	6.27c	1.10	22.98c
.35	7.31c	1.15	29.02c
.40	8.36c	1.20	25.06c
.45	9.40c	1.25	26.11c
.50	10.45c	1.30	27.16c
.55	11.49c	1.35	28.21c
.60	12.54c	1.40	29.24c
.65	13.58c	1.45	30.29c
.70	14.63c	1.50	31.33c
.75	15.67c	1.75	36.56c
.80	16.72c	2.00	41.79c
.85	17.76c	2.25	47.01c
.90	18.80c	2.50	52.23c
.95	19.85c	2.75	57.46c

This table shows corn to have to be as low as 20 cents a bushel in order for molasses to have a feeding value of 4.18 cents per gallon. With corn at 60 cents a bushel, molasses has a feeding value of 22.54 cents per gallon.

Summary
1. All mules on the Sugar Station are treated for worms once each year.
2. Molasses is mixed with the ground whole ear corn at time of feeding.
3. No case of digestive disturbance has occurred during more than 12 months of continuous molasses feeding at levels varying from 3 to 9 pounds per mule.
4. Molasses is approximately equal to corn grain as a feed for farm work mules.
5. Molasses is usually cheaper than corn.

THE
SUGAR

Dr. Chas. E. Coates,
Baton Rouge, La.
BULLETIN

Entered as second-class matter April 13, 1925, at the postoffice at
New Orleans, La., under Act of March 6, 1879.

We stand for the encouragement of Home Industries as against foreign competition.

| Vol. 9 | NEW ORLEANS, LA., SEPTEMBER 15, 1931 | No. 24 |

THE ANNUAL MEETING
of the
AMERICAN SUGAR CANE LEAGUE
of the
U. S. A., Inc.
will be held on
Thursday, September 24th, 1931
at 1:30 P. M.
at the office of the League
407 Carondelet St., New Orleans

Annual reports will be submitted and there will be an election of officers and of members of the Executive Committee to serve during the ensuing fiscal year.

The activities of the American Sugar Cane League are constantly enlarging in scope and in their beneficial effects on the Louisiana sugar industry, and at the annual meeting an opportunity is afforded to every member of the organization to express himself concerning the past and future work of the League.

LET EVERY MEMBER OF THE LEAGUE ATTEND

☞ Note that the annual meeting will be held on *Thursday* and not on the usual monthly meeting day, which is Wednesday. This is because the charter requires that the annual meeting shall be held the last *Thursday* in September.

ACCEPT THIS PUBLICATION AS YOUR INVITATION TO ATTEND

THE
SUGAR
BULLETIN

407 Carondelet St., New Orleans

Issued on the 1st and 15th of each month. Official Organ of the American
Sugar Cane League of the U. S. A., in which are consolidated
The Louisiana Sugar Planters' Assn.
The American Cane Growers' Assn.
The Producers & Mfgrs. Protective Assn.
Subscription Price, 50 Cents Per Year.

Reginald Dykers, General Manager & Editor of the Bulletin
301 Nola Bldg., New Orleans
Frank L. Barker, Secretary and Treasurer
Lockport, La.
C. J. Bourg, Manager Washington Office
810 Union Trust Building

CHAIRMEN OF COMMITTEES:
C. D. Kemper, Franklin, La.
President of the League and Ex-Officio Chairman of Executive Committee
Percy A. Lemann, Donaldsonville, La.
Chairman Agricultural Committee
David W. Pipes, Jr., Houma, La.
Chairman Industrial Committee
Frank L. Barker, Lockport, La.
Chairman Finance Committee.
Edward J. Gay, Plaquemine, La.
Chairman Tariff Committee
H. Langdon Laws, Cinclare, La.
Chairman Legislative Committee
J. C. LeBourgeois, New Orleans, La.
Chairman Freight Rate Committee
R. H. Chadwick, Bayou Goula, La.
Chairman Membership Committee
A. H. Rosenfeld, New Orleans, La.
Chairman Publicity Committee

Members of the League desiring action on, or information on, any subject are invited to communicate with
the League or with the Chairman of the Committee
to which it seems to appertain.

Low Cutting of Cane

As we all know, nobody has devoted his time and
thought more assiduously to the benefit of the Louisiana sugar industry than Mr. T. E. Holloway, the
Senior Entomologist at the Sugar Cane Insect Laboratory in New Orleans. Every now and then he
advances some idea that he thinks may help us, and
which he asks us to try. He now suggests that
we have not given enough thought to the fact that
tall sugar cane stubble is a source of borer infestation, and he has been talking this over with Mr. Elliott Jones of the American Sugar Cane League's
Agricultural Committee, and it was agreed between
them that something ought to be published in the
SUGAR BULLETIN to draw attention to the marked
benefits, of more than one kind, that will result
from lower cutting of cane. We are glad to print
Mr. Holloway's statement, made verbally to us in
the shape of an interview, as follows:

"I have tried to bring out from time to time," said
Mr. Holloway, "that tall sugar cane stubble is a
source of borer infestation. With the present methods of cutting it is practically impossible to get the
cane cut flush with the ground, and the result is
that tall stubble is left in which many borers pass
the winter. To remedy this, I recently proposed in
the SUGAR BULLETIN that we experiment with a me-

chanical cane knife, or cane saw, but this suggestion
apparently did not meet with the approval of the
planters.

"I was talking with Mr. Elliott Jones at Southdown Plantation the other day, and it was Mr.
Jones' opinion that the importance of low cutting has
not been sufficiently emphasized. Mr. Jones, however, would obtain this effect by cutting the cane in
the usual way and then going over it immediately
with a stubble shaver. It is very likely that this
would destroy a number of borers, although it would
not be as good as cutting the cane low in the first
place. The planter would continue to lose the base of
the stalk, which is richest in sugar. As for the borer,
some of the pieces of stubble would dry out and
others might be frozen, but other pieces might fall
in protected situations and the borers in these would
probably survive. Some borers would undoubtedly
be killed, but without seeing the method tried I could
not say whether most of them would be killed or not.
The experiment is worth trying, however, and perhaps a large percentage of the borers would perish.

"I hope that I may be pardoned for referring
again to the mechanical cane knife. A working
model of this machine is offered to the sugar industry by a machinist in New Orleans for the insignificant sum of $125. This model would not be just
what I have in mind, but it would be sufficient for
a plantation test. Perhaps the machine as constructed might not be a success, but it might serve
as a guide to a model which would be successful.

"I shall be very glad to see both the mechanical
cane knife made and tried and the trial of Mr. Jones'
idea concerning stubble shaving immediately after
cutting."

Cane Roots

The Editor of the SUGAR BULLETIN has had the
pleasure of reading Louisiana Bulletin No. 223, b
Dr. T. C. Ryker and Dr. C. W. Edgerton of th
Louisiana Experiment Station staff, entitled "Studie
on Sugar Cane Roots." The purpose of Bulletin No
223 is to call attention to the obvious importance o
the roots of the cane as a factor in the growth an
development of the stalk. After reading it one i
impressed with the thought that probably we hav
not been devoting enough attention to the safety o
the roots and the encouragement of the roots and th
guidance of the roots. The authors of Bulletin No
223 point out that from 85% to 90% of the roots of th
cane spread themselves in the upper 14 inches of soi
and the greater part of the root distribution is in th
portion of the soil from 3 inches to 8 inches belov
the surface. In this shallow area the roots grow ou
laterally, so that they are easily cut by cultivatior
Such cutting is highly detrimental.

It is not attempted in Bulletin No. 223 to explai
just why the greatest root development is in thi
shallow area near the surface, but the authors see
to imply by indirection that probably this is so be
cause the soil is not loose below that depth and th
roots do not readily penetrate it. This theory is a
least a plausible one, so plausible that a demonstra
tion on an industrial scale of fields loosened by dee
tillage 18 to 20 inches should be made. It is quit
conceivable that if the soil was so conditioned tha
the roots could penetrate it they would tend to g

downward instead of growing laterally and in such case they would be safer from injury. Cane with 50% of its root system running down instead of sideways might be far better cane. The question of whether a large percentage of the roots will run down instead of sideways, if the soil is loosened up more deeply than it ordinarily is ought to be answered. Perhaps it has already been answered. The SUGAR BULLETIN will be glad to publish any information sent to it on this subject.

Have You Filled Out This Blank?

Professor William Whipple, in charge of the instruction in steam engineering at the Louisiana State University, has interested himself in the great loss of sugar that occurs every year in Louisiana through improper mill work. Professor Whipple's efforts to reduce this loss have the co-operation and approval of the Contact Committee of the American Sugar Cane League, and the first step he has taken is to collect data as to the sizes and settings of all the mills and crushers in the Louisiana sugar district, the grooving of the rolls, setting of turnplates, and so on. Professor Whipple has mailed suitable blank forms to all the Louisiana mills and has asked that these forms be filled out and returned to him. If any mill has not received a form Professor Whipple should be notified and he will send one at once.

The report of Professor Whipple, when completed, will show the effect of various factors on the capacity and efficiency of the mills. It will be prepared solely for the purpose of preventing some of the serious losses of sugar in the bagasse that now occur, and no carelessness nor indifference should be shown in relation to the blanks. If received they should be at once filled out and returned to Professor Whipple at the Louisiana State University, Baton Rouge. If not received, or if lost or mislaid, duplicates will be sent on application.

One of the shortcomings of human nature is to show inadequate appreciation and responsiveness in cases of this sort. It is hoped that Professor Whipple will not be discouraged by the neglect of those who receive his blanks to fill them out and return them to him as he requests.

Producing New Varieties of Sugarcane

By G. B. Sartoris, Pathologist, Division of Sugar Plant Investigations, Bureau of Plant Industry.

Coincident with the introduction of new varieties of sugarcane in Louisiana during the past few years cane planters have become greatly interested in the subject and it is believed that they may be interested in a description of the methods followed in producing and selecting new varieties at the United States Sugar Plant Field Station located at Canal Point, Florida. No attempt will be made to go into a detailed description of the technique of sugarcane breeding, which has been developed as a result of laborious and accurate research, which has been carried on for more than half a century in numerous countries in which sugarcane is grown, but a brief non-technical description of the fertilization of the sugarcane flower, the germination of the seed, and the care and selection of seedling varieties will serve to indicate the procedure followed and the enormous amount of detailed and laborious work involved in breeding new varieties.

The actual breeding season at Canal Point extends throughout the period November to January, inclusive, but the propagation, culture and study of new seedling varieties and of both locally bred and imported varieties intended for use for breeding purposes is carried on throughout the year.

Cross Fertilization of Sugarcane

The sugarcane tassel is composed of several hundred flowers, each of which possesses both male and female organs, but the flowers are so small that it is not practical to attempt to remove the male organs and in cross fertilization the entire tassel is used as a unit. Nearly all varieties of cane which produce tassels have fertile eggs but many varieties do not have fertile pollen and are incapable of producing seed unless they are fertilized with fertile pollen from another variety. Such varieties are known as females, and those varieties which have fertile pollen are known as males. Male varieties, that is, varieties having both fertile eggs and fertile pollen, are capable of producing seed as the result of self-fertilization, but the chances for producing new varieties possessing disease-resistant and other essential characteristics are greatly enhanced by the controlled fertilization of male and female varieties which have been carefully selected for their desirable characteristics. Obviously, the sex of the varieties selected for breeding purposes is the first thing which must be determined. Early morning is the best time for this work, and portions of the tassels which are out far enough to be used in crossing are collected at sunrise and the fertility of the pollen is ascertained by examining it under the microscope.

After the sex of the varieties has been determined, pairs of varieties possessing the best possible combinations of disease-resistant, early-maturity, high yield, and other desirable characteristics are cross-fertilized. Stalks of the male parent carrying flowering tassels are cut and the cut end of the stalks immediately placed in water. Several inches of the end of the stalks are cut off under water and each stalk immediately transferred to an individual glass jar filled with sulphurous acid solution of suitable

strength. Twelve stalks of the male parent are ordinarily used but if this number is not available, as many as are in the proper stage of development are used. The jars are placed in a suitable rack provided with a cross bar for securely holding the stalks and tassel in an upright position.

The racks are then placed in the field and the tassels are securely fastened slightly above the tassels of the female parents in such manner that they will remain fixed in the proper position regardless of the direction and intensity of the wind. If the stalks of the male parents are not long enough to permit the tassels to reach the tassels of the female parents the racks are placed upon scaffolds. Each stalk will use nearly a quart of the sulphurous acid solution each twenty-four hours, and the supply must be replenished daily. Once each week a node of the stalk is cut off under water and the stalk immediately placed in a clean jar filled with the solution. The male tassels, which continue to shed fertile pollen for ten to fifteen days, remain in position until the flowering period is over and if at the end of that time the female tassels are still receptive fresh male tassels are set up. After all of the flowers on the female tassel have opened the male tassels are removed. The stalks bearing the female tassels remain in the field until the seed is mature enough to harvest. The seed at the top of the tassel matures first and in view of the fact that it is liable to be blown away by wind the tassel is harvested as soon as the seed at the top begins to blow away.

In such cases as it is not desirable to set up a cross in the field, stalks bearing the female and the male tassels are cut and placed in separate racks. The racks may be placed in the field between rows of cane which are not in flower, or may be placed in the greenhouse. The cross is set up in the same manner as in the field, the racks being placed side by side and the male tassels arranged slightly above the females and securely tied in place. After the female flowers have been pollenated the male tassels are removed and the female tassels retained in the racks until the seed matures. Twenty-five to thirty days elapse before the seed matures, and during this period the stalks are kept alive in the solution of sulphurous acid.

One of the male tassels used in a cross, which would be self-fertilized as a result of its having both fertile eggs and fertile pollen, is retained as a check upon the fertility of its pollen. If the seed produced by this tassel is viable it is reasonably certain that the flowers of the female tassels have been fertilized by fertile pollen from the male tassels used.

Cross-fertilization is the method usually followed in breeding new varieties but self-fertilization, that is, the pollenization of the fertile eggs of the flowers of male tassels by fertile pollen from the same tassel, is frequently resorted to especially in the case of male parents which possess unusually favorable characteristics.

Handling and Germinating Sugarcane Seed

The terms sugarcane "seed" and "seed cane" are frequently misused and the difference between them should be clearly understood. Sugarcane seed denotes the actual seed produced by the sexual union of the male cell, or sperm, and the female cell, or egg, following fertilization of the female cell by fertile

(Continued on page 6.)

pollen and is comparable to the seed produced from grass, rice, corn, and other plants. The propagation of sugarcane by sugarcane seed is called sexual reproduction. "Seed cane" denotes the stalks of sugarcane, or cuttings of the stalks bearing one or more buds, or "eyes," used for planting in connection with the propagation or commercial culture of sugarcane. This method of reproducing sugarcane is called a sexual or vegetative propagation.

Sugarcane seed is never used for commercial planting because it is difficult to obtain, is not very fertile, retains its viability for only a comparatively short period of time, and does not reproduce true to type. Each sugar cane seed, no matter whether produced as the result of self-fertilization or cross-fertilization, upon germinating gives rise to a new variety of sugarcane and, therefore, the seed is used in connection with the production of new varieties only.

The total number of seeds germinated each year throughout all of the countries in which sugarcane breeding is carried on runs into the millions and from the myriads of seedlings produced a few of the most promising ones are selected for commercial trial. It is by this method that disease-resisting, high sugar yielding varieties particularly adapted for culture under conditions existing in various countries in which cane is grown have been and are being produced. Once a variety is produced it can be propagated true to type for an indefinite period of years by planting cuttings or "seed cane." All of the cane of a single variety, even though it may be planted to thousands of acres, came from a single sugarcane seed.

The sugarcane tassels which have been self or cross-fertilized are harvested as soon as the seed at the top of the tassel is mature, and placed in paper or muslin bags to dry. The bags are placed in the sun and the tassels are frequently turned in order to facilitate drying. If the weather is unfavorable the tassels are dried by artificial means. It is necessary to thoroughly dry the tassels in order to permit easy separation of the seed but drying must be completed in eight or ten days because the viability of the seed is liable to decrease if it is stored for a longer time. Each seed is surrounded by the glumes, at the base of which are many fine silky hairs which completely surround them. A mass of unthreshed sugarcane seed has the appearance of a mass of short silky fibers, and is sometimes called "fluff," or "fuzz." The seed itself is golden yellow in color and extremely small.

In Florida, sugarcane seed is planted in the greenhouse. About three inches of moist, sterilized muck soil is placed in a "flat," or box, 16 by 22 inches and 4 inches deep, and a layer of unthreshed seed about one-fourth inch in depth is spread over it and lightly pressed in order to bring it closely in contact with the soil. The mat of unthreshed seed has somewhat the appearance of a slightly soiled layer of raw cotton. A little sterilized muck soil is sprinkled over the surface and the seed is watered. The seed must be kept thoroughly moist but if the soil is permitted to become soggy it is liable to rot and, therefore, it must be sprinkled lightly several times each day. The seed begins to germinate in four or five days but if none of it germinates after ten or fifteen days the "flat" is discarded.

Formerly, all seed was planted in an unthreshed condition but it has been ascertained that much more satisfactory results are obtained if threshed seed is

(Continued on page 8)

planted. Planting threshed seed not only permits contact of all of the seed with the soil but greatly lessens the danger of growth of harmful fungi, the frequent appearance, of which in the mat of un-threshed seed resulted in loss of seed and seedlings. A recent valuable improvement in technique permits of the satisfactory separation of the seed from the glumes and fine silky hairs and threshed seed is now ordinarily used for planting. The seed is scattered over the surface of the moist, sterilized muck in a "flat" and lightly pressed into the soil. The seeds are lightly sprinkled several times each day and if they are fertile they will germinate in three or four days.

When the seeds germinate they send up a single blade which has the appearance of grass. Several thousands of seed are planted in each flat but only a small percentage of them are fertile and even in the case of good germination—when the flat has the appearance of a newly planted lawn—there may be not more than 1500 to 2000 seedlings. The number of seedlings varies greatly depending upon the fertility of the seed, and in some of the flats no seedlings appear, in others there may be from 10 to 20 seedlings, and in others from 100 to 2000 seedlings.

Care and Selection of Sugarcane Seedlings

Young sugarcane seedlings grow slowly at first but after six or eight weeks their root systems have developed sufficiently to permit the transfer of individual seedlings from the "flats" in which the seed was germinated to small pots. At that time the seedlings are usually from four to six inches tall. In view of the great number of seedlings produced each season, the total number of which from all of the crosses made may range as high as 60,000, it is not practicable to attempt to pot a large percentage of them, and the usual procedure is to pot 200 of the most vigorous seedlings from the best crosses and 100 from other crosses. As many as 6000 individual seedlings may be potted each season.

The seedlings are transplanted in four-inch flower pots filled with sterilized muck soil, thoroughly watered, and the pots placed upon benches in a greenhouse. The seedlings are watered at least twice each day and are frequently lightly cultivated throughout the six or eight weeks during which they remain in the pots. At the end of this period the seedlings are about a foot in height, have developed good root systems, and have usually developed several suckers. During May and June they are transferred to the field nursery, care being taken to avoid disturbing the soil around the roots, where they are planted in rows in which the seedlings are spaced 4½ feet apart. The plants ordinarily continue to grow at a normal rate, and from this time on the care and culture of the seedlings is the same as for plants grown from cuttings.

Sugarcane reaches full growth and maturity in from twelve to fourteen months from the time that the seed is formed and, therefore, at Canal Point, Florida, it is January or February of the following year before final selection of seedlings for field trial may be made. Study of the seedlings is begun when the young plants are potted and is continued until the final selections are made. Each seedling is studied as an individual, and all of the seedlings from each cross are studied as a group in order to deter-

(Concluded on page 10)

mine the value of the cross and the advisability of making further crosses with the parent varieties which were used. The following characters are studied for each seedling transferred from the pots to the field nursery: Number of stalks in the stool, height and diameter of stalk, pithiness of stalk, erectness of stalk, width of leaves, erectness of leaves, stripping, vigor and general habit of growth, and apparent resistance to mosaic and other diseases. Seedlings possessing the most promising characteristics are selected and are further examined for specific gravity of the stalk and total solids (Brix) in the juice. When this data has been obtained the temporary selections are again examined upon a basis of the above-mentioned characters and final selection is made upon a basis of the seedlings which possess the most promising characteristics. The varieties finally selectedare given "C.P." numbers and cuttings of them are shipped to the U. S. Sugar Plant Field Station at Houma, La.; to the Louisiana Agricultural Experiment Station at Baton Rouge, La., and to the U. S. Sugar Plant Field Laboratory at Cairo, Georgia, for propagation and for trial in comparison with the varieties grown commercially in these states. Trials of the varieties for commercial culture in Florida are also carried on by the Agronomic Division of the U. S. Sugar Plant Field Station at Canal Point, Florida.

List of Members of the American Sugar Cane League of the U. S. A., Inc., Who Have Paid Their Dues· for the Year 1931

Abadie, Gaston
Accardo, Nick & Sons
Achee, Samuel P.
Ackal & Ben Placide
Ackal & Paul Placide
Ackers, Charles
Ackers, Henry
Ackers, William
Acme Veneer Co.
Acosta, Mack
Acosta, Olivan
Adam, August
Adams, Alfred
Adams, Arthur
Adams, Eddie
Adams, Ives
Adeline Sugar Factory Co.
Adras & Anitus
Aiken, Albert
Aguillard, J. M.
Albert, Cleque
Alciatore & Leon Celestin
Alciator & Elphege Datis
Alciator & Theodore Guillot
Alciatore & Ursin Guillot
Alciator, Jules
Alciator & Olgus Maturin
Alciator & H. Meloncon
Alciatore & Anatole Sonnier
Alciatore & Clement Sonnier
Alexandre, Albert
Alexander, Daniel
Alexander, Dave
Alexander, Ernest
Alexander, George
Alexander, Joseph
Alexander, Polerin
Alexander, Victor
Alexander, Walter
Alexis, Guillaume
Alfred, Louis
Alleman, Adam
Allemand, Alex.
Ally & Braquet
American Bank & Trust Co.
American Cyanamid Co.
American Molasses Company
Anderson, Mrs. Jacob
Andra, F.
Andrews, Nicholas
Angelle, Darnley
Angelle & Duplecien
Angelle, Gaston
Angelle, Lucien
Angelle, Paul, Jr.
Angelle, Paul, Sr.
Anita Planting Co.
Anselmo, Sam
Anthony, Amos
Anthony, Antoine & Shaw & Fed. Cr. Assn.
Anthony & Boutte
Anthony & Co.
Anthony & Federal Credit Assn.
Anthony, George
Anthony, Joe & Shaw & Fed. Cr. Assn.
Anthony, Neville
Anthony, Roosevelt
Anthony & Rice Gro. Cr. Assn.
Anti-Rust Paint Co. of La.
Antin, Joe & Wm. Chauvin
Antoine & Shaw
Arboneaux, Howard
Arcement, Albert
Arcement, Willie
Arceneaux, Alexis
Arceneaux, Geo. D.
Arceneaux, Ives
Archange, Lucy
Armantor & Derouen
Armantor, Rodney
Arthur & Paye
Ascension Auto Company
Aucoin, L. & G.
August, Ignace
Autin, Gibson
Aymar & Ransonet
Babin, Albert
Babin, A. R. & Blouin
Babin, Ashlie & Richard
Babin, Ashville
Babin, Belonie
Babin, C. & A. C. Duboin
Babin, Clovis
Babin, Deonie
Babin, G. P.
Babin, J. E.
Babin, Lucien
Babin, Luke B.
Babin, Marcellin
Babin, Phillips
Babin, S. B.
Babin, T.
Babin, W. A.

Babineaux, Joseph
Badeaux, E. J.
Baez, David
Bailey, J. H.
Baker, L. P.
Baker, R. L.
Banasto, Chita
Bank of St. Martinville
Banker, M. J.
Banks & Williams
Baptiste, Emile
Barabin, Abraham & Rose Peyton
Barbier, Alcide
Barbier, Ernest
Barker Barge Line
Barnes, Henry
Barnes, Henry & V. Jones
Baronne, Frank
Barras, A.
Barras, Alex, Jr.
Barras & Breaux
Barras, Charles
Barras, Darneville
Barras, Edward
Barras, J. B. & Bro.
Barras, John
Barras, Wilfred
Barrilleaux, A.
Barrilleaux, Alphonse
Barrilleaux & Breaux
Barrilleaux, G. & Sons
Barrilleaux, Henry H.
Barrilleaux & Picard
Barrios, Joseph
Barron, Mrs. B.
Barrs, Henry
Barton, P. B.
Bastion, Paul
Battaglia & Broussard
Battaglia, Joe
Battaglio, Leonard
Battalia & LeGrange
Baudin, F. & Babin
Baudoin, F. & LeBlanc
Bay Chemical Co., Inc.
Baye, Joseph
Bayer, Alexander
Bayer, John
Bazet, R. A.
Beatty, Willie
Beaullieu, Frank
Beck, James D.
Becnel, Estate Antoine
Becnel, Charles
Becnel & Pillara
Becnel, Robert
Begnaud, Donadien
Begnaud, Narcisse
Belanger, Adam
Belanger, James G.
Belanger, Joachin
Belanier, Alcee
Belisle, C. A.
Bell, Dave
Bellanger, Leo
Bellanger, Mitchell
Belle Terre, Inc.
Bend Field Plantation
Bennett, Albert
Benoit, Felicien
Benoit, Est. Jos.
Benoit, Leonce
Benoit, Noah
Benoit, Wilfred
Beorque & Armantor
Beorque, Frank
Berard, Aleus
Berard & LeBlanc
Berard, Louie
Berard, Simon
Berard, Walter
Bergeron, Alcide
Bergeron, George
Bergeron, Mrs. Joseph
Bergeron, Olivier
Bergeron, Paul
Bergeron, Willie
Bernard, Carlos, Jr.
Bernard, Charles & C. O. Chaisson
Bernard, Dumas
Bernard, Edwin
Bernard, Ignace
Bernard & LeBlanc
Bernard, Rouel
Bernard, Tom
Bernard, Willie
Bernis, Alexie
Bernis, Cyrus
Bernis, E. J.
Bertrand, Charles
Bertrand, Emahuel
Bertrand, Harriet
Bertrand, L.

Bertrand, Lastie
Bertrand & Patin
Beuche, Rene
Beyt, J. L.
Bijeaux, Achille
Bijeaux, Joseph
Bienvenu, Mrs. P. A.
Billeaud Sugar Factory
Bilello, Anthony
Bilello, Chas.
Billew, William
Bishop, P. G.
Bizette, Francis
Black, Robert
Blanchard, Adam
Blanchard, Adrien
Blanchard, Alfred
Blanchard, Ambroise
Blanchard, Caesaire
Blanchard, E. D., Sr.
Blanchard & Gonsoulin
Blanchard, Mrs. Joe
Blanchard Planting Co., Ltd.
Blanchet, Mrs. M. & Wilson Landry
Blaze, Elie & Cyrus DeBlane
Blouin, Joseph
Blum, Leopold
Boas & Evans
Boatner, C. J.
Bodin, Claerfalt
Bodin, Denis & J. O.
Bodin, Fernand
Bodin, Gregoire
Bodin, Joseph B.
Bodin, J. U.
Bodin, Est. Jules O.
Bodin, Paul
Bodin, Robert
Bodin, Severin
Bomer-Blanks Lumber Co.
Bonin, Alcide
Bonin, Anatole
Bonin, Anatole, Jr.
Bonin, Camille
Bonin, Deluke & Fage
Bonin, Eraste
Bonin, F. & Fages
Bonin, Pelicien
Bonin, F. & First National Bank
Bonin & Terradet
Bonin, Ulysse
Boniol, W. C.
Borel, Adrien
Borel, Charles
Borel, Hervilitan
Borne Bros.
Bory, C.
Boudoin, Merille
Boudreaux, Adrien
Boudreaux, Albert
Boudreaux, Alcide
Boudreaux, Alex.
Boudreaux, Aroema
Boudreaux, Blanchard
Boudreaux Bros.
Boudreaux, Charles C.
Boudreaux, Clophas
Boudreaux & Delaune
Boudreaux, M.
Boudreaux, F. & Hebert
Boudreaux, Fosten
Boudreaux, Fostin
Boudreaux, Fosten & Mrs. Clay
Boudreaux, Homer
Boudreaux, J. F.
Boudreaux, John F.
Boudreaux, John K.
Boudreaux, Joseph
Boudreaux, Lawless
Boudreaux, Lenes & Ed Meyers
Boudreaux, Leo
Boudreaux, Nathan J.
Boudreaux, Nelson J.
Boudreaux, Oda & Ed. Meyers
Boudreaux, Oleus
Boudreaux, Oneal
Boudreaux, Sabin
Boudreaux, Ulysses
Bourda, Anthony & Policar, J.
Bourda, Charles
Bourda, Louis
Bourg, John
Bourg, Oscar A.
Bourgeois, Carlyle
Bourgeois, Charles
Bourgeois, Claude
Bourgeois, Donate
Bourgeois & Mrs. Dugas
Bourgeois, E. F.
Bourgeois & Falgout
Bourgeois, Ferdinand & Falgout
Bourgeois, Mrs. Jos.

Bourgeois, Mrs. Joe & Wilson Hartman
Bourgeois, Julia
Bourgeois, K.
Bourgeois & McGowan
Bourgeois, Rene
Bourgeois, S. J.
Bourgeois & Smith
Bourgeois, St. Paul
Bourgeois, St. Paul & Domingues
Bourgeois, St. Paul & Joseph
Bourgeois, Taylor & Breaux
Bourgeois, Taylor & Falgout
Bourgeois & Toupa
Bourgeois, Wilfred
Bourk, Daniel
Bourk, Mrs. Simillian
Bourk, Suberbielle
Bourque, Augustin
Bourque, Jean
Bourreague, Rene
Boutte & Abadie
Boutte, August
Boutte, Charles
Boutte, Clovis & Ansler
Boutte, E. M.
Boutte, Fernest
Boutte, H. C., R. Dupleix & Mrs. Blanchet
Boutte, Joe
Boutte, Loreal
Boutte, Mary
Boutte, Mose.
Boutte, Oscar
Boutte, Remus & L. Boutte
Boutte, Remus & L. LeBlanc
Boutte, Rene
Boutte, Sidney
Boutte, Zenor
Boyance, Dellas
Boyance, Dulva
Boyance, Willie
Boyard, Lamont
Boyd & Blaze
Boyd, Wm.
Boye, Alexzon
Boye, Gabriel
Brame, Chester E.
Braquet & Dugas
Braquet, Henry
Braquet, J. J.
Braquet & Oubre
Braquet & Prince
Braquet, Willie
Brassieu, Noah
Braud, Calice
Braud, Charles
Braud, Dennis
Braud, Dorza
Braud, Emile
Braud, Frederick
Braud & Mire
Braud, Ulysses
Brazan, Louis
Breaux, Ademar
Breaux, Alfred
Breaux, Arthur
Breaux & DeBlane
Breaux, E. & Stewart
Breaux, Elie
Breaux, Felix
Breaux, Ferdinand
Breaux, Ferdinand & Gonsoulin
Breaux, Ferdinand & Son
Breaux, Geo. & Theodore Pellerin
Breaux, Giles & Morceline LeBlanc
Breaux & Gonsoulin
Breaux, H. A. & Louviere
Breaux, Harry
Breaux, Ignace
Breaux, Mrs. Lizin & Son
Breaux, Luzin
Breaux, Pierre
Breaux & Weeks
Breaux, Whitney
Brien, A. E.
Brou, C. & Sons
Brou, F. & H.
Broussard, Adolph
Broussard, Allison & Alberta Lewis
Broussard, Alpha
Broussard, Amand
Broussard, Armand
Broussard, Armand & Dugas
Broussard, Arnold
Broussard, Arnold & Willie Thomas
Broussard, Aromis & Bonin
Broussard, B. B.
Broussard, Bernard
Broussard & Bonin

Broussard, Charles
Broussard, Clarence
Broussard, Clomaire
Broussard, Damas
Broussard, Damas, Jr.
Broussard & Derouen
Broussard, Eddie
Broussard, Edmond
Broussard, Elick
Broussard, Everard
Broussard, F. O.
Broussard, Guilman
Broussard & Guesser
Broussard, H. C. & Aikens
Broussard, Homer
Broussard, Isaac
Broussard, Mrs. J. O. & Landry
Broussard & James
Broussard, John
Broussard & Jones
Broussard, Joseph
Broussard, Jules
Broussard, Laodice
Broussard, Lodice & S.
Broussard, Loto
Broussard, Lucien
Broussard, Marcel
Broussard, Martin
Broussard, Mignes & Gordy
Broussard, Neuville
Broussard, Numa
Broussard, Odey & Nic Delcambre
Broussard, Otto
Broussard, P. E.
Broussard, Pearl
Broussard, Philo & L. Broussard
Broussard, Pierre
Broussard, Prosper
Broussard, Renie
Broussard & Savoy
Broussard, Severin
Broussard, Simeon
Broussard, Sims
Broussard, Theobal
Broussard, Whitney
Broussard, Willie
Brown, Ashmond
Brown, George
Brown, William
Bruce, Emile & Joseph
Bruns, Joe
Brupbacher, Robert
Bryant, F. E.
Bubenzer, H. K.
Bugg, T. H.
Bullion, J. R.
Burden Bros.
Burguieres, The J. M. Co., Ltd.
Burguieres, Jules M.
Burleigh, Robert
Burke, Walter J.
Burrowes, H. S.
Butler, Bazel
Butler, Louis & Robert Stuart
Caballero, Augustin
Caesaire & LeBlanc
Cage, John
Caire, E. J.
Caire & Graugnard
Callahan, D.
Callahan & V. Jones
Callahan, Leo
Callegan, A. & Sons
Callegan, E. & Sons
Callegan, Sylvester
Callegan, Willie
Callier, David
Calois, Alfred
Calois, George
Calois, O.
Calumet Plantation
Cambre, Edwin
Canal Bank & Trust Co.
Cantrelle, Paul
Carnell, Victor
Caronna, Martin
Caronna, Martin & Amy
Carrier, Arthur
Carrier, Leonce
Carrier, Dallas
Carrouche, Frank J.
Carter, Celestin
Carticuglia, Sam
Caruso, L.
Casseigne, P. A.
Castagnos Cane Loader Co., Inc.
Castille, James
Catalan, Oscar
Catalano, Arthur
Catalone, Frank
Catherine Sugar Co., Inc.
Caville, Alexcide
Celestin, Huval
Celestine Plantation, Inc.
Central Farms & Shipping Co.

Chaission, C. O.
Chaission, C. O. & Chas. Bernard
Chaission, C. O. & James Toups, Jr.
Chaisson, Guy
Chaisson, Horace
Chaisson, Ives
Chaisson, Joe M.
Chaisson, Joe M. & Mrs. Marie Borbier
Chaisson, Leon
Chaisson, Zepherin
Chalmette Petroleum Corp.
Champagne, Albert
Champagne, Alces
Champagne, Arcadie
Champagne & Davis
Champagne, Denis, Jr.
Champagne, Dennis, Sr.
Champagne, Devillier
Champagne, Dewey
Champagne & Frederick
Champagne, George
Champagne, John
Champagne, Jos.
Champagne, L. J.
Champagne & Louis
Champagne, Robert D.
Champagne, Willie
Chaney, L. C.
Charles, John
Charles, Joseph & Broussard
Charles, Murphy
Charles, Steven
Charley & Shaw & Fed. Cr. Assn.
Charpentier & Chauvin
Charpentier, Edwin J.
Charpentier, F. & R. P. Duplantis
Charpentier, F. & T. Duplantis
Charpentier, Frank
Chastant, Evalture
Chastagbuerm, Ozar
Chastant & Blanchard
Chastant & Toups
Chastant & Doucette
Chauvin, Clay
Chauvin, William
Chenovert, F.
Chequelin, S. G.
Chotin, Andre
Chotin, Eclide
Christy, Ed.
Christy, Eugene
Christy, Fred & Marchand
Christy, J. P.
Christy, W. A.
Christy, Wilford
Christy & Wilson
Cinclare Central Factory
Citizen, M.
Clark, Albert & Francis
Clause, O. & C.
Clause, O. & C. Tenant
Clement & Wooster
Cline, J. F.
Cline, W. M.
Clements, Joe
Cline, Fred
Clotida Plantation
Clovelly Farms
Coates, C. E.
Coe, Dana G.
Cole, Clifton
Coles, J. B.
Colia & Landry
Colia & Williams
Collette, A. & F. Freud
Collette, Ansmore
Colietti, Ross
Colthrop, L. H.
Comeaux, Adolph
Comeaux, Adolph & Jessie Evans
Comeaux, Camille
Comeaux, Entine
Comeaux, L. J.
Comeaux, O. D.
Comeaux, Ophil
Connor, Edgar
Continiglia, Sam
Conrad, J. J.
Consolidated Companies, Inc.
Cooper, H. E. & Jenkins
Cooper, L. & Christy
Cooper, L. & York
Cooper, Jim & E. LeGrange
Cormier, Paul
Cornier, Charles
Cornish, Mose
Costello, Carlton
Costello, Lewis
Costello, Lewis & Mrs. Lee Gonsoulin
Costello, Octave
Courts, F. F.
Courville, Henry

Courville, Mrs. Louis
Crapito Brothers
Cremaldo, Cosimo
Cretien, Prosper
Crochet & Braquet
Crochet & Crochet
Crochet, Dennis
Crochet, Robert
Crochet, Romain
Crochet, Stanley
Crochet, Wilfred
Crofton, Joe
Cureau, C.
Curet, A. B.
Cushenbury, Bill
Cutrera, Joe
Dagethare, Alcie
Daigle, Albert
Daigle, Aurelian
Daigle, Crepin
Daigle, Jules
Daigle, Lucien
Daigle, Oseme & Joe Daigle
Daigle, Oseme & Pierre Barrios
Daigle & Sears
Daigle, Webster
Daigre, Joe
Daily & Roady
Daisy, Tom
Danos, Clement
Danos, Joseph
Dansereau, H. C.
Darby, Ferdinand
Darby & Gajan
Darby, Jules
Dargradingo, Arthur
Darville & Christy
Darville, James
Darville, John
Daucet & Kling
Daunis, Edgar
Dauphine, Ladie
Dauset, Ramie & Braquet
Dautreuille, Martin
David, Alphee
David, Augustin & LeBlanc
David & Cormier
David, Edwin
David & Hill
David, Lamartine
David & Laurent
David & Lee
David, Phillius
David, Sallustin
David, Theo.
David, Theo. & L. Bourque
David, Theo. & J. Garden
David, Theo. & Paul Proveaux
Davis, Henry
Davis, Rufus
DeBlanc & Anthony
DeBlanc, Cyrus
DeBlanc, David
DeBlanc & Emare
DeBlanc, Geo. & Armair Broussard
DeBlanc, Geo. & Tom Kilegan
DeBlanc, & Johnny Owen
DeBlanc & Tom
Debonie & Fyge
Decuir, A. C.
Decuir, A. C. & David Baez
Decuir & Bourque
Decuir, F. & Broussard
Decuir & Granger
Decuir & Mouton
Decuir, Oscar
Decuir, Wm. & Jefferson
Dejean, Leonard
Delahoussaye, Augustin, Mrs.
Delahoussaye, Frank
Delahoussaye & Legnon
Delatte, John M.
Delaune, E. A.
Delaune, Elvira, Miss
Delaune, Fred
Delaune, J. N.
Delaune & Johnson
Delaune, Melvin
Delaune, S. J.
Delaune, T. J.
Delaune, Max V.
Delbert, A. F.
Delcambre, Albert
Delcambre & Decuir
Delcambre, Ignes
Delcambre, Onelia
Delcambre, Rudolph
Delcambre, Whitney
Demus, A. L.
Denova, Angelos
Derouen, Ackling & A. Boutte
Derouen, Ackling & Aurelien LeBlanc
Derouen, Alfred
Derouen, Alfred, Jr.
Derouen, Alfred & Ned
McIlhenny

Derouen, Alphee & Co.
Derouen & Aristie
Derouen & Boudreaux
Derouen & Broussard
Derouen & Clairphe
Derouen, Claude
Derouen & Comeaux
Derouen & Eorard
Derouen & Eraste
Derouen & Estie
Derouen & Ferdinaud
Derouen & Gilbert
Derouen, Hameton & Blanchard
Derouen, Harrison
Derouen, Joseph
Derouen & Joseph
Derouen & Kerlegan
Derouen & Leonce
Derouen & Lockhous
Derouen & Louis
Derouen & Nelson
Derouen & Nora
Derouen, Oneil
Derouen & Paul
Derouen & Pine
Derouen & Prevost
Derouen, Mrs. Treville
Derouen & Viator
Derouen, Wilson
Derouen, Wright & Simons
Desarmeaux, Demas
Desermeaux, Sidney & Westley Bodin
Deslatte, Arthur
Deslattes, Mrs. Clay
Deslatte & DeBlanc
Deslattes, Robert & Cyrus DeBlanc
DiBenedetto, Frank
Dickinson, E. F.
Dies, Chris, Jr.
Dies, Moise
Dile, Agnes
Dill, Wm. A.
Dionne, Leodias
Dipuma, Carlo
Dixon, C. B.
Dixon, John
Dixon, Wm.
Dodds, H. H.
Dodson, W. R.
Doherty, Thomas
Doiron, Emile
Doiron, Numa
Dolsey & Geoffray
Domergeaux, Antoine
Domingue, A.
Dominick, Hillans
Dominick & Blanchard
Dominick, Clmae
Dominick, Clet
Dominick, Cora
Dominick & Donnel
Dominick, Elsia
Dominique, Oniel
Dominick, Porteuls
Dominick, William
Dominique, Lawrence
Donaldson, Theo.
Donier, J. A.
Dore, Silvien
Doriet, E. & Eugene Dupuy
Dornier, Felix
Dornier, Jos. R.
Doucet & Braquet
Doucette & Chastant
Douzette & Kling
Drake, Willie
Dressel, Emile
Dubois Bros. & Guilliot
Dubois, Clovis
Ducos, Mrs. Elie
Duet, Donatien
Duff, F. Deane
Dufrene, Alfred
Dufrene, Ulysses
Dugas, A. & Ganucheau
Dugas, Anthony
Dugas, Antoine
Dugas, Armas
Dugas & Broussard
Dugas, Carlos
Dugas, Chas.
Dugas, Charles & Bonin
Dugas, Clesme
Dugas, Dennis
Dugas, Dennis & Ganuchaux
Dugas, Dumas
Dugas, Edwin
Dugas, Edwin & Father
Dugas & F. Elico
Dugas, Elie
Dugas, Ernest
Dugas, Euclide
Dugas, Gilbert & A. C. Duboin
Dugas, Henry
Dugas, Ide
Dugas, Joe & Ganucheau
Dugas & LeBlanc, Ltd.

Jaccuzza, Joe
Jack, Horace
Jacko, Leon
Jackson, J. M.
Jackson, Louisa
Jackson, Mine
Jacob, Willie
Jacobs, Joseph
Jacquet & Broussard
Jacquet, Willie
James, Arthur
James & Becnel
James, C. I.
James, Cornelius
James, Fergust
James, J. N.
James, Jos.
James, Louis
James & Morse
James & Murry
Jarreau, Alberic
Jarreau, Alfred
Jarreau, Aristide
Jarreau, Joseph
Jarreau, Numa
Jarreau, Raphael
Jarreau, Richard
Jeanerette Lumber & Shingle Co.
Jean Louis & Anthony
Jean Louis, Bridget
Jean Louis, Camelia & Jean Louis
Jean Louis, Peter
Jean Louis, Pierre
Jean Louis, Pierre & Anthony
Jean Louis & Son
Jean Minuette & Boutte
Jean Minuette, E. T.
Jean Minuette & Landry
Jean Minuette, Ulger
Jeanpierre, Alfred
Jeanpierre, Batiste
Jeanpierre, D.
Jefferson, E. C.
Jefferson & LeBlanc
Jeffrey, Robert
Jenkins, Harry
Jenkins, Mary
Jennings, Ludd
Jernigan, Wm. P., Jr.
Jewell, Emanuel
Jewell, J. L.
Joe & Marcel
John & Bernard

Johnson, Albert
Johnson, Allen
Johnson, Eddie
Johnson, Eddie & V. Jones
Johnson, Henderson
Johnson, Henry
Johnson, W. H.
Johnson, Willie
Jones, D. & Alcide Goulas
Jones, Freeman
Jones, Isaac
Jones, Josh
Jones & Laughlin Steel Corp.
Jones, LeBon
Jones, LeBen & Regis LeGrange
Jones, Lulu
Jones, Oseme
Jones, Paul F.
Jones, Peter
Jones, Peter & Mrs. Louis Levy
Jones, V.
Jones & Vincent
Joseph, Alle
Joseph, Armond
Joseph, H. & Landry
Joseph, Pierce
Joseph, Pierre
Joseph, W. & Landry
Judice, Clovice
Judice, Delma
Judice, E. J.
Judice, Emplis
Judice, Enoe
Judice, George
Judice, Guilliam
Judice, Gustave
Judice, Leed
Judice, Mrs. Mary Ann & Caronna
Judice, Octave
Judice, Paul
Judice, Rene
Judice, Willie
Julmire & Judice
Kahao, M. J.
Kahn, Emile
Kappel, A. C.
Karlegan, A. & DeBlanc
Kearny, J. Watts & Sons
Keen, John R.
Keller, A. J.
Keller, L. & Co.
Kelley, Shafter & George Placide
Kennison, Noah

Kern, Sidney
Kibbe & Romero
Kidder, Alverez
Kidder, Lester
Kilgore Plantation
Kimbrough Sons, Inc.
King, Tom
Klibert, Marie
Kliempeter, Leon R.
Kleinpeter, T. G.
Kling, Derouen & A. Boutte
Kling & Borodeaux
Kling & G. Segura
Kling & Walet & Felix Abraham
Kling & Walet & Dugas
Kling & Walet & Alcede Green
Kling & Walet & Bernard Green
Kling & Walet & Edward Green
Kling & Walet & Arrel Louviere
Kling & Walet & Bertin Louviere
Kling & Walet & Ovide Louviere
Kling & Walet & Sedeol Louviere
Kling & Walet & George Oubre
Kling & Walet & Junius Oubre
Kling & Walet & Archie Polk
Kling & Walet & Saterfield Polk
Kling & Walet & Eugler Segura
Klots, Sol
Knatt, Morning
Knight, Allen
Knobloch, Charles
Knobloch, D. & E.
Knobloch, G. & M.
Knobloch, T. J.
Koeh, C. J.
Kocke, Elray
Kramer, Jos. F.
Kramer, Wilbur H.
Kreiger, William, Mrs.
LaBauve, T. A.
LaBauve, Ursin & Son
Labbee, Jos.
Labello, Jack
Labiche, Desire
Labiche, Milton
Labiche, Numa
Labiche, Numa & Mrs. Bonin
Labiche, Numa & D. Boudier
LaGrange, Henry
Lagarde, Klebert

Lagarde, L. & P.
Lagrange & Braquet
LaGrange, Placide
Lalande, Angelas
Lalande, Rossana
Lalande, T. D.
Lanaux, O. J.
Lanclos, Alex.
Lanclos, Ben
Lanclos, Colon
Lanclos, Leonce
Lancon, Albert
Lancon, Alcide
Lancon, Alphonse
Lancon, Antoine
Lancon, Charlie
Lancon, Charley & Alberta Lewis
Lancon, Charles, Jr., & Alberta Lewis
Lancon, Lucien
Lancon, Luke
Lancon, Mrs. P.
Lancos & Mrs. Halleman
Lancy, Ida
Landry, A.
Landry, Abadee
Landry & Abel
Landry, Albert
Landry, Amilcar
Landry, A. O.
Landry, Aristide
Landry & Badeaux
Landry & Bourgue
Landry & Baudlon
Landry & Boyance
Landry & Broussard
Landry, Camille
Landry & Carrol
Landry & Champagne
Landry & Chanley
Landry, Clarence
Landry, Clet
Landry, Clet & Braquet
Landry & Cliford
Landry & Clotis
Landry & Comeaux
Landry & Cormier
Landry & Deneause
Landry & Drosin
Landry, Elie
Landry, E. N. & A. G.
Landry, Ernest
Landry, Eulgere
Landry, Everard

Landry, Felix
Landry, Fernand
Landry, F. U.
Landry, G.
Landry, Mrs. G. & Eddie
Landry, Gaston
Landry, Henry
Landry & Jackson
Landry, Joseph
Landry, Joseph No. 2
Landry, J. T.
Landry & Langlinais
Landry & Laviolette
Landry & LeBlanc
Landry, Leon J.
Landry, Leo
Landry, Leonard
Landry, Leuce
Landry & Lopez
Landry, Louis
Landry, Louis & Bernadette
Landry, Louis & Braquet
Landry, Ludovice
Landry & Meyers
Landry & Miguez
Landry, Neles
Landry, Neville
Landry & Oliva
Landry & Pesson
Landry, Philip
Landry & Pierre
Landry & Reaux
Landry & Renard
Landry, Rufus & Landry
Landry, Sam
Landry & Segura
Landry, Sims
Landry & Smith
Landry, Telles
Landry, Theo. E.
Landry, T. J.
Landry & Trahan
Landry, Ulger
Landry, Ulysse
Landry, Ulysse & Champagne
Landry, Ussah
Landry & Vallot
Landry, Wallace
Landry & Walter
Landry, Will B.
Landry, Will B. & Shaw
Landry & Willie
Landry & Williams
Langlois, Alex
Langlois, Gaston

Langlois, Roselus
Lanier, Mrs. J. A.
Lannie & Smith
Lanoux, Ambrose
Lanoux & Dorville
Lanoux, O. J.
Lapelle, Albert J.
Laparouse, Expodie
Laperouse, Fred
Lapeyrouse, Adolph
Laport, Antoine
LaSalle, Mrs. C. L. & M. Dorris
Lashbrook, Mrs. May P.
Lasseigne, Alphonse
Lasseigne, Clet
Lasseigne, Lucien
Lasseigne, Vallery
Lastra, Alex.
Latiolais, Aldus
Latiolais, Clebert
Latiolais, Clerbert
Latiolais, Oscar
Latiolais, Pierre
Latour, Laurence
Laurel Ridge P. & M. Co.
Laurel Valley Sugars, Inc.
Laviolette, Dolsy
Laviolet, Emile
Laviolette, Laureal
Lawless, Wm.
Lawrason, Chas. M.
Laws, Harry L. & Co.
Laws & LeBlanc
Lebeau, Amilcar
Lebeau, Hazael
LeBlanc, Abel
LeBlanc, Albert J.
LeBlanc, Alcie & Simon
LeBlanc, Arthur
LeBlanc & Bernard
LeBlanc, Blanc
LeBlanc & Chastant
LeBlanc, Claude & Burleigh
LeBlanc, Clebert
LeBlanc, Clement
LeBlanc, Clifford & Burleigh
LeBlanc, Delno
LeBlanc, Dortles
LeBlanc, Duprelon
LeBlanc, Edgar
LeBlanc, Edral
LeBlanc & Emare
LeBlanc, Ernest B.
LeBlanc, E. J.

LeBlanc, Etis
LeBlanc, Mrs. Euphine
LeBlanc, Evariste
LeBlanc, Felix
LeBlanc, George
LeBlanc, Harrington
LeBlanc, J. Clarence
LeBlanc, J. B.
LeBlanc, E. & Jeanerette Lbr. Co.
LeBlanc & LeBlanc
LeBlanc, Leonard
LeBlanc, Louis
LeBlanc, Lucien
LeBlanc, Madios
LeBlanc & Melancon
LeBlanc, Marceline & Gileq Breaux
LeBlanc, Marceline & Clovis Bourgeois
LeBlanc, Marcellius
LeBlanc, Odie
LeBlanc, P. & A.
LeBlanc, P. D.
LeBlanc, Pierre
Le Blanc, Mrs. Salvador
Le Blanc, Sedatal
LeBlanc & Simon
LeBlanc, Simon & Burleigh
LeBlanc & Smith
LeBlanc, Theophile
LeBlanc & Tom
Le Blanc, Ulysse & Sons
LeBlanc, Wallace
LeBlanc, Wilfred
LeBourgeois Brokerage Co., Inc.
LeBourgeois & Clarence
LeBourgeois, H. W.
LeBourgeois, J. C., Jr.
LeBourgeois, L. P.
LeBourgeois, P. & Henry
LeBourgeois, Raoul
LeBourgeois & Romero
Lecompte, Claude
Ledet, Arsane
Ledet, Augustine
Ledet & Burleigh
Ledet, C. A.
Ledet, Edmond
Ledet, Etienne
Ledet, Felix
Ledet, John
Ledet, Mrs. J. P.
Ledet, Martial

Lee, Alex & DeBlanc
Lee, Junius & DeBlanc
Lee, Noah & DeBlanc
Lee, Willie & DeBlanc
Leed & Mitchell
Lefaux, Ed.
Lege & Vallot
Legendre, Leo
Legget & Dube
Legnon, A. L.
Legnon, Gaston
Legnon, M. & Goldberg
Legnon, T. L.
LeGrange, D.
LeGrange, Emile
LeGrange, Homer
LeGrange, Homer & St. Mary Bank
Leitemeyer, Fred M.
Leitmeyer & Martin
Lejeune, Jos.
Lejeune, J. S. & D.
Lejeunne, O. A.
Lejeunne, O. A. & Deslattes
Lejeunne, W. R.
Leleaux, Lue
Leleux & Bourque
Leleux, Mrs. Delphine
Leleux, Emare
Leleux, Jos. & Jos. Greene
Leleux, Niles
Leleux, Ovide
Leleux, Ozar
Leleux, Paul
Leleux, Theo.
Leleux, U. D.
Lemaire & Trahan
Lemaire, T. C.
Lemann, Percy A.
Lens, Frank
Leonard, Amilcar
Leonard, George
Leonard, Paul
Leonard & Ransonnet
Lepre, Peter
Lett, Frank M.
Levert Bros.
Levert, Ed.
Levert, Shirley Co,
Levert-St. John, Inc.
Levron, Victor
Lewis, Agnes & Bessie
Lewis, Alcia & Armstrong
Lewis, Alcide
Lewis, Alcide, Jr.

Morvant, E. L.
Morvant, Evariste
Moses, Joe
Moss, Asa
Moss, Asa, Jr.
Mouton, Rousseau
Munson, Stephen C.
Murphy, James L.
Murry, Ella
Mustache, Lucas
Myers, Joe
McCarthy, Charles A.
McHugh, James K.
McIlhenny, E. A.
McIntyre, T. T.
Naquin, Arthur
Naquin, Eugene
Naquin, Frank
Naquin, H. B.
Naquin, Leo
Naquin, Leon
Naquin, Leonie
Narcisse, Etienne
National Food Products Co.
Nelson, H. & Dalbor
Nelson, Horace
Nettles, C. H.
Neuville, Eusebe
Neuville, M. O.
New Orleans Coffee Co., Ltd.
Nicaisse & Bernard
Nicholas, Wesley
Nightshed, Jack
Noel, Alcide
Noel, Dalton
Noel, Julien
Noel, Wilfred
Norris, Clemire
Norris & Linnartz
Norris & Touchet
Norton, S.
Oak Alley Farms
Oakhill Plantation
O'Brien, Lillie
O'Brien & Migues
Odom, I. L.
O'Donnell Bros., Inc.
Okey, Chas. W.
Olinde, Etienne
Oliva & Vallo
Oliveor, Geo.
Olivier, Albert
Olivier, Alcide
Olivier, Amadie
Olivier, Archille & Landry

Olivier & Boutte
Olivier, Charles & Gabriel
Olivier & Dalbor
Olivier, Joseph R.
Olivier, Joseph & Legnon
Olivier, Jules
Olivier, Nicaisse
Olivier, Rene
Olivier, Victor
Olivier & Walet
Ontine & Darby
Orange Grove Sugar Co., Inc.
Orgeron, Ernest
Orgeron, Leon
Orgeron, Wilfred
Orphe, Bob
Orphe, Lionel
Oubre & Braquet
Oubre & Dugas
Oubre, Eustace
Oubre, Fernand
Oubre, Joe
Oubre, Laurent
Oubre, Louis
Oubre, Louis & Prince
Oubre, Oscar
Oubre, Price & Grivat
Oubre, Sidney
Oubre & Sons
Oubre, O. & Vaufrey Plantation
Ourso, Fred
Ourso, Martin
Ourso, Robert
Owen, W. L.
Owens, John
Painter, Horace
Palo Alto Co., Inc.
Parent, Daniel
Parent, S. J.
Parent, Mrs. Sim.
Parm, Andrew
Parm, R. A.
Parr, Ernest
Parr, Paul
Parsson & Miguez
Patin, Albin
Patin, Alexis, Jr.
Patin, Aloxson
Patin, Anatole
Patin, Clobus
Patin, George
Patin, Polemon
Patin, Robert
Patin, Sam
Patout & Delahoussaye

Patout, Henry
Patout, M. A. & Son, Ltd.
Patout, Sidney
Patson, Onile & V. Jones
Patterson, C. T. Co., Inc.
Paxton, J. R.
Paye & Arthur
Pellegrin, Theo., Mrs.
Pellegrin, Willie
Pellerin, Edmond
Pellerin, Charles
Pellerin, Mrs. & Ganuchaux
Pelletier, Fernand
Peltier, C.
Peltier, Leo & Ganuchaux
Peltier, V. & Sons
Penick & Ford, Limited, Inc.
Pepper, Clarence
Pepper, Richard
Pepper, Richard & Geo. Robichaux
Perdue, L. E.
Perrilait, H.
Perkins, Eddie
Perry, Sam
Pertuit, Alex., Jr.
Pertuit, Edmond
Pesson, Alfred R.
Pesson & Dartes
Pesson, Fernand
Pesson, Louis
Peter, Joe
Peter & Mayer
Peyton, James H.
Peyton, James H. & Goldberg
Peyton, Harra & V. Jos.
Peyton, R. & Vivien Joe
Philip, Bastien
Phillips, Ed.
Phillips, Octave
Picard & Geismar, Receiver
Picard, H. M.
Picard, Joe
Pickney, Harry
Pickney, Mary
Pierce, Frank
Pierce, Franklin
Pierce, Ignace
Pierce, Sidney
Pierce, Willie
Pierce, Willie & Dave Uzee
Pierre & Breaux
Pierre, Jean Louis
Pierre & Moresi
Pillaro, Jake

Pitre, Augustine
Pitre, Felix & Federal Land Bank
Pitre, Mrs. Jules
Pitre, Sidney
Placide, Ben & G.
Placide, Cecelia
Placide, Cecelia & Augusta
Placide, Cecile & Edison Jones
Placide, Cecile & Shafter Kelly
Placide, George & Cecelia
Placide, George & Shafter Kelly
Placide, Gustave & Bernard
Placide, Gustave & Paul
Placide, Gustave & Romeald
Placide, Joe
Placide, Tilman & G. Lewis
Placide, Tilman & James Lewis
Placide, Wilbert & Lydia Stewart
Plaisance & Daviet
Plaisance, Emile
Plaisance, Lee
Plaisance & Theriot
Plessila, Sidney
Plessila, Sidney & Domingue
Poleder, Emily
Poleran & Paul Segura
Policar & Kling
Polite, Ben
Polite, Joe
Polk, Earl
Polk, John
Polk & LaSalle
Polozolo, Frank
Ponsano, Charles
Ponsano, Robert
Pontiff, D. J.
Pontiff, D. J. & St. Mary Bank
Poplar Grove Planting & Refining Co., Inc.
Porter, C. V.
Pourciau, A. R.
Pourciau, L. E.
Pourciau, P. L.
Pourciau, Raphael
Powers, V. D.
Pracide & A. Bourda
Prejeant, Leonie
Prevost, Arnold
Prevost, Solange
Price, Octave
Primeaux, Clodis
Primeaux, Hotley
Prince & Braquet

Prince, Leon
Prodas & Oubre
Provost, Charley & Frank
Provist, E. & Son
Provost, Euzebe
Provost, Joe
Pugh, Preston
Punch, J. B.
Punch, Lucien
Punch, Sylvere
Punch, Sylvest
Quereau & Evans
Quereau & Metz
Quereau & Porter
Raceland Bank & Trust Co.
Ragget, Victor
Rainold, E. A., Inc.
Ramsey & Porter
Randaitt, Sam
Randolph, Mrs. Albert
Randolph, Leu
Rands, R. D.
Ransonet & Braquet
Ransonet & Dugas
Ransonet, Lazard & Leonard
Ransonet, Leonard
Ransonet, Leonard & Louis
Ransonnet & Louviere
Ransonet, Sidney
Ransonet, Willie
Rathe, Anderson
Rathe, Edward
Rawlies, Lilia
Raymond Bros.
Raymond, O. & Raymond
Reaux, Elias
Red Top Farm
Reed, Bill
Reed, Linen
Reese, Wm.
Remond, Gustave
Renard, Edvard
Renard & Suire
Renaudet, O.
Rescue Plantation
Rescue Plantation & Francis
Reulet, Mrs. Jos. & Son
Reulet, Louis
Reynaud, F. Co., Inc.
Rice Growers Credit Corp.
Richard, Amede
Richard, Arthur
Richard, C. J.
Richard, Edgar
Richard, E. G.

Richard, Mrs. Henry
Richard, James
Richard, Joe
Richard, Joel
Richard, Ovide
Richard, Prosper
Richard, Thiel
Richard, Ulrice
Richards, Evariste
Richerson, Melton
Ridgefield, Inc.
Ringold, Levy
Rivet, Ed.
Rivet, Eugene
Rivet, Taylor
Roane, S. B.
Roane, S. B. & Joseph
Roberson, Clyde
Roberson, Sidney
Robert, Alfred
Robert, Anthony
Robert, Gilbert
Robert, Hanley
Robert, Joseph
Robert, Sidney
Roberts, Paul & Co.
Roberts, W. B.
Robertson, Arthur
Robertson, C. & Agnes Lewis
Robertson, Philip
Robichaux, Albert
Robichaux, Alvin & Walter
Robichaux, Armogene
Robichaux, Arthur
Robichaux, Carlos
Robichaux & Delcambre
Robichaux, Est. E. G.
Robichaux, E. G. Co., Ltd.
Robichaux, Frank
Robichaux, Henry
Robichaux, Heywood
Robichaux, John
Robichaux, John & Realty
    Operators, Inc.
Robichaux, Octave
Robichaux, R.
Robichaux, Roy
Robichaux, Sam
Robichaux, Thomas
Robichaux, Ulysse
Robichaux, Walter & John
Robichaux, Robert
Robicheaux, Wickliff
Robin, Arista
Robin, Clemiel

Robin, Theo.
Robinson, Philip
Rochon, Homer
Rochon, Joseph
Roadney, Tony
Rodrigue, Albert
Rodrigue, Alcide
Rodrigue, Joe
Rodrigue, Philip
Rodrigues, Lucien
Rodriguez, Alcide
Roger, Clame
Roger & Lancon
Roger, Leon
Romeald & G. Placide
Romero & Abadie
Romero, Arthur
Romero & Broussard
Romero, C.
Romero, C. & Co.
Romero & Chaston
Romero, Clement
Romero & Deslatte
Romero, Dupre
Romero, Estave & Matha Blan-
    chet
Romero, H.
Romero, H. & Company
Romero, Ignace
Romero, Mrs. Jos.
Romero & LeBlanc
Romero, Ovey & Johnnie Lewis
Romero, Pierre
Romero & Raphael
Romero & Segura
Romero & Alpha Vallot
Romero & Vallot
Ronsonnet, L. & Annie Lewis
Ronsonnet, L. & Bessie Lewis
Ronsonnet, L. & Olivier
Ronsonnet, O. & Olivier & Pa.
    zout
Ropailo, Tony
Ropello, Veto
Ross, Ben
Ronsonnet, Leonie & Alberta
    Lewis
Roth, Ben
Roussel, Numa
Roy, Albert
Roy, Ferd.
Roy, Forrest
Roy, Garfield
Roy, J. A.
Rye, Alfred

Rye, Wilfred
Saison, Adam
Saizan, Joseph
Samonie, Sidney
Sanches Brothers
Sanchez, Omer
Sanches, Robert
Sanders, A. A., Inc.
Sapp, Legi
Savignol, C.
Savoie, Arthur & Brothers
Savoie, Arthur & Smith
Savoie, Audressy
Savoie, E.
Savoie, Elles
Savoie, Eugene
Savoie, H. & A.
Savoie, Silevin
Savoy & Arthur
Savoy, Charles
Savoy, Lodice & Joseph Gabriel
Savoy, Lodice & Francis
    LeBlanc
Savoy, Lodice & Edier Viator
Savoy, Joseph
Savoy, Sam
Savoy, Vincent
Schawb, Disera
Schexnayder, Ernest
Schexnayder, F. & Co.
Schexnayder, Felix
Schexnayder, Mrs. Felix
Schillemore & Nico
Schillemore & Joe Vallot
Schillemore & Whitney
Scioneaux, Lubin
Scioneaux, Wilson
Schweiger, Philip E.
Scott & Erwin
Scott, Henry
Scott, Harry & St. Mary. Bank
Scott, P. E.
Scott, Rachael
Scott, Robert
Scott, W. C.
Scotts, Willie
Scull, Julia
Sealy, H. S.
Sealy, Heywood
Sealy & Scharff
Sealy, Scharff & Lewis
Sedatole, Luxion
Segura, Adonis & Marine
Segura, Adran
Segura, Ambrose

Segura, Anitus
Segura, Anitus & Marcel De-
  ronen
Segura, Arvillian
Segura, Arvillian & Brown
Segura & Bonin
Segura, Conston
Segura & Darby
Segura, Gaston
Segura, Gerard
Segura & Girole
Segura, Horace
Segura, Howard
Segura & Jacky
Segura, Joseph
Segura, Jos. & Alcide Romero
Segura & Landry
Segura, Lee
Segura, Lee & E. Viator
Segura & Lorance
Segura, Maurice
Segura & Mitchel
Segura, Morise
Segura, Ontim & Adolph Darby
Segura, Paul
Segura, Paul & Oda Romero
Segura & Placide
Segura, Policare
Segura & Rochel
Segura & Romero
Segura & Viator
Segura, Whitney
Segura, Willie
Senette, Thos. E.
Sentierre & Achee
Sentierre, Albert
Seraphim, Gilbert
Settia, Arthur
Sevin, Mrs. S.
Shadyside Operators, Inc.
Shaw & Landry
Shaw & Ransonet
Shaw & Wallace
Shell Hill Planting Co.
Shell Petroleum Corporation
Shines, Samuel
Shines, Simuel
Sias, Eusebe & Broussard
Sigue, Arthemus
Segue, George
Sigue, Thomas
Simon & Decourt
Simon, Francis
Simon & Girard
Simon, Joseph J.

Simon, Joe, Jr.
Simon, Michel
Simon & Shaw
Simon, Zenor
Simoneaux, D. A.
Simoneaux, D. A. & Co.
Simoneaux, Dozilla
Simoneaux, Emile
Simoneaux & Louviere
Simoneaux, O. J.
Simoneaux, Odon
Simoneaux, Simon & Sou
Sims, H. L.
Size, Joseph
Smart, Dan
Smart, Marshal
Smedes Bros., Inc.
Smillion & Marcel
Smith, C. & Alec Moore
Smith, C. & Felix Boudreaux
Smith, C. L. & Willie Dupuy
Smith, David
Smith, E. D.
Smith, Edward
Smith, James
Smith, Marshall
Smith, McGregor
Smith & Moore
Smith, Rodney
Smith, T. Baker
Smith, Urias
Snyers, A. C.
Sompey, Leo
Sonier, Clay
Sonier, Laurent
Sonier, Lovincy
Sonnier, Seville
Sparrow, Valmon & Davis
Speligene, Chris
Stakelum, Pat Iron Works
Standard Sugars Co., Inc.
Standard Supply & Hardware
  Co.
Stansberry, L. & Annie Lewis
State Agricultural Credit Corp.,
  Inc.
Stauffer, Eshleman & Co., Ltd.
Stein, Cleveland
Stein, Mrs. Michel
Sterling Sugars, Inc.
Stevenson, Grant
Stewart, Harrison
Stewart, R. J.
Stewart, Robert
Stoufflet, Adolph

St. Germaine, Louis
St. Joseph Planting & Mfg. Co.
St. Julien, Anatole
St. Julien & Broussard
St. Julien, James
St. Julien & Jefferson
St. Julien & Treaville
St. Martin, Nelson
St. Martin & Perret
St. Martin, Peter B.
St. Martin, Robert J.
St. Mary Hardware Co., Inc.
Stokes, Doff
St. Romain, Euzebe
St. Romain, Stanley
Suire, Honore
Suire, Ignace
Suire, Louis
Suire, Noah
Suire, Pervis
Suire, Renoudet
Sunier, Lule
Sunier, Oscar
Sunier, Oscar & Sules
Supple's, J. Sons Planting Co.,
  Ltd.
Suttle, Octave
Swindler, Frank
Taggart, W. G.
Takewell, Mrs. David & William
  Chauvin
Talbot, Myrtle
Talbot, Myrtle & Charley
Talbot, Rodolph
Talbot, Willie
Talbot, Willie J.
Talbot, Willy & Jolibois
Talenion, Edgar
Tally Ho, Inc.
Tanner, W. H.
Tassere, Raoul
Tassin, C. C.
Tate, Jessie, Sr.
Taussant, Homer & Miss M.
  Wooster
Tausin, Anders
Tausin, Arthur
Tausin & Gonsoulin
Tausin, Hypolite
Tausin & Ganuchaux
Tausin & Gonsoulin
Tausin, Louis
Tausin & Quereau
Tausin & Tausin
Taylor, William

Telesmar & Smillian
Templet, Redolph
Tenny, John
Terrebonne Ice Co.
Terrebonne Motor Co., Inc.
Terregrosse, L. J.
Terrodat, Leonce
Texas & Pacific Railway Co.
Thayer, L. L.
Therance, Francois
Therenet, Andre
Theriot, Mrs. C.
Theriot, Leonce & Claude Via-
  tor
Theriot, Louis, Sr.
Theriot, Mrs. R. & Brown
Thiac, Charles N.
Thibaut, A. & J. N.
Thibaut, B. & D.
Thibaut, D.
Thibodeaux, Albert
Thibodeaux, Alexander
Thibodeaux, Alfred
Thibodeaux, Alphius
Thibodeaux, Armadie
Thibodaux Boiler Works
Thibodaux, Charles
Thibodeaux, Chotard
Thibodaux, Emile
Thibodeaux, Gaston
Thibodaux, John
Thibodeaux, John No. 2
Thibodeaux, Julius
Thibodaux, L. C.
Thibodeaux & Leitmeyer
Thibodeaux, M. & Leitmeyer
Thibodaux, Marcello
Thibodeaux, Meluse
Thibodeaux, Toneal
Thibodaux, Wallace
Thibodeaux, Walter
Thomas & Delcambre
Thomas & Geoffrey
Thomas & Godfrey
Thomas, Henry
Thomas, Robert
Thompson, Maguel
Tillman & Lydia
Tillison, Samuel
Torras, B.
Torres Brothers
Toups, Alcide
Toups, Camille
Toups, Edgar E.